B.R. Ambedkar

'This is a unique book ... [it] fills a major gap in the studies of the first pan-Indian Dalit leader, Bhim Rao Ambedkar. It offers an in-depth view, not only of ... political mobilization and public policies ... but also of his sociological thought—a pioneering reading of the hierarchical arrangement ... it shows the relevance of a man who has become the most popular icon of Indian politics and a world view that has become one of the guiding principles for today's social change.'

—Christophe Jaffrelot, Director,
Centre d'Études et de Recherches Internationales (CERI), Paris

'This is a comprehensive collection of Ambedkar's ideas and initiatives.... The principles invoked in these writings have a wider application than the immediate context suggested.... These writings advance a normative defence and justification of preferential policies nearly fifty years before these arguments found wider circulation in the public domain world-wide.'

—Valerian Rodrigues, Professor,
Centre for Political Studies, Jawaharlal Nehru University, New Delhi

B.R. Ambedkar
Perspectives on Social Exclusion
and Inclusive Policies

SUKHADEO THORAT
and
NARENDER KUMAR

OXFORD
UNIVERSITY PRESS

OXFORD
UNIVERSITY PRESS

22 Workspace, 2nd Floor, 1/22 Asaf Ali Road, New Delhi 110002, India

Oxford University Press is a department of the University of Oxford.
It furthers the University's objective of excellence in research, scholarship,
and education by publishing worldwide in

Oxford New York
Auckland Cape Town Dar es Salaam Hong Kong Karachi
Kuala Lumpur Madrid Melbourne Mexico City Nairobi
New Delhi Shanghai Taipei Toronto

With offices in
Argentina Austria Brazil Chile Czech Republic France Greece
Guatemala Hungary Italy Japan Poland Portugal Singapore
South Korea Switzerland Thailand Turkey Ukraine Vietnam

Oxford is a registered trade mark of Oxford University Press
in the UK and in certain other countries.

Published in India
by Oxford University Press, New Delhi

ISBN-13: 978-0-19-806350-6
ISBN-10: 0-19-806350-4

Typeset in ACaslon Regular 10.5/12.5
by Eleven Arts, Keshav Puram, Delhi 110 035
Printed in India by Replika Press Pvt. Ltd.

Dedicated to
Babasaheb Dr Bhimrao Ambedkar

Contents

PART II: CONSTITUTIONAL REFORMS: SEEKING POLITICAL REPRESENTATION, 1930–3

PART III: EXTENDING THE REPRESENTATION: EMPLOYMENT AND EDUCATION, 1934–46

Foreword

OF CONSTITUTIONS AND CONSTITUTIONAL MOMENTS: THE RISE OF AFFIRMATIVE ACTION IN INDIA

About four years ago I was approached by a diplomat from the United States State Department based in India about participating in a teleconference with scholars at the newly established Institute of Dalit Studies in New Delhi on affirmative action. The diplomat informed me that the Indian participants in the teleconference would have a great deal to learn from the USA experience with such policies. I responded, much to the diplomat's surprise, that India had a much longer experience with affirmative action than US, and one of the great missed opportunities was the failure of policymakers in the USA to examine India's history of affirmative action before such policies were adopted and implemented in America in the late 1960s and early 1970s.

At the federal level India has had a policy of affirmative action (or reservations or compensatory discrimination) on behalf of the untouchables (Dalits) and tribals since 1948. Some Indian states had adopted caste based reservations considerably earlier; for example, Tamil Nadu had developed a system of caste-based quotas in 1921. The federal policy reserving seats for untouchables and tribals in the Indian Parliament, state legislative assemblies, civil service positions, and university faculty appointments and student admissions is the product of provisions written directly into the post-independence Indian constitution by Bhimrao Ambedkar (1891–1956). Ambedkar, the greatest figure in the struggle for emancipation of the untouchables from the yoke of caste Hinduism, is the central subject of this superb volume by Sukhadeo Thorat and Narender Kumar.

The long history of struggle that led to the emergence of India's reservation policy as a mechanism of inclusion for the segment of the Indian population that has been subjected to social abuse, dispossession, indignity, impoverishment and discrimination for millennia demands careful attention; that is precisely what this volume does, taking the reader from Jyotirao Phule's development of the first school in India that would serve untouchable youths in 1848 to the first years of implementation of the new constitution in the 1950s. The twisting and twisted position of the British colonial authorities with respect to Hindu caste system also is given complex treatment here. Still it is Ambedkar's intellectual and political contributions that lie at the heart of the development of the reservation policy that prevails in India to this day, and it is his contributions that are the primary object of this study.

From the perspective of this black American, the notion of the militant Dalit leader having a direct hand in the construction of the Indian Constitution and having the ability to write the reservation system explicitly into the Constitution is an astonishing moment. It is roughly equivalent to a circumstance in the late 1860s where the black militant Frederick Douglass would have been given the authority to design the post-Civil War reconstruction programme for the ex-slaves in the USA, including the delivery of forty acres and a mule to each family of formerly enslaved blacks.

Ambedkar's personal story is remarkable in its own right. The fourteenth child born into an untouchable family that had a moderately more open range of opportunities than other Dalits because Ambedkar's father was employed in the British East India Company army. A brilliant student who was subjected to intense socio-economic discrimination from his early years, Ambedkar somehow managed to earn a law degree in Britain and a PhD in economics from Columbia University in the USA. When the time came to craft the post-independence constitution, not only was there political utility in having Ambedkar play a key role in writing the document, but then he was possibly most qualified individual among many to do so.

However the most significant of Ambedkar's intellectual and political contribution was the articulation of affirmative action policy in legislature, education, employment, and other spheres. This seems startlingly radical by USA norms. I recall the firestorm that was raised when President Bill Clinton nominated the black female law professor, Lani Guinier, for appointment as the head of the Civil Rights Division of the US Department of Justice. In her academic writings Guinier had had the temerity to contemplate alternative voting schemes to majority rule that would have preserved a greater level of influence for minorities who otherwise would be consistently outvoted. Her ideas were seized upon by the political right to create an image of Guinier as anti-democratic and a minority chauvinist—rather than someone exploring ways to insure that the voices of minorities are actually heard in a democracy.

To put it bluntly, India has had a far more aggressive and well-developed system of affirmative action than the USA. While the Indian system has not been extended to private sector employment as it has in the USA, it has included the parliamentary system from the outset—an arena that has never been the purview of affirmative action in the US. The Indian system is a quota system rather than a more timid system of preferential boosts of the sort used in America. And the Indian system is inscribed in the national constitution, precluding the more whimsical status it possesses in the USA. The volume at hand tells the story of how affirmative action in India came to be in comprehensive and compelling fashion. We are fortunate that Thorat and Kumar have written it for us.

USA   William Darity Jr.
30 November 2007   Duke University

Preface and Acknowledgements

Academicians, policy makers, and the government are engaged in an intensive discussion on developing a solution to the problems of social groups which have historically suffered from social exclusion and the resultant deprivation and poverty. The Indian government has developed a formal 'Equal Opportunity Policy' in the form of 'Reservation' for the Scheduled Castes (SCs) and Scheduled Tribes (STs). This has also been extended on a selective basis for Other Backward Castes/Classes (OBCs), semi-nomadic and de-notified tribes, women, and physically challenged persons. Currently we are searching for alternative ways to extend the reservation to the private sector for SCs, STs, and OBCs in central higher education institutions, and also address similar demands by lower caste people, now converted to Christianity and Islam.

Among those who devoted their intellectual and political efforts and were instrumental in developing equal opportunity policy in the form of reservation, Babasaheb Bhimrao Ambedkar occupied a central place. In fact he could be considered the architect of the present reservation policy. Ambedkar was a pioneer in so far as he was instrumental in piloting the concept of reservation policy at all India level in the early 1930s in the form of the Poona Pact initiating the beginning with representation for SC/ST in central and state Legislatures. Though there were attempts at provincial level in early twentieth century but they remained confined to the provinces like Kolhapur, Baroda, Travancore, Cochin etc.

Ambedkar's intellectual efforts in developing inclusive policy had focused on two interrelated aspects. Firstly, it included an interpretation of the institution of caste system and untouchability, its exclusionary character and consequences on the excluded and discriminated groups reflected in lack of access to resources, employment, education, civil rights, and high level of poverty. Secondly, based on the interpretation of caste system and untouchability it addressed the issue of remedies against discriminations and exclusion.

Given this pioneering contribution of Ambedkar, it is imperative that we study his perspective and vision and draw lessons for our present efforts to develop inclusive policy for groups suffering from exclusion in various magnitude such as SC/ST, semi-nomadic and de-notified Tribes, OBCs, women, religious minorities, and other similar groups.

Although there are some studies on Ambedkar's perspective on this theme, much of his basic academic writings are not placed in the mainstream academic domain. Ambedkar's writings on this theme are hidden in the massive literature that he produced. The present book for the first times tries to present this literature at one place in a systematic historical sequence. Based on this literature, it also provides insight into Ambedkar's interpretation of the institution of caste system and untouchability and the solutions to the problem of Indian society arising out of processes of social exclusion. The book presents the original texts and also interpretations of those texts on the problem of social exclusion and inclusive policies.

Most of the original writings of Ambedkar have been picked up from the collected works of Ambedkar, published by the Government of Maharashtra as *Babasaheb Ambedkar Writings and Speeches* in twenty-one volumes. We express our gratitude to the Dr. Babasaheb Ambedkar, Mahatma Jotirao Phule, Rajarshri Sahu Charitrya Sadhane Prakashan Samiti and particularly to the Education Secretary, Government of Maharashtra for granting us permission to utilize the available material. Many other institutions and persons supported us in this endeavour and we express our gratitude to all of them.

This volume forms a part of an ongoing academic programme on 'social exclusion' which has been initiated by Indian Institute of Dalit Studies, New Delhi. We acknowledge their support. The staff at the Indian Institute of Dalit Studies particularly Narendra Kumar gave his time for scanning and typing the script. We are grateful to them.

Narender Kumar, the co-editor of the book did a major part of the work while he was Visiting Scholar at the Centre for the Study of Law and Governance, Jawaharlal Nehru University. We therefore thank the Chairperson of the Centre, Amita Singh for her support. Discussion on Ambedkar's views regarding political representation with Valerian Rodrigues of the Centre for Political Studies, Jawaharlal Nehru University, has been fruitful. We express gratefulness to him as well.

We thank the Oxford University Press for understanding the significance of the work and readily accepting it for publication.

Sukhadeo Thorat
Narender Kumar

Abbreviations

API	Associated Press of India
BAWS	Vasant Moon (ed.) *Dr. Babasaheb Ambedkar: Writings and Speeches*
CP	Central Provinces
DC(s)	Depressed Class(es)
GOI	Government of India
HMG	Her Majesty's Government
ICS	Indian Civil Service
OBC(s)	Other Backward Classes
RTC(s)	Round Table Conference(s)
SC(s)	Scheduled Caste(s)
ST(s)	Scheduled Tribe(s)

Introduction
Historical Overview (1919–55)

In recent years, the use of equal opportunity policy in the form of reservation, as a means of inclusion of socially excluded groups in India has become a subject of lively discussion. This discussion has been revived due to initiative by government for reservation in private sector for Scheduled Castes (SCs) and Scheduled Tribes (STs), extension of reservation for Other Backward Classes (OBCs) in the higher education institutes managed or funded by the State and similar demands by Dalit Christians and Muslims. The discussion covers a wide range of issues ranging from the characterization of Indian society, problem of socially disadvantaged groups, such as Dalits, OBCs, religious minorities, women, and other excluded groups, and the possible remedies against discrimination and deprivation. In this context a number of questions have been raised: what policies are warranted to overcome the problem arising out of historical denial of equal rights? What should be the nature of such policies? Which spheres should such policies cover—employment, education, housing, business, and other spheres? Should it be extended to private sector, or remain confined to state sector? Should these policies be targeted to poor within the socially disadvantaged or to apply to group as whole? How long should such policies continue?

Ambedkar's Legacy

Ambedkar being the architect of the present reservation policy, his efforts to introduce this policy needs careful consideration. He could be considered a pioneer who introduced the concept of a reservation policy at the all India level in early 1930s, although there were attempts at the provincial level, about which we shall discuss latter. In fact the articulation and systematic framing of various types of remedies against discrimination including reservation/affirmative action policies for discriminated groups, internationally, emerged only during the 1950s and 1960s, and since Ambedkar developed a framework for such policies and got them implemented as early as 1930s (in the form of Poona Pact) he could be considered a pioneer of inclusive policies in the world.

It was in 1919 that Ambedkar for the first time submitted a statement to the Southborough Committee on the demands of the Untouchables in the political sphere in the Legislative Council. In 1928, he submitted a memorandum to the Simon Commission to safeguard the interests of Depressed Classes (DCs). Later, appearing at the Round Table Conferences (RTCs) in 1930–2, he once again demanded social and political safeguards to protect the interests of excluded groups. In 1942, Ambedkar's interventions became wider. While writing to the Institute of Pacific Studies and to the Cripps Mission, he demanded adequate representation in the Public Services of the State. Prior to the formation of the Constituent Assembly, he presented two major memorandums—first to the Governor General in 1945 and second to the Cabinet Mission Plan in 1946. On the eve of the formation of the Constituent Assembly, a comprehensive plan on the multidimensional aspects of SCs position in the free India was presented by him. Though the contribution in the 1930s and 1940s had already set the stage for the reservation policy. At the time of Constitution-making, he being the chairman of the Drafting Committee piloted the reservation policy.

Thus Ambedkar's intellectual and political efforts for reservation policy, which began in 1919, were instrumental in developing a policy in 1932 in the form of Poona Pact. The reservation policy which began in 1932 in Legislature got extended to public employment and education in the 1940s and finally came into its present form with acceptance of the Constitution of India in 1950. Ambedkar undoubtedly was the architect of the reservation policy at the all India level. In view of this it is absolutely relevant and necessary to look into the intellectual contribution of Ambedkar on this issue and to draw lessons for the current discussion, and attempts to extend reservation for SCs/STs in the private sector, for OBCs in education, and measures on similar lines for minorities and women.

This volume attempts to put forth Ambedkar's understanding and his efforts to develop solutions to the problems of Indian society arising out of institutions of caste and untouchability and to develop socially inclusive policies for the excluded groups in the contemporary context. To provide the readers with an opportunity to have insight about the original writings of Ambedkar on this issue, the book provides both the original texts and interpretations of those texts on the problem of social exclusion and inclusive policies.

In the scheme of presentation, first we discuss Ambedkar's interpretation of caste and untouchability including the consequences for lower castes. Secondly, we describe Ambedkar's efforts through various memorandums, statements etc. to the government to highlight the problems of marginalized sections and to develop comprehensive remedies in the form of inclusive policies during 1919 through 1950. Thirdly, we indicate lessons for present day efforts of the government to extend the same to private sector and other disadvantaged groups.

INTERPRETING CASTE AND PROBLEM OF EXCLUDED GROUPS

For Ambedkar, understanding the nature of the institutions of caste and untouchability were essential for recognizing the consequences for the excluded groups. We therefore first discuss Ambedkar's interpretation of the caste system and untouchability, which forms the base for the inclusive policies suggested by him.

Ambedkar believed, in its classical form the caste system involved in itself social, economic, cultural, and political frameworks of governance of Hindu society. In 1916, Ambedkar developed a theory of caste system looking at its origin and growth, which was followed by a theory of the origin of untouchability in 1948 and a theory about the origin of Shudras; and then he wrote a number of essays, which discuss the features of caste system and the institution of untouchability. 'Castes in India' (*BAWS* 1979, vol. 1: 3–22), 'Annihilation of Caste' (*BAWS* 1979, vol. 1: 23–96), 'The Untouchables: Who Were They and Why They Became Untouchables' *(BAWS* 1994, vol. 7: 239–381), 'Who Were Shudras' (*BAWS* 1994, vol. 7: 1–226), 'Philosophy of Hinduism' (*BAWS* 1987, vol. 3: 1–94), 'The Hindu Social Order—Its Essential Features' (*BAWS* 1987, vol. 3: 95–115), 'The Hindu Social Order—Its Unique Features' (*BAWS* 1987, vol. 3: 116–29) are used to capture the Ambedkar's interpretation of caste system and untouchability.

Ambedkar identified six attributes of the caste system, which made it exclusive in character and brought a peculiar system of governance to Hindu society. It divides Hindu population in social groups called castes. The castes are then made endogamous, restricting marriage within the caste. It assigned civil, cultural, educational, and economic rights, for each caste and continuance by heredity without freedom to change. The entitlements of rights is however unequal across the castes. The entitlement of rights is also hierarchical—rights going down from high caste to low caste. Further, some occupations or economic activities are treated as superior and others as inferior, thus maintaining hierarchy based on purity and impurity. It also provides a mechanism for enforcement of the system in terms of social ostracism, through a provision of social and economic penalties, including social and economic boycott. Finally, the caste system also draws justification from some elements of Hindu religious philosophy such as making the divine origin of the caste system and its linkages with the concepts of karma and rebirth.

The most pertinent principle of caste-system is the fixation of rights and continuance thereof by heredity. For instance, in the economic field every member must follow the occupation assigned to the caste to which he/she belonged (for details see *BAWS* 1987, vol. 3: The Hindu Social Order: Its Essential Features). It left no scope for individual capabilities, choices, or inclinations. In other societies, economic stratification existed with the freedom to move from one occupation to another. Such free social mobility prevented isolation and exclusion. Thus, it is not so much the existence of classes or segmentation, rather the idea of isolation and exclusiveness, which is inimical to a free social order.

An equally important principle feature of the caste system is the unequal entitlements of various rights among the castes. In fact, inequality in distribution of rights is the core feature of the caste system. The lower castes suffered the most. The way social and economic rights are assigned, it left little scope to the lower castes for social and economic improvement, as they are deprived of the rights to choose occupation, acquire property, and receive education (for details see ibid.).

Yet another feature is hierarchical and graded entitlements of various rights to different castes insofar as the rights increase in ascending order from Untouchable to Brahmin. In this hierarchial arrangement castes are artfully interlinked in such a manner that the rights and privileges of higher castes become the disabilities of lower castes, particularly the former Untouchables and other lower castes. In this sense, in Ambedkar's view caste cannot exist in a single form. Caste can exist only as a plural number, interlinked to each other in unequal measures of social, religious, and economic relations and rights.

In this particular hierarchy, the Brahmins are not only placed at the top but are considered 'superior social beings' worthy of special entitlements, rights, and privileges. At the bottom, the Untouchables and lower castes are treated as 'sub-human beings or lesser human beings' considered unworthy of any rights. In fact, the disabilities they suffer are so severe that they are physically and socially isolated and excluded from the rest of society. Isolation and exclusion of Untouchables is a unique feature of the Hindu social order. Ambedkar argued that classes or social groups are common to all societies, but as long as the classes or social groups do not practice isolation and exclusion they are only non-social in their relations towards one another. 'Isolation and exclusiveness' makes them anti-social and inimical to one another (ibid.).

In this context, it is necessary to recognize that while the Hindu social order provides no social and economic rights to the deprived castes, it gives multiple privileges and rights to the higher castes, particularly the Brahmins. For instance, teaching of the Vedas, officiating at a sacrifice and receiving grants and presents are the exclusive rights or occupations of Brahmins. However, unlike other castes, there is no restriction on them to take up other occupations if the situation demands, except of course, the occupations of the Untouchables. This unique feature of exclusive privilege for Brahmins, and denial of minimum rights to lower castes, particularly to Untouchables, is important to understand the present inter-caste economic inequality, particularly between Brahmins and others (ibid.).

Denial of equal access to education is another core feature of the caste system. In Ambedkar's view, the concept of formal education in the Hindu social order was quite narrow (ibid.). Formal education was confined to the study of the Vedas in schools which were established for this purpose. The State did not hold itself responsible for opening establishments for the study of arts and sciences that concerned the life of merchants and artisans. In the absence of a formal educational system, each caste managed to transmit to its progeny the traditional ways of doing things. Therefore, illiteracy became an inherent part of the caste system by a process that was indirect but internal to Hinduism, observed Ambedkar. It was a direct result of the rule relating to the rights to teach and study the Vedas. Brahmins, Kshatriyas, and Vaishyas could study the Vedas but Brahmins alone had the right to teach them. Shudras were allowed to neither study the Vedas nor hear them. The successors of Manu made contravention of this bar an offence punishable with direct penalties. The series of penalties against the study of the Vedas by the deprived castes gave rise to illiteracy and ignorance in secular life (ibid.). It was not so much the access or right to read the Vedas that mattered for the deprived castes, but the denial of the right to education and opportunities to develop human capabilities. In this way, reading and writing became incidental to the study of the Vedas. The net result of this was that reading and writing became the right of the high castes and illiteracy the destiny of the low castes. In this context, Ambedkar observed:

The ancient world may be said to have been guilty for failing to take the responsibility for the education of the masses. But never has any society been guilty for closing to the generality of the people the study of the books of its religion. Never has society made any attempt to declare that an attempt made by the common man to acquire knowledge shall be punishable as a crime. Manu is the only divine law giver who has denied the common man the right to knowledge (*BAWS* 1987, vol. 3: 43).

Analysing the economic relations under the caste system, particularly those between high and lower castes in the economic sense, the Hindu social order involves a slave-like character for the lower castes. In Ambedkar's view, a slave is a person who accepts from another the purpose which controls his conduct. In this sense, a slave is not an end in himself; he or she is only a means of fulfilling the end desire of others. In their economic significance, the rules put an interdict on the economic independence of the deprived castes. They were required to serve others, not themselves, which means they were not allowed to strive for economic independence, but had to forever remain economically dependent on others. Besides this, the Hindu social order also recognized slavery in a more direct form. Manu recognized seven types of slaves; Narada recognized 13 types (ibid.). What is, however, important in Ambedkar's view is that both brought graded inequality into the system of slavery and, therefore, it was not a free system. In the Hindu scheme of slavery, Shudras could be made slaves of the three higher castes, but the higher castes could not be slaves of Shudras. A Brahmin might become the slave of another Brahmin (at least in theory), but not of a Kshatriya, Vaishya, or Shudra. He might, however, hold as his slave anyone belonging to the four varnas. This hierarchical bar to enslaving anyone from a higher caste applied to all castes.

How did this social order sustain and maintain? The caste system provided the mechanism, through social and economic penalties, to sustain and maintain the system. The instruments of social and economic boycott are the main forms of penalties laid down against the violation of the codes of the system.

To put it in brief, Ambedkar's interpretation of the Hindu social order as a system of governance in general, and a system of production, organization, and distribution in particular is based on three inter-related elements. These included fixed rights, unequal and hierarchical (or graded) division of social and economic rights across castes, and provision of strong instruments of social and economic ostracization to sustain the rigid system with a philosophical justification in Hindu religion.

Ambedkar believed that whatever may have been the purpose behind the origin of the caste system, in its later classical form, it certainly involved an economic motive, the main purpose of which was exploitation rather than economic efficiency of any sort. The manner in which the rules concerning the right to property, occupation, employment, wages, education, social status of occupation, dignity of labour, rules governing graded slavery, and other economic relations were defined, these involved essentially an element of economic exploitation, particularly of castes located at the bottom of the caste hierarchy. This, in fact, implied that the caste system was primarily based on the principle of economic inequality and exploitation. The economic inequality (as much as socio-cultural inequality) under the Hindu social order has not emerged as a matter of indirect historical consequences, but as a direct outcome of its governing principles, and in fact it formed its core doctrine.

The most important point, however, is about the role of some philosophical elements of Hinduism that provided 'divine' justification for the origin and sustenance of the Hindu social system. Deepak Lal recognized the negative role of some religious principles when he observed that 'obviously the religious, philosophical and ritual elements in Hinduism are equally (if not more) important in perpetuating the system'. Lal did not however elaborate this point and simply added that 'the relative primacy of one or other factor in originating or perpetuating the system is not of importance for my purpose. What is important is that the economic and non-economic aspects of the system mutually reinforced each other' (Lal 1988: 73). Ambedkar, on the other hand, located the role of some religious and social principles of Hinduism in providing divine support and justification to the doctrine of inequality in the social, cultural, economic, and religious spheres. In Ambedkar's view, it is this justification which has provided an abiding strength for the sustenance of the Hindu social order. Nowhere in the world, according to Ambedkar, have social and religious ideologies intertwined in the economic sphere as much in the Hindu social order. He observed:

Nowhere has society consecrated its occupations—the ways of getting a living. Economic activity has always remained outside the sanctity of religion. Hunting society was not without a religion but hunting as an occupation was not consecrated by religion and made sacred. Pastoral society was not without religion. But pasturage was not consecrated by religion and made sacred. Farming as an occupation did not become consecrated by religion and made sacred. Feudalism with its gradations, with its lords, villains and serfs, was purely social in character. There was nothing sacred about it. The Hindus are the only people in the world whose social relations are consecrated by religion and made sacred, eternal and inviolate. The Hindus are the only people in the world whose economic order—the relation of workman to workman—is consecrated by religion and made sacred, eternal and inviolate. It is not therefore enough to say that the Hindus are a people with a sacred code of religion. So are the Zoroastrians, Israelites, Christians and Muslims. All these have sacred codes. But they do not prescribe, nor do they consecrate a particular form of social structure—the relationship between man and man in a concrete form—and make it sacred and inviolate. The Hindus are singular in this respect. This is what has given the Hindu social order its abiding strength to defy the ravages and the onslaught of time (*BAWS* 1987, vol. 3: 129).

The religious intervention in social and economic sphere, however, was not positive in nature such that it promoted or facilitated social and economic justice. Unfortunately, the Hindu social philosophy as a form of social governance of human society, far from promoting just order, promoted the opposite. While summarizing the centrality of the philosophy of Hinduism, Ambedkar observed:

Religious ideals as a form of divine governance for human society fall into two classes, one in which 'Society' is the centre and the other in which the

'Individual' is the Centre, and for the former the appropriate test of what is good and what is right i. e. text of moral order is utility while for the latter the test is justice. Now the reason why the philosophy of Hinduism does not answer the test either of utility or of justice is because the religious ideal of Hinduism for divine governance of human society is an ideal which falls into a separate class by itself. It is an ideal in which the individual is not the centre. The centre of the ideal is neither individual nor society. It is a class; it is a class of supermen called Brahmins. Those who will bear the dominant and devastating fact in mind will understand why philosophy of Hinduism is not founded on individual justice or social utility. The philosophy of Hinduism is founded on totally different principles. To the question what is right and what is good the answer that the philosophy of Hinduism gives is remarkable. It holds that to be right and good the act must serve the interest of a class of supermen, namely the Brahmins. Anything, which serves the interest of this class, is alone entitled to be called good (*BAWS* 1987, vol. 3: 72).

This, in Ambedkar's view, is the core of the social philosophy of Hinduism. It teaches that what is right for one particular class is the only thing treated as morally right and good. It is also important to recognize that in this social framework there is no difference between legal philosophy (law) and moral philosophy (morality). This arose because in social aspects of Hinduism there is no distinction between legal and moral. Moral is legal and legal is moral which is also social and individual.

CONSEQUENCES OF CASTE SYSTEM

The caste system's characteristic of fixed social and economic rights for each caste, implies 'exclusion' of one caste from having social interaction with, and undertaking the occupations of other castes. Exclusion and discrimination are thus an obvious consequence of this system. The unequal and hierarchical assignment of civil, cultural, occupational, and property rights among castes implies that although every caste, except those at the top of the caste order, suffer in various magnitude from an unequal division of social and economic rights, the 'Untouchables' (SCs), who are located at the bottom of the caste hierarchy, suffer most as they are excluded from access to any economic rights except manual labour or service to the castes above them (*BAWS* 1987, vol. 3). The concept of 'untouchability' adds additional dimensions to the social and economic discrimination and exclusion of this social group as they are prohibited from social intercourse and participation in several social and economic activities due to the stigma of pollution associated with their caste.

The caste system is not merely a division of labour but also the division of labourers into watertight compartments without any opportunity for inter-occupational mobility. Ambedkar argued that division of labour is needed in a civilized society, but that no civilized society had division of labour accompanied by division of labourers. The matter does not end with the division of labourers but also is accompanied by hierarchy in occupations graded one above the other leading to social and economic gradation of labourers. This involves the subordination of natural human powers and inclination to the exigencies of social rules. Another wrong it does is to dissociate intelligence from work and recreate contempt for physical labour.

The caste-based economic order entails adverse consequences on economic growth and income distribution. The market failure associated with caste-based market discrimination not only adversely affects economic growth, but also generates unequal income distribution and induced poverty particularly among discriminated social groups. For an optimum economic outcome, an efficient functioning of markets for labour and other factors of production is of central importance. Fixed and compulsory caste-based division of occupations thus results in immobility of factors of production and imperfections in labour and other markets. Thus, far from promoting competitive market condition, caste-based division of labour and occupation creates segmented and monopolistic market situations and produces less than optimum economic outcome (*BAWS* 1987, vol. 3).

Negative consequences of the economics of caste system are particularly pronounced in terms of income distribution and poverty experienced by the excluded/discriminated groups. Since property rights are assigned unequally across castes, income distribution is generally skewed along caste lines. The impact on 'Untouchables' and lower caste is far more serious as they are excluded from access to property rights and often from education. Thus the consequences of the caste system are denial of equal rights, exclusion, discrimination, and subordination of one by another caste. And if any group suffers more than the other, it is the Untouchables who suffer not only from denial of property rights but also human dignity.

POLICIES FOR SOCIAL INCLUSION: A HISTORICAL REVIEW

As mentioned earlier, the efforts for the social inclusion of excluded groups took place at various junctures of history, but it was only in the nineteenth century that some sort of legal framework was initiated by the British and some of the rulers of the Indian provinces. So in this section we discuss the efforts in formulation of policies for the social inclusion of deprived sections of the society. It is divided into two parts, the first discusses pre-Ambedkar efforts and the second focuses on the attempts made by Ambedkar and the actual policy initiations by the State.

Pre-Ambedkar Efforts

Ambedkar is obviously the architect of the present reservation policy. However, prior to him, there were some instances where not only the British but also the rulers of Indian provinces like Kolhapur, Baroda, Travancore, and Cochin, realized the need to introduce educational and employment rights in nineteenth- and twentieth-century India for the non-Brahmins. The social reformer Mahatma Phuley had opened schools for the education of non-Brahmins including the Untouchables and women in Poona in nineteenth century.

Education has been the social privilege of the upper strata of the society in India. It was not only influenced by them but was also under their control. Commenting on this, Mahatma Phuley remarked 'for want of education intellect deteriorated; for want of intellect morality decayed; for want of progress, wealth vanished; for want of wealth Shudras perished and all these sorrows sprang from illiteracy' (Kshirsagar 1994: 44). The establishment of British rule in India introduced a western system of education, which was based on the principle of open access and universalistic criterion of admittance. The Woods' Despatch of 1854, perhaps could be considered the first of its kind in the process of British efforts to impart education among the socially discriminated sections. The Court of Directors' order quashing the practice of refusing admission on caste grounds may be cited here, which said, 'all schools maintained at the sole cost of the Government shall be open to all classes of its subjects without distinction' (Sinha 1986: 42). Prior to this, it was Phuley who for the first time opened schools for the Untouchables as early as in 1848. However, it was Maharaja Sayajirao Gaekwad of Baroda, who started schools in his province as a part of State effort in 1883 (Keer 1990: 4). However he had to depend on Muslim teachers for these schools as the caste-Hindu teachers would not accept the teaching posts in such schools (*Maharashitriya Dnyana Kosh*, Part VII: 644). It was a scholarship awarded to Ambedkar by the king of Baroda which enabled him to study abroad. In 1885 Sir Richard Temple, the governor of Bombay proposed to reserve fifty per cent of free scholarships for Muslim and backward Hindu castes because, it was felt that the scholarships based on the sole criterion of merit would perpetuate the Brahmin monopoly on the educational system (Jain 1990).

The demand for higher education was followed by the demand for representation in Public Services by the backward castes. This was voiced by the non-Brahmin Movement in Bombay, Madras, Mysore, and to some extent in Travancore. There was a time, when the Bombay government recognized that the recruitment from amongst the advanced classes should be stopped till an adequate number of Backward Classes were recruited to the services. This, however, was not implemented. However, in Madras, a system of communal rotation was introduced to accord representation to all the backward class groups in order to remove inequalities of representation in the services. Similarly, in Mysore orders for removing inequalities of representation in the State services were issued in 1895 that certain reservation of posts should be earmarked for all communities except Brahmins who till then had a virtual monopoly on the entire services (Mysore Government Circular No. 218–98 dated 19/21 January 1895). It was realized in Mysore early enough that reservation for backward communities did not by itself ensure equitable distribution over the whole range of communities included in this group. In actual practice it was found that the more backward among them did not receive sufficient representation. The government, therefore, evolved a policy that would give representation to all communities by according representation to the unrepresented first, the under-represented next, and the represented last. The governments of Travancore and Cochin States had followed a policy of representation to the several communities in the State approximately in proportion to their population (First Backward Class Commission Report 1955: 129–30).

The Maharaja of Kolhapur, Shahuji was inspired by the efforts of Mahatma Phuley for social reforms. He first realized that the non-Brahmins needed education and for this he founded boarding houses and also encouraged the low caste leadership to do the same for the students of their castes (Jaffrelot 2003: 159). It was way back in 1902 that he reserved fifty per cent of vacancies in the state administration for members of the backward communities (Mudaliar n. d.: 21). He became the pioneer for having provided primary education free and compulsory as early as in 1917 for the benefit of non-Brahmins including the Untouchables (ibid.). In 1919, he categorically issued a 'Hujur Order' directing the educational institutions that 'any Untouchable student joining any state aided or helped educational institution should be treated respectfully like a gentleman and taken into school rooms. If any man in the state education staff has any objection to his doing so, he must send in his resignation within six weeks from the receipt of this order.' (Quoted by Vundru in '100 Years of Reservations: Appraisal and Assessment' 2003: 72).

A committee of the British government under the Chairmanship of Sir Leslie Miller, the then Chief Justice reviewed the question in 1918. The government accepted the recommendations and directed that the proportion of members of backward communities in all headquarters and district offices of all departments should be hiked to fifty per cent of the total strength. To achieve the same, standing instructions were issued to the appointing authorities to give preference to the candidates of the backward communities in making initial appointments, so long as those candidates possessed the prescribed qualifications (First Backward Class Commission Report 1955: 129–30).

The Indian Councils Act 1861 was a commencement of a legislative devolution system by which members were appointed to the Legislative Council through nomination. The Indian Councils Act 1892 further liberalized the parliamentary system by not only increasing the number of members but also enhancing the powers of the members to ask questions of public importance. Here started not only nomination of official and non-official members but also their election (Johari 1988: 29–69). It was under these circumstances that in 1906, a delegation of Muslim community under the leadership of Aga Khan met Lord Minto, the then Viceroy and Governor General of India and demanded special representation for the Muslims. In the address, he raised mainly the following issues—

1. Muslim community is a distinct community in terms of religion and history.
2. It needs 'fair share' of representation in the Legislative Councils.

3. Due proportion of Muslims to be nominated in the gazetted and the subordinate and ministerial services of all Indian provinces.
4. Representation in the Provincial Councils, Viceroy's Council and Executive Council.
5. Establishment of a Mohamedan university and fellow in the Senate and Syndicates of Indian universities (Allana 1988: 5–15).

Lord Minto promptly responded to the demands and assured the delegation by saying that 'the Mohamedan community may rest assured that their political rights and interests as a community will be safeguarded in any administrative organisation with which I am concerned....' (ibid.: 20). In the similar vein, Lord Morley, Secretary of State for India at another occasion said, 'Let us not forget that the difference between Mohamedanism and Hinduism is not a mere difference of articles of religious faith and dogma. It is a difference of life, in tradition, in history, in all the social things as well as articles of belief that constitute a community ...' (ibid.: 24).

It was under these circumstances that the GOI Act 1909, popularly known as Morley-Minto Reforms was introduced. The Act further enlarged the size of Legislative Councils and introduced the system of Separate Electorates, whereby representation was bestowed upon different communities, classes, and interests viz., University Senates and Chambers of Commerce and Muslim community. It was here for the first time that Muslim community on the basis of religious and social differentiation acquired Separate Electorates but no other community, not even Europeans or Sikhs were given Separate Electorates at this juncture. It marked a beginning of separate representation of various minority communities in the Legislatures.

Situating the Caste and Discrimination Question
The Untouchable question had not gained any substantial place till the GOI Act 1909. But it was being acknowledged that they were a category apart suffering from social exclusion. It did amount to treating them equal as in the field of education without commensurate special considerations. This situation is well explained by Eleanor Zealliot in the following words:

The granting of an electorate for Muslims in which they alone would vote brought the idea of communal electorate for minorities to the forefront in the minds of all communities which feared their submersion in a government run by the dominant caste-Hindu community. The granting of special electorates to the Muslim community also made numbers important. Whether the vast number of Untouchables were truly Hindu and to be counted as such, or not, became an important question for the first time (Quoted by Galanter 1984: 26).

Ambedkar's Efforts and Role, 1919–55

After completing his education at Columbia University in USA and The University of London in UK, Ambedkar returned to India in 1917. It was a time when the British were expanding the participation of various groups in the administration and Legislatures. It was in 1919 that Ambedkar for the first time appeared for the rights of DCs. It was the formative stage of reservation policy that culminated in a proper and exhaustive policy in the Constitution of India in 1950, for which Ambedkar made systematic intellectual efforts.

A systematic articulation of arguments in favour of remedies against caste discrimination was put forth by Ambedkar in his first statement, to the Southborough Committee in January 1919 at the time of the reform in the Government of India Act 1919. About ten years later an attempt was made to revise the 1919 Act, through a series of RTCs. Ambedkar submitted two statements to the Simon Commission in 29 May 1928. During the RTCs in 1930–2 he made various interventions through memorandums in the meetings of the conference which ultimately led to acceptance of reservation in the Central and State Legislatures. It was in 1940s that the reservation policy took the definite shape it has today. While the final formation came at the time of framing of India's Constitution in 1947 that spelled out broader issues of safeguards, these statements and interventions, indeed, provide insights to the evolution of reservation policy for SCs. An analysis of these interventions reveal the origin of reservation policy in India and also lessons for the present discussion. These documents in their intellectual exercise are fundamental to the understanding of the malady of Hindu society and the remedies proposed by Ambedkar against denial of equal opportunity and incessant discrimination to Untouchables and similar other groups.

After looking into the writings of Ambedkar, we divide these into five phases: (1) *Prologue to the Problem of Indian Society—Seeking Solution: 1919–29*, (2) *Constitutional Reforms—Seeking Political Representation: 1930–3*, (3) *Extending the Representation—Employment and Education:*

1934–46, (4) *India's Constitution—Provisions for Social Inclusion and Empowerment: 1947–50*, and (5) *Post-Constitution Reflections: 1951–6*.

PROLOGUE TO THE PROBLEM OF INDIAN SOCIETY— SEEKING SOLUTION, 1919–29

As mentioned prior to Ambedkar's intervention in 1919, a few major developments had taken place, which include recognition of Muslims as minority by providing them Separate Electorates, and recognition of the fact by the British that Indians need to be given some political rights for establishment of self-government under the British. It was in this context that various communities like Sikhs, Anglo-Indians, and Untouchables, started demanding their separate representation in the Legislature.

First Effort at Southborough Committee, 1919

As mentioned earlier, it was in 1919 that Ambedkar, for the first time, intervened in the formulation of British policies with regard to DCs by presenting a written statement to the Southborough Committee (*BAWS* 1979, vol. 1: 247–77) appointed to look into the claims of various communities to get franchise rights for representation in Legislatures.

The first challenge before Ambedkar was how to establish the fact that the Untouchables were a distinct community in Indian society against the popular belief that Untouchables and Hindus were same, having no separate interests. Thus during this effort, he raised three important issues concerning Untouchables, namely—the position of Untouchables vis-à-vis other castes; need to have equal rights; and the methods to ensure equal rights. In his maiden attempt he proceeded within this framework. On the issue of separate identity of Untouchables his arguments to the Southborough Committee can be summarized as follows:

1. As religion divides the Hindus, Muslims, Parses, Christians, etc., to become a community, similarly caste divides Hindus into low caste and higher castes. The matter does not end with division of castes but it further divides them into Touchables and the Untouchables.
2. To become a community, there have to be common aims, beliefs, customs, etc., among the members of the community, which was missing among the Untouchables and the caste-Hindus.

3. Non-Brahmins may also be facing the intellectual superiority of Brahmins but it differs in terms of rights with the Untouchables, who need protection not from confiscation of their property but from the confiscation of their personality itself.

4. The theological bias even among the non-Brahmins for the Untouchables is so high that they rejected to function under the leadership of Untouchable officers i. e., denial of Marathas to work under the Mahar officers.

Having shown the distinct identity of Untouchables, the next important concern was to bring out their social conditions which prevented them even to become citizens and thus Ambedkar grounded the case of Untouchables in the denial of citizenship rights. Ambedkar argued:

Not only the untouchability arrested the growth of personality of Untouchables but also comes in the way of their 'material well-being'. It deprived them of certain civil rights. The Untouchable is not even a citizen. Citizenship is bundle of rights such as personal liberty, personal security, right to hold private property, equality before law, liberty of conscience, freedom of opinion, and speech, right of assembly, right of representation in country's government, and right to hold office under the state. The untouchability of Untouchables puts these rights far beyond their reach (*BAWS* 1979, vol. 1: 256).

Ambedkar was well aware that under the present system of franchise Untouchables would hardly have voting rights and that is why he demanded removal of uniformity in franchise because they 'have no modes of acquiring wealth'. For this purpose he found a solution in lowering the conditions of franchise but left it to the Committee to decide the qualifications of franchise to DCs. So far as representation was concerned, there were two possibilities suggested: either to reserve seats in plural constituencies for communities who otherwise cannot secure personal representation or grant communal electorates on the lines of Muslim representation. He argued that 'communal remedy was an exceptional remedy for an exceptional situation and it could have been rejected if the divisions were not real and did not matter.'

The evidence before the Southborough Committee by Ambedkar had no substantial impact on the GOI Act 1919 so far as separate political representation through elections is concerned. But he was able to convince that there was a community that had distinct identity and needed separate representation. It was provided in the form of representation through nomination to the DCs. A provision was incorporated in the Act itself that 'at the expiration of ten years after the passing of this Act, a statutory commission would be appointed to enquire into the working of the system of government, the growth of education and the development of representative institutions in British India....' In this context, a commission was appointed in 1928 under the Chairmanship of Simon. It provided another opportunity for Ambedkar to plead the case of DCs but this time, he not only insisted upon separate political representation through election and adoption of alternative franchise system but also to take measures to protect their civil rights. The safeguards were also sought in the field of education and employment in the Public Services with the State.

Second Effort at Simon Commission, 1928

While submitting a statement (*BAWS* 1982, vol. 2: 430–46) concerning safeguards for the protection of the DCs as minority to the Simon Commission, Ambedkar articulating the concerns observed:

Injustice had been done to the DCs in 1909 by completely ignoring their representation and in 1919 Act by giving them minimal representation as compared to their population in the Legislative Council, which was endorsed by Chelmsford Report and Muddiman Committee respectively. Moreover, their representation was based on the process of nomination that was emphatically opposed during 1919. The standing of the community in terms of economic and educational status instead of numerical strength should be taken into account in determining its quota of representation. Thus the lower the standing of a community the greater the electoral advantage to it over the rest (*BAWS* 1982, vol. 2: 437).

Thus Ambedkar did not want the numerical strength of a community to be the benchmark for representation but the economic and educational standing, that is the lower the economic and educational standing the higher the representation and vice-versa. In the opinion of Ambedkar there were two major objections raised by various quarters against the application of the principle of election to the DCs—difficulty in forming constituencies, and difficulty in getting a sufficiently large electorate. The first objection was termed to be absurd as the Muslims and Europeans also did not have unified constituencies but scattered ones. And the second objection could be tackled with adult suffrage in case of DCs instead of qualifications of property and education that debarred them from participating in electing their representatives, was asserted by him (*BAWS* 1982, vol. 2: 441).

There appear two major shifts in Ambedkar's assertion—one, that the DCs would not insist upon communal electorates if reserved seats were carved out in the general constituencies and two, instead of leaving the conditions of franchise for them on the Commission he argued for adult suffrage, and in its absence insisted for Separate Electorates.

Appearing for Evidence before the Southborough Committee, Ambedkar outlined the kind of social system prevailing in India vis-à-vis DCs and why Untouchables as a distinct community needed to have separate representation in the councils, and the same was re-emphasized during 1928. However, there was an addition of promulgating safeguards by incorporating protection of rights through guarantees so that the rights not only remained on paper but also got secured through guarantees. The guarantees proposed by him included:

1. That the education of the DCs shall be recognized as the first charge on the revenues of the Province and that an equitable and just proportion of the total grant for education should be earmarked for the benefit of the DCs.
2. That the right of the DCs to unrestricted recruitment in the army, navy, and the police shall be recognized without any limitation as to caste.
3. That for a period of 30 years the right of the DCs for priority in the matter of the recruitments to all posts, gazetted as well as non-gazetted in all civil services shall be recognized.
4. That the right of the DCs to the appointment of a special inspector of police from amongst themselves for every District shall be recognized.
5. That the right of the DCs to effective representation (as defined above) on the Local Bodies shall be recognized by the Provincial Government.
6. That the right of the DCs to appeal to the Government of India in cases of violation of these rights by the Provincial Government shall be recognized and the Government of India shall be given the power to compel the Provincial Government to conform to the law in the matter (*BAWS* 1982, vol. 2: 442)

Ambedkar argued that representative government without a system of guarantees could be a most dangerous experiment for minorities. Taking instances of post-war history and guarantee clauses for the benefit of the minorities in case of Austria, Hungary, and Romania, he insisted that if representative government among European people was so weak in spite of secularization of politics then, how weak it could be in India, where politics was nothing but theology in practice. He argued that it was against this theology that the DCs needed to be protected.

Ambedkar's Opinion on British Education Policy vis-à-vis Depressed Classes

Questioning the sincerity of the government in the matter of promoting the education of the DCs, and putting the efforts in the right direction, while presenting their case (*BAWS* 1982, vol. 2: 425–8), he suggested some of the measures which the government must adopt in the present context. Such measures included—modifying compulsory primary education act in a way that the DCs were inspired to get education; making primary education obligatory; and applying the recommendations made by the Hunter Commission regarding the education of the Muslims to the DCs to make their educational progress a fact, and securing entry in the Public Service to the DCs to induce them to get an education (*BAWS* 1982, vol. 2: 427–8). At this juncture, Ambedkar's concern was to insist that the DCs also have the right to education provided by the State.

Public Services and Ambedkar's Interventions

In a separate report on Public Services to the Simon Commission (*BAWS* 1982, vol. 2: 393–9), Ambedkar argued that the Untouchables, having been virtually excluded from the services would prefer the system of appointments by selection, to the system of selection by open competition. The Brahmins were vehemently opposing this on the ground of efficiency. Recalling the case for Indianization of administration—to prefer Indians as compared to Europeans—demanded by Gokhale, Ambedkar argued that this demand did not rest on efficient administration, but on good administration. Similar was the case for other than Brahmins then. He further argued that efficiency through competitive exams pre-supposed that the educational system of the State was sufficiently democratic and facilities for education were sufficiently used by all classes. Moreover, democracy needed not only efficient government but also good government and it required the representation of various groups in the administration. Supplementing the argument, he added that as struggles for equality were going on between the Brahmins and non-Brahmins, between Hindus and Muslims, and between Touchables and Untouchables, they were bound to be partisan, and expansion of administration from diverse social groups was mandatory to avoid the ill effects of this. Presenting the case he suggested that a certain number of vacancies in Class I and Class II services to be filled by system of nomination with a pass examination for other than Brahmins. Also, posting an increasing number of DC officers at the headquarters. Ambedkar also suggested constitution of a Central Recruitment Board as an application registering agency, so that applicants come in touch with the offices.

Concluding this period of Ambedkar's interventions, we observe that there is articulation of the problems of DCs by showing how they differ as a community from the rest of the population in general, and from Hindus in particular. There are references of social discrimination and denial of civil rights to DCs but this was a juvenile stage of argument. The emphasis was more on political representation and less on civil rights. The questions of education and Public Services were raised but the solutions were more in the context of equal rights, and did not emphasize on legal safeguards against violation of rights.

CONSTITUTIONAL REFORMS: SEEKING POLITICAL REPRESENTATION, 1930–3

The second phase of Ambedkar's efforts surround RTCs held during 1930 and 1933. This period is marked by two breakthroughs. Firstly, after being nominated to the RTCs, his concerns got enlarged from the Bombay Province to the All India level. Secondly, the concerns got widened not only in terms of geographical space but also in terms of issues and their remedies. He came down heavily on the role of the British in the first RTC and argued that they had been 'not only indifferent but also incompetent' in taking decisions on providing equal rights to Untouchables. Taking a strong stand on the issue, he emphatically said that though the problems of DCs were rooted in social mechanism, these need political instead of social solutions. The following remarks show the kind of disappointment Ambedkar felt during his initial intervention at the first RTC:

We feel that nobody can remove our grievances as well as we can, and we cannot remove them unless we get political power in our own hands. No share of political power can evidently come to us so long as the British government remains as it is only in Swaraj constitution that we stand any chance of getting power into our own hands, without which we cannot bring salvation to our people ...

Depressed by the Government, suppressed by the Hindu and disregarded by the Muslim, we are left in a most intolerable position of utter helplessness to which I am sure there is no parallel and to which I was bound to call attention (*BAWS* 1982, vol. 2: 506–7).

Thus, here the idea was to show how maliciously Hindu society treated Untouchables, and the government ignored their concerns and why they needed equality of opportunity and protection of civil rights through political representation. The assertions in the arguments were more vigorous, pressing, and comprehensible during this period than at the time of evidence before the Southborough Committee and statements before the Simon Commission. Representation through co-option or nomination was opposed again to enable effective representation.

For the British government, all the minorities were on a common footing but Ambedkar asserted that the social standing of one minority differed from the other. Although minorities had many things in common but the DC suffered from one more handicap in the form of Untouchability and social ostracism that was missing for others and this made their case special. The disabilities were so rampant and effective as if imposed by law, was stated by him.

Ambedkar and Rao Bahadur Srinivasan jointly presented a design of political safeguards for the protection of the DCs at the first RTC (*BAWS* 1982, vol. 2: 528–53). This could be seen as the first systematic presentation of problems and their solutions where clear conditions were cited. It comprised of equal rights, legal safeguards against discrimination or violation of rights, and mechanism for equal share and participation in public life, that is, representation in services, education, and Legislatures. Ambedkar declared that without such provisions, the future Constitution of India would be incomplete (*BAWS* 1982, vol. 2: 546).

Equal rights were seen in terms of citizenship rights so that untouchability did not become an obstacle in practicing right to equality. It was made clear that mere provision of equal rights was not going to help. And to secure equality, there was 'a need to have adequate penalties from interference in the enjoyment of declared rights'. Social boycott had been an effective weapon in the hands of caste-Hindus, where a complete alienation or segregation could take place in the public sphere if the DCs tried to exercise equal rights. Discrimination being so rampant, it was suggested that there should be protection against discrimination through legislation or Executive order so that no civil place should treat them unequally (*BAWS* 1982, vol. 2: 548–50).

The memorandum for the first time clearly advocated for— (1) adequate representation in the Legislatures, and (2) adequate representation in Public Services.[1] Ambedkar remarked that even if adequately represented in the legislatures, DCs would remain in minority and sheer political representation could not help them effectively. So if injustice to their interests and neglect of their vital needs takes place then the Governor General in Council or Secretary of State as appellate authority should adopt a reprisal mechanism as monitoring authorities. Another solution for addressing the interests and promoting the welfare of DCs was requested in the form of Special Departmental Care in the inchargeship of a minister. Moreover, having representation of the DCs in the Cabinet so that even the general policy of the government was prepared by looking into the safeguard for their interests (*BAWS* 1982, vol. 2: 554). Thus for the first time a demand for not only proper representation in the Legislatures but also in the Cabinet and a special department to care for the rights of DC under a minister was proposed.

There could be no tangible progress due to deliberations at the first RTC. Winding up the conference, Prime Minister MacDonald expected co-operation in future from the sections absent from the conference. Though the first RTC was adjourned without any decision, the representatives of the DC did succeed in convincing the conference that they were entitled to be recognized as a separate entity for political and constitutional purposes with other minority groups (Chatterjee 1996: 235).

In September 1931 the second RTC was held to solve the problems of various groups in India. Ambedkar and Rao Bahadur Srinivasan submitted another memorandum (*BAWS* 1982, vol. 2: 652–72) redefining and clarifying further the details of special representation. Some of the important demands were—(1) Special representation in the Provincial Legislatures and in Federal Legislatures, in proportion to their population (2) Separate Electorates not to be altered except in case of referendum by themselves, and such a referendum to take place only after twenty years and under universal adult suffrage (3) DCs not only to have Separate Electorates but also to be represented by themselves (4) DCs to be defined strictly on the basis of the system of Untouchability, and (5) Changing the nomenclature of DCs to non-caste-Hindus, Protestant Hindus, Non-conformist Hindus, etc. (*BAWS* 1982, vol. 2: 669–72).

The second RTC witnessed a major contentious discussion between Mahatma Gandhi and Ambedkar. Gandhiji had remarked during the meeting in the Federal Committee held prior to the meeting of the Minorities Committee that he would consider Separate Electorates only for Muslims and the Sikhs. However, the representatives of DCs, Anglo-Indians and Indian Christians contested this position in the meeting of the Minorities Committee. On the question of treating DC as a separate entity and providing them Separate Electorates, Ambedkar was confronted with the arguments of Gandhiji viz. 'will the Untouchables remain Untouchables in the times to come as the Muslims to remain Muslims and Sikhs as Sikhs ...', and 'I would resist it (Separate Electorates for Untouchables).' (Proceeding of sub-committee, vol. II sub-committee No. II Minorities, India Round Table Conference 1930–1: 77–8).

In the meantime, a note (*BAWS* 1982, vol. 2: 491–502) was submitted by Ambedkar to the Indian Franchise Committee, popularly known as Lothian Committee, on the question of the confusion prevailing on defining DCs vis-à-vis Untouchables and who need to be known as Untouchables. The Untouchable, he opined, was an unclean person not fit for social interaction. He remarked that Untouchability is not merely in the literal sense of the term, 'where pollution by touch' test is applied but it also has notional sense of application. He argued further that if we apply only the literal sense then people should take into account purification modes adopted in case touch with an Untouchable takes place. But in situations where touch is not considered to go for purification, there also exist the distinctions of pure and impure, which infers that untouchability is not confined to literal sense of the term, rather it needs to be understood in the notional sense of the term as well. In his analysis he said it was absurd to claim that untouchability was on the decline. The literal form of untouchability may be diminishing and not vanishing, whereas, the notional form of untouchability still prevailed because it was based on the religious dogma, and the Hindu considers observing untouchability adherence to his religion (*BAWS* 1982, vol. 2: 494).

A lack of compromise between the leaders of Indian groups made the British Prime Minister adjourn the second RTC *sine die* with a suggestion to put a signed requisition authorizing the Prime Minister to arbitrate and give decision on the communal issue. Gandhi signed this but Ambedkar refused to do so asserting that the demands of the Untouchables were so reasonable having no need for arbitration (*BAWS* 1982, vol. 2: 74).

Communal Award and Poona Pact

Meanwhile, the British Prime Minister, Ramsay MacDonald, announced his decision known as Communal Award on 4 August 1932 to impart Separate Electorates to the DCs. Along with it he also declared that he would be glad to accept any other solution of the communal problem acceptable to all communities. The Award conceded Separate Electorates to the Muslims, Sikhs, Indian Christians, Anglo-Indians, and Europeans. Labour, commerce, industry, mining and planting, land holders and universities were also given separate constituencies and fixed seats. It suggested the formation of general constituencies, where all voters except Muslims, Sikhs, Christians, Anglo-Indians or Europeans were entitled to vote. It was for the first time that DCs were recognized as a minority.

The notable features of the Award were:

1. There shall be Separate Electorates for the DCs earmarked from the General Constituencies.
2. The DCs will not only vote for the election of DCs representatives but also for the Hindu candidates of General Constituencies. Thus they will get weightage of having two votes.
3. The system of Separate Electorates will last only for twenty years.
4. This system can be abolished with the mutually agreed alternative mechanism (*BAWS* 1990, vol. 9: 80–1).

The granting of Communal Electorate to the DCs touched Mahatma Gandhi so deeply that he declared 'fast' till the decision was reverted. Writing a letter to the British Prime Minister he said that Separate Electorates were equally harmful for the DCs and Hinduism. Responding to the letter the Prime Minister remarked the following:

1. The decision should be acceptable to you as signatory to the agreement to have left the question of electorates to the government due to contradictory views of Indian representatives at the second RTC.
2. It is misunderstanding that the electorates will have a split between Hindus and Untouchables rather two votes have been accorded to DCs so that they

not only elect their own representatives but also vote for Hindu candidates in the general constituencies. The two stage election of DCs representatives will make Hindus also to vote for them for their final election.

3. There is no communal electorate for the DCs as for other groups like Muslims, Christians, Sikhs etc.

4. The Separate Electorates for the DCs not based on their population (which is higher than the electorates assigned) but to secure Spokespersons for them.

5. Again the agreement of the communities concerned (DCs and Hindus) can substitute other electoral arrangements for those that Government devised in a sincere endeavour to weigh the conflicting claims on their just merits (ibid.: 83–6).

It was on the fifth day of the fast that leaders of both sides that is, Hindus and the DC agreed on a formula that is known as the Poona Pact, signed on 25 September 1932, by Ambedkar on behalf of the DCs and by Madan Mohan Malaviya on behalf of the caste-Hindus. The substance of the Poona Pact was the reservation of seats based on Joint Electorates to the DCs out of the seats classified as general seats. All members of the DCs who were registered on the general electoral roll of certain constituencies had to elect a panel of four candidates belonging to their own community, and the four persons who received the highest number of votes in this primary election were to be the candidates for election to the reserved seat, but the candidate finally elected to the reserved seat was to be elected by the general electorate including the DCs. The number of seats reserved for the DCs under the Poona Pact was practically double the number reserved under the Communal Award (Joint Committee on Indian Constitutional Reforms, vol. I: 96)

Apart from this, there was a provision for 18 per cent reservation for the DC in the Central Legislature of British India. The DCs were not to be discriminated against while being considered for appointments to Public Services. However, there was no fixed percentage of seats for them at this juncture. Every province was to earmark adequate educational grants for providing educational facilities to the members of the DC (*BAWS* 1990, vol. 9: 85–8).

We observe that during the RTCs, Ambedkar's arguments became more voluble and determined, and solutions to the problems more precise and specific. At the same time, the solutions were confined to improving the present conditions. On the front of education and employment, there were proposals put by Ambedkar. Consequently there had been the acceptance of general rules for the participation of the DCs in the educational and employment spheres. However on the political front the Separate Electorates could not be accepted, and Ambedkar accepted to the propositions of Joint Electorates for the DCs.

EXTENDING THE REPRESENTATION—EMPLOYMENT AND EDUCATION, 1934–46

Although the RTC and its culmination in the Poona Pact had given space in Central and Provincial Legislatures, but in Ambedkar's view, it was not complete in terms of safeguards. Though, Ambedkar made some references to the Pact afterwards but he avoided any overt comment on it immediately. On 4 February 1940, he came out openly against the Pact saying that 'Safeguards under Poona Pact are inadequate.' It was again after a gap of two years that Ambedkar raised the issue of safeguarding the interests of SCs in a comprehensive way while submitting a memorandum (*BAWS* 1991, vol. 10: 405–42) to the Governor General on 29 November 1942 as Member of the Executive Council.

The arrival of the Cripps Mission to India on 22 March 1942 to negotiate with Indian political parties to find a solution of the constitutional crisis arising out of resignation by the Congress Ministries and secure their co-operation in the efforts of the Second World War provided an opportunity to Ambedkar to put forth his demands. It proposed constituting a Constituent Assembly. It was an important and historical opportunity to demand representation for the SCs, who did not have adequate representation in the Legislatures.

Ambedkar submitted a fresh proposal. The memorandum was divided into four parts where the first part dealt with political grievances, second with educational grievances, third with grievances of neglect of publicity and role in government contacts and the fourth with the duty of the government towards distressed people. The political grievances were further divided into four parts—(1) inadequate representation in the Central Legislature, (2) inadequate representation in the Central Executive, (3) absence of representation in the Public Services, and (4) absence of representation in the Federal Public Services Commission.

Using statistics, he argued that the representation in the Central Assembly was so low that out of 141 elected and nominated members only two belonged to SCs (representing 40 million of population) and among them also, one was officially nominated. What could two representatives do among 141. Ambedkar reminded that at the second RTC the Hindus did not oppose this demand. Coming out with a solution for this, he suggested that whenever there occurred vacancies in the Central Assembly, such vacancies should go to increase the representation of SCs and same could be done in the Central Executive.

The representation in political institutions was inadequate, it was almost absent in the Public Services where out of 1056 Indian Civil Service officials only 1 belonged to SC. Ambedkar pointed to the prevalence of communal representation in Public Services for the minorities and absence of it in case of SCs. And it was due to two factors—(1) absence of declaration of SCs to be Minority, and (2) non-fixation of a particular quota for them. It brought out that in case of other minorities the Public Services were made a matter of obligation, whereas in case of SCs, it had been a matter of discretion of government functionaries.

Further, the following issues were raised in the Memorandum

1. The European officials are blissfully ignorant about the special protection of SCs, and the Hindu self-interest combined with age-old prejudice keeps the percentage of SCs in Public Services almost absent.
2. Public Services are vital avenue for employment for SCs because all other openings are blocked due to age-old customs of not allowing SCs to adopt any occupation not assigned to them.
3. The hope for employment in Public Services gives them government patronage in encouraging spread of education.
4. In modern times administration has not only power to execute but also to legislate and it makes the need for representation of SC in the hostile, unjust and prejudiced Public Services significant (*BAWS* 1991, vol. 10: 417–25).

Evaluating the situation of SCs in the Public Services, he termed the condition not only deplorable but also intolerable because there was a virtual absence of SCs in the Indian Civil Services. Another important problem mentioned by Ambedkar related to the composition of appointing authorities, which were mainly comprised of Europeans and Hindus or Muslims. He observed that the interests of the SCs will continue to be neglected and suffered until there was a solution of these problems in 1942, and he suggested the following solutions:

1. Declare that they (SC) are a minority for the purpose of services like the other communities,
2. Fix 13.5 per cent as the proportion of annual vacancies in the I. C. S. and both in the Central Services that are recruited on an all India basis and that are recruited locally as the share to which they are entitled and which (for consideration of) in equity and justice should be reserved for them. Unless this is done the Scheduled Castes will never get their due share in Public Services,
3. Appointment of a Scheduled Caste officer to see that the provisions made in the interests of the Scheduled Castes in this behalf are carried by all Departments concerned (*BAWS* 1991, vol. 10: 420, 423).

Thus it was in 1942 that Ambedkar demanded proportional representation of SCs in the Public Services.

With regard to education, Ambedkar expressed himself in detail while submitting a report to the Simon Commission. This time the emphasis was more on solutions than on describing the evolution of educational policy of the British and its neglect of application to SCs. Bringing out the significance of education, Ambedkar opined that howsoever numerous the SCs might get ministerial posts, it will not have particular consequence for their community. It was necessary that they are represented in the Executive/administration and it could be achieved by high degree of education. He emphasized for education more in the field of science and technology than elsewhere. The solutions offered were the following:

1. An annual grant of Rs. 2 lakhs for scholarships for Scheduled Caste students taking science and technology courses tenable at the universities or other scientific and technical training institutions in India.
2. An annual grant of 1 lakh of rupees to be spent on scholarships for the education of Scheduled Caste students for Science and Technology in foreign universities in England, the Dominions, in Europe and in America.
3. One-tenth of the total admission should be reserved for the SC in the School of Mines and granting the admitted students free-ships and scholarships.

4. As the GOI spends 3 lakhs per annum on the University of Aligarh and University of Benares—the institutions of Muslims and Hindus, same amount be spent on advanced education of SC annually.
5. Appointing two Members of SC on the Central Advisory Board of Education to make the board interested for them.
6. SCs are generally unskilled labour and have lack of technical knowledge so to train them they should have—1. Apprenticeships in Government Printing Presses, and 2. Apprenticeships in Railway Workshops (*BAWS* 1991, vol. 10: 427–32).

On the request of the Institute of Pacific Studies in 1943, Ambedkar wrote a paper on the problems and solutions of the SCs (*BAWS* 1990, vol. 9: 403–25). Apart from re-emphasizing the questions raised in the memorandum to the Governor General on the grievances of the SCs, he also mentioned about another important issue, namely forming separate settlements for the habitation of SCs. The idea behind this was that separate villages in terms of territory could be created where there would be no distinction on the basis of high and low, Touchable and Untouchable. To realize this, it was suggested that a commission should be appointed and it should be provided with a fixed amount to carry on the scheme. On another occasion, addressing session of the Scheduled Castes Federation of India in 1945 (*BAWS* 1979, vol. 1: 355–79), Ambedkar preferred to speak on the communal problem facing India with reference to a deadlock between Hindus and the Muslims on the question of the Constituent Assembly. He maintained that the majority in India is a communal majority that is fixed and unchanging, not a political majority, which keeps changing with time and space. During the address he also referred to the question of SCs, as part of minority community problem. Commenting on the existing state of affairs, he regretted that:

there is a community economically poor, socially degraded, educationally backward and which is exploited, oppressed and tyrannized without shame and without remorse, disowned by society, unowned by Government and which has no security for protection and no guarantee for justice, fair play and equal opportunity. Such a community is told that it can have no safeguards, not because it has no case for safeguards but only because the bully on whom the bill of rights is presented thinks that because the community is not politically organized to have sanctions behind its demand he can successfully bluff (*BAWS* 1979, vol. 1: 366).

Regarding representation in the Public Services, he maintained that there was already administrative practice to give representation to the minorities as per the Resolutions of 1934[2] and 1943[3] which need to be converted into statutory obligation through a schedule in the Constitution. To make the Executive representative and efficient, he suggested— (1) the quantum of representation in the Executive should be as per their population, and it should be constituted in a way that it has a mandate, not only from the majority but also from the minorities in the Legislature, (2) the Executive should be non-parliamentary in the sense that it is not removable before the term of the Legislature, (3) the positions in the Executive should be so filled that the prime minister represents not the majority but the whole house and the persons representing a particular minority community should have the confidence of the members of his community in the Legislature, and (4) the Prime Minister and his Cabinet should be elected by a single transferable vote and the representatives of the Cabinet of minority community should be elected by the members of the minority communities of the Legislature. Lord Wavell, the Governor General of India had proposed for Indianization of the Executive Council vis-à-vis full self-government to the Indian people. Responding to this Ambedkar on 7 June 1945 gave a proposal (*BAWS* 2003, vol. 17, no. 2: 166–70) where he alleged that the SCs have not been appropriately represented in the Council and it was low not only in terms of their proportion in the population but also in terms of their needs (as their social standing is peculiar and vulnerable).

The political parties in India termed the Wavell's Plan as disappointing and unacceptable since it offered nothing materially different from the Cripps Plan. In the meantime, the British government sent a three member delegation of cabinet ministers known as the Cabinet Mission Plan on 23 March 1946 with a twofold mission— (1) to negotiate a settlement on the basis of which the Indian Constitution would be framed, (2) setting up of a national government in favour of which transference of power would take place. The Cabinet Mission met various leaders and Ambedkar presented a memorandum (*BAWS* 2003, vol. 17, no. 2: 171–81) on behalf of the All India Scheduled Castes Federation on 5 April 1946. This memorandum was also based on the resolutions adopted by the working committee of the Federation. In the memorandum it was categorically mentioned that the SCs would not accept any constitution which did not contain:

1. True and adequate representation in all the Legislatures and Executives both at the provincial and central levels.
2. Election through Separate Electorates.
3. Adequate representation in the Public Services and Public Service Commissions at the federal and provincial levels.
4. Provision of adequate sum in the annual budgets of the provincial and Central governments for the higher education of SCs.
5. Provision of new and separate settlements.

Justifying the provision of Separate Electorates, it was mentioned that it had been a very old demand of the SCs and had got approval of the British government in 1932. Ambedkar also argued that between the two, namely, present political representation and Separate Electorates, the latter is superior as it has potential to select better representation.

On 16 May 1946 the Cabinet Mission submitted its report including solutions for the political problems of India. The proposals got appreciation from the Congress leaders and Gandhiji described it as 'the best document the British Government could have produced in the circumstances' (quoted in Johari 1988: 161). On the contrary, minorities including the SC leaders criticized the Cabinet Mission's proposals, for not giving adequate attention to their demands. SCs were not recognized as minorities, and the demand of Separate Electorates was set aside. Responding to this, Ambedkar wrote a letter to Prime Minister Attlee 'to reconsider the matter of SCs and make a declaration that they are an important minority to avert a possible danger to their position in the new Constitution' (*BAWS* 1991, vol. 10: 514).

In October 1946, Ambedkar went to meet Attlee and Churchill and took a memorandum (*BAWS* 1991, vol. 10: 512–14) to circulate. Terming the decisions of the Mission as most galling and astounding, he brought few facts to light:

1. The Untouchables denied right to send their genuine representatives in the Central Executive as one of them appointed by the Congress and the other by the Muslim League.
2. The Cabinet had to have two members of SC as per Shimla Agreement in 1945 but denied in 1946 by the Cabinet Mission.
3. Separate Electorates as the necessary condition for the representation of SC that was denied.

To save the Untouchables from the 'impending peril', Ambedkar suggested the following measures:

1. Declaring Untouchables as minority.
2. Instituting a machinery to examine whether the safeguards for minorities framed by the Constituent Assembly are adequate and real.
3. Circumscribing the power of the future Indian Legislature to do away with minority safeguards by bare majority (*BAWS* 2003, vol. 17, no. 2: 173–4).

To sum up, during 1934–46 Ambedkar's efforts were focused on the extension of reservation to public employment and education. Some other solutions also had significant additions from the previous articulations, such as separate settlements, re-emphasizing on the Separate Electorates, and asking for a share in the government contacts carried out by private contractors. The most important aspect of interventions during this period has been to put a check on the future Legislatures and Executives to end the safeguards agreed upon, that was further elaborated in the memorandum to the Constituent Assembly in the next phase of interventions.

India's Constitution—Provisions for Social Inclusion and Empowerment, 1947–50

In this phase, Ambedkar's efforts to put inclusive policies for excluded groups during the making of the Constitution for free India by the Constituent Assembly have been discussed. It was the time when the future course of history was to be set in motion. As earlier mentioned, Ambedkar termed the Cabinet Mission's recommendations regarding SCs as most galling and astounding for two major reasons— (1) not declaring them as minorities and (2) not accepting their long-standing demand of Separate Electorates. It was in this context that Ambedkar presented a memorandum (*BAWS* 1979, vol. 1: 391–450) on the safeguards of SCs to the Constituent Assembly on behalf of the All India Scheduled Castes Federation in 1946. However, he was appointed the Chairman of the Drafting Committee of the Assembly on 23 December 1947, and drafted and debated the provisions for safeguarding the interests of the SCs in particular and other marginalized sections in general.

The Memorandum presented to the Constituent Assembly could be thought of as a small constitution for the protection of common citizenry, and attempted to established social democracy and State Socialism. Ambedkar suggested a dual strategy for adopting 'Inclusive Policy' referring to it as 'Safeguards Against Economic Exploitation' and

'Safeguards Against Social Discrimination and Isolation'. Here, we observe the widening and maturing perspectives of Ambedkar's formulations. He suggested separate remedies against social discrimination and remedies against economic exploitation. A number of measures are suggested as remedies against social discrimination, the focus of which is equal participation in multiple spheres. As a remedy against economic exploitation he proposed to adopt State Socialism as a general solution to the problem of poverty and economic exploitation. And it is through this policy that he expected to emancipate the poor in general and SCs in particular and compensate for historical exclusion.

The problem of discriminated groups was twofold for him. Firstly, this was related to the lack of access to income earning capital assets like agricultural land and capital, services necessary for business, employment and education and skill, due to denial of the same in the past. The second relates to the continuation of discrimination in the labour and other markets, in some forms, if not in its original form. If the problem is twofold then it requires a dual solution—one set of remedies as compensation for the historical denial of economic rights, and a second set of remedies to provide safeguards against discrimination in the present in various market and non-market transactions, and ensuring due share and participation in employment, education, business, and other supportive services.

To address the problem of 'structural inequalities', Ambedkar suggested measures for the equalization of economic opportunities for poor in general and low castes in particular. These were equal access to land and capital, opportunity for employment, provision of education and health, and use of economic planning as an instrument to promote equalization policy. Such a policy for the poor in general will create an egalitarian basis for the economic and social empowerment of excluded sections and compensate for the historical denial of right of property, business, equality in employment and education etc.

Revealing the limitation of improved ownership of income earning assets and education to empower the excluded group for using business opportunities and employment, Ambedkar pointed out that the continuation of the discriminatory working of markets, including the labour market, private education, and housing services may not in practice enable them to make use of these opportunities. Therefore Ambedkar suggested a complementary remedy of 'Equal and Fair Opportunity' to ensure fair access to employment, capital assets, and social needs like education and housing canalized through market and non-market channels. The Equal Opportunity policy suggested by Ambedkar carried four main attributes—(1) legal safeguards in the form of laws against discrimination in economic, social, and other spheres, (2) continuous pro-active measures to ensure fair share and participation in various spheres like Legislature, Executive, employment, education, and other public spheres for discriminated groups in the form of reservation policy both in public and private spheres, (3) the 'Equal Opportunity policy' to ensure due share in business, employment, education, housing, and other services and (4) together the policy of 'Economic and Social Empowerment and Equal Opportunity' will help to address the problem of poor in general and the dual problem of discriminated groups.

Here, we observe that Ambedkar's proposals had become more clear, systematic and forthright with arguments more focused and sharpened. While proposing protection against discrimination, he argued that government officials and private employers were in a habit of discrimination on the basis of race, creed, social status and other factors and this needed to be treated as an offence as it primarily affected SCs. Above all it functioned to stop the SCs from utilizing even the common places of the village.

The demand for Separate Electorates was reiterated with adult franchise and cumulative voting system so that true representatives are elected, all adults participate in their election, and SCs determine not only their own representatives but have a say in electing others to the legislative bodies. He proposed political representation not only in the Legislature but also in the Executive as per their population. He further emphasized that no minority should be given more representation than its proportion in the population. Even if this had to be given in unavoidable circumstances then it was to be granted by carving out the representation of the majority and not the share of the minority community (the rationale behind this was that Muslims were given more representation than their population and it was cut from the proportion of other minorities).

The government was to take special responsibility and make adequate provisions in the budgets of state and the central governments for the education of the SCs. Here, the responsibility for secondary and college education was put on the States and to fund foreign education of the SCs on the Union government. However, the responsibility of primary education was bestowed upon the state governments with a fixed amount as per population. It was pointed out that these demands were not new but contained in the Poona Pact; the only addition was regarding the fixing of amount as per the population of the SCs.

Regarding the Public Services, the propositions were—proportional representation to their population; compulsory recruitment with minimum qualifications, education, age and other criteria; continuing the concessions on the basis of Resolutions of 1934 and 1943; and, having one member of SCs in the Public Service Commission or the Committee constituted for filling up of vacancies. The argument put forth here was Clause 8 of the Poona Pact guaranteeing fair representation to SCs in the Public Services. The only addition now proposed was to have it as per population proportion.

The demand for Separate Settlements was once again raised in the memorandum to the Cabinet Mission Plan submitted by Ambedkar. The proposition contained three aspects—(1) establishment of a Separate Settlement Commission, (2) starting with a fund of Rs 5 crores for the purpose, and (3) giving power to the Commission to purchase any land offered for sale and use it for the purpose. The argument was justified by the circumstances under which the Untouchables lived separated from the village but dependent on the villagers for their livelihood, and meted out indignities as well as injustices.

One of the most crucial propositions was the section on the safeguards against amendments in the safeguards. The guarantees to protect the rights were proposed because without guarantees, rights have no meaning. And it was in this light that Ambedkar proposed safeguards to amend the provisions containing protection of SCs.

This memorandum to the Constituent Assembly was submitted at a time when Ambedkar was not Chairman of the Drafting Committee. However, in late 1947 he assumed this office. The wisdom of the Constituent Assembly had by now become favourable to the rights of the Policy of Reservation, under which, on the political front the seats were reserved for SCs/STs in the Parliament and the State Assemblies. Referring to an agreement arrived at in the very beginning of the meeting of the Constituent Assembly, Ambedkar mentioned that a give and take formula was adopted so that the minorities would not press for Separate Electorates, and the majority would not oppose reserved seats for the minorities (*BAWS* 1990, vol. 9: 530–2). It meant that Ambedkar did follow the agreement to avoid any further confusion on the issue and as per situation did not press for Separate Electorates, which he favoured. It shows that though Ambedkar did not really favour reservation over Separate Electorates for representation to the SCs, but in the given circumstances he had little option but to accept the arrangement. At the same time, he kept it open for future generations to choose what they desired.

On the question of reservations in Public Services, the wisdom of the Constituent Assembly was in favour of some safeguards for the SCs. However, there was a difference of opinion on the methods to be adopted. Ambedkar, summarizing the opinion of the House made two points namely—that there shall be equality of opportunity for all the citizens and, there must at the same time be a provision made for the entry of certain communities which have so far been outside the administration. Subsequently, Article 10 of the draft constitution that became Article 16 in the present Constitution was adopted and both the views got combined (Saxena 1981: 386–88). It was on the consent of two communities—Muslims and Christians, in the Advisory Committee that they were not treated as minorities for the purpose of political representation (Saxena 1981: 391). After a vehement discussion on the issue, during the third reading on Article 16, the word 'Backward' instead of Minorities was used and specific safeguards for the claims of the SCs/STs was provided in Article 335. Moreover 'it was left to the government to make provisions for other Backward communities which have not been included' was remarked by Ambedkar in the Constituent Assembly while discussing Article 10 of the draft constitution.

Participating in the debate, he remarked, 'with regard to the minorities, there is a special reference to that in article 296, where it has been laid down that some provision will be made with regard to the minorities. Of course we did not lay down any proportion. That is quite clear from the section itself, but we have not omitted the minorities from consideration.' These observations reveal that the makers of the Constitution had been conscious of the status of other backward castes and minorities, but due to the prevailing circumstances a clear strategy was not adopted.

This phase saw widening of the perspectives of Ambedkar's formulations and the actual policy measures. The most significant contribution of Ambedkar had been the proposal through the Memorandum known as 'States and Minorities' submitted to the Constituent Assembly. This proposal talked of separate remedies against social discrimination and remedies against economic exploitation. A number of measures were suggested as remedies against social discrimination, the focus of which was equal participation in multiple spheres. As a remedy against economic exploitation he proposed to adopt State Socialism as a general solution to the problem of poverty and economic exploitation. And it is through this policy that he expected to emancipate the poor in general and SCs in particular, and compensate for the historical exclusion.

POST-CONSTITUTION REFLECTIONS, 1951–6

This phase deals with the contributions of Ambedkar after the formulation of a reservation policy and other safeguards adopted by the Constitution of India. This was the phase where the policy being implemented and the flaws in the execution, and also the need to conceptualize the areas left out in the Constitution were coming to the fore. The first intervention by Ambedkar in the post-Constitution period comes in the form of intercession on the judicial interpretation of Article 16(4) of the Constitution vis-à-vis the communal government order of the Madras government involving reservation for the Backward Classes (including OBCs) in educational institutions. It was in the light of the judgment by the Supreme Court regarding Article 16(4) that the Constitution (First Amendment) Bill was introduced by Ambedkar as law minister. This amendment (*BAWS* 1997, vol. 15: 329–34) apart from other articles introduced Article 15(4) providing that 'nothing in this article or in clause (2) of Article 29 shall prevent the State from making any special provision for the advancement of any socially and educationally Backward Classes of citizens or for the Scheduled Castes and the Scheduled Tribes.' It was the first concrete step towards making reservations for the Other Backward Classes (OBCs). Secondly, he suggested measures through the Election Manifesto of the Scheduled Castes Federation in October 1951 (*BAWS* 2003, vol. 17, no. 1: 385–403) on the eve of the first general elections of India. This can be divided into three parts where the first dealt with the Principles, second with the Policy, and the third with the Programme of the Party. Apart from dealing with the general principles, it clearly mentioned that the equality of opportunity will be upheld for every Indian but it will be subject to the provision that 'those who had none in the past shall have priority over those who had'. It was to supplement the redemption from oppression and exploitation of man by another man, of one class by another class and of nation by another nation. It was an attempt to adopt compensatory policies for historical exclusion of the discriminated groups and ensure them equal rights. This could also be seen as extending State measures to the other marginalized sections like OBCs and minorities. The proposition to provide cultivable land to the landless was also given priority whereby the State was to be interventionist to protect the rights of the common masses.

On the policy front, the party was not to be tied to any 'ism' but adopt any plan of social and economic betterment of the people provided it was consistent with its principles. In the programme of the party, the first priority was given to education, next to the services in civil and military administration. In case of education, while primary and secondary education was important, advanced education of high order which would enable the excluded groups to fit themselves for high level position was equally vital. In the matter of services, reservation was insisted upon subject to minimum qualifications. In the case of the traditional occupational pattern he mentioned that in spite of considerable development of industries, there had been little change in the occupational structure of the social groups. It was suggested that landless labour could be handed over cultivable wasteland, and the necessary infrastructure be provided by the State to benefit these groups.

On a debate of the report of the Commissioner for SCs/STs for 1953 (*BAWS* 1997, vol. 15: 895–918), Ambedkar commented comprehensively on the functioning of the safeguards for these sections in the Republican India. Apart from being concerned to implement the existing policies of the government, he again touched upon matters relating to State interventions in the areas where there had been no safeguards. He maintained that as the government has not taken land into its own hands and created land proprietors, hence it could not take away land and distribute equally among the masses. Therefore the only way out was to amend the Constitution and put the cultivation of wasteland within the purview of the Central government so that it was utilized for the benefit of the landless. The second suggestion was to levy a salt tax and develop wasteland, and settle the SCs on that land. He even suggested that the money coming out of the salt tax could be kept out of Budget and be spent on a scheme in the name of Mahatma Gandhi like 'Gandhi Welfare Scheme' that would give relief to the people whom he wanted to elevate. In probably the last of his comments, Ambedkar, while writing on the linguistic states in 1955 (*BAWS* 1979, vol. 1: 167–70) argued that caste has a great potential to convert people into majority and minority, and the majority, not taking a shape of political majority, but has immense potential to turn into a communal majority.

SUMMING UP

Thus, a close look at the various interventions by Ambedkar during 1919–54 captures his understanding about the problem of deprived castes. He reiterated his position that the problems of Untouchables are rooted in the historical denial of basic human rights. Therefore he grounded the justification for remedies against caste discrimination of Untouchables in a citizenship framework. If initial efforts involved creating awareness among the British regarding the position of Untouchables and demands to give citizenship rights, the second phase took him towards assertion for of rights with wide description and explanations in terms of political representation in the form of Separate Electorates. In the third phase, we see the extension of representation and participation in the sphere of education and employment. The fourth phase of interventions came at the time of the making of the Constitution. This in fact saw his greatest achievements as it had a general framework which involved acceptance of the principles of non-discrimination, legal abolition of untouchability, recognition of the problem, particularly the educational and economic backwardness of the low castes and the responsibility on the State to protect the interests of the SCs/STs and take measures for their upliftment. In the last phase of interventions, he gets back to re-assertion and rejuvenation whether it was in the sphere of political representation in the Legislatures or enlarging the spheres of State interventions.

We also see a broadening of the solution ever since Ambedkar first articulated it in 1919, which in latter years took a definite shape. Ambedkar came up with two set of remedies, one against social discrimination and another against economic exploitation. This laid the foundation of recognition of the problem, responsibility on the State, and the need to take various measures. The remedies against social discrimination include the provision of equal rights to all, legal safeguards against violation of rights in term of punitive measures, measures to ensure equal access and participation (through reservation policy) in civil, political, and economic spheres, and in addition a definite strategy by the State for the development and empowerment of the poor in general and Untouchables in particular, to compensate for exclusion in the past. Ambedkar laid emphasis on monitoring mechanisms to implement and supervise the measures and the participation of Untouchables in policy and decision-making process and monitoring mechanisms.

AMBEDKAR'S SOLUTIONS FOR SOCIAL INCLUSION

The above discussion establishes that Ambedkar had been concerned with the problem of lower castes from 1919 onwards and argued that their problem had been deeply entrenched in the institution of the caste system and untouchability which involved the denial of human rights. So the remedies against discrimination were placed with the framework of citizenship rights. Therefore what follows is the summary of the policies he suggested for social inclusion.

Claim for Equal Rights

Though, in his first memorandum Ambedkar demanded political representation, however, he started with a claim for equal rights to the Untouchables that he called 'citizenship rights'. He understood that it was in the absence of these rights that they were not treated as equals and as a consequence suffered from discrimination, exploitation, seclusion and exclusion in multiple ways in society. And without having a claim on such rights their position would lack the primary conditions of participating in socio-political developments. His focus on the claims for equal rights could be seen through his following arguments:

The Untouchable is not even a citizen. Citizenship is a bundle of rights such as personal liberty, personal security, rights to hold private property, equality before law, liberty of conscience, freedom of opinion and speech, right of assembly, right of representation in a country's Government and right to hold office under the State. The British Government by gradual growth may be said to have conceded these rights at least in theory to its Indian subjects. The right of representation and the right to hold office under the State are the two most important rights that make up citizenship. But the untouchability of the

Untouchables puts these rights far beyond their reach. In a few places they do not even possess such insignificant rights as personal liberty and personal security, and equality before law is not always assured to them. These are the interests of the Untouchables. And as can be easily seen they can be represented by the Untouchables alone. They are distinctively their own interests and none else can truly voice them. A free trade interest can be voiced by a Brahmin, a Mohammedan or a Maratha equally well. But none of these can speak for the interests of the Untouchables because they are not Untouchables. Unsociability constitutes a definite set of interests, which the Untouchables alone can speak for. Hence it is evident that we must find the Untouchables to represent their grievances which are their interests and, secondly, we must find them in such numbers as will constitute a force sufficient to claim redress (*BAWS* 1979, vol. 1: 256).

Not only did he diagnose the problem of Untouchables but also analysed the cause behind the denial of these basic conditions of human life. He found its prevalence in the social code that prevented them from claiming equality in all spheres. While presenting the case before the Simon Commission in 1928, he expressed the following sentiments:

The Depressed Classes cannot be employed in the army, navy and the police because such employment is opposed to the religious notions of the majority. They cannot be admitted in schools because their entry is opposed to the religious notions of the majority. They cannot avail themselves of government dispensaries, because will not let them cause pollution to their person's or to their dispensaries. They cannot live a cleaner and higher life, because to live above their prescribed station is opposed to the religious notions of the majority. So rigorous is the enforcement of the Social Code against the Depressed Classes that any attempt on the part of the Depressed Classes to exercise their elementary rights of citizenship only ends in provoking the majority, to practice the worst form of social tyranny known to history. It will be admitted that when society is itself a tyrant, its means of tyrannising are not restricted to the acts which it may do by the hands of its functionaries and it leaves fewer means of escape penetrating much more deeply into the details of life, and enslaving the soul itself (*BAWS* 1982, vol. 2: 445–6).

Thus he located the reason for the denial of equal rights in the social code that was being practiced against the Untouchables throughout a major part of history. Therefore, Ambedkar grounded his justification for remedies against caste discrimination of Untouchables on the denial of citizenship rights. The denial of citizenship rights was seen as rooted in the denial of basic human rights essential for the growth of human beings. This view had become the core of his arguments, not merely during his initial interventions in 1919, 1928, and 1932 but also while submitting a memorandum to the Constituent Assembly for the free India in 1947, when he went to the extent of saying that 'unequal treatment has been the inescapable fate of the Untouchables in India' and observed that 'In a country like India where it is possible for discrimination to be practiced on a vast scale and in a relentless manner, fundamental rights have no meaning' (*BAWS* 1979, vol. 1: 407–8).

Legal Safeguards Against Discrimination and Violation of Rights
Equal rights have no meaning without sufficient safeguards in one form or the other. These safeguards have to be through adequate legal protection in case of violation of such rights. Ambedkar stated that claims of equality of opportunity have no meaning in Indian social conditions, which do not allow equality to prevail, and efforts by Untouchables to secure equal rights are vehemently opposed by the so-called higher castes. The equality of opportunity is conflicted not only by the common masses of caste-Hindus but also by those in government at various levels of the helm of affairs of the State. Consequently the remedy lies not merely in having equal rights for the Untouchables as possessed by others but rather in having a device that provides legal ways and methods to claim rights if violation takes place and impose penalties against infringement of rights as rights without guarantee to exercise them have no meaning, if the society at large does not allow the rights to be protected. Though, Ambedkar did not talk of remedies against abuse of rights in his first memorandum to the Southborough Commission but he mentioned this in 1928:

That the right of the Depressed Classes to appeal to the Government of India in cases of violation of these rights by the Provincial Government shall be recognized and the Government of India shall be given the power to compel the Provincial Government to conform to the law in the matter ... the benefit of the minorities bear eloquent testimony to the fact that the minorities cannot depend upon the representative form of Government but must seek protection in the form of guarantees of their rights (*BAWS* 1982, vol. 2: 442–3).

These measures were to be applicable not only on government functionaries but in the private sector. With regard to the private sector he wrote that 'discrimination against citizens by the government officers in the public administration or by private employers in factories and commercial concerns on the grounds of race or creed or social status should be treated as offences'. The legal protection was demanded not only in vicinity of employment in the public and private domains but also in the daily activities of community life, where social boycott of the DCs was exercised by others to prevent them from enjoyment of civil rights.

Ambedkar was concerned with the protection of DCs not only against the violation of rights by individuals or by society but also protection against grave fears of discrimination either by legislation or by Executive order being made in the future. Therefore, he argued, that they will consent themselves to majority rule only when it is rendered impossible in law for the Legislature or the Executive to make any invidious discrimination against them. Ambedkar could visualize the apathy of the Legislatures or Executives of the future for the Untouchables due to societal attitudes as the caste-Hindus would control such institutions and its adverse impact on the safeguards for Untouchables. Here he is found to be critical towards the so-called secular institutions established by the State (*BAWS* 1982, vol. 2: 550).

Measures for Equal Opportunity and Participation

The measures in the form of equal rights and legal safeguards against violation of rights also suffer from limitation in ensuring due share in various spheres of society. These merely restrain members of society to take steps putting minorities or underprivileged sections in a disadvantageous position in the public domain. This may not enable the Untouchables to enjoy just access and participate in social, economic, and political processes due to the prevalence of the practice of discrimination and opposition by the higher castes. In this context, Ambedkar observed, 'in a country like India, where it is possible for discrimination to practise on a vast scale and in a relentless manner, fundamental rights have no meaning'. Thus in addition to legal safeguards against discrimination, protection against discrimination becomes significant and this could be possible only through equal access and participation in Legislature, Executive, educational institutions, government services and other spheres in proportion to their population through an instrument of reservation policy.

The following argument is testimony to this when he said:

It is not enough to be electors only. It is necessary to be law-makers; otherwise who can be law-makers will be masters of those who can only be electors....

One crux of popular Government is the representation of interests and opinions. The other crux is personal representation.... (*BAWS* 1979, vol. 1: 251–2).

In addition to due share in Legislature, Executive, educational institutions, and Public Services, Ambedkar also proposed fair participation of the lower caste in policy and decision-making and also in the monitoring of policies and programmes.

Policies for Empowerment to Compensate for Historical Exclusion and Denial of Equal Rights

From the foregoing discussion, it becomes evident that Ambedkar strived for a threefold approach to provide safeguards against the denial of equal rights to the lower castes in the present. These include— claims for equal rights; remedies against the violation of rights in terms of legal provision; and measures for equal access, share and participation in Legislature, Executive, administration, education and other public domains for discriminated groups in the form of reservation policy.

Nevertheless, he could visualize that lack of access to income earning capital assets, employment, education, poverty, etc., as an outcome of historical denials of equal rights. Although, the above-mentioned measures could work as safeguards against discrimination in the present but they could not overcome poverty and deprivation caused by historical exclusion and denial of economic rights in the past for a long period of time, reflected in lack of income earning assets (agricultural land and non-land assets), education, employment, and lack of basic civil amenities for the SCs. The anti-discriminatory measures do serve as safeguards against discrimination in the present but have their limitation in overcoming the deprivation caused by a historical denial of economic and social rights in the past for long time leading to lack of education, lack of access to agricultural land, business, employment, etc. Therefore, certain strategies are required to compensate the discriminated group of Untouchables for historical denial of ownership of resources, employment, education, service, and social requirements. Ambedkar observed that the kind of situation in which Untouchables are placed, unless the agenda for equalization of opportunities is realized in practice through an egalitarian economic system and definite policy, and determined efforts on the part of government, their upliftment will remain a sanctimonious hope (*BAWS* 1982, vol. 2: 553).

For the overall development of discriminated groups as well as other poor sections, in addition to reservation, Ambedkar suggested the political and economic system to remove structural inequalities, and the effective role of SCs in policy making and governance. On the first, Ambedkar entrusted the State with the task of providing access to agricultural land and capital to the SCs and other poor. He suggested the more radical remedy of equalization in the form of 'State Socialism' in agriculture and industry to protect deprived groups against economic exploitation. In this regard, Ambedkar observed:

The main purpose behind the clause is to put an obligation on the State to plan the economic life of the people on the lines which would lead to highest point of productivity without closing every avenue to the private sector and provide for the equitable distribution of wealth. The plan set out in the clause proposes State ownership in agriculture with collectivised method of cultivation and a modified form of State Socialism in the field of industry. It places squarely on the shoulders of the State the obligation to supply capital necessary for agriculture as well as for industry (*BAWS* 1979, vol. 1: 408).

For Ambedkar, to remove the structural inequalities governing the economic life of the people was necessary and this could be done through State Socialism where there is State ownership in agriculture with collective farming. On similar lines, he proposed a modified form of State Socialism for industries. He did not propose to monopolize all the fields by the State but to have a say in the major areas so that the inequalities could be reduced. With this kind of arrangement, the State would have the duty of reorganizing the economic life of people by which not only socially discriminated groups like SC/ST and OBC would be benefited but also the general masses of poor would get advantage of state interventions in deciding their economic life.

On the second, Ambedkar suggested a statutory obligation to maintain a separate administrative division to deal with their problems—that is 'to watch the interests of the Depressed Classes and promoting their welfare'. In this context, he observed:

There can be no doubt that in view of these circumstances the uplift of the Depressed Classes will remain a pious hope unless the task is placed in the forefront of all governmental activities and unless equalization of opportunities is realized in practice by a definite policy and determined effort on the part of the Government (*BAWS* 1982, vol. 2: 553–4).

To summarize the central points of Ambedkar's position, we observe that he suggested two sets of remedies. One set of remedies against continuing caste discrimination in the present, and another set of remedies against the historical deprivation due to the denial of economic, civil, and cultural rights in the past. In the first, three safeguards are suggested against the continuing practice of untouchability and caste discrimination. Safeguards against present discrimination included the provision of equal rights, legal safeguards in the form of preventive laws against the violation of the rights and continuous pro-active measures for fair share and participation in Legislature, Executive, Public Services, education, and other public spheres for discriminated groups of Untouchables in the form of reservation policy. The second set of remedies included measures to address the problems of deprivation due to historical exclusion from access to resources, education, and employment. Ambedkar suggested more fundamental measures for addressing the problem of 'structural inequalities' and suggested special developmental measures of equalization of economic opportunities for the poor in general and low castes in particular. These included State ownership of land and its equal distribution by the State to all, and state ownership of key basic industries, banks, and insurances and instruments of economic planning to implement development policies. Equal rights, in Ambedkar's view would provide the legal framework, overturning the unequal customary legal framework of the institution of caste and untouchability. Punitive laws would provide protection against violation of laws against discrimination in the public and private spheres, and the pro-active measures would provide fair share, participation and representation through reservation in public spheres as a safeguard against present discrimination. The developmental measures directed towards equalization of opportunities in economic resources and employment, as compensatory measures for past denial of economic and education rights would help to empower the poor and discriminated groups and reduce inequalities between them and rest of the sections in Indian society. Ambedkar emphasized the need for provisions in the Constitution as well as statutory provision, with clear responsibility on the State to develop strategies for development of the Untouchables. In addition, he also emphasized the need to have their representation in decision-making process and administrative machinery to monitor policy measures and programmes. Representing the interests of Dalits was not enough. Ambedkar believed that their interests could be meaningfully ensured by their own representation and participation in decision-making process at all levels. He recommended the participation of Dalits in the democratic polity at all levels from legislation to the execution of policies, which would regulate the working of modern Indian society. In this manner, in the conceptual scheme of Ambedkar, representation and participation were central.

His arguments for equal access in the form of reservation in the Indian conditions are an innovative and original formulation to bring together the requirements of representation and participation of marginalized groups through an elaborate system of rights. For guaranteeing participatory democracy and equal opportunity, the provision with respect to rights needed to be embodied in the Constitution. He was aware that if a society practices discrimination, then the impetus for change should be located in both State and private domains. Given the historical exclusion and isolation of certain groups, Ambedkar favoured a fair policy of inclusion in the democratic polity, economy and society and cultural life of the society.

The inclusive policy was not to be confined to the public sector only as has been done through the reservation policy in the spheres of education, Public Services, and politics. Ambedkar insisted that safeguards against discrimination be extended to the private domain as well, as discrimination also widely persisted in the private domain.

Lessons for Inclusive Development Policy

Ambedkar's interpretation of the caste system with regard to its exclusionary character and consequences has important lessons for the contemporary efforts to develop inclusive policies, not only for groups suffering from the institutions of caste and untouchability but also the groups suffering from discrimination associated with other group identities like ethnicity, religion, gender, and other forms of exclusion. It is recognized that 'group based exclusion' essentially generates outcomes which are detrimental for the excluded groups. Exclusion results in deprivation and poverty insofar as it involves denial of equal rights to persons from these groups. By doing so, it also leads to inter-group inequalities and generates potential for inter-group conflict. Recent literature also points towards the adverse consequences of market discrimination on economic growth.

Given these adverse consequences on economic growth, income distribution, and inter-group conflicts; reducing discrimination becomes imperative as it is likely to induce economic growth, reduce poverty and inequality, and minimize the potential for inter-group conflict.

Views on the remedies against economic discrimination, however, differ. Mainstream economists suggest market competition as a solution to the problem of market failure associated with discrimination. It is argued that in highly competitive market situations, discrimination will be transitory as there are costs associated with discrimination to the firm/employer, which result in lowering of profits. Others, on the other hand, point out that for several reasons market discrimination may persist over long periods of time. Even if the markets are sufficiently competitive, discrimination will still persist—if all firms practice discrimination—the likelihood of which is always high. The persistence of labour market discrimination in high-income countries over long periods of time attests to this. But more importantly, in practice, markets are generally characterized by imperfections and monopoly power. Such monopolies provide enough power to the firms to discriminate in various markets.

Since discrimination will persist, an interventionist policy to remedy market failure associated with discrimination is pertinent. Interventionist policy is required, both to improve competitiveness and also to provide safeguards against market and non-market discrimination. Interventions will be necessary in all markets, namely, land, labour, capital, product, and consumer and non-market transitions in education and housing.

In the Indian context, given the multiple forms of exclusion associated with group identities like caste, ethnicity, gender, and religion in various spheres of economy, polity, society and culture, it is important to formulate an inclusive policy to overcome deprivation associated with multiple forms of discrimination. To develop inclusive policies for multiple groups suffering from exclusion associated with caste, ethnicity, religion, gender and other forms of exclusion is an issue, which is currently being discussed by the Indian government and policymakers. It is to be recognized that the nature of inclusive policies will be necessarily governed by the exclusionary character of Indian society. It would further depend on the forms and spheres of discrimination and their specific consequences on discriminated groups.

As regards Hindu society, the principle of 'graded inequality' implies that not all castes suffer equally from the hierarchical entitlement of rights. While the castes located at the bottom of the caste hierarchy, namely, the former Untouchables suffer the most, the OBCs follow closely. The OBCs in all probability do not suffer from the notion of Untouchability, but they have historically faced exclusion in education, employment, and in certain other social spheres.

In case of religions other than Hinduism, the lower castes converted to Christianity and Islam probably face discrimination, although not in a similar fashion to the Hindu low castes. Certain religious minorities, particularly the Muslims, also probably face discrimination in a number of spheres, but due to lack of studies in the area we do not have clear idea about the forms and spheres of discrimination. Similarly, women also face exclusion, and it varies depending upon their caste and religious backgrounds. Some groups such as tribal and semi-nomadic tribes also suffer from physical and social isolation/ exclusion due to their ethnic backgrounds. An important issue, therefore, is to develop group-specific inclusive policies to overcome the consequences of discrimination. Currently, we are discussing alternative ways of overcoming deprivation suffered by excluded groups such as the SCs, STs, OBCs, low castes converted to Christianity and Islam, and religious minorities such as Muslims and women in the public and the private domain.

In this context, there is a lot to be learnt from Ambedkar's approach and the latter developments in social science literature on social exclusion for the devising inclusive policies. Ambedkar's perspective on 'inclusive policy' incorporates a dual strategy. He refers to these as 'safeguards against economic exploitation' and 'safeguards against social discrimination and isolation' in his last systematic treatise on this theme (Ambedkar 1947).

In Ambedkar's view, the problem of discriminated groups is two-fold. First is the lack of access to income earning capital assets, businesses, employment, and education due to the denial of the same in the past—the consequences of which are visible even in contemporary times. Second is the continuation of discrimination in the present, in various market and non-market transactions in one form or the other, if not in their full original forms. Some discriminated groups also face exclusion in civil and cultural spheres. Therefore, policies for discriminated groups require a dual solution—one set of remedies for the historical denial of economic, social and educational rights (the consequences of which were carried forward and are visible today) as a compensation for that denial in the past, and a second set of remedies to provide safeguards against continuing forms of discrimination in the present.

The first strategy includes fundamental measures for addressing the problem of 'structural inequalities' created by the caste system and involves the creation of an 'egalitarian economic structure', which will ensure equal access to income earning capital assets and economic opportunities for the poor in general and the discriminated persons in particular. This includes creating an economic structure which will ensure equal access to land, capital, employment, and the provision of education and health services. This policy for generality of the poor, in Ambedkar's view, will also create an egalitarian structural base for the economic and social empowerment of excluded groups as well.

This strategy of 'egalitarian economic structure' will enable and enhance the capacity of excluded groups to participate in the economic and social development processes of the nation. However, such a strategy has its limitations. Improved ownership of income earning assets will empower excluded groups to make use of business opportunities. However, the discriminatory working of factor markets, and private education and housing services, may not in practice enable them to make actual use of such opportunities. Similarly, educational and skill development will enhance the employability of discriminated groups, but the discriminatory working of the employment market may not automatically and necessarily translate to the actual employment of these groups. Therefore, in addition to the strategy of creating a 'Egalitarian Economic Structure', Ambedkar suggested a complementary strategy of 'Equal Opportunity' to ensure fair share and access to employment, capital assets, and social needs like education and housing canalized through market and non-market institutions. They are not mutually exclusive, but complementary to each other. The 'Equal Opportunity Policy' suggested by Ambedkar is characterized by four main attributes. Firstly, legal safeguards in the form of laws against discrimination in economic, social, and other spheres so that persons may use them in event of discrimination. Secondly, the incorporation of pro-active measures for discriminated groups to ensure fair access to income earning capital assets, employment, and education, both in the public and the private spheres, and also in the Legislature, Executive and other public spheres, in the form of reservation policy.

The enactment of such an 'Equal Opportunity Policy' will ensure a due share for discriminated groups in businesses, employment, education, housing, and other services. Together, the dual policies of 'Egalitarian Economic Structure' and of 'Equal Opportunities' will enable addressing the problems of the poor discriminated groups. Third, is the provision of adequate representation and participation in the Executive, and in administration for decision-making and monitoring. In Ambedkar's view, representing the interests of discriminated groups by others is not enough, their interests could be meaningfully ensured by their own representation and participation in decision-making processes and monitoring, with others at all levels. Therefore, the participation of the discriminated groups in the democratic polity at all levels from legislation to execution of policies is necessary. In the strategic scheme of inclusive policies suggested by Ambedkar, representation and participation of discriminated groups in the Executive, and in administration for decision-making and monitoring remains crucial and central. Fourthly, the provision of rights to be embodied in the Constitution remained at the core of Ambedkar's perspective. In Ambedkar's view, if a society practices discrimination, then the impetus for change should ideally emanate from the State. This requires provisions in the Constitution and in other statutory forms, with clear responsibility on the State to develop policies against discrimination and for the development of discriminated groups, both in the public and private sectors.

Thus, the 'Inclusive Policy' proposed by Ambedkar has these four components, which include creating an egalitarian economic structure, which will provide a base for equal economic and social opportunities for the the poor, including discriminated groups; equal opportunity policy in terms of reservation for discriminated groups with adequate legal safeguards against discrimination; the participation of discriminated groups in governance through a fair share in Legislature, Executive and administration involving decision-making and monitoring processes; and finally responsibility on the State to undertake such policies with a clear provision in the Constitution and in other statutory forms.

An Equal Opportunity Policy will be of a different nature for various 'discriminated groups' depending on the forms and spheres of discrimination and their social, economic and educational consequences on discriminated groups. An equal opportunity policy, therefore, may not be the same for groups such as the former Untouchables; OBCs; lower-caste converts to Christianity and Islam; ethnic groups like tribals; religious minorities such as Muslims; women; and others. This will be necessarily governed by a reasonable understanding about the forms, spheres and nature of exclusion and discrimination suffered by various excluded and discriminated groups and their specific socio-economic and educational situation. This will enable us to develop more enlightened and well-grounded equal opportunity policies. In this sense our economy, polity, society, culture, and governance will have to be more participatory and representative of various castes, ethnicities, religions and women. This will make our democracy more inclusive, vibrant and consequential to all the citizens.

NOTES

1. Adequate representation was not to be merely in quantitative terms but similar terms as determined for other minorities.
2. The Government of India Resolution for the representation of Minorities in the Services.
3. The Government of India Resolution for representation of Scheduled Castes in the Services.

   No. 23/5/42-Ests(S). In pursuance of the undertaking given in the Central Legislative Assembly in 1942, the Government of India have carefully reviewed the policy which they have followed since 1934 in regard to the representation of Depressed Classes, since described in the Government of India Act, 1935 as 'Scheduled Castes', in services under their administrative control. In their Resolution No. F. 14/17-B/33, dated the 4th July 1934, the Government of India stated that in the then state of general education among these classes they did not consider that any useful purpose would be served by reserving for them a definite percentage of vacancies. In order, however, to secure fair representation for Scheduled Castes they directed that duly qualified members of these classes might be nominated to a Public Service even though recruitment to that service was being made by competition. Various measures have been taken since then to secure increased representation of the Scheduled Castes in the Public Services. The results obtained so far have, however, not been substantial. While the Government of India recognize that this is mainly due to the difficulty of getting suitably qualified candidates, they now consider that the reservation of a definite percentage of vacancies might provide the necessary stimulus to candidates of these castes to obtain better qualifications and thus make themselves eligible for various government posts and services. It is believed that the grant of age concessions and the reduction of prescribed fees might also help to secure qualified candidates from among members of the Scheduled Castes. The Government of India have accordingly decided to prescribe the rules mentioned in paragraph 4 below.

The following rules will therefore be observed in future in order to secure better representation of the Scheduled Castes in Public Services:

1. 8 1/3 per cent of all vacancies to be filled by direct recruitment of Indians in the Central and Subordinate Services to which recruitment is made on an all-India basis will be reserved for Scheduled Castes candidates.

2. In the case of services to which recruitment is made by local areas or circles and not on an all-India basis, e. g., subordinate posts in the Railways, Posts and Telegraphs Department, the Customs Services, the Income-Tax Department, etc., the total reservation for India as a whole of 8 1/3 percent of vacancies for Scheduled Castes candidates will be obtained by fixing a percentage for each local area or circle having regard to the population of Scheduled Castes in the area or circle concerned and the rules for recruitment adopted by the Provincial Government of the area or circle concerned.

3. When recruitment is made by open competition and Scheduled Castes candidates obtain fewer vacancies than are reserved for them, the difference will, if possible, be made up by the nomination of duly qualified candidates of those castes.

4. If Scheduled Castes candidates obtain less than the number of vacancies reserved for them in open competition and duly qualified candidates of these castes are not available, or not available in sufficient numbers, for nomination, the remaining vacancies reserved for such candidates will be treated as unreserved; but a corresponding number of vacancies will be reserved for them in that year under clause (1) or clause (2) above.

5. If duly qualified candidates of the Scheduled Castes are again not available to fill the vacancies carried forward from the previous year under clause (4) the vacancies not filled by them will be treated as unreserved.

6. In all cases, a minimum standard of qualification will be prescribed and the reservation will be subject to this condition.

7. The maximum age limit prescribed for appointment to a service or post will be increased by three years in the case of candidates belonging to the Scheduled Castes.

8. The fees prescribed for admission to any examination or selection will be reduced to one-fourth in the case of candidates belonging to the Scheduled Castes.

9. The orders contained in the foregoing rules will also apply to temporary vacancies lasting three months or longer, including vacancies in permanent posts filled temporarily by persons not permanently employed in Government service.

10. For the purposes of these roles a person shall be held to be a member of the Scheduled Castes if he belongs to a caste which under the Government of India (Scheduled Castes) Order, 1936, has been declared to be a Scheduled Caste for the area in which he and his family ordinarily reside.

Part I

Prologue to the Problem of
Indian Society
Seeking Solution, 1919–29

Introduction

In this section, we discuss the initial articulations made by Ambedkar to safeguard the interests of the DCs vis-à-vis GOI Act 1919 and the Simon Commission in 1928–9. During this period he gave following evidences and statements to suggest the policy measures to safeguard the interests of DCs:

1. Evidence before the Southborough Committee on Franchise (with regard to constitutional reforms and political representation of minorities): 27 January 1919.
2. Statement concerning the safeguards for the protection of the interests of the Depressed Classes as a minority in the Bombay Presidency (before Indian Statutory Commission—Simon Commission): 29 May 1928.
3. Statement concerning the state of education of the Depressed Classes in the Bombay Presidency (before Indian Statutory Commission—Simon Commission): 29 May 1928.
4. Evidence of Dr. Ambedkar before the Indian Statutory Commission (before Indian Statutory Commission—Simon Commission): 23 October 1928.
5. Report on the Constitution of the Government of Bombay Presidency (before Indian Statutory Commission—Simon Commission): 17 May 1929.
6. Indianization of Services (before Indian Statutory Commission—Simon Commission): 17 May 1929.

Ambedkar emerged in the background of a few major developments, viz., recognition of Muslims as minorities by providing them Separate Electorates, demand for the autonomy of the provinces, recognition of the fact by the British that Indians need to be given some political rights for establishing self-government under the British. It was under this context that various communities like Sikhs, Anglo-Indians, and Untouchables, started demand for their separate representation in the Legislature.

Thus, it was in 1919 that Ambedkar for the first time intervened in the formulation of British policies with regard to DCs by presenting a written statement to the Southborough Committee appointed to look into the claims of various communities to franchise for representation in Legislatures. The Muslims had already got Separate Electorates after their representation to Lord Minto in 1906 under the leadership of Aga Khan (Allana 1988). Ambedkar had a daunting task of representing the claims of the Untouchables as a separate entity detached from Hindu society.

SOUTHBOROUGH COMMITTEE—FIRST EFFORT

The first challenge before Ambedkar was how to establish the fact that the Untouchables are a distinct community against the popular belief of Untouchables being part of Hindu society, having no separate interests. In this regard his arguments to the Southborough Committee (*BAWS* 1979, vol. 1: 247–77) were:

1. There was a lack of communality of aims, beliefs, customs etc. among the Untouchables and the caste-Hindus.
2. As religion divides the Hindus, Muslims, Parses, Christians etc. similarly caste divides Hindus into low caste and higher castes on the one hand and Touchables and the Untouchables on the other.
3. Non-Brahmins may also be facing the intellectual superiority of Brahmins but the Untouchables need protection not from confiscation of their property but from the confiscation of their personality itself.

After showing the distinct identity of Untouchables, the next concern for Ambedkar was to bring out their social conditions which prevented them even to become citizens. Thus Ambedkar grounded the case of Untouchables against oppression in denial of citizenship rights.

Ambedkar further argued that to make the popular government successful, the constituencies and the franchises have to transmit the social forces and that would require personal representation of the communities concerned that is, the Untouchables. On the same lines, territorial representation was considered to be inadequate because as electors, the people will go by their mere sympathy towards a candidate that is decided by community considerations and it leaves the minor groups or minorities without personal representation. And the personal representation would make possible popular government. And a popular government need to fulfill two conditions—it should represent interests and opinions and, it should give personal representation, whereas territorial representation fails to provide the second one completely, the first one depends on whims and fancies of the representatives of majority community.

He discarded the solution of Untouchable representation in the form of co-option and nomination as these were considered to be against political education restricting the freedom of the representatives. The evidence before the Southborough by Ambedkar had three substantial impacts on the GOI Act 1919 except separate political representation through elections is concerned. Among the achievements were—Untouchables were a separate entity in Indian society, Untouchables were in desperate need of rights to protect them from discrimination, and Ambedkar was nominated to the Bombay Legislative Council that gave representation to the Untouchables.

Simon Commission—Second Effort

The GOI Act 1919 had made a provision that after ten years of passing of this Act, a statutory commission would be appointed to enquire into the working of the system of government, the growth of education, and the development of representative institutions in British India. Thus a Commission was appointed in 1928 (*BAWS* 1982, vol. 2: 430–46) under the chairmanship of Mr Simon. It provided another opportunity for Ambedkar to plead the case of DCs. He insisted upon separate political representation through election and to adopt alternative franchise system. With this he also emphasized to take measures to protect their civil rights. The safeguards were also sought in the field of education and employment in the Public Services with State.

He further argued that the DCs would not insist upon communal electorates if reserved seats were carved out in the general constituencies. It was repetition of his plea during 1919 for representation. However, for franchise now he did not leave it to the wish of the commission to decide the franchise conditions for the DCs but argued for adult suffrage and in its absence he insisted upon Separate Electorates.

While giving evidence before the Southborough Committee, Ambedkar delineated the rationale to have separate representation in the Councils and it was reaffirmed again during 1928. There had been a significant addition to safeguards the interests of the DCs by incorporating protection of rights through guarantees so that the rights get secured through. These guarantees were demanded not only in political sphere but also in education, Public Services particularly in the army, navy and police as well as in matter of appealing before the government in case of violtion of these rights.

Ambedkar on British Education Policy

Concerned with promoting the education of the DCs, Ambedkar suggested some measures (*BAWS* 1982, vol. 2: 425–8) like abolishing Compulsory Primary Education Act that stopped transfer of primary education to the school boards leading to inspiration among the DCs to get educated, making primary education obligatory and enforcing the admission to primary strictly, replicating the recommendations of Hunter Commission regarding the education of the Mohammendans on the DCs to make their educational progress a reality and entry in the Public Service to the DCs to encourage them to take education (*BAWS* vol. 2: 427–8).

Evidence before the Simon Commission

On 28 May, Ambedkar gave written statements to the Simon Commission and on 23 October, he gave evidence before the Commission (*BAWS* 1982, vol. 2: 459–89) by appearing personally. While repeating major arguments of his statements before the Commission like treating DCs as distinct minority and acknowledging their need for greater protection than any other community, he gave many instances of social ostracism of them in Poona, Ratnagiri, Collaba, through boycott by the shopkeepers, stopping them to perform their duties as village servants, denial of equal rights in using basic amenities like public dispensaries, taking away the lands cultivated by them so that they revert to their dirty and unclean jobs.

Ambedkar's Interventions and Public Services

A separate report (*BAWS*, 1982, vol. 2: 393–9) presented by Ambedkar argued that the Untouchables having been virtually excluded from the services would prefer the system of appointments by selection to the system of selection by open competition. Recalling the case for

Indianization of administration to prefer Indians as compared to Europeans demanded by Gokhale, Ambedkar argued that this demand did not rest on efficient administration, but on good administration. Similar was the case for other than Brahmins then. Moreover, democracy needed not only efficient government but good government as well and it required representation of various groups in the administration. Supplementing the argument, he added that as the struggles for equality were going on between the Brahmins and non-Brahmins, between Hindus and Muslims, between Touchables and Untouchables, they were bound to be partisan, and to avoid the ill effects of it, expansion of administration from diverse social groups was mandatory. Presenting the case before the Simon Commission, he suggested the following remedies:

1. A certain number of vacancies in Class I and Class II services be filled by system of nomination with a pass examination for other than Brahmins.
2. Posting increasing number of officers from them at the headquarters.
3. Constitution of a Central Recruitment Board as an application registering agency so that applicants come in touch with the offices.

It was here for the first time that he clearly and categorically proposed to accept constituencies with reserved seats for the DCs instead of Separate Electorates in the form of communal electorates, if they were accorded adult franchise. He insisted that the franchise of not only the DCs but also communities like Muslims, Marathas, should be expanded so that the equal qualification for the Brahmins and the others at present did not give leverage to the former.

While concluding this period of Ambedkar's two major interventions, one to the Southborough Committee and the other to Simon Commission, we observe that he was able to lay a concrete foundation of making the British government understand the urgent need to address the problems of the DCs. He raised that the problems of DCs differed from rest of the population in general and from Hindus in particular. He also said that the DCs not only have separate identity but face acute social discrimination and complete denial of civil rights absent in case of other minorities/discriminated groups. In the first intervention the emphasis had been more on political representation but before the Simon Commission the issue of civil rights violations became important. Though questions of education and Public Services were raised, the solutions were more in the context of equal rights and not as safeguards against violation of rights.

So far as the achievements of this period are concerned, the government recognized that Untouchables were a separate entity in the Indian society who were in desperate need of protection of their rights due to acute social discrimination and denial of civil rights. The separate political representation was given to them by nominating Ambedkar to the Bombay Legislative Council giving representation to the Untouchables.

1

Evidence before the Southborough Committee*
27 January 1919

'The most difficult and the most momentous question of Government (is) how to transmit the force of individual opinion and preference into public action. This is the crux of popular institutions.' So says Professor A. B. Hart. But this is only half the definition of popular Government. It is therefore necessary to emphasize the other half which is equal if not more in importance. As the Government is the most important field for the exercise of individual capacities, it is in the interest of the people that no person as such should be denied the opportunity of actively participating in the process of Government. That is to say popular Government is not only Government for the people but by the people. To express the same in a different way, representation of opinions by itself is not sufficient to constitute popular Government. To cover its true meaning it requires personal representation as well. It is because the former is often found without the latter that the Franchise Committee has to see in devising the franchises and constituencies for a popular Government in India, it provides for both, that is, representation of opinions and representation of persons. Any scheme of franchise and constituency that fails to bring this about fails to create a popular Government.

Success in this task will ultimately depend upon the accuracy of the *de facto* conception of the society which is to be given the popular form of Government. *De facto* India was well portrayed by Lord Dufferin when he described it as a:

Population ... composed of a large number of distinct nationalities, professing various religions, practicing diverse rites, speaking different languages, while many of them ... still further separated from one another by discordant prejudices, by conflicting sources of usages, and even antagonistic material interests. But perhaps the most patent characteristic of our Indian cosmos is its division into two mighty political communities as distant from each other as the poles apart—On the one hand the Hindus—with their elaborate caste distinctions—on the other hand, the Mohammedans—with their social equality. To these must be added a host of minor nationalities most of them numbering millions—almost as widely differentiated from one another by ethnological or political distinctions as are the Hindus from the Mohammedans, such as Sikhs, with their warlike habits and traditions and their enthusiastic religious beliefs, the Rohillas, the Pathans, the Assamese, the Baluchis and other wild and martial tribes on our frontiers, the hillmen dwelling in the folds of the Himalayas, our subjects in Burma, Mongol in race and Buddhist in religion, the Gonds, Mhars, Bheels and other non-Aryan people in the centre and south of India, and the enterprising Parsees, with their rapidly developing manufactures and commercial interests. Again, amongst these numerous communities may be found, at one and the same moment, all the various stages of civilization through which mankind has passed from the pre-historic ages to the present days.

Englishmen have all along insisted that India is unfit for representative Government because of the division of her population into castes and creeds. This does not carry conviction with the advanced wing of Indian politicians. When they say that there are also social divisions in Europe as there are in India they are amply supported by facts. The social divisions of India are equaled, if not outdone, in a country like the United States of America. Corresponding to those in the former, we have in the latter men bonded together in a criminal conspiracy and trust or combinations that prey upon the public. Not only are there political sub-divisions but also industrial, scientific, and religious associations, differing in their aims and their attitudes towards each other. Apart from political parties with diverse ends, social sets, cliques and gangs we find in the United States of America more permanent divisions of the population such as the Poles, Dutch, Swedes, Germans, Russians, etc., each with its own language, religious and moral codes and traditions. If social divisions unfit a country for representative Government, it should unfit the United States of America as much as India. But if with all the social divisions, the United States of America is fit for representative Government, why not India ? Ask the Indian politicians, so entrenched, it is difficult to dislodge them, and show that the social divisions of India are of a different kind or grant them their contention. Without these two there is no third alternative possible.

In my opinion their contention cannot be granted for the social divisions of India do matter in politics. How they matter can be best shown by understanding when they don't matter. Men live in a community by virtue of the things they have in common. What they must have in common in order to form a community are aims, beliefs, aspirations, knowledge, a common understanding; or to use the language of the Sociologists, they must be like-minded. But how do they come to have these things in common or how do they become like-minded? Certainly, not by sharing with another as one would do in the case of a piece of cake. To cultivate an attitude similar to others or to be like-minded with others is to be in communication with them or to participate in their activity. Persons do not become like-minded by merely living in physical proximity, any more than they cease to be like-minded by being distant from each other. Participation in a group is the only way of being like-minded with the group. Each group tends to create its own distinctive type of like-mindedness, but where there are more groups than one to be brought into political union, there would be conflict among the differently like-minded? And so long as the groups remain isolated the conflict is bound to continue and prevent the harmony of action. It is the isolation of the groups that is the chief evil. Where the groups allow of endosmosis they cease to be evil. For endosmosis among the groups makes possible a resocialization of once socialized attitudes. In place of the old, it creates a new like-mindedness, which is representative of the interests, aims, and aspirations of all the various groups concerned. Like-mindedness is essential for a harmonious life, social or political and, as has just been shown, it depends upon the extent of communication, participation or endosmosis. Applying this test to the divisions in India, we must pronounce upon them as constituting an obstacle in the path of realizing a harmonious political life.

The groups or divisions each with its set like-mindedness that are sure to be in conflict may be given as follows: (1) Hindus (2) Mohammedans (3) Christians (4) Parsees (5) Jews, etc.

Except the Hindus the rest of the divisions are marked by such complete freedom of communication from within that we may expect their members to be perfectly like-minded with respect to one another. Regarding the Hindus, however, the analysis must be carried on a little farther. The significant fact about the Hindus is that before they are Hindus they are members of some caste. The castes are so exclusive and isolated that the consciousness of being a Hindu would be the chief guide of a Hindu's activity towards non-Hindu. But as against a Hindu of a different caste his caste-consciousness would be the chief guide of activity. From this, it is plain that as between two Hindus, caste-like-mindedness is more powerful than the like-mindedness due to their both being Hindus. Thus from within the Hindus, as from without, there is likely to be a conflict of like-minded persons. There are some who argue that this conflict runs through the whole gamut of the caste system. But this is protesting too much. From the point of view of communication the Hindus, in spite of castes, divide themselves into two significant groups—the touchables and the Untouchables. The touchables have enough communication between them to enable us to say that the conflict of like-mindedness so far as they are concerned is not much to be dreaded. But there is a real difference and consequent conflict between the like-mindedness of the touchables and the Untouchables. Untouchability is the strongest ban on the endosmosis between them. Their complete isolation accounts for the acuteness of the difference of like mindedness.

The real social divisions of India then are:

1. Touchable Hindus
2. Untouchable Hindus
3. Mohammedans
4. Christians
5. Parsees
6. Jews

It will not do good to ignore these real divisions in devising a system of policy, if the policy is to take the form of popular Government. But if the success of popular Government depends upon how well the constituencies and franchises transmit the social forces and how well they secure personal representation; we must first study the form which the conflict between these groups will assume in an election.

In a territorial constituency, which will group together voters belonging to the above groups, a majority of votes will declare a candidate to be a representative for the constituency in question. Now the question arises: is such a candidate, a true representative of the groups, covered by the territorial constituency? Is he a true mirror of the mind of the constituency? Is he a representative of all the interests in the constituency? To be concrete, will a Hindu candidate represent Mohammedan interests? At this stage it must be recalled that the various divisions described above are held together by a community of interests which are non-secular or purely religious. We cannot say that each division is held together by a community of interests which are secular or material. If so, then for secular purposes the groups will be broken up. From the point of view of material interests, there are no such people as Mohammedans, Parsees, Hindus, etc. There will be in each of these groups landlords, labourers, capitalists, free traders, protectionists, etc., each of the groups having community of interests which are material will be composed of Hindus, Mohammedans, Parsees, etc. Consequently, a Hindu candidate can very well represent the material interests of the Mohammedans and *vice versa*. There is thus no conflict of material interest in the main among the communities as such. If we suppose that religious interests in future will occupy a subordinate place in the affairs of men, the secular interests of a group can be well represented by a candidate from another group.

From this point of view a territorial constituency will be sufficient for a popular Government. A little more consideration will show that it will be sufficient for only one-half the definition of popular Government. How true it is, will be shown presently. In an electoral fight between the various groups in a territorial constituency the voters will discriminate in favour of a candidate with whom they are in sympathy. But with whom they will be in sympathy is determined for them in advance. Given two candidates belonging to different groups but purporting to represent the same interest, the voters will mark their votes on the person belonging to the same community. Any group yielding a large number of electors will have its own candidate elected. This discrimination on the part of the voters, though it may not leave unrepresented the interests of the members of the minor groups, leaves them without any chance of personal representation.

To those who are busy in devising schemes for the proper and adequate representation of interests and opinions dilating on the importance of personal representation is likely to seem idle. But personal representation is not therefore unimportant in recent times 'Government for the people' has claimed more attention than 'Government by the people'. In fact there are instances to show that 'Government for the people' can exist in the best sense of the phrase without there being a 'Government by the people'. Yet all political theorists will unanimously condemn such a form of Government. And the why of it is important to know. It will be granted that each kind of association, as it is an educative environment, exercises a formative influence on the active dispositions of its members. Consequently, what one is as a person is what one is as associated with others. A Government for the people, but not by the people, is sure to educate some into masters and others into subjects; because it is by the reflex effects of association that one can feel and measure the growth of personality. The growth of personality is the highest aim of society. Social arrangement must secure free initiative and opportunity to every individual to assume any role he is capable of assuming provided it is socially desirable. A new rule is a renewal and growth of personality. But when an association—and a Government is after all an association—is such that in it every role cannot be assumed by all, it tends to develop the personality of the few at the cost of the many—a result scrupulously to be avoided in the interest of Democracy. To be specific, it is not enough to be electors only. It is necessary to be law-makers; otherwise who can be law-makers will be masters of those who can only be electors.

Territorial constituencies are therefore objected to, and rightly, on the ground that they do nothing to prevent this absurd outcome. They erroneously suppose that electors will vote on the programmes of the candidates without any regard for their persona. As a matter of fact, the electors before they are electors are primarily members of a group. The persona of the candidates does matter with them. Naturally, therefore, as members of a group they prefer the candidate who belongs to their group to another candidate who does not belong to their group though both of them claim to represent the same interest. As a result of this preference the electors of a large group are destined to rise to a higher position of becoming eventual law-makers, while the electors of a smaller group for no fault of theirs are doomed to a lower position of remaining electors. One crux of popular Government is the representation of interests and opinions. The other crux is personal representation. Territorial constituencies fail to create popular Government because they fail to secure personal representation to members of minor groups.

If this is a correct analysis as to how the social divisions operate to the prejudice of the political life of some communities, never was a more improper remedy advocated to meet the situation than proportional representation. Proportional representation is intended to give proportionate representation to views. It presupposes that voters vote for a candidate because of his views and not because of his persona. Proportional representation is ill-suited for the purpose in hand.

We have therefore two possible methods of meeting the situation; either to reserve seats in plural constituencies for those minorities that cannot otherwise secure personal representation or grant communal electorates. Both have their usefulness. So far as the representation of the Mohammedans is concerned, it is highly desirable that they should participate in a general election with seats reserved for them in plural constituencies. The angularity of the division that separates the Hindus and Mohammedans is already sharp and communal representation, it may be urged, sharpens it the more. Communal election, however, seems to be a settled fact, so far as the Mohammedans are concerned and nothing is likely to alter it, even though alteration is likely to be beneficial.

But this argument is mainly intended to concern itself with the representation of the Hindus in general, and of the Untouchable Hindus in particular. The discussion of the representation of the Hindus may be best introduced by a quotation which expresses the newer consciousness that has arisen in the various Hindu groups. It is said:

A community may claim representation only on the ground of separate interests which require protection. In India, such interests are of three kinds only: either they arise out of religious antipathies which are pretty strong in India, or out of the backward state of a community in educational matters, or out of the socio-religious disabilities to which a community may be subject. Confining ourselves to the Hindu communities there are certain communities who, besides being very Backward, are suffering under a great social tyranny. The Untouchable classes must have their own men in the Council Hall to fight for the redress of their grievances. The non-Brahmins as a class are subjected to the social and intellectual domination of the Brahmin priesthood and may therefore rightly advocate separate representation.

From this it will be seen that the new consciousness among the Hindus while acknowledging the separate interests of the Untouchables does not accept the position that the touchable Hindus form a group by themselves. The new consciousness insists on dividing the touchable group into Brahmins and non-Brahmins each with its own separate interests. Separate Electorates or reserved seats in mixed electorates are demanded for the three groups in which the Hindus are divided.

Before dealing with the problems of the representation of the Untouchables something will be said on the question of the Brahmins and non-Brahmins.

That the non-Brahmins are 'backward in educational matters' cannot be said in any way to be their special interest. It is the general interest of all even of those Brahmins who are educationally backward. 'The intellectual domination of the Brahmins' is not a matter that affects the non-Brahmins alone. It affects all and it is therefore the interest of all. What remains then as a special interest for the non-Brahmins to require their protection?

The case for separate representation for non-Brahmins fails because they cannot prove to have a common non-Brahmin interest.

But do they fail to secure personal representation? This can be best shown by reference to figures—

Caste of voters Local Board	Group I		Group II	
	No. of voters for the Local Boards of the districts of Belgaum, Bijapur and Dharwar	Total population of the three districts	No. of voters for the Local Boards of the districts of Ratnagiri and Kolaba	Total population of the two districts
1	2	3	4	5
Brahmins	4600	85739	4477	89786
Lingayats	12730	933123	-	-
Marathas	1074	255526	3667	446077
Mahars	22	196751	33	138738
Mohammedans	661	295838	1169	106273
Others	4241	1065821	2837	1016930
Total	23328	2832798	12183	1797804

Reducing the above figures to the basis of a thousand we have the following interesting result:

Name of Castes	Group I			Group II		
	Proportion of population of a caste thousand of the population covered	Proportion of voters of a caste to every thousand of the population of the same caste	Proportion of voters of a caste to every thousand of voters	Proportion of population of a caste to every thousand of the population covered	Proportion of voters of a caste to every thousand of the population of the same caste	Proportion of voters of a caste to every thousand of voters
1	2	3	4	5	6	7
Brahmins	30.2	53.7	197.2	50.8	49.8	367.4
Lingayats	329.4	13.6	545.7	–	–	–
Marathas	90.2	4.2	46.0	248.8	8.2	300.9
Mahars	69.5	0.1	0.9	74.5	0.2	2.7
Mohammedans	104.4	2.2	28.3	59.2	10.9	95.9
Others	376.2	3.9	181.3	562.2	2.8	232.8

Note: Compiled by Ambedkar

So arranged, the conclusions to be drawn from these figures are highly important.

1. The Brahmins, given a uniform franchise for all, though a small minority so far as numbers are concerned becomes a majority so far as the total of voters is concerned as is the case in Group II.

2. Though with a uniform franchise the non-Brahmin communities like the Lingayats and Marathas do not fail to figure on the voters' list, the proportion of their voters to their population is insignificant as compared with the proportion which the Brahmin voters bear to the Brahmin population.

The proportion of the Brahmins to their voters is really extravagant. It is justified neither by faith in them nor by their own numbers. The Lingayats though they can legitimately complain that the proportion of their voters is small will succeed in securing personal representation. The Marathas though larger in numbers than the Brahmins, besides the very small proportion of their voters suffer on the voters' list and very likely will fail to secure personal representation for themselves. So argued, the case for special provision of the Marathas can be sustained and should be admitted.

The question is what form the provision should take. In my opinion such provision instead of taking the form of Separate Electorates of reserved seats should take the form of a low pitched franchise. The franchise for the non-Brahmin should be lower than that for the Brahmin. By this arrangement the Marathas would improve their position on the voters' list and the altogether favoured position of the Brahmin would be equalized. It is in the interest of all that the Brahmin should not play such a preponderant part in politics as he has been doing hitherto. He has exerted a pernicious influence on the social life of the country and it is in the interest of all that his pernicious influence should be kept at a minimum in politics. As he is the most exclusive he is most anti-social.

Even the authors of the report on constitutional reforms are not in favour of a limited or uniform franchise. They say, 'We consider that the limitations of the franchise, which it is obviously desirable to make as broad as possible, should be determined rather with reference to practical difficulties than to any prior considerations as to the degree of education or amount of income which may be held to constitute a qualification. It is possible that owing to unequal distribution of population and wealth it may be necessary to differentiate the qualifications for a vote not merely between provinces, but between different parts of the same province' (p. 147). To this I should like to add that we should differentiate the qualifications for a vote not merely between provinces or parts thereof but between communities of the same provinces. Without this differentiation some communities with a small but wealthy or educated population will secure more votes than a large community consisting of poor and uneducated members. Uniformity in franchise should be dispensed with. An important result will be that communal representation or reservation of seats for some non-Brahmin communities who are now clamouring for it would be avoided.

The Untouchables are usually regarded as objects of pity but they are ignored in any political scheme on the score that they have no interests to protect. And yet their interests are the greatest. Not that they have large property to protect from confiscation. But they have their very *persona* confiscated. The socio-religious disabilities have dehumanized the Untouchables and their interests at stake are therefore the interests of humanity. The interests of property are nothing before such primary interests.

If one agrees with the definition of slave as given by Plato, who defines him as one who accepts from another the purposes which control his conduct, the Untouchables are really slaves. The Untouchables are so socialized as never to complain of their low estate. Still less do they ever dream of trying to improve their lot, by forcing the other classes to treat them with that common respect which one man owes to another. The idea that they have been born to their lot is so ingrained in their mind that it never occurs to them to think that their fate is anything but irrevocable. Nothing will ever persuade them that men are all made of the same clay, or that they have the right to insist on better treatment than that meted out to them.

The exact description of the treatment cannot be attempted. The word Untouchable is an epitome of their ills and sufferings. Not only has untouchability arrested the growth of their personality but also it comes in the way of their material well-being. It has also deprived them of certain civil rights. For instance, in Konkan the Untouchables are prohibited from using the public road. If some high caste man happens to cross him, he has to be out of the way and stand at such a distance that his shadow will not fall on the high caste man. The Untouchable is not even a citizen. Citizenship is a bundle of rights such as (1) personal liberty, (2) personal security, (3) rights to hold private property, (4) equality before law, (5) liberty of conscience, (6) freedom of opinion and speech, (7) right of assembly, (8) right of representation in a country's Government and (9) right to hold office under the State. The British Government by gradual growth may be said to have conceded these rights at least in theory to its Indian subjects. The right of representation and the right to hold office under the State are the two most important rights that make up citizenship. But the untouchability of the Untouchables puts these rights far beyond their reach. In a few places they do not even possess such insignificant rights as personal liberty and personal security, and equality before law is not always assured to them. These are the interests of the Untouchables. And as can be easily seen they can be represented by the Untouchables alone. They are distinctively their own interests and none else can truly voice them. A free trade interest can be voiced by a Brahmin, a Mohammedan or a Maratha equally well. But none of these can speak for the interests of the Untouchables because they are not Untouchables. Untouchability constitutes a definite set of interests which the Untouchables alone can speak for. Hence it is evident that we must find the Untouchables to represent their grievances which are their interests and, secondly, we must find them in such numbers as will constitute a force sufficient to claim redress.

Now, will a general territorial electorate provide for the adequate return of the Untouchables to the law-making body? Referring back to the figures we find that the Untouchables (represented in the table by the Mahars), though they formed 69.4 in every thousand of the population, did not claim even a voter from their class. Under such circumstances it is impossible for them to elect their own man in a general electorate. On the other hand they must despair of any votes being cast by the touchable Hindus for an Untouchable candidate. The gradation of castes produces a certain theological basis which cuts the Untouchables both ways: in the minds of the lower orders it creates a preference for the higher orders while it creates contempt for the lower orders in the minds of the higher orders. Thus the ascending scale of preference and the descending scale of hatred and contempt beggars the Untouchables both ways. Without giving a single vote to the Untouchables, the touchables are sure to make a large draft on the already meagre voting strength of the Untouchables.

So situated, the Untouchables with the largest interests at stake will be the greatest sufferers in a general territorial electorate. To give them an opening special provision shall have to be made for their adequate representation....

The total population of the Bombay Presidency by the Census of 1911 (British districts only) is 19, 626, 477. Of this the Untouchable population is 1, 627, 980 or 8 per cent of the total. Assuming for the present the Bombay Legislative Council to consist of 100 elected members, the Untouchables. should have 8 representatives to represent them in the Council. If we distribute one representative to every 200,000 of the people (which is just the ratio of 100 representatives to the 20 millions of the population), then the Untouchables can by right claim 8 representatives to themselves. But the Untouchables of the Bombay Presidency may be allowed to elect 9 members in all....

It may be objected that though 8 representatives are not in excess to the Untouchable population it may be in excess to the voting strength of Untouchables. That the Untouchables are a poor community and that under the same franchise they yield per thousand a smaller proportion of voters than other communities is a fact. But if the grave position of the Untouchables is admitted instead of restricting their number of representatives, the aim should be to increase the number of their voters, i.e., we must aim at lowering the franchise so far as the Untouchables are concerned.

What the franchise should be is a very important question. There is a line of argument which urges that franchise should be given to those only who can be expected to make an intelligent use of it. As against this view it can be said in the words of Prof. L. T. Hobhouse that it is true that 'the success of democracy depends on the response of voters to the opportunities given to them. But conversely the opportunities must be given in order to call forth the response. The exercise of popular Government is itself all education ... enfranchisement itself may precisely be the stimulus needed to awaken interest. The ballot alone effectively liberates the quiet citizen from the tyranny of the shouter and the wire-puller. An impression of existing inertness alone is not a sufficient reason for withholding responsible Government or restricting the area of suffrage.' Taking into consideration that suffrage is an education and that there are groups with unequal distribution of wealth and education among them and that these groups are not sympathetically like-minded, the authors of the reports rightly argue that the case for uniformity of franchise cannot be sustained.

But in the case of the Untouchables there are as few reasons for curtailing the number of their representatives as the reasons for widening their electorate are many. If under a given franchise the Untouchables do not muster strong as electors, it is not their fault. The very untouchability attached to their person is a bar to their moral and material progress. The principal modes of acquiring wealth are trade, industry or service. The Untouchables can engage in none of these because of their untouchability. From an Untouchable trader no Hindu will buy. An Untouchable cannot be engaged in lucrative service. Military service had been the monopoly of the Untouchables since the days of the East India Company. They had joined the Army in such large numbers that the Marquis Tweedledale in his note which he submitted to the Indian Army Commission of 1859 wrote, 'It should never be forgotten that India was conquered with the help of the low-caste men.' But after the mutiny when the British were able to secure soldiers from the ranks of the Marathas, the position of the low-caste men who had been the prop of the Bombay Army became precarious, not because the Marathas were better soldiers but because their theological bias prevented them from serving under low-caste officers. The prejudice was so strong that even the non-caste British had to stop recruitment from the Untouchable classes. In like manner, the Untouchables are refused service in the Police Force. In a great many of the Government offices it is impossible for an Untouchable to get a place. Even in the mills a distinction is observed. The Untouchables are not admitted in Weaving Departments of the Cotton Mills though many of them are professional weavers. An instance at hand may be cited from the school system of the Bombay Municipality. This most cosmopolitan city ruled by a Corporation with a greater freedom than any other Corporation in India has two different sets of schools ... one for the children of touchables and the other for those of the Untouchables. This in itself is a point worthy of note. But there is something yet more noteworthy. Following the division of schools it has divided its teaching staff into Untouchables and touchables. As the Untouchable teachers are short of the demand, some of the Untouchable schools are manned by teachers from the touchable class. The heart-killing fun of it is that if there is a higher grade open in Untouchable school service, as there is bound to be because of few Untouchable trained teachers, a touchable teacher can be thrust into the grade. But if a higher grade is open in the touchable school service, no Untouchable teacher can be thrust into that grade. He must wait till a vacancy occurs in the Untouchable service!!! Such is the ethics of the Hindu social life. Under it if the Untouchables are poor, the committee, it may be hoped, will not deny them representation because of their small electoral roll but will see its way to grant them adequate representation to enable the Untouchables to remove the evil conditions that bring about their poverty. At present when all the avenues of acquiring wealth are closed, it is unwise to require from the Untouchables a high property qualification. To deny them the opportunities of acquiring wealth and then to ask from them a property qualification is to add insult to injury. Just what sort of franchise and just what pitch are required to produce sufficient voting strength from the Untouchables? In absence of data, I leave it to the Committee to decide. It would be better to pitch the franchise so low as to educate into political life as many Untouchables as possible. They are too degraded to be conscious of themselves. I only wish to emphasize that in deciding upon the representation of the Untouchables the Committee looking to their interests at stake will not let the extent of the electorate govern the number of representatives, but will rather let the number of representatives govern the extension of the electorate.

In this connection it would not be improper to remind the Committee of Lord Morley who is reported to have said that 'the object of Government was that the Legislative Councils should represent truly and effectively with reasonable approach to the balance of real social forces, the wishes and needs of the communities concerned. This could not be done by Algebra, Arithmetic, Geometry or Logic, but by a wide outlook. He saw no harm as to a compromise that while numbers should be the main factor in determining the extent of representation modifying causes might influence the number of representatives.' It is therefore proposed that the Untouchables of the Bombay Presidency should be allowed to elect 9 members through the constituencies made up as above. These 9 members will further form a constituency to elect one member from among themselves to represent the Untouchables in the Imperial Legislative Council leaving 8 members to represent the Untouchables in the Bombay Legislative Council.

Besides communal electorates there are other schemes in the field for the representation of the Untouchables. It would not be proper to close this statement without a word of comment on those Schemes.

The Congress has denied communal representation except in the case of Mohammedans and it also denies the extensive use of nomination; the only way then left open to the Untouchables is to fight in a general electorate. Now this is as it should be if all were equally free to fight. To educate the Untouchables by Shashtras into pro-touchables and the touchables into anti-Untouchables and then to propose that the two should fight out at an open poll is to betray signs of mental aberration or a mentality fed on cunning. But it must never be forgotten that the

Congress is largely composed of men who are by design political Radicals and social Tories. Their chant is that the social and the political are two distinct things having no bearing on each other. To them the social and the political are two suits and can be worn one at a time as the season demands. Such a psychology has to be laughed at because it is too interested to be seriously taken into consideration either for acceptance or for rejection. As it pays to believe in it, it will die a hard death. Starting from this unnatural premise the Congress activities have been quite natural. Those who attend the Congress do not care to attend the National Social Conference held in the same pandal. In fact those who attend the Congress had once started a campaign to refuse the use of the pandal to the Conference which was once refused the pandal in the city of Poona, the roosting place of the intelligentsia of our Presidency. As the Congress is a non-national or anti-national body, its views on communal electorates are worthy of no serious consideration.

The moderates in their separate meeting have been more kindly than just. They proposed the reservation of seats for backward communities in plural constituencies. They have not specified the number of seats for the Untouchables. But the general sense of many enlightened moderates and others kindly inclined is that one or two representatives of the Untouchables in the Legislative Council would suffice. It is impossible to agree with these gentlemen though they are entitled to gratitude for this much sympathy. One or two representatives of the Untouchables are as good as having none. A Legislative Council is not an old curiosity shop. It will be a Council with powers to make or mar the fortunes of society. How can one or two Untouchables carry a legislative measure to improve their condition or prevent a legislative measure worsening their state? To be frank, the Untouchables cannot expect much good from the political power to be given over to the high caste-Hindus. Though the power may not be used against the Untouchables and one cannot be altogether sure of this, it may not be used for their betterment. A Legislative Council may be sovereign to do anything it likes, but what it will like to do depends upon its own character. The English Parliament, we may be certain, though it is sovereign to do anything, will not make the preservation of blue-eyed babies illegal. The Sultan will not, though he can, change the religion of Mohammed just as the Pope will not, though he can, overthrow the religion of Christ. In the same way Legislature, mainly composed of high caste men, will not pass a law removing untouchability, sanctioning inter-marriages, removing the ban on the use of public streets, public temples, public schools; in short, cleansing the person of the Untouchables. This is not because they cannot, but chiefly because they will not. A Legislature is the product of a certain social condition and its power is determined by whatever determines society. This is too obvious to be denied. What may happen in future can be guessed from what has happened in the past. The high caste men in the Council do not like any social question being brought before the Legislature, as may be seen from the fact of the Resolution introduced by the Honourable Mr. Dadabhoy in 1916 in the Imperial Legislative Council. That it was adversely criticized by many who claimed to evince some interest in the Untouchables is too well known to need repetition. But what is not well known is that though the resolution was lost the mover was not pardoned; for the very moving of such a nasty resolution was regarded as a sin. At a subsequent election the mover had to make room for the Honourable Mr. Khaparde, who once wrote in an article: 'Those who work for the elevation of the Untouchables are themselves degraded.'

Isn't this sympathy of the higher castes for the Untouchables, sympathy with a vengeance ?

Those who tell that one or two members would suffice for the Untouchables fail to grasp the true import of political right. The chief import of a political right though technically summed up in the power to vote does lie either in voting upon for laws or for those who make laws; neither does it consist in the right to speak for or against a certain measure nor in being able to say 'yea or nay' upon roll-call; to be able to put into a ballot-box a piece of paper with a number of names written thereon is an act which, like those mentioned above, of itself possesses no value which stamps it as inherently superior to many of the most ordinary transactions of daily life. They are educative but as much as any transaction is. The chief significance of suffrage or a political right consists in a chance for active and direct participation in the regulation of the terms upon which associated life shall be sustained. Now the terms upon which the associated life between the touchables and Untouchables is carried on today are the most ignominious to the former and highly detrimental to the latter. To make effective the capacities of a people there must be the power to fix the social conditions of their exercise. If the conditions are too obdurate, it is in the interest of the Untouchables as well as of the touchables that the conditions should be revised. The Untouchables must be in a position to influence the revision. Looking to the gravity of their interests, they should get their representation as proposed in proportion to their population. One or two is only kind but neither just nor sufficient. As Lord Morley says in an earlier quotation, 'needs not numbers should govern the extent of representations.'

Recently there is brought into the forefront a rival scheme for the representation of the Untouchables by the Depressed Class Mission. The scheme is known as co-option. The scheme proposes that the representatives of the Untouchables should be nominated by the co-option of the elected members of the Council. Whether one should laugh or cry at the solicitude of the Mission for the Untouchables it is rather 'difficult to decide'. To cry is to believe that such a silly scheme would ever be adopted. The best way is to laugh it out. From the scheme can be easily seen that what is sometimes called benevolent interest in others may be an unwilling mask for an attempt to dictate to them what their good shall be, instead of an endeavour to agree with them so that they may seek and find the good of their own choice. The Mission, it must be said, was started with the intention of improving the condition of the Depressed Classes by emancipating them from the social tyranny of their high caste masters. But the Mission has fallen on such bad times that it is forced to advocate a scheme by which its wards or their representatives will be bounden slaves of their past masters. The masters and the mission have thus met and evolved a scheme which will keep the Depressed Classes eternally depressed without any hope of deliverance. Such tactics do not deceive the Untouchables ignorant as they are; less will they deceive the Franchise Committee. From another point of view the scheme of the Mission is unacceptable. It is aggravating to see the Mission proposing a scheme for the representation of the Untouchables while persistently refusing to admit an Untouchable in its governing council. Interested and officious as it is, its scheme must be rejected.

Nomination even though by Government in itself to be preferred to the former kind of nomination, is to be objected to from the standpoint of the Untouchables. Apart from restricting the freedom of the representatives it fails to give political education which is the urgent need of all communities, much more of the Untouchables.

At this stage we must consider the argument against communal representation. The first argument raised by the authors of the report is to the effect 'that the history of self-government among the nations who have developed it is decisively against' communal representation. But on an earlier page the authors say that the difference of caste and creeds must be taken 'into account as presenting a feature of Indian

Society which is out of harmony with the ideas on which elsewhere in the world representative institutions rest.' (page 97). In writing the former the later analysis of the situation must have vanished from their minds, else we must say that the authors could hold two opposing views at the same time. Presented in juxtaposition, the authors must be expected to agree to communal representation on the score of an exceptional remedy required to meet an exceptional situation.

Another and chief argument against communal representation is that it will perpetuate social divisions. The fun of it is that those who uphold the social divisions are the loudest in their expression of this adverse argument. The committee will please note that those who are the opponents of communal representation on this score are also the staunchest opponents of Mr. Patel's Inter-Caste Marriage Bill as a caste-breaking bill. The sincerity of those who bring forward this argument is seriously to be doubted. But as even the authors of the report have put it as a second count against communal representation, this particular argument must be met if possible.

Does communal representation perpetuate social divisions? If you look upon communal representation as making electoral Colleges of social divisions, the criticism may be said to be valid. This is true only if it is presupposed that the divisions are no real divisions and that they don't matter. This is as false a pre-supposition as that of inviting India which is made when it is said that Englishmen are unsocial. Communal Representation is a device to ward off the evil effects of the divisions. To those who, while agreeing to this particular benefit of communal representation, object to it on the score that it perpetuates the divisions it can be shown that there is another perspective from which it can be said that communal representation instead of perpetuating the social divisions is one of the ways of dissolving them.

While communal electorates will be co-terminous with social divisions their chief effect will be to bring together men from diverse castes who would not otherwise mix together into the Legislative Council. The Legislative Council will thus become a new cycle of participation in which the representatives of various castes who were erstwhile isolated and therefore anti-social will be thrown into an associated life. An active participation in an associated life, in its turn, will not leave unaffected the dispositions and attitudes of those who participate. A caste or a religious group today is a certain attitude. So long as each caste or a group remains isolated its attitude remains fossilized. But the moment the several castes and groups begin to have contact and co-operation with one another the resocialization of the fossilized attitude is bound to be the result. If the Hindus become resocialized with regard to their attitude towards Mohammedans, Christians, etc., and the Mohammedans, Christians, etc., become resocialized with regard to their attitudes towards the Hindus, or the touchable Hindus with regard to the Untouchables, caste and divisions will vanish. If caste is an attitude and it is nothing else, it must be said to be dissolved when that particular attitude symbolizing the caste is dissolved. But the existing set attitude representing the diverse castes and groups will be dissolved only if the diverse groups meet together and take part in a common activity. Such changes of disposition and attitudes will not be ephemeral but will, in their turn influence associated life outside the Council Hall. The more opportunities are created for such conjoint activities the better. The resocialization will then be on a larger scale and bring about a speedier end of caste and groups. Thus those who condemn communal representation on the score of perpetuating the existing divisions will welcome it, on reflection, as a potent solvent for dissolving them.

The importance and necessity of communal and adequate representation of Untouchables is beyond question. The depth of emotion with which the Untouchables speak on this topic must have been easily gauged when the Untouchables of the Madras Presidency told Mr. Montagu that there would be bloodshed if Home Rule for India was not accompanied by communal representation to the Untouchables. The authors of the Report however are actuated by a faith in the intelligentsia to effect all reforms for the elevation of the Untouchables from permanent degradation and ostracism. They say 'they find the educated Indian organizing effort not for political ends alone but for various forms of public and social service.' As the authors have connived at the demands of the Untouchables on this score it is but proper to investigate whether their faith is well grounded. On education and its social value the words of Joseph Addison are not too stale to be recalled. He said, 'There can be no greater injury to human society than that good talent among men should be held Honourable to those who are endowed with them without any regard how they are applied. The Gifts of Nature and the Accomplishments of Art are valuable but as they are exerted in the interest of virtue or governed by the Rules of Honour, we ought to abstract our minds from the observation of an excellence in those we converse with, till we have taken some notice or received some good information of the Disposition of their Minds, otherwise they make us fond of those whom our reason and judgment will tell us we ought to abhor.'

Statistics will show that the intelligentsia and the Brahmin caste are exchangeable terms. The disposition of the intelligentsia is a Brahmin disposition. Its outlook is a Brahmin outlook. Though he has learned to speak in the name of all, the Brahmin leader is in no sense a leader of the people. He is a leader of his caste at best, for he feels for them as he does for no other people. It is not intended to say that there are no Brahmins who feel for the Untouchables. To be just, there are a few more moderate and rational Brahmins who admit the frightful nature of the institution of untouchability in the abstract and perceive the dangers to society with which it is fraught. But the great majority of the Brahmins are those who doggedly deny the horrors of the system in the teeth of such a mass of evidence as never was brought to bear on any other subject and to which the experience of every day contributes its immense amount; who, when they speak of freedom, mean the freedom to oppress their kind and to be savage, merciless and cruel, and whose inalienable rights can only have their growth in the wrongs of the Untouchables. Their delicate gentility will neither bear the Englishmen as superior nor will it brook the Untouchables as equal. 'I will not tolerate a man above me, and of those below none must approach too near' sums up the true spirit of their social as well as political creed. Those who speak against the anti-social spirit of the Brahmin leaders are often cautioned that in their denunciation they do not pay sufficient regard to the existence of the first class of Brahmin leaders. This is no doubt the case. Noble but very rare instances of personal and pecuniary sacrifice may be found among them just as may be found to be tender in the exercise of their unnatural power. Still it is to be feared that this injustice is inseparable from the state of things with which humanity and truth are invoked to deal. The miserable state of the Untouchables is not a bit more tolerable because some tender hearts are bound to show sympathy, nor can the indignant tide of honest wrath stand still because in its course it overwhelms a few who are comparatively innocent among a host of guilty.

The trend of nationalism in India does not warrant us to believe that the few who are sympathetic will grow in volume. On the other hand it is the host of guilty that time is sure to multiply. With the growth of political agitation, the agitation for social reform has subsided and has even vanished. The Prarthana Samaj, the Brahmo Samaj with their elevating influence have become things of the past. The future has few things like these in store. The growth of education if it is confined to one class, will not necessarily lead to liberalism. It may lead to the justification and conservation of class interest; and instead of creating the liberators of the downtrodden, it may create champions of the past and the supporters of the *status quo*. Isn't this the effect of education so far ? That it will take a new course in future *ceteris paribus,* there is no ground to believe. Therefore, instead of leaving the Untouchables to the mercy of the higher castes, the wiser policy would be to give power to the Untouchables themselves who are anxious, not like others, to usurp power but only to assert their natural place in society.

This gigantic world war, however motivated, has yielded what is known as the principle of self-determination which is to govern international relations of the future. It is happy to note that the pronouncement of the 20th August 1917 declared the application of the principle to India—a principle which enunciates the rule that every people must be free to determine the conditions under which it is to live. It would be a sign of imperfect realization of the significance of this principle if its application were restricted to international relations, because discord does not exist between nations alone, but there is also discord between classes from within a nation. Wittingly our Indian politicians in their political speeches and harangues hold on to 'the *de jure* conception of the Indian people'. By the *de jure* conception they conceive of the Indian people as by nature one and emphasize the qualities such as praiseworthy community of purpose and welfare, loyalty to public ends and mutuality of sympathy which accompany this unity. How the *de jure* and *de facto* conceptions conflict, it is hoped, the committee will not fail to realize. As an instance the following may be noted. The moral evil to the Indian people of their conquest and subjugation by the British is a theme which is very attractive to the Brahmin politicians, who never fail to make capital out of it. The moral evils were once portrayed by John Shore in his 'Notes on Indian Affairs' written in 1832. The late Honourable Mr. Gokhale once voiced the same feeling when speaking about the 'excessive costliness of the foreign agency'. He said:

There is a moral evil which, if anything, is even greater. A kind ol dwarfing or stunting of the Indian race is going on under the present system. We must live all the days of our life in an atmosphere of inferiority and the tallest of us must bend, in order that the exigencies, of the existing system may be satisfied. The upward impulse, if I may use such an expression, which every schoolboy at Eton and Harrow may feel, that he may one day be a Gladstone or Napoleon or a Wellington, and which may draw forth the best efforts of which he is capable, is denied to us. The full height to which our manhood is capable of rising can never be reached by us under the present system. The moral elevation which every self-governing people feel cannot be felt by us. Our administrative and military talents must gradually disappear, owing to sheer disuse till at last our lot as hewers of wood and drawers of water in our own country, is stereotyped.

I beg to invite the attention of the Committee whether these sentiments which have been voiced by a Brahmin (a noble Brahmin to be sure) to the disgrace of the British bureaucracy cannot be more fittingly voiced by the Untouchables to the disgrace of the Brahmin oligarchy? May it be said to the credit of the bureaucracy, that it has disproved the charge of being wooden and shown itself susceptible to feeling by proposing changes in the system of the Government which has dwarfed the personality of those for whom it was devised. But can the oligarchy claim anything half as noble? Their belief is that the Hindu social system has been perfected for all time by their ancestors who had the superhuman vision of all eternity and supernatural power for making infinite provision for future ages. This deep ingrained ethnocentrism has prevented a reconstruction of Hindu Society and stood in the way of a revision of vested rights for the common good. A farce of a conference for the removal of untouchability was enacted in March 1918 in Bombay. Doctor Kurtakoti, the Shankaracharya of Karvir fame, though promised to attend, left for Northern India just a day or two before the conference met, on some urgent business. Mr. Tilak is credited with a short speech at the conference which has for the good luck of Mr. Tilak remained unreported. But this was only lip sympathy shown to hoodwink the Untouchables for when the draft of the proclamation removing untouchability was presented to Mr. Tilak, it is known on creditable evidence that he refused to honour it with his signature.

Here is disclosed a patent disharmony within a nation and therefore a proper field for the application of the principle of self determination. If the advanced classes are clamouring for its application to India and if the powers that we have sanctioned it, however partially, to ward off the future stunting and dwarfing of the Indian people, may not the Untouchables with justice claim its benefit in their own interest? Admitting the necessity of self-determination for the Untouchables communal representation cannot be withheld from them, for communal representation and self-determination are but two different phrases which express the same notion.

2

Statement for the Protection of the Depressed Classes as a Minority in the Bombay Presidency*
29 May 1928

Protection Through Adequate Representation

Preliminary

The Sabha feels relieved of great anxiety by the decision of Parliament not to appoint an Indian on the Statutory Commission. The agitation for the appointment of an Indian would have been proper if the Commission had to consider a common Indian demand for self-government. But the fact is that the Commission shall have to consider not one demand, but a variety of demands made by the different interests prevailing in the country. That being the case the agitation should have been for a representation of all such interests on the Commission. The Sabha desires to point out that nothing could have satisfied the Depressed Classes better than the appointment of Indians representing various interests in the country, including their own, on the Statutory Commission. The demand for representation on the Statutory Commission was not, however, of such a nature and the Sabha, therefore, could not feel at one with those who urged it. The Sabha, it is true, did not agitate as it should have done, in conformity with its own views, for the representation of the Depressed Classes on the Commission. But that was because the Sabha felt that it was too much to hope for in a country where those in charge of the affairs from the Viceroy downwards have cultivated the habit of recognizing the noisy few and forgetting the dumb millions. To use the language of Burke, because half a dozen politicians, like grasshoppers under a fera, make the field ring with their importunate chink, whilst the masses, like thousands of great cattle, are reposing beneath the shadow of the oak, chew the cud and are silent, the Government of India imagines that the politicians who make the noise are the only inhabitants of the field—that, of course, they are many in number—or that, after all, they are other than the little, shrivelled, meagre, hopping, though loud and troublesome insects of the hour. But there was also another reason why the Sabha did not press for its views. In the opinion of the Sabha this exclusion of Indians from the Statutory Commission was no small mercy to the Depressed Classes. For, by their non-appointment the Depressed Classes are, at any rate, saved the prejudice that would have otherwise been caused to their case, which the Sabha has hereby undertaken to place before the Commission.

Injustice Done to the Depressed Classes in 1919

The Montagu Chelmsford Report recognized fully (para. 151) that the existence of the social differences and divisions formed 'a feature of Indian Society which is out of harmony with the ideas on which elsewhere in the world representative institutions rest' and the authors of the Report (para. 153) held that they 'have to be taken into account and they must lead us to adjust the forms of popular Government familiar elsewhere to the special conditions of Indian life.' In accordance with this, the authors of the Report, in order to pacify the Depressed Classes who had stoutly opposed the introduction of the Reforms, undertook to safeguard their interests as will be seen from the following statement in paragraph 155 of their Report in which they say:

We have shown that the political education of the Ryot cannot be very rapid and may be a very difficult process. Till it is complete he must be exposed to the risk of oppression by people who are stronger and cleverer than he is; and until it is clear that his interests can safely be left in his own hands or that the Legislative Council represent and consider his interests, we must retain power to protect him. *So with the Depressed Classes, we intend to make the best arrangements we can for their representation in order that they too may ultimately learn the lesson of self-protection.* But if it is found that their interests suffer and that they do not share in the general progress, we must retain the means in our hand of helping them....

The Sabha regrets that all these promises were thrown to the wind by the Southborough Committee which was subsequently appointed to devise franchise, frame constituencies and to recommend what adjustments were needed to be made in the form of the proposed popular Government as a consequence of the peculiar social conditions prevalent in India. So grossly indifferent was the Southborough Committee to the problem of making adequate provision for safeguarding the interests of the Depressed Classes that even the Government of India which was not over-particular in this matter felt called upon in paragraph 13 of their Despatch on the Report of the Southborough Committee to observe: 'We accept the proposals (for non-official nomination) generally. But there is one Community whose case appears to us to require more consideration than the Committee gave it.' The Report on Indian Constitutional Reforms clearly recognized the problem of the Depressed Classes and gave a pledge respecting them. The castes described as 'Hindus—others' in the Committee's Report though they are defined in varying terms, are broadly speaking all the same kind of people. Except for differences in the rigidity of their exclusion they are all more or less in the position of the Madras *Panchamas*, definitely outside that part of the Hindu Community which is allowed access to their temples. They amount to about one-fifth of the total population, and have not been represented at all in the Morley-Minto Councils. *The Committee's Report mentions the Depressed Classes twice, but only to explain that in the absence of satisfactory electorates they have been provided for by nomination. It does not discuss the position of these people or their capacity for looking after themselves. Nor does it explain the amount of nomination which it suggests for them. Paragraph 24 of the Report (of the Franchise Committee) justifies the restrictions of the nominated seats on grounds which do not suggest that the Committee were referring to the Depressed Classes.* The measure of representation which they propose for this Community is as follows:

Province	Total population in millions	Population of Depressed Classes in millions	Total seats	Seats for the Depressed Classes
Madras	39.8	6.3	120	2
Bombay	19.5	0.6	113	1
Bengal	45.0	9.9	127	1
United Provinces	47.0	10.1	120	1
Punjab	19.5	1.7	85	–
Bihar and Orissa	32.6	9.3	100	1
Central Provinces	12.0	3.7	72	1
Assam	6.0	0.3	54	–
Total	221.4	41.9	791	7

Note: Compiled by B.R. Ambedkar.

These figures speak for themselves. It is suggested that the one-fifth of the entire population of British India should be allotted seven seats out of practically 800. It is true that in all the Councils there will be roughly a one-sixth proportion of officials who may be expected to bear in mind the interests of the depressed (?); but that arrangement is not, in our opinion, what the Report on Reforms aims at. The authors stated that the Depressed Classes should also learn the lesson of self-protection. It is surely fancifull to hope that this result can be expected from including a single member of the Community in an Assembly where there are 60 to 90 caste-Hindus. To make good the principles of paragraphs 151, 152, 154 and 155 of the Report we must treat the out-castes more generously....

The Sabha feels happy that it is not alone in its opinion as to the injustice done to the Depressed Classes by the framers of the Reforms Scheme of 1919. This opinion was also shared by the Muddiman Committee which was appointed two years afterwards to report upon the possibility of improving and enlarging the scheme of Reforms. That Committee admitted in its Report (Paragraph 64) that the representation granted to the Depressed Classes under the Scheme was inadequate.

Extent of Representation that Must be Granted to the Depressed Classes

What then should be the extent of the representation of the Depressed Classes which can be said to be adequate?...

In either case the demand of the Sabha is for 22 representatives of the Depressed Classes in a Council composed of 140 members. The Sabha desires to state emphatically that this much representation to the Depressed Classes in a Council of 140 is only just. The Sabha is aware that some people are likely to call such a demand as a very large one. Such a view must however be deemed to be the result of prejudice against the Depressed Classes. It cannot be said to be founded upon any definite reason. The Sabha thinks that an exact idea as to the population of the Depressed Classes would be a sufficient corrective to views of this sort. *For, it must be admitted that population is a measure by which to evaluate the representation that is to be granted to any community.* The computation of the exact strength of the Depressed Classes is therefore a matter of considerable importance. The Depressed Classes of the Bombay Presidency have already suffered an injustice at the hands of the Southborough Committee in 1919.... So small was the strength of the Depressed Classes shown by the Southborough Committee that even the paltry suggestion of the Government of India to give two representatives to the Depressed Classes in the Bombay Legislative Council failed to have any effect. Similar attempt is now being made in responsible quarters to whittle down the population of the Depressed Classes. For instance, Mr. Bajpai speaking on behalf of the Government of India in the Legislative Assembly on the 23rd February 1928 said 'that the population of the Depressed Classes in India was much exaggerated and that the real strength of the Depressed Classes was only $28^1/_2$ millions and not 60 millions' as used to be stated theretofore. The Sabha fears that the Commission may fall into the same error in which the Southborough Committee fell and may in consequence make proposals based upon such erroneous calculation. The Sabha therefore desires to draw the attention of the Commission to what the Director of the Census of India has to say in this connection. In Chapter XI of Volume I of the *Census of India 1921* the Director observes:

Paragraph 193. It has been usual in recent years to speak of a certain section of the community as the 'Depressed Classes'. So far as I am aware the term has no final definition, nor is it certain exactly whom it covers. In the *Quinquennial Review of the Progress of Education* from 1912 to 1917 (Chapter XVIII paragraph 505), the Depressed Classes are specifically dealt with the point of view of educational assistance and progress, and in Appendix XIII to that Report a list of the castes and tribes constituting this section of the community is given. The total population classed according to these lists as depressed amounted to 31 million persons or 19 p.c. of the Hindu and Tribal population of British India. There is undoubtedly some danger in giving offence by making in a public report social distinctions which may be deemed invidious; but in view of the lists already prepared and the fact that the 'depressed' have especially in South India, attained a class consciousness and a class organization, are served by special missions, 'raised' by philanthropic societies and officially represented in the Legislative Assemblies, it certainly seems advisable to face the facts and to attempt to obtain some statistical estimate of their numbers. I, therefore, asked Provincial Superintendents to let me have an estimate based on Census figures of the *approximate* strength of the castes who were usually included in the category of 'depressed'. I received lists of some sorts from all Provinces and States except the United Provinces, whose extreme delicacy of official sentiment shrank from facing the task of attempting even a rough estimate. The figures given are not based on exactly uniform criteria, as a different view is taken of the position of the same group in different parts of India, and I have had in some cases to modify the estimate on the basis of the figures in the educational report and of information from the 1911 reports and tables. *They are also subject to the general defect which has dreads been explained, that the total strength of any caste is not recorded.* The marginal statement [reproduced below] gives, however, a rough estimate of the *minimum* numbers which may be considered to form the 'Depressed Classes' of the Hindu Community. The total of these provincial figures adds up to about 53 millions. *This, however, must be taken as a low and conservative estimate since it does not include (1) the full strength of the castes and tribes concerned and (2) the tribal aborigines most recently absorbed in Hinduism, many of whom are considered impure.* We may *confidently* place the numbers of the Depressed Classes, all of whom are considered impure, at something between 55 and 60 millions in India proper....

... This cautious and considered estimate of the Director of Census must supersede all guesses and surmises regarding the strength of the Depressed Classes in the different Provinces of India. It destroys the validity of the estimate of Mr. Bajpai. For, it has been arrived at after scrutinizing the figures that have appeared in the Provincial Educational Reports which Mr. Bajpai says have formed the basis of his statement. Its correctness must be admitted. For, as the Director says it was arrived at after a deliberate investigation. The Sabha must therefore insist upon the Statutory Commission accepting these figures in preference to any other. According to this estimate the minimum strength of the Depressed Classes in the Bombay Presidency is 28, 00, 000 souls or 10.8 p.c. of the total population. On the basis of their strength alone the Depressed Classes are entitled to 15 seats out of a total of 140.

If the strength of a community was the only factor governing the extent of the representation to be granted to it, then the demand for the seven extra seats for the Depressed Classes would no doubt appear to be one for an unearned increment. *It must however be recognized that the strength of the community cannot be taken as the sole factor in determining matters of this sort. The standing of a community is no less an important factor to be taken into account in determining its quota of representation.* The standing of the community must mean its power to protect itself in the social struggle. That power would obviously depend upon the educational and economic status of the community. It follows from the recognition of the principle that *the lower the standing of a community the greater is the electoral advantage it must get over the rest.* There can be no two opinions that the standing of the Depressed Classes both educational and economical is the lowest in this Presidency. Consequently they are entitled to some electoral advantage over what they are entitled to on the basis of their strength. This electoral advantage must be greater in the case of the Depressed Classes than in the case of any other community of equal strength and standing; because no community can be said to form a submerged class in the same sense in which the Depressed Classes do. Nor can any class be said to be burdened with those grave disabilities which form the common lot of the Depressed Classes and which prevent them from rising above their degraded station in life. This is one reason why the Sabha feels justified in asking for this increment in representation. There is also another reason which the Sabha thinks must justify the extra representation claimed by it for the Depressed Classes. The representation of a minority, if it is to protect the minority, must also be effective. If not, it would be a farce. To escape this reproach it must be recognized that *if a minority is to be protected then there must be enough representatives of the minority to save it from being entirely submerged.* To put the same thing in the form of a proposition, the effectiveness of a minority representation depends upon its being large enough to have the sense of not being entirely overwhelmed. In claiming this extra representation the Depressed Classes, the Sabha thinks, are entitled to invoke this principle in their favour, in common with the rest of the minorities in the country.

Necessity for Impartial Treatment of All Minority Communities

These principles governing the extent of representation are those which have been laid down by the Government of India in their despatch reviewing the Report of the Southborough Committee. The Sabha desires to point out that the case of the Depressed Classes was more deserving of the application of such principles than that of any other community that could have been thought of in the whole of India. In practice, however, the benefit of these principles was rigorously denied to the Depressed Classes all throughout India and was literally showered upon a community like the Mahomedans holding a stronger and better position in the country than can be predicated of the Depressed Classes. To point out one such instance of unequal treatment the Sabha would invite the attention of the Commission to the two following cases:

Provinces	Moslem population	Seats for Moslem	Depressed Classes population	Seats for Depressed Classes
Central Provinces	574276	11	3060232	2
Bombay Presidency	1207443	7	1627980	1

Howsoever indignant one may feel over the perpetration of such injustice to the Depressed Classes the Government of India does not blush at it. For, it had avowedly enunciated those principles for the very limited purpose of applying them to the Mahomedans only. This was due, as everyone knows, to the distinction the Government of India made in the political importance of the different communities. The Sabha protests against this grading of the citizens of a country on the basis of their political importance, there can be no safe and secure rule except the one that that all communities are politically of equal importance. This invidious distinction is at the root of all the communal troubles and is destructive of the principle of equal opportunity. The introduction of this principle in the governance of India at the time when the Ist installment of Reforms was granted by Parliament was disastrous to the interests of the Depressed Classes. The Sabha is glad to find the present Secretary of State recognizing the existence of the Depressed Classes as a problem for serious consideration in the decision that may now be taken with regard to the enlargement of the scope of the Political Reforms already introduced. But the Sabha is anxious to point out that such recognition would be of no consequence to the Depressed Classes if it is not reflected in the changes that may now be introduced into the framework of the constitution of the country.

Mode of Representation

The Sabha is opposed to the principle of nomination and would insist upon the extension of the principle of election to the Depressed Classes. Election is not only correct in principle from the standpoint of responsible Government, but is also necessary in practice from the standpoint of political education. Every community must have an opportunity for political education which cannot well be secured otherwise than by the exercise of the vote. It must be regarded as unfortunate that the Depressed Classes who need such education, more than any other community, should be denied an opportunity to take their share in the rapidly developing political life of India. There is also another reason why election in the case of the Depressed Classes is a necessity. Ministership is a very important privilege and the Depressed Classes cannot afford to forego the same. No great benefit can come to them from the introduction of Political Reforms unless they can find a place in the Cabinet of the country, from where they can influence the policy of the Government. This opportunity will be denied to them so long as they are denied the opportunity of electing their own representatives. For under responsible Government nominated members must continue to be ineligible for office. A system of representation like that of nomination which deprives the Depressed Classes of this right must stand self-condemned.

Two objections are usually urged against the application of the principle of election to the Depressed Classes.

Difficulty in Forming Constituencies
This objection, the Sabha thinks, must be ruled out of serious consideration as not being honest. If difficulty in the matter of forming constituencies was a consideration which led Government to prefer nomination to election in the matter of the representation of the Depressed Classes, it is difficult to understand how the Government ventured to apply the principle of election to the Moslems and the Europeans. These communities are not less-scattered than the Depressed Classes and no constituencies can be formed for them including the existing one, which cannot be condemned as absurd from a logical point of view. All the same, the Government of Bombay did abandon its aesthetic sense and undertook to form asymmetrical constituencies for these communities when it found impossible to form symmetrical ones. All these difficulties in regard to the formation of the constituencies for the Depressed Classes are, however, set at rest under the scheme of representation outlined by the Sabha. The problem being thus simplified, no objection ought now to be raised for the substitution of the principle of nomination by the principle of election.

Difficulty in Getting a Sufficiently Large Electorate
Will there be a sufficient number of electors in any constituency to make the election of the Depressed Classes to the Council a real election? By way of pointing out a difficulty in substituting election for nomination this question is usually raised and answered in the negative. The difficulty

would no doubt be there if it is decided that the existing pitch of the franchise is not to be touched and so long as the pitch continues where it now is, the Sabha must admit that the number of electors among the Depressed Classes will be very few. But the Sabha thinks that the existing pitch of the franchise is unjustifiable on every ground. It has turned responsible Government into a mockery. It means a Government of the whole Presidency of two crores of people by a minority of seven lakhs who happen to have the good fortune of being voters under the existing franchise. Such a state of things is clearly vicious and cannot be allowed to continue in future, if there is to be responsible Government, not merely in name but also in fact. It is to be regretted that the question of franchise does not seem to have been adequately pressed by the class that is most vocal in demanding Reforms. Democracy is alleged to be the aim of that class, but if the truth be told, in the words of the Government of Burma,

they are in favour of democratic institutions mainly because they are making an appeal to a democratic nation. They could not very well call for democracy and leave the *Demos* out. Their chief interest in the Reforms is centered in the powers that they expect to gain over the Executive. The broad franchise and responsible voting in its true sense by the rural electors is not at all the central idea of their demand. As long as their own class will furnish the Legislative Councillors who will exercise the—desired control, it is immaterial to them whether these represent few or many voters.

Whether or not this is the correct diagnosis of the difference of the Indian politicians to the important question of franchise, the fact remains that the question of franchise occupies in Congress politics a very subordinate place as compared to the question of the transfer of powers. In the opinion of the Sabha, this attitude of the Congress politicians is a reversal of the true relationship between the question of the franchise and the question of transfer of power. It must be admitted that the dictum of the Government of India that the forces which now hold the administration together cannot be withdrawn before satisfactory substitutes are ready to take their place, must find acceptance in all quarters which are willing to look at things from a proper perspective. Now these substitutes must obviously be the electors; it follows, therefore that the degree and the kind of responsibility which can be introduced into the Government of the country will depend upon the strength of the electors. So vital is this question of the franchise that upon its determination alone can depend the degree of the transfer of political power. What should be the franchise is therefore a most important question. In the way in which it is determined at present the Sabha wishes to point out that the principle aim of representative Government has been lost sight of altogether. *Franchise means the right to determine the terms of associated life.* Franchise can mean nothing else. If that is the meaning of franchise, then it follows that it should be given to those who by reason of their weak power of bargaining are exposed to the risk of having the terms of associated life fixed by superior forces in a manner unfavourable to them. If this is true, then the very exigencies of representative Government demand that the franchise, if the term is properly understood, must be fixed so low as to bring it within the reach of the large majority, of the poor and the oppressed sections of society. Indeed adult franchise is the only system of franchise which can be in keeping with the true meaning of that term. The Sabha would, however, be content if the franchise for the Legislative Council is fixed at the same level as that for the Taluka Local Board in the rural parts and Rs. 3 rental per month in urban parts of the Presidency. The fear often entertained on the part of the Government that such a lowering of the franchise will bring in a large part of unintelligent people is without foundation. Large property is not incompatible with ignorance. Nor is abject poverty incompatible with high degree of intelligence. Property may as well dull the edge of intelligence. On the other hand poverty does and often must stimulate intelligence. Consequently the adherence of the Government to a high property qualification as an insurance against ignorance is nothing but a superstition, which is sedulously cultivated by the classes and fostered by the Government in order to deprive the masses of their right to the making of their Government.

System of Election

Free election in general constituencies is, in the opinion of the Sabha, out of the question so far as the Depressed Classes are concerned. On the other hand the Sabha does not wish to ask for Communal electorates, in its opinion, it would be sufficient if the Depressed Classes are provided with reserved seats in the general constituencies. In the case of the candidates for election from the Depressed Classes the Sabha would urge the total abandonment of the residential qualification and a partial relaxation in the condition as to deposit.

Representation in the Assembly

The Sabha respectfully protests against the non-recognition of the right of the Depressed Classes in the Legislative Assembly in 1919. The Government of India, is still supreme in important matters which are directly under its control or under the Reserved half of the Provincial Governments. Even in respect of the Transferred subjects it continues to have the power of superintendence. It is, therefore, obvious that in the direction of such large powers the Depressed Classes should have some voice and the Sabha would, therefore, claim that three members from the Depressed Classes of the Bombay Presidency should be elected to the Legislative Assembly by their representatives in the Local Legislative Council.

PROTECTION THROUGH GUARANTEES

In addition to the demand for adequate representation the Sabha feels that it must also demand the inclusion of clauses in the constitution of the country and as a fundamental part thereof guaranteeing the civil rights of the Depressed Classes as a minority in the Bombay Presidency. Such guarantees must cover the recognition of the following propositions concerning the interests of the Depressed Classes:

1. That the education of the Depressed Classes shall be recognized as the first charge on the revenues of the Province and that an equitable and just proportion of the total grant for education should be earmarked for the benefit of the Depressed Classes.
2. That the right of the Depressed Classes to unrestricted recruitment in the army, navy, and the police shall be recognized without any limitation as to caste.
3. That for a period of 30 years the right of the Depressed Classes for priority in the matter of the recruitments to all posts, gazetted as well as non-gazetted in all civil services shall be recognized.
4. That the right of the Depressed Classes to the appointment of a special inspector of police from amongst themselves for every District shall be recognized.
5. That the right of the Depressed Classes to effective representation (as defined above) on the Local Bodies shall be recognized by the Provincial Government.
6. That the right of the Depressed Classes to appeal to the Government of India in cases of violation of these rights by the Provincial

Government shall be recognized and the Government of India shall be given the power to compel the Provincial Government to conform to the law in the matter.

Justification for Such Guarantees

It may be argued that as the Depressed Classes have been given adequate representation in the Council, there can be no danger to their rights, as there can be in the case of an unrepresented minority. Why then should there be these guarantees? The Sabha demurs to this much faith in the efficacy of a representative form of Government to effectively protect a minority from the tyranny of the majority. In this connection the Sabha would like to invite the attention of the Commission to the views of John Stuart Mill who has observed that 'the notion that the people have no need to limit their power over themselves, might seem axiomatic, when popular Government was the thing only dreamt about or read of as having existed at some distant period of past.... It was now perceived that such phrases as self-government, and the power of the people over themselves, do not express the true state of the case. The people who exercise the power are not always the same people over whom it is exercised; and the self-government spoken of is not the government of each by himself, but of each by all the rest. The will of the people, moreover, practically means the will of the most numerous or the most active part of the people, the majority or those who succeed in making themselves accepted as the majority; the people, consequently, may desire to oppress a part of their number; and precautions are as much needed against this, as against any other abuse of power. The limitation, therefore, of the power of Government over individuals loses none of its importance when the holders of power are regularly accountable to the community that is to the strongest party therein. This view of things, recommending itself equally to the intelligence of thinkers and to the inclination of those important classes in European Society to whose real or supposed interests democracy is adverse, has had no difficulty in establishing itself; and in political speculations the tyranny of the majority included amongst the evils against which the Society requires to be on its guard.'

From this it is obvious that representative Government cannot altogether do away with the necessity of such guarantees for the protection of the interests of the minorities in a nation. Indeed it may safely be asserted that a representative form of Government far from being a means of affording protection to the minorities must be deemed to be so very inadequate for that purpose that its introduction without a system of guarantees being made a part thereof was looked upon as a most dangerous experiment. The postwar history of Europe abounds in such cases. The peace treaties between the allied powers and Czechoslovakia, Austria, Hungary, Rumania and the Polish German Convention relating to Upper Silesia with their guarantee clauses for the benefit of the minorities bear eloquent testimony to the fact that the minorities cannot depend upon the representative form of Government but must seek protection in the form of guarantees of their rights.

If representative Government is so weak when operating among European peoples, where the secularization of politics has gone far further, how much weaker must it be in India where politics is nothing but theology in action. It is this theology against which the Depressed Classes must seek to be protected. How destructive is this theology of true citizenship has nowhere been described so well as in the Note by the Hon'ble Sir Alexander Cardew, K.C.S.I., I.C.S., to the Government of India contained in the letter No. 1146 (Reforms) dated the 31st December 1918. The following extracts are made from that Note:

[...] 2. It may first be asked whether the democratic idea is in accordance with the prevailing philosophy of the people of India. The fundamental principle of the modern democratic State is the recognition of the value of the individual and the belief that as each individual has but one life, full opportunity should be accorded to each to attain his maximum development in that life. Neither of these propositions is accepted in the current philosophy of India. This rather holds that the present life is for each only one of a series of existences; that the position of each individual in this life has been determined for him by his merit or demerit in previous births; and that, therefore, his place in the social organism is irrevocably fixed and cannot be changed. It may therefore be safely asserted that the root notions of democracy run counter to all the ideas which for thousands of years have formed the common stock of popular belief in India.

3. Closely connected with the doctrine, that each man's place in the present birth has been determined by his actions in the past existences is the institution of caste which has the effect of stereotyping and fixing unalterably the position of each individual in the social scale. Thus a man born a Brahman cannot be

other than a Brahman and a man born Pariah can never be other than a Pariah. Equality of opportunity is impossible under such conditions and it is neither recognized nor desired by Indian public opinion.

4. At the apex of the caste pyramid stands the Brahman. This caste, originally representing, at least in Southern India, a racial difference, has established through a long period of time its absolute supremacy over all other castes. The Brahman's claim to supremacy is based not only on race and intellect but also on the injunctions of religion. The sanctity of a Brahman's person and religious merit to be obtained by feeding him, paying for his education, providing money for the marriage of his daughters, endowing him with land, has been an established belief in India for centuries. Brahmans.... possessed numberless privileges....

6. With such predominance in most walks of life, it is not surprising that the Brahman has easily secured control in politics. No representative of the great Pariah community nor of the Christian community has ever sat or would ever have a chance of sitting, for one of these constituencies. This experience strongly suggests that the political machine in the future as in the past will be under the control of the Brahmans, unless special measures are resorted to, to secure adequate representation of the other classes....

8. Next to the Brahman *sed longo intervello* comes the great group of Hindu-castes, some higher, some lower, generally grouped together as non-Brahmans but all equally exclusive and largely antagonistic to one another. It is notorious that if a member of one of these castes attains to a position of influence he fills the offices in his gifts with his fellow castemen. The Standing Orders of the Government recognize this tendency and contain directions to counteract it. The joint report is not ignorant of this, for it says, 'there runs through Indian Society a series of cleavages of religion, race and caste which constantly threaten its solidarity.' These distinctions of castes do not merely threaten the solidarity of Indian Society—they prevent such solidarity from ever existing.

9. Below both the Brahmans and the non-Brahman caste-Hindus, come the low castes or more correctly the persons of no castes who number *in* this Presidency [*i.e.* Madras] some ten millions of people. For convenience they may be referred to as the Panchama or Pariah community. These people are regarded, not merely as belonging to a lower class, but as conveying by their very presence an actual pollution which requires purificatory religious ceremonies....

13. The difficulty of introducing democratic institutions into a society such as this, illiterate, divided into hard and fast castes, with Brahman at the top, with the various Non-Brahman Hindu castes in the middle and the low castes liable to be oppressed impartially by both, at the bottom must be very great. Nor does this difficulty seem to have been sufficiently realized by the

writers of the Joint Report. *Surely the first essential of any scheme of reform is that adequate safeguard should be provided for the good government of the inarticulate masses of the population....*

If this is a correct description of the existing state of affairs then the Minorities of Europe cannot be said to have a better case for obtaining guarantees of their rights than the Depressed Classes. *Many people in the world have fallen low by force of circumstances. The Depressed Classes on the other hand form a solitary case of a people who have remained fallen because their rise is opposed to religious notions of the majority of their countrymen.* Much was made before the Muddiman Committee by certain persons of the resolutions passed by the various Legislative Councils, throwing open wells, dispensaries and dharamshalas to members of Depressed Classes and of the circulars issued by Ministers of Education requiring children of the Depressed Classes to be admitted to schools in common with the rest. But what a mockery such resolutions and circulars are will be apparent to the Commission from the perusal of Annexure A to this statement. It will illustrate the attitude of the majority towards the Depressed Classes as evidenced by incidents reported from time to time in the various newspapers in the country (item Nos. 1 and 10). From a perusal of these news items it will be realized that the Depressed Classes cannot be employed in the army, navy and the police because such employment is opposed to the religious notions of the majority (item No. 8). They cannot be admitted in schools because their entry is opposed to the religious notions of the majority (item No. 12). They cannot avail themselves of government dispensaries, because the majority will not let them cause pollution to their person's or to their dispensaries (item Nos. 2 and 5). They cannot live a cleaner and higher life, because to live above their prescribed station is opposed to the religious notions of the majority (item Nos. 1 and 6). So rigorous is the enforcement of the Social Code against the Depressed Classes that any attempt on the part of the Depressed Classes to exercise their elementary rights of citizenship only ends in provoking the majority, to practice the worst form of social tyranny known to history (item Nos. 4, 7 and 11). It will be admitted that when society is itself a tyrant, its means of tyrannizing are not restricted to the acts which it may do by the hands of its functionaries and it leaves fewer means of escape penetrating much more deeply into the details of life, and enslaving the soul itself. Protection against such tyranny is usually to be found in the Police power of the state. But unfortunately in any struggle in which the Depressed Classes are on the one side and the upper class of Hindus on the other, the Police power is always in league with the tyrant majority (item No. 11), for the simple reason that the Depressed Classes have no footing whatsoever in the Police or in the Magistracy of the country.

In view of this, it is unfair to the Depressed Classes to be lulled into the belief that their interests would be safe in the hands of their countrymen, because some Councils have passed resolutions and some of the Ministers have issued circulars favouring the Depressed Classes. The Sabha desires to caution the Commission against being lured into forming a better opinion of the Hindu majority from its best instances. Pictures of loving exercise of authority on one side, loving submission to it on the other, of superior wisdom ordering all things for the greatest good of the dependants are very gratifying to read. But such pictures would be to the purpose only if any one from the Depressed Classes denied the existence of good men in the Hindu society. Nobody among the Depressed Classes doubts that there would be great and universal happiness under the government of a good Hindu. But the fact is that laws and institutions require to be adapted not to good men but to bad. From this point of view, it is safer to grant the minority the necessary protection by the inclusion of guarantee clauses than to leave it unprotected on the fanciful ground that the tyrant majority has in it a few good men sympathetic to the minority. Such guarantees may be looked down upon by persons other than the Depressed Classes as being unnecessary; but from the standpoint of the Depressed Classes it is but an essential safeguard. There is such an enormous dread of the Reforms prevalent amongst the Depressed Classes that they have from the very beginning opposed their introduction. So strong was their feeling against the Reforms that in one of the addresses presented to Mr. Montagu the Depressed Classes declared 'we shall fight to the last drop of our blood, against any attempt to transfer the seat of authority in this country from the British hands to the so-called high class Hindus.' Nothing can allay such fears as the system of guarantees can do. Government is based upon faith and not upon reason. If the Depressed Classes can have no faith in the new constitution it is statesmanship to buy that faith if it can be done so with the concession of guarantees herein demanded.

3

Statement on Education of the Depressed Classes in the Bombay Presidency*
29 May 1928

... The Reforms Act came into force in 1921. Education was made a transferred subject in charge of a minister and a rapid advance in education was naturally expected at his hands. The Backward Classes had, however, their doubts as to whether any benefit would accrue to them from the transfer of education to the control of the ministers. Already they had suffered in the matter of education at the hand of the bureaucracy. In the first period of existence the bureaucracy did not permit them to receive the benefits of education. In the second period the bureaucracy did not help them to get education. All the same the bureaucracy was too much enlightened to deny the principle that the Backward Classes had a right to education. The Backward Classes were not prepared to predicate the same enlightenment of the Indian intelligentsia which was struggling to replace the bureaucracy. As the Indian intelligentsia had its roots in the part in which the Backward Class had no recognized rights, the latter were apprehensive that the past may again be made to live in the present.

Unfortunately their doubts came true and it may be truly said that under the Reforms the Backward Classes in the Bombay Presidency have fallen from purgatory to hell. This may appear to be a very strong commentary on the existing situation. But the situation for the Backward Classes of the Bombay Presidency created by the Compulsory Primary Education Act (Bombay Act No. IV of 1923) can hardly be described in any other words. The Compulsory Primary Education Act is in a very important sense a 'fraud'. It was claimed for the Act, it was calculated to change the character of the primary education from being voluntary to compulsory. The Act does nothing of the kind. A reference to section 10 of the Act is sufficient to expose the 'fraud'. The system is as voluntary as it was before and will remain so indefinitely. For, not only there is no obligation to make it compulsory, there is even no time limit fixed within which to fulfill the obligation. Apart from this the Compulsory Primary Education Act has made a most extravagant change in the administrative machinery for the control of Primary Education. Hitherto the control and management of Primary Education was entrusted to the Provincial Government and the whole of the expenditure on primary education was defrayed out of Provincial revenues except a small grant by the Local Boards amounting to one-third of their revenue from certain defined sources. Under the Compulsory Primary Education Act the position is reversed. The control and management of Primary Education is now entrusted to District School Boards (which are committees of District Local Boards) and instead of the Local Boards giving grants to the Provincial Government the Provincial Government is required to give a grant to the District School Board. Such extravagant and wild was the spirit in which this change was conceived that the Act gives to these School Boards power to appoint its own Executive officer—a privilege which is denied even to such an advanced Corporation as the Municipality of Bombay.

The Sabha thinks that this change is a most revolutionary change and is bound to be detrimental to the best interest of the Presidency and particularly of the Backward Classes. It must be borne in mind that the vital necessity of education has not been realized by all the classes of the population. The popular belief is that education is nobody's concern except that of the Brahmins. It is only a few, who have taken to politics that care for the spread of education. The School Board must be drawn from the many uniformed villagers who being brought up in the tradition that education is the concern of the Brahmins only must be indifferent to it and are bound to be opposed to make it compulsory. Education if it is to be efficiently administered must for some time to come, remain with the Provincial Government under the direct control of the Legislative Council where the few politicians who know the necessity of education are likely to be. The transfer of education from the Education Department to the School Boards, therefore, means transfer from well-trusted quarters to unworthy hands. But if the transfer is harmful to the progress of education in general, it is detrimental to the interests of the Backward Classes in particular. It must be borne in mind that although there may be some doubts as to whether the generality of the people do or do not believe in education, one thing is certain that they do not believe in the education of the Backward Classes. As to the attitude of the higher classes towards the extension of elementary education to the lower classes of the community the Hunter Commission observed:

Several witnesses have replied that positive hostility is shown to the admission of low caste boys to school. A Madras witness mentions the case of a school for Cherumans, the ancient slave caste, being established at Calicut, but the Nayars and Tiyas used to waylay the boys as they went to school and snatch their books out of their hands. In our discussion on this subject it was brought to our notice that in some parts of the Central Provinces and of Bombay special objections were entertained by the rural communities to the instruction of low castes on the ground that education would advance them in life and induce them to seek emancipation from their present servile condition. In his report for the year 1896–97 the Director of Public Instruction, Bombay quoted a case in which the action of the Local Officers of the Kaira District in requiring the admission of low caste pupils led to five or six large schools being closed for years and to the huts and crops of the low caste people being burnt in one village and to the imposition of a heavy punitive post on that village for two years.

Such being the attitude of the rural communities, how can it be expected that the School Boards drawn as they largely will be from the rural communities will discharge, faithfully, their trust in the matter of the education of the Depressed Classes ? To give the School Boards the control over the education of the Backward Classes is to make the prosecutor the ruler. No wonder that Resolutions are passed by the Backward Classes condemning the transfer of the control of Primary Education to the School Boards. It would have given some relief if the School Boards were manned by representatives of the Depressed Classes in adequate numbers. But that is not the case. The representation of the Depressed Classes in self-governing bodies from the Council down to the Local Boards has been planned by the Government after the manner of a curator who is not anxious to keep more than one specimen of each species in his Museum. Government nominates one member from the Depressed Classes to the District Local Board out of some forty members and the School Board is directed to co-opt one member from the Depressed Classes. In the principle of co-option there is always the danger of the wrong man being co-opted—a danger which the Depressed Classes of East Khandesh have had to face in the recent

School Board elections. But supposing the right man is co-opted, what can a single individual do in a hostile group of 15 which is the maximum strength of a School Board?

If Government is sincere in the matter of promoting the education of the Depressed Classes then there are certain measures which Government must adopt. The Sabha has its own convictions as to what Government should do in this connection and would like to state the same in the form of proportions as follows:

1. Unless the Compulsory Primary Education Act is abolished and the transfer of Primary Education to the School Boards is stopped, the Sabha fears that education of the Depressed Classes will receive a great setback.

2. Unless compulsion in the matter of Primary Education is made obligatory and unless the admission to primary schools is strictly enforced, conditions essential for educational progress of the Backward Classes will not come into existence.

3. Unless the recommendations made by the Hunter Commission regarding the education of the Mohamedans are applied to the Depressed Classes their educational progress will not be an accomplished fact.

4. Unless entry in the Public Service is secured to the Depressed Classes there will be no inducement for them to take education.

In making these comments upon the management of the educational affairs of the Presidency under the Reform and their bearing upon the Depressed Classes the Sabha is not oblivious to the special provisions made for the education of the Depressed Classes in the form of a few hostels and a few scholarships for higher education. But the Sabha begs to point out that it is useless to make provision for higher education of the Depressed Classes unless steps are taken to ensure the growth of Primary Education. Besides there is no guarantee that such concessions will continue. On the other hand that depends a great deal upon the policy of the particular Minister in charge of Education and upon the voting strength of the Depressed Classes in the Legislative Council, both of which are uncertain factors and cannot be depended upon.

4

Evidence before the Indian Statutory Commission*
23 October 1928

... *Dr. Ambedkar*: The first thing I would like to submit is that we claim that we must be treated as a distinct minority, separate from the Hindu community. Our minority character has been hitherto concealed by our inclusion in the Hindu community, but as a matter of fact there is really *no* link between the Depressed Classes and the Hindu community. The first point, therefore, I would stress before the Conference is that we must be regarded as a distinct and independent minority. Secondly, I should like to submit that the Depressed Classes minority needs far greater political protection than any other minority in British India for the simple reason that it is educationally very backward, that it is economically poor, socially enslaved, and suffers from certain grave political disabilities, from which no other community suffers.... Then I would submit that, as a matter of demand for our political protection, we claim representation on the same basis as the Mahomedan minority. We claim reserved seats if accompanied by adult franchise.

Chairman: And if there is no adult franchise?

Dr. Ambedkar: Then we would ask for Separate Electorates. Further, we would like to have certain safeguards either in the constitution, if it possible, or else in the way of advice in the instrument to the Governor regarding the education of the Depressed Classes and their entry into the Public Services?

...

Dr. Ambedkar: On that point I should like to say this, that our experience so far as the administration of the law is concerned is very bitter. I wish to say most emphatically that in many cases the law is administered to the disadvantage of the depressed class man. I would like to give a concrete case of what actually happened in one of the districts, without, of course, mentioning names. The Bombay Government annually lets out its forest lands for cultivation to the villages on certain stated terms. Now we discovered that in the allotment of those forest lands the depressed class man, who was often a landless labourer or with very little land, and who was clamouring for some sort of economic stability, never came in for a share. The Mamlatdars, who were really in charge of distributing the lands, showed absolute favouritism to the caste-Hindus as against the depressed class man. Last year in one district we organized and sent a deputation to the Assistant Deputy Collector of that district, placing before him our grievances with respect to these forest lands. He issued a circular to the Mamlatdars saying that the applications from the Depressed Classes should be considered. Now, some of the Mamlatdars, to show they were acting up to the circular, did give some lands to the Depressed Classes. But we found that they rather fooled us, if I may say so. What they did was, on paper they allotted a very large amount of land to the Depressed Classes and a very small amount of land to the caste-Hindus, but when we came to see actually what was allotted to us we found that the land allotted to the Depressed Classes was all rocky and unfit for cultivation and the depressed class people would not take it for anything, and the land allotted to the caste-Hindus though small, was all rich and fertile. Now I think that is a most fragrant abuse of the administrative power which is entrusted to the officials, and I personally attach far more importance to good administration of law than to more efficient administration of law.

Chairman: I imagine that the application of what you have told us, which is interesting, to our present inquiry is really this—because, of course, it is no part of the function of this Commission to interfere in day-by-day administration?

Dr. Ambedkar: No.

Chairman: You are using it as an argument to support your view that the Depressed Classes should have a full representation?

Dr. Ambedkar: In the services.

Chairman: That is your point?

Dr. Ambedkar: That is my point. I will give some instances of what happens in judicial courts actually in this Presidency. I happened to defend a depressed class man in one of the courts, and, to my great surprise, I found that the man had to stand outside the court behind a little window, outside the wall, and he would not come in simply because, as he said, 'It is all right so far as you are concerned, but after you have left there will be terrible social ostracism if I enter the court.'

Chairman: It was the client who did not want to come in?

Dr. Ambedkar: Who dare not come in.

Chairman: What sort of social ostracism had he in mind?

Dr. Ambedkar: The social ostracism would be that if he went back to the village there would be the boycott of the shopkeepers; nobody would sell him grain. The villagers would stop his dues as a village servant. He would not be allowed to come into the village. The depressed class people always live on the border of the village, not in the centre or in the midst. ...

...The Depressed Classes have been dubbed to be unfit for association because of certain unclean habits. That is the allegation of the upper classes. That is to say, they eat the meat of the dead animals and they are not clean, and so on. In this Presidency during the last two years I started a campaign to purify the Depressed Classes, so to say, and to persuade them to give up some of their dirty habits. But, to my great misfortune, I found the whole caste-Hindu population up against me when in a matter like this I expected the utmost co-operation from them. But when I began to analyse the basis of their opposition I found that they insisted upon the depressed class people doing the unclean things because giving up doing these things meant that the Depressed Classes are exceeding their social status and rivalling the upper class. For instance, in the Colaba and Ratnagiri districts the whole of the Mahar population have given up the eating of the meat of dead animals, but the tyranny and social oppression that is going on against them is simply unspeakable; there is a complete economic and social boycott. The lands they had been cultivating for years past have been taken away from them by their caste-Hindu landlords. Every sort of pressure, social and economic, has been brought to bear upon the Depressed Classes in order to compel them to resume their dirty habits. The officials, who are all caste-Hindus, give no protection to the Depressed Classes, whose condition has really become pitiable, and all this because they sought to give up their dirty habits. Instead of getting co-operation I find that the members of the upper classes are up against me, and they say 'these evil habits of the Depressed Classes are all insignia of their inferiority and they must remain.'...

Chairman: Coming to medical relief, will you kindly enlighten us as to the kind of medical relief the depressed class men are getting?

Dr. Ambedkar: They are not allowed entry into the dispensary, unless the case is a very serious one; such as for instance, the non-admission would bring the officer's conduct to the notice of the higher authorities. Ordinarily the medicine is dispensed out.

Chairman: I suppose you are talking of dispensaries in the mofussil?

Dr. Ambedkar: Yes, Government dispensaries....

Rao Bahadur Rajah: Will you kindly enlighten us as to the attitude of the schoolmasters or the Education Department or the managers of schools towards the children of the Depressed Classes?

Dr. Ambedkar: There is a circular issued by Dr. Paranjpye when he was Minister of Education in this Presidency to the effect that children of Depressed Classes should be admitted in all schools. But our experience is that circular has not been carried out at all. It is true that in the report of the Director of Public Instruction it is stated that that circular has been carried into effect; but I beg to differ from that view. It is not a correct statement of facts as they exist today. There is an incident here at Poona which took place only a few days ago, at Deoo, where the children of the Depressed Classes were refused admission and when they insisted on it the village proclaimed social boycott against the Depressed Classes....

5

On Electorates and Franchise*
17 May 1929

... In making my suggestions for the recasting of the electoral system I have allowed myself to be guided by three considerations: (1) Not to be led away by the fatal simplicity of many a politician in India that the electoral system should be purely territorial and should have no relation with the social conditions of the country (2) Not to recognize any interest, social or economic, for special representation which is able to secure representation through territorial electorates (3) When any interest is recognized as deserving of special representation, its manner of representation shall be such as will not permit the representatives of such interest the freedom to form a separate group.

Of these three considerations the second obviously depends upon the pitch of the franchise. In another part of this Report I have recommended the introduction of adult suffrage. I am confident that it will be accepted. I make my recommendations therefore on that basis. But in case it is not, and if the restricted franchise continues, it will call for different recommendations, which I also propose to make. For the reasons given above and following the last mentioned consideration I suggest that—

1. If adult suffrage is granted there shall be territorial representation except in the case of the Mohamedans, the Depressed Classes, and the Anglo-Indians.
2. If the franchise continues to be restricted, all representation shall be territorial except in the case of the Mohamedans, the Depressed Classes. Anglo-Indians, the Marathas and the allied castes and labour.
3. That such special representation shall be by general electorates and reserved seats and of labour by electorate made up of registered trade unions.

From these suggestions it will be seen that I am for the abolition of all class electorates, such as those for (1) Inamdars and Sardars (2)

Trade and Commerce, whether Indian or European (3) Indian Christians, and (4) Industry; and merge them in the general electorates. There is nothing to prevent them from having their voice heard in the Councils by the ordinary channel. Secondly, although I am for securing the special representation of certain classes, I am against their representation through Separate Electorates. Territorial Electorates and Separate Electorates are the two extremes which must be avoided in any scheme of representation that may be devised for the introduction of a democratic form of government in this most undemocratic country. The golden mean is the system of Joint Electorates with reserved seats. Less than that would be insufficient, more than that would defeat the ends of good government. For obvious reasons I make an exception in the case of the European community. They may be allowed to have their special electorates. But they shall be general electorates and not class electorates.

DISTRIBUTION OF SEATS AMONG THE MINORITIES

The quota of seats assigned by my colleagues to the different minorities is given below in the tabular form:

Minority	No. of seats out of 140	
	General	Special
Europeans	2	5
Anglo-Indians	2	Nil
Indian Christians	1	Nil
Depressed Classes	10	Nil
Mohamedans	43	2

Note: Compiled by B.R. Ambedkar

From this table it will be seen that in distributing the seats among the different minorities, my colleagues have not acted upon any uniform principle. Nor does it appear that they have striven to do justice to the minorities concerned. This is clear if we compare the treatment given by my colleagues to the Mohamedans with the treatment they have given to the Depressed Classes. Mohamedans form 19 per cent of the population of the Presidency. My colleagues have proposed to give them over 31 per cent, of the total representation provided for the Legislative Council. The Depressed Classes on the other hand who form according to the most conservative estimate 8 per cent, of the total population of the Presidency are allowed only 7 per cent of the total seats in the Council. The reasons for this discrimination are difficult to comprehend. Of the two minorities the Mohamedan minority is undoubtedly stronger in numbers, in wealth and in education. Besides being weak in numbers, wealth and education, the Depressed Classes are burdened with disabilities from which the Mohamedans are absolutely free. The Depressed Classes cannot take water from public watering places even if they are maintained out of public funds; the Mohamedans can. The Depressed Classes, by virtue of their untouchability, cannot enter the Police, the Army and the Navy, although the Government of India Act lays down that no individual shall be denied his right to any public office by reason of his caste, creed or colour. The Mohamedans have not only an open door in the matter of Public Service, but that in certain departments they have secured the largest share. The Depressed Classes are not admitted in Public schools even though they are maintained out of public money; there is no such bar against the Mohamedans. The touch of a Depressed Class man causes pollution; the touch of a Mohamedan does not; that trade and industry are open to a Mohamedan while they are closed to a man from the Depressed Classes. The Mohamedan does not bear the stigma of inferiority as does a man from the Depressed Classes with the result that the Mohamedan is free to dress as he likes, to live as he likes and to do what he likes. This freedom the Depressed Class man is denied. A Depressed Class man may not wear clothes better than the villagers even though he may have the economic competence to pay for its cost. He must live in a hut. A Depressed Class man may not make much display of wealth and splendour even on ceremonial occasions and may certainly not take the bridegroom on a horse in procession through the main streets. Any act contrary to the customary code or beyond his status is bound to be visited by the wrath of the whole body of villagers amongst whom he happens to live. The Depressed Class man is far often subject to the tyranny of the majority than the Mohamedan is. The reason is that the Mohamedan who has all the elementary rights of a human being accorded to him, has no cause for quarrel against the majority, except when a religious issue comes to the front. But the position of the Depressed Class man is totally different. His life which is one incessant struggle for the acquisition of the rights of a human being, is a constant challenge to the majority which denies him these rights. The result is that he is constantly in antagonism with the majority. This is not all. If on any occasion the Mohamedan is visited by the tyranny of the majority, he has on his side the long arm of the Police and the Magistracy. But when the Depressed Class man is a victim of the tyranny of the majority, the arm of the Police or of the Magistracy seldom comes to his rescue. On the contrary it works in league with the majority to his detriment, for the simple reason that the Mohamedan can count many of their kith and kin in the Police and the Magistracy of the Province; while the Depressed Classes have no one from them in these departments. And be it noted that the Depressed Classes have not merely to bear the brunt of the orthodox Hindu force. They have also to count against the Mohamedans. It is ordinarily supposed that the Mohamedan is free from social prejudices of the Hindus against the Depressed Classes. Nothing can be a greater error than this. Leaving aside the urban areas the Mohamedan in the rural parts is as much affected by the poison as the Hindu. The fracas that took place at Harkul, a village in the Mangaon Taluka of the Kolaba District, is an instance in point. In this district the Depressed Classes launched a campaign of social elevation and resolved to give up certain unclean practices which have marked them out as persons of inferior status. The Hindus of the district, who had formerly preached to these people the abandonment of these unclean practices as a necessary condition of their uplift, turned upon these poor people and tyrannized them by bringing to bear upon them a social and economic boycott. But it was never expected that the Mohamedans of the district would follow their Hindu neighbours. On the contrary it was the hope of the Depressed Classes that in their struggle with the touchable Hindus the Mohamedans would act as their friends. But these hopes of theirs were dashed to pieces. For, it was soon found that the Mohamedans, although they did not observe untouchability, were as much infected as the Hindus with the noxious belief that the Depressed Classes were born to an inferior social status and that their attempt to raise themselves above it by giving up their unclean habits was an affront and an insult which required to be put down. As a result many were the fights that took place between the Mohamedans and the Depressed Classes of the district, in one of which, at Harkul, a Depressed Class man actually lost his life.

It is therefore clear that the problem of the Depressed Classes is far greater than the problem of the Mohamedans. The Mohamedans may be backward in the race, although they are so forward that in education at least they are second only to the advanced Hindus. But they are certainly not handicapped, so that with effort and encouragement they can hope to rise. The Depressed Classes, on the other hand, are not merely backward, they are also handicapped, so that no effort or encouragement will enable them to rise unless the handicap is first removed. That being the difference between the two, whatever degree of political power that may be necessary for the Mohamedans to change their backward state, the Depressed Classes will require twice as much if not more to do so. Yet my colleagues have reversed the proportion of their representation. The Mohamedans, who are 19 per cent, and who form a strong minority, are given 31 per cent of seats in the Council, while the Depressed Classes, who form 8 per cent of the population on the most conservative estimates, are given only 7 per cent of the seats in the Council which, in fact, is 1 per cent less than their population ratio of 72. There is a view that the problem of the Depressed Classes is a social problem and that its solution must be sought for in the social field. I am surprised that this view prevails even in high quarters. I am afraid that those who hold this view forget that every problem in human society is a social problem. The drink problem, the problem of wages, of hours of work; of housing, of unemployment insurance are all social problems. In the same sense the problem of untouchability is also a social problem. But the question is not whether the problem is a social problem. The question is whether the use of political power can solve that problem. To that question my answer is emphatically in the affirmative. True enough that the State in India will not be able to compel touchables and Untouchables to be members of one family whether they like it or not. Nor will the State be able to make them love by an Act of the Legislature or embrace by order in Council of the Executive. But short of that the State can remove all obstacles which make Untouchables remain in their degraded condition. If this view is correct, then no community has a greater need for adequate political representation than the Depressed Classes....

6

On Indianization of Services[*]
17 May 1929

It is notorious that the Public Services of the country in so far as they are open to Indians have become by reason of various circumstances a close preserve for the Brahmins and allied castes. The Non-Brahmins, the Depressed Classes and the Mohamedans are virtually excluded from them. They are carrying on an intense agitation for securing for themselves what they regard as a due share of the Public Services. With that purpose in view they prefer the system of appointment by selection to the system of appointment by open competition. This is vehemently opposed by the Brahmins and the allied castes on the ground that the interests of the State require efficiency and that should be the only consideration in the matters of appointment to public offices and that caste and creed should count for nothing. Relying only the educational merit as the only test which can be taken to guarantee efficiency, they insist that public offices should be filled on the basis of competitive examinations. Such a system it is claimed serves the ends of efficiency without in any way prohibiting the entry of the Backward Classes in the Public Services. For the competitive examination being open to all castes and creeds it leaves the door open to a candidate from these communities if he satisfies the requisite test.

The attitude of the Brahmin and allied castes towards this question has no doubt the appearance of fairness. The system of competitive examination relied upon may result in fairness to all castes and creeds under a given set of circumstances. But those circumstances presuppose that the educational system of the State is sufficiently democratic and is such that facilities for education are sufficiently widespread and sufficiently used to permit all classes from which good public servants are likely to be forthcoming to complete. Otherwise even with the system of open competition large classes are sure to be left out in the cold. This basic condition is conspicuous by its absence in India, so that to invite Backward Classes to rely upon the results of competitive examination as a means of entry into the Public Services is to practise a delusion upon them and very rightly the Backward Classes have refused to be deceived by it.

Assuming therefore that the entry of the Backward Classes in the Public Services cannot be secured by making it dependent upon open competition, the first question that arises for consideration is, have the Backward Classes a case for a favoured treatment? Unless they can make good their case they can no expect any modification of the accepted principles of recruitment by considerations other than those of efficiency pure and simple. In regard to this important question I have no hesitation in stating that the Backward Classes have a case which is overwhelming.

First of all those who lay exclusive stress upon efficiency as the basis for recruitment in Public Services do not seem to have adequate conception of what is covered by administration in modern times. To them administration appears to be nothing more than the process of applying law as enacted by the Legislature. Beyond question that is a very incomplete understanding of its scope and significance. Administration in modern times involves far more than the scrutiny of statutes for the sake of knowing the regulations of the State. Often times under the pressure of time or from convenience a government department is now-a-days entrusted with wide powers of rule-making for the purpose of administering a particular law. In such cases it is obvious that administration cannot merely consist in applying the law. It includes the making up of rules which have the force of law and of working them out. This system of legislation by delegation has become a very common feature of all modern governments and is likely to be on the increase in years to come. It must be accepted as beyond dispute that such wide powers of rule-making affecting the welfare of large classes of people cannot be safely left into the hands of the administrators drawn from one particular class which as a matter of fact is opposed to the rest of the population in its motives and interests, does not sympathize with the living forces operating in them, is not charged with their wants, pains, cravings and desires and is inimical to their aspirations, simply because it comes out best by the test of education.

But even assuming that administration involves nothing more than the process of applying the law as enacted by the Legislature it does not in the least weaken the case of the Backward Classes. For, officers who are drawn from a particular caste and in whose mind consciousness of caste sits closer than conscientious regard to public duty, may easily prostitute their offices to the aggrandizement of their community and to the detriment of the general public. Take the ordinary case of a Mamlatdar, administering the law relating to the letting of Government lands for cultivation. He is no doubt merely applying the law. But in applying he may pick and choose the lessees according to his predilection and very possibly may decide against lessees on grounds which may be communal in fact although they may be non-communal in appearance. Take another illustration of an officer placed in charge of the census department in which capacity he is called upon to decide questions of nomenclature of the various communities and of their social status. An officer in charge of this department by reason of his being a member of particular caste in the course of his administration may do injustice to a rival community by refusing to it the nomenclature or the status that belongs to it. Instances of favouritism, particularly on the grounds of caste and creed are of common occurrence though they are always excused on some other plausible ground. But I like to quote one which pertains to the Vishwakarmans of the Madras Presidency. It is related in their letter to the Reforms Enquiry Committee of 1924 in which they complained that 'a Brahmin member of the Madras Executive Council Sir (then Mr) P. Siwaswami Ayyar—when he was in charge of the portfolio of law issued a Government Order objecting to the suffix "Acharya" usually adopted by the Vishwakarmans in their names and seeking to enforce in its place the word "Asry", which is weighed with common odium. Though there was neither necessity nor authority to justify the action taken by the law member, the Government Order was published by the law department as if on the recommendation of the Spelling Mistakes Committee. It happened to be our misfortune that the non-official members of this Committee were drawn largely from the Brahmin community, who never knew how to respect the rights of their sister communities and never informed us of the line of action that they were decided upon. It was dealt more or less as the stab in the dark.'

This is inevitable. Class rule must mean rule in terms of class interests and class prejudices. If such results are inevitable then it must raise a query in the minds of all honest people whether efficient government has also given a good government? If not, what is the remedy? My view is that the disadvantages arising from the class bias of the officers belonging to Brahmin and allied castes has outweighed all advantages attending on their upon their efficiency and that on the total they have done more harm than good. As the remedy, the one I see is a proper admixture of the different communities in the Public Service. This may perhaps import a small degree of inefficiency. But it will supply a most valuable corrective to the evils of class bias. This has become all the more necessary because of the social struggles that are now going on in the country. The struggles between the Brahmins and the non-Brahmins, between Hindus and Mohamedans, between Touchables and Untouchables for the destruction of all inequalities and the establishment of equality, with all their bitterness, cannot leave the judges, magistrates, civil servants and the police without being influenced in their judgment as to the right or wrong of these struggles. Being members of the struggling communities they are bound to be partisans, with the, result that there may be a great loss in the confidence reposed by the public in their servants.

So far I have considered the case of the Backward Classes on grounds of administrative utility. But there are also moral grounds why entry into the Public Service should be secured to them. The moral evils arising out of the exclusion of a person from the Public Service were never so well portrayed as by the late Mr. Gokhale. In the course of a telling speech he observed,

The excessive costliness of the foreign agency is not however its only evil. There is a moral evil, which, if anything, is even greater. A kind of dwarfing or stunting of the Indian race is going on under the present system. We must live all the days of our life in an atmosphere of inferiority and tallest of us must bend in order that the exigencies of the existing system may be satisfied. The upward impulse, if I may use such an expression, which every school-boy at Eton or Harrow may feel that he may one day be a Gladstone, a Nelson, or a Wellington, and which may draw forth the best efforts of which he is capable, is denied to us. The full height to which our manhood is capable of rising can never be reached by us under the present system. The moral elevation which every self-governing people feel cannot be felt by us. Our administrative and military talents must gradually disappear, owing to sheer disuse, till at last our lot, as hewers of wood and drawers of water in our own country, is stereotyped.

Now what one would like to ask those who deny the justice of the case of the Backward Classes for entry into the Public Service is whether it is not open to the Backward Classes to allege against the Brahmins and allied castes all that was alleged by the late Mr. Gokhale on behalf of Indian people against the foreign agency? Is it not open to the Depressed Classes, the non-Brahmins and the Mohamedans to say that by their exclusion from the Public Service a kind of dwarfing or stunting of their communities is going on? Can they not complain that as a result of their exclusion they are obliged to live all the days of their lives in an atmosphere of inferiority, and that the tallest of them has to bend in order that the exigencies of the existing system may be satisfied? Can they not assert that the upward impulses which every school-boy of the Brahmanical community feels that he may one day be a Sinha, a Sastri, a Ranade or a Paranjpye, and which may draw forth from him the best efforts of which he is capable is denied to them? Can they not indignantly assert that the full height to which their manhood is capable of rising can never be reached by them under the present system? Can they not lament that the moral elevation which every self-governing people feel cannot be felt by them and that their administrative talents must gradually disappear owing to sheer disgust till at last their lot as hewers of wood and drawers of water in their own country is stereotyped? The answers to these queries cannot but be in the affirmative. If to exclude the advanced communities from entering into Public Service of the country was a moral wrong, the exclusion of the backward communities from the same field must also be a moral wrong, and if it is a moral wrong it must be righted.

These are the considerations which lead me to find in favour of the Backward Classes. It will be noticed that these considerations are in no way different from the considerations that were urged in favour of Indianisation. The case for Indianisation, it must be remembered, did not rest upon efficient administration. It rested upon considerations of good administration. It was not challenged that the Indian was inferior to the European in the qualities that go into the make-up of an efficient administrator. It was not denied that the European bureaucracy had improved their roads, constructed canals on more scientific principles, effected transportation by rail, carried their letters by penny post, flashed their messages by lightning, improved their currency, regulated their weights and measures, corrected their notions of geography, astronomy and medicine, and stopped their internal quarrels. Nothing can be a greater testimony to the fact that the European bureaucracy constituted the most efficient government possible. All the same the European bureaucracy, efficient though it was, was condemned as it was found to be wanting in those qualities which make for human administration. It is therefore somewhat strange that those who clamoured for Indianization should oppose the stream flowing in the direction of the Backward Classes, forgetting that the case for Indianization also includes the case for the Backward Classes. Be that as it may, I attach far more importance to this than I attach either to Provincial Autonomy or to complete responsibility in the Provincial Executive. I would not be prepared to allow the devolution of such large powers if I felt that those powers are likely to fall in the hands of any one particular community to the exclusion of the rest. That being my view I suggest that the following steps should be taken for the materialisation of my recommendations:

1. A certain number of vacancies in the Superior Services, Class I and Class II, and also in the Subordinate Services, should every year be filled by system of nomination with a pass examination. These nominations should be filled on the recommendation of a select committee composed of persons competent to judge of the fitness of a candidate and working in conjunction with the Civil Service officer referred to above. Such nominations shall be reserved to the Depressed Class, the Mohamedans and the Non-Brahmins in the order of preference herein indicated until their numbers in the services reach a certain proportion.

2. That steps should be taken to post an increasing number of officers belonging to these communities at the headquarters.

3. That a Central Recruitment Board should be constituted as a central agency for registering all applications for appointments and vacancies and putting applicants in touch with the offices where vacancies exist or occur from time to time. It is essential to put the man and the job in touch if this desire is to be achieved. The absence of such a Board is the reason why the efforts of the Government of Bombay in this connection have not achieved the success which was expected of them.

Part II

Constitutional Reforms
Seeking Political Representation, 1930–3

Introduction

The initial efforts made by Ambedkar to formulate policies for DCs saw his articulations during 1919–29, where his emphasis had been to draw attention towards—their distinct identity as a community; need for granting equal rights to them; need for their political representation either with Separate Electorates or with reserved seats with adult suffrage; making primary education of DCs obligatory and other arrangements for their educational development; and, participation in Public Services. The British government appointed the Simon Commission and it submitted its report to the British government in 1930 when the Labour Party had formed government. The Labour government of Britain, which came into office following the general election in May 1929, announced its intention of giving the Dominion Status to India and also of convening a RTC to invite various groups for their opinion on constitutional reforms. The Indian Viceroy made an announcement on 31 October 1929 for inviting representatives of different parties and interests in British India and representatives of the Indian States for the purpose of a conference and discussion with regard both to the British Indian and All-Indian problems (*Indian Quarterly Register* 1929, vol. 2: 47–8).

It gave yet another opportunity to Ambedkar to put forth the grievances of the DCs before the Conference. During this period, he intervened and presented following statements:

1. Need for Political Power for Depressed Classes: 20 November 1930.
2. In Sub-Committee No. III (Minorities): 31 December 1930.
3. A Scheme of Safeguards for the Protection of Depressed Classes: 31 December 1930.
4. Report of Sub-Committee No. III: 16 January 1931.
5. Demand for Specific and Concrete Provisions for Safeguards of Depressed Classes in the Future Constitution: 19 January 1931.
6. In the Minorities Committee: 8 October 1931.
7. Provisions for a Settlement of the Communal Problem: 8 October 1931.

8. Supplementary Memorandum on the Claims of Depressed Classes for Special Representation: 4 November 1931.
9. Note Submitted to the Indian Franchise Committee: 1 May 1932.
10. Poona Pact Correspondence between Gandhiji and British: August–September 1932.
11. Statement on Gandhiji's Fast: 19 September 1932.

The first RTC was held in the absence of Congress but other major interests like Muslims, Christians, etc., participated in it. Emphasizing the need for political representation for the DCs, Ambedkar again presented their inhuman conditions where there was not only possibility of discrimination in public life but it actually worked out as a denial of all equality of opportunity and denial of most elementary civic rights of human existence.

Ambedkar and Rao Bahadur R. Srinivasan jointly presented a design of political safeguards for the protection of the DCs (*BAWS* 1982, vol. 2: 528–53). This was the first systematic presentation of problems and their solutions in terms of equal rights, legal safeguards against discrimination or violation of rights and mechanism for fair share and participation in public life that is representation in services and Legislatures.

It was made clear that mere provision of equal rights would not help and to secure equality, there was 'a need to have adequate pains and penalties from interference in the enjoyment of declared rights.' Social boycott had been an effective weapon where a complete alienation or segregation could take place in public sphere if the DCs tried to exercise equal rights with the fellow beings. Three stages of solutions were suggested—(1) punishment for threatening a boycott, (2) punishment for instigating or promoting a boycott, and (3) punishment for boycott. Discrimination being so rampant, it was suggested that there should be protection against discrimination through legislation or Executive order so that no civil places should treat them unequally (*BAWS* 1982, vol. 2: 548–50).

The memorandum for the first time clearly advocated adequate representation in the Legislatures and Public Services. Another solution was requested in the form of Special Departmental Care in the in chargeship of a minister and having representation of the DCs in the Cabinet so that even the general policy of the government was prepared to safeguard their interests. The Governor General or Secretary of State was to function as appellate authority to adopt reprisal measures.

Though the first RTC was adjourned without any decision, the representatives of the DCs did succeed in convincing the conference that they were entitled to recognition as a separate entity for political and constitutional purposes. Specifying the claims of DCs, Ambedkar and Rao Bahadur Srinivasan submitted another memorandum at the second RTC. Here, apart from the earlier demands they explained how to change the Separate Electorates to other system in future and also to change the nomenclature of DCs to other terms like non-caste-Hindus, protestant Hindus, non-conformist Hindus, etc.

Yet another significant aspect of the second RTC was a fierce debate between Mahatma Gandhi and Ambedkar on the Separate Electorates to the DCs (*BAWS* 1982, vol. 2: 659–63). On the question of treating DC as a separate entity and providing them Separate Electorates, Ambedkar was confronted with the arguments such as 'will the Untouchables remain Untouchables in the times to come as the Muslims to remain Muslims and Sikhs as Sikhs ...', and 'I would resist it (Separate Electorates for Untouchables) with my life' by Gandhiji.

Meanwhile, a note (*BAWS* 1982, vol. 2: 491–502) was submitted by Ambedkar to the Indian Franchise Committee, on the question of the confusion prevailing on defining DCs vis-à-vis Untouchables and who needed to be known as Untouchables. He argued that the literal form of untouchability may be diminishing and not vanishing, however, the notional form of untouchability still prevailed.

Subsequently, lack of compromise between the leaders of Indian groups made the British prime minister to adjourn the Conference *sine die* with a suggestion to put a signed requisition authorizing the prime minister to arbitrate and give decision on the communal issue.

COMMUNAL AWARD AND POONA PACT

The British Prime Minister, Ramsay MacDonald, announced his decision known as Communal Award on 4 August 1932 to impart Separate Electorates to the DCs. The award also proposed that caste-Hindus and Untouchables could suggest some other arrangement with each other's consent and the government will agree to such an agreement. Gandhiji commenced his 'fast unto death' on 20 September 1932 against the award leading to Poona Pact signed on 25 September 1932, by Ambedkar on behalf of the DCs and by Madan Mohan Malaviya on behalf of the caste-Hindus. The substance of the Poona Pact was the reservation of seats based on Joint Electorates to the DCs out of the seats classified as general seats. The Pact also provided—(1) 18 per cent reservation for DCs in the Central and State Legislatures, (2) no discrimination for appointment to Public Services, and (3) to earmark adequate educational grants for education of DCs.

Concluding the efforts during second phase in which Ambedkar participated in the discussion at the RTCs, we observe the following issues being raised by him:

1. The DCs needed not merely political representation but adequate political representation in terms of their standing in population.
2. The need was not confined to political spheres but the spheres of Public Services also had to have adequate representation.
3. There was a need to have special department to care the interests of DCs in the charge-ship of a Minister.
4. The need was to define Untouchables strictly on the basis of the system of untouchability.
5. The British accepted for the first time that the DCs should be treated as minority that was not accepted earlier.
6. The DCs were given Separate Electorates by the British but denied due to fast by Gandhi and subsequent agreement with Ambedkar.

And we find some of the achievements during this period. On the front of education and employment, proposals were put by Ambedkar. Consequently there had been acceptance of general rules for the participation of the DCs in the educational and employment spheres. However on the political front for the representation of the DCs, the Separate Electorates were not granted and a new arrangement was approved under Poona Pact. Here, for the DC representation two-step election—where only DC voters were to elect four candidates to contest the final election, where both the general and the DC electorates were to elect one candidate, was adopted. This was mid-way between Separate and Joint Electorates for the DCs.

7

During Round Table Conferences
20 November 1930

NEED FOR POLITICAL POWER FOR DEPRESSED CLASSES
(*BAWS* 1982, VOL. 2: 503–9)

Dr. B.R. Ambedkar: Mr. Chairman.... The point of view I will try to put as briefly as I can. It is this that the bureaucratic form of Government in India should be replaced by a Government which will be a Government of the people, by the people and for the people. This statement of the view of the Depressed Classes I am sure will be received with some surprise in certain quarters. The tie that bounds the Depressed Classes to the British has been of a unique character. The Depressed Classes welcomed the British as their deliverers from age long tyranny and oppression by the orthodox Hindus. They fought their battles against the Hindus, the Mussalmans and the Sikhs and won for them this great Empire of India. The British, on their side, assumed the role of trustees for the Depressed Classes. In view of such an intimate relationship between the parties, this change in the attitude of the Depressed Classes towards British Rule in India is undoubtedly a most momentous phenomenon. But the reasons for this change of attitude are not far to seek. We have not taken this decision simply because we wish to throw in our lot with the majority. Indeed, as you know, there is not much love lost between the majority and the particular minority I represent. Ours is an independent decision. We have judged of the existing administration solely in the light of our own circumstances and we have found it wanting in some of the most essential elements of a good Government. When we compare our present position with the one which it was our lot to bear in Indian society of the pre-British days, we find that, instead of marching on, we are only marking time. Before the British, we were in the loathsome condition due to our untouchability. Has the British Government done anything to remove it? Before the British, we could not enter the temple. Can we enter now? Before the British, we were denied entry into the Police

Force. Does the British Government admit us in the Force? Before the British, we were not allowed to serve in the Military. Is that career now open to us? To none of these questions can we give an affirmative answer. That the British, who have held so large a sway over us for such a long time, have done some good we cheerfully acknowledge. But there is certainly no fundamental change in our position. Indeed, so far as we were concerned, the British Government has accepted the social arrangements as it found them, and has preserved them faithfully in the manner of the Chinese tailor who, when given an old coat as a pattern, produced with pride an exact replica, rents, patches and all. Our wrongs have remained as open sores and they have not been righted, although 150 years of British rule have rolled away.

We do not accuse the British of indifference or want of sympathy. What we do find is that they are quite incompetent to tackle our problems. If the case was one of indifference only it would have been a matter of small moment, and it would not have made such a profound change in our attitude. But what we have come to realize on a deeper analysis of the situation is that it is not merely a case of indifference, rather it is a case of sheer incompetence to undertake the task. The Depressed Classes find that the British Government in India suffers from two very serious limitations. There is first of all an internal limitation which arises from the character, motives and interests of those who are in power. It is not because they cannot help us in these things but because it is against their character, motives and interests to do so. The second consideration that limits its authority is the mortal fear it has of external resistance. The Government of India does realize the necessity of removing the social evils which are eating into the vitals of Indian society and which have blighted the lives of the downtrodden classes for so many years. The Government of India does realise that the landlords are squeezing the masses dry, and the capitalists are not giving the labourers a living wage and decent conditions of work. Yet it is a most painful thing that it has not dared to touch any of these evils. Why? Is it because it has no legal powers to remove them? No. The reason why it does not intervene is because it is afraid that its intervention to amend the existing code of social and economic life will give rise to resistance. Of what good is such a Government to anybody? Under a Government, paralysed between two such limitations, much that goes to make life good must remain held up. We must have a Government in which the men in power will give their undivided allegiance to the best interest of the country. We must have a Government in which men in power, knowing where obedience will end and resistance will begin, will not be afraid to amend the social and economic code of life which the dictates of justice and expediency so urgently call for. This role the British Government will never be able to play. It is only a Government which is of the people, for the people and by the people that will make this possible.

These are some of the questions raised by the Depressed Classes and the answers which in their view these questions seem to carry. This is therefore the inevitable conclusion which the Depressed Classes have come to: namely, that the bureaucratic Government of India, with the best of motives, will remain powerless to effect any change so far as our particular grievances are concerned. We feel that nobody can remove our grievances as well as we can, and we cannot remove them unless we get political power in our own hands. No share of this political power can evidently come to us so long as the British Government remains as it is only in a Swaraj constitution that we stand any chance of getting the political power into our own hands, without which we cannot bring salvation to our people.

There is one thing, Sir, to which I wish to draw your particular attention. It is this. I have not used the expression Dominion Status in placing before you the point of view of the Depressed Classes. I have avoided using it, not because I do not understand its implications nor does the omission mean that the Depressed Classes object to India's attaining Dominion Status. My chief ground for not using it is that it does not convey the full content of what the Depressed Classes stand for. The Depressed Classes, while they stand for Dominion Status with safeguards, wish to lay all the emphasis they can on one question and one question alone. And that question is, how will Dominion India function? Where will the centre of political power be? Who will have it? Will the Depressed Classes be heirs to it? These are the questions that form their chief concern. The Depressed Classes feel that they will get no shred of the political power unless the political machinery for the new constitution is of a special make. In the construction of that machine certain hard facts of Indian social life must not be lost sight of. It must be recognized that Indian society is a gradation of castes forming an ascending scale of revenges and a descending scale of contempt—a system which gives no scope for the growth of that sentiment of equality and fraternity so essential for a democratic form of Government. It must also be recognized that while the intelligentsia is a very important part of Indian society, it is drawn from its upper strata and although it speaks in the name of the country and leads the political movement, it has not shed the narrow particularism of the class from which it is drawn. In other words what the Depressed Classes wish to urge is that the political mechanism must take account of and must have a definite relation to the psychology of the society for which it is devised. Otherwise you are likely to produce a constitution which, however symmetrical, will be truncated one and a total misfit to the society for which it is designed.

There is one point with which I should like to deal before I close this matter. We are often reminded that the problem of the Depressed Classes is a social problem and that its solution lies elsewhere than in politics. We take strong exception to this view. We hold that the problem of Depressed Classes will never be solved unless they get political power in their own hands. If this is true, and I do not think that the contrary can be maintained, then problem of Depressed Classes is I submit eminently; a political problem and must be treated as such. We know that political power is passing from the British into the hands of those who wield such tremendous economic, social and religious sway over our existence. We are willing that it may happen, though the idea of Swaraj recalls to the mind of many of us the tyrannies, oppressions and injustices practised upon us in the past and fear of their recurrence under Swaraj. We are prepared to take the inevitable risk of the situation in the hope that we shall be installed, in adequate proportion, as the political sovereigns of the country along with our fellow countrymen. But we will consent to that on one condition and that is that the settlement of our problems is not left to time. I am afraid the Depressed Classes have waited too long for time to work its miracle. At every successive step taken by the British Government to widen the scope of representative Government the Depressed Classes have been systematically left out. No thought has been given to their claim for political power. I protest with all the emphasis I can that we will not stand this any longer. The settlement of our problem must be a part of the general political settlement and must not be left over to the shifting sands of the sympathy and goodwill of the rulers of the future. The reasons why the Depressed Classes insist upon it are obvious. Everyone of us knows that the man in possession is more powerful than the man who is out of possession. Everyone of us also knows that those in possession of power seldom abdicate in favour of those who are out of it. We cannot therefore hope for the effectuation of the settlement of our social problem. If we allow power to slip into the hands of those who stand to lose by settlement unless we are to have another revolution to dethrone those, whom we today help to ascend the throne of power and prestige. We prefer being despised for too anxious apprehensions, than ruined by too confident a security, and I think it would be just and proper for us to insist that the best guarantee for the settlement of our problem is the adjustment of the political machine itself so as to give us a hold on it, and not the will of those who are contriving to be left in unfettered control of that machine.

What adjustments of the political machine the Depressed Classes want for their safety and protection I will place before the Conference at the proper time. All I will say at the present moment is that, although we want responsible Government, we do not want a Government that will only mean a change of masters. Let the Legislature be fully and really representative if your Executive is going to be fully responsible.

I am sorry Mr. President. I had to speak in such plain words. But I saw no help. The Depressed Classes have had no friend. The Government has all along used them only as an excuse for its continued existence. The Hindus claim them only to deny them or, better still, to appropriate rights. The Muhammadans refuse to recognize their separate existence, because they fear that their privileges may be curtailed by the admission of a rival. Depressed by the Government, suppressed by the Hindu and disregarded by the Muslim, we are left in a most intolerable position of utter helplessness to which I am sure there is no parallel and to which I was bound, to call attention....

8

In Sub-Committee No. III (Minorities)*
31 December 1930

Dr. B.R. Ambedkar: Mr. Chairman, I am sure you will readily agree that the task which has fallen upon me to represent the case of the Depressed Classes is a heavy one. I think it is for the first time that the case of the Depressed Classes from the political point of view has come to be considered. The disabilities of the Depressed Classes were mentioned in almost every dispatch that was recorded by the Government of India in connection with the political advancement of the country; but the dispatches only mentioned the difficulties and never attempted to give any solution of those difficulties. The problem was just allowed to rest there. In view of that, and in view of other matters, namely, that in a Committee consisting of so many members we are only two to voice the grievances of 43 millions of people, and grievances which the Committee will agree are unparallel by the case of any other community that exists in India, I submit that the task is really an enormous one, and I should have expected more latitude in the matter of time allowed to me for presenting this case. But I anticipated that probably such would be the fate that would befall me, as it did, of course, at the Plenary Session; and, in anticipation of that, I and my colleague, Rao Bahadur Srinivasan, thought it advisable to submit to this Conference a written memorandum giving in clear-cut language what the Depressed Classes desire by way of political safeguards in the future constitution of India. That memorandum has already been submitted and circulated among the members of this Committee, and I hope everyone of them has received it. In view of this fact, that the case of the Depressed Classes is in the possession of the members of this Committee, I do not wish to ask indulgence from the Chairman for a larger period to present the case. I will therefore summarise, only to emphasize, what I have stated in the memorandum which is already in the hands of the members of the Committee.

BAWS 1982, vol. 2: 528–34.

Sir, the first observation that I will make is this, that although there are various minority communities in India which require political recognition, it has to be understood that the minorities are not on the same plane, that they differ from each other. They differ in the social standing which each minority occupies *vis-à-vis* the majority community. We have, for instance, the Parsee community, which is the smallest community in India, and yet, *vis-à-vis* its social standing with the majority community, it is probably the highest in order of precedence.

On the other hand, if you take the Depressed Classes, they are a minority which comes next to the great Muslim minority in India, and yet their social standard is lower than the social standard of ordinary human beings.

Again, if you take the minorities and classify them on the basis of social and political rights, you will find that there are certain minorities, which are in enjoyment of social and political rights, and the fact that they are in a minority does not necessarily stand in the way of their full and free enjoyment of those civic rights. But if you take the case of the Depressed Classes, the position is totally different. They have in certain matters no rights, and, where they have any, the majority community will not permit them to enjoy them.

My first submission to this Committee, then, is that it should realize that although, to use an illustration, the minorities are all in the same boat, yet the most important fact to remember is that they are not all in the same class in the same boat; some are travelling in 'A' Class, some in 'B' Class and some in 'C', and so on. I have not the slightest doubt in my mind that the Depressed Classes, though they are a minority and are to that extent in the same boat as other minorities, are not even in 'C' or 'D' Class but are actually in the hold.

Starting from that point of view, I agree that, in some respects, the position of the Depressed Classes is similar to that of the other minorities in India. The Depressed Classes, along with the other minorities, fear that under any future Constitution of India by which majority rule will be established and there can be no shadow of doubt that that majority rule will be the rule of the orthodox Hindus—there is great danger of that majority with its orthodox Hindu beliefs and prejudices contravening the dictates of justice, equality and good conscience, there is a great danger that the minorities may be discriminated against either in legislation or administration or in the other public rights of citizenship, and therefore it is necessary to safeguard the position of the minorities in such a manner that the discrimination which is feared shall not take place.

From that point of view, however, what is asked is that the minorities shall have representation in the Legislature and the Executive, that they shall have representation in the Public Services of the country, and that the constitution shall provide that there shall be imposed on the future Legislatures of India, both Central and Provincial, certain limitations on their legislative power which will prevent the majorities from abusing their legislative power in such a manner as to enact laws which would create discrimination between one citizen and another. I say, this circumstance—this danger of discrimination is common to all minorities, and I, as a representative of the Depressed Classes, join with the demand, which the other minorities have made in this regard.

Now, Sir, I will come to those circumstances which mark off the Depressed Classes and the other minority communities in India. I will at once say that the way in which the position of the Depressed Classes differs from the position of the other minority communities in India is this, that in the first place the Depressed Classes are not entitled, under present circumstances, to certain civic rights which the other minorities by law enjoy. In other words, in the existing situation the Depressed Classes suffer from what are called civic disabilities. I will give you just one or two illustrations because I know I have not much time at my disposal.

Take the case of employment in the Police or in the Army. In the Government of India Act it is provided that no subject of His Majesty shall be deprived of the right of being employed in any Public Service by reason of his caste, creed or colour. Having regard to that, it is obvious that every member of the Depressed Class community who is capable, who is in a position to satisfy the test laid down for employment in any public department, should have the right to enter that public department. But what do we find? We find this. If a Depressed Class man applies for service in the Police Department today, he is told point-blank by the Executive officers of the Government that no member of the Depressed Classes can be employed in the Police Service, because he is an Untouchable person. In the case of the Military the same situation obtains. Up to 1892 practically the whole of the Madras Army and the whole of the Bombay Army consisted of members drawn from the Depressed Classes. All the great wars in the history of India have been fought with the help of sepoys drawn from the Depressed Classes, both in the Bombay Presidency and in Madras. Yet in 1892 a rule or regulation was made which debarred the Depressed Classes from entry into the Military Service, and even today, if you ask a question in the Legislative Council as to why this is done, the answer is that the bar of untouchability does create insuperable difficulties in the recruitment of these classes.

I am quite sure that this disability is as effective as if it was imposed by law, and the section in the Government of India Act, which says that all His Majesty's subjects shall have free entry into employment provided they are otherwise fit, is altogether set at naught.

I can cite many other cases. For instance, there is the difficulty the Depressed Classes find in getting themselves accommodated in public inn when they are travelling, the difficulty they find in being taken in an omnibus when travelling from one place to another, the difficulty they find in securing entry to public schools to which they have themselves contributed, the difficulty they find in drawing water from a well for the building of which they have paid taxes, and so on. But I need not go into all these cases. The one circumstance which distinguishes the position of the Depressed Classes from that of the other minorities is that they suffer from civic disabilities which are as effective as though they, were imposed by law.

The second and, in my opinion, the most hideous distinction which marks the Depressed Classes is that the Depressed Classes are subject to social persecution unknown in any other part of the world. In that connection I want to read to the Sub-Committee a small extract from the Report of a Committee appointed by the Government of Bombay in the year 1928 to investigate into the position of the Depressed Classes. That Committee tried to find out whether there were any impediments in the way of the Depressed Classes enjoying such rights as the law gave them in common with other citizens of the State....

A third thing (the other two mentioned in Memorandum submitted by Ambedkar and Rao Bahadur Srinivasan on Depressd Classes and Social Boycott in the next chapter) which the Depressed Classes fear more than any other community is that whatever representation they may be granted in the new Legislature, they will always be in a very small minority, and consequently, having regard to the apathetic attitude of the orthodox classes towards the Depressed Classes, there is always the danger of the interests of the Depressed Classes, being neglected altogether, or some action taken which may ultimately prove to be prejudicial to their interests.

As against these special circumstances which affect the Depressed Classes, we propose the following safeguards. First *of* all, we want a fundamental right enacted in the constitution, which will declare 'untouchability' to be illegal for all public purposes. We must be emancipated, so to say from this social curse before we can at all consent to the constitution; and secondly, this fundamental right must also invalidate and nullify all such discriminations as may have been made hitherto. Next, we want legislation against the social persecution to which have drawn your attention just now, and for this we have provided in the document which we have submitted by certain clauses which are based upon an Act, which now prevails in Burma. I need not go into that detail just for the moment. Then what we want is this, that liability of the Executive officers of the Crown for acts of tyranny or oppression shall be made effective. Today under sections 110 and 111 of the Government of India Act that liability is not real. And lastly, what we want is a right to appeal against acts of neglect and prejudice to the Central Government and failing that, to the Secretary of State and a Special Department in the Government of India to take charge of our welfare.

This is, in general, the cases for the Depressed Classes, and the safeguards that they want. Let me just say a word or two as regards the most important of them, namely—their right to adequate representation in the Legislature. Now, on the question of the granting of representation of the Depressed Classes, we are absolutely unanimous that that representation shall be by election and not by nomination. The system of nomination has produced in the case of the Depressed Classes results which we all say, are abdominable. The system has been abused in a manner in which it was never expected that it would be abused, and it has never given the Depressed Classes the real and independent representation, which they must have as their safeguard. Under no circumstances, therefore, will the Depressed Classes accept representation by nomination.

As to the question of Joint or Separate Electorates, our position is this—that if you give us adult universal suffrage the Depressed Classes, barring a short transitional period which they want for their organization, will be prepared to accept Joint Electorates and reserved seats; but if you do not give us adult suffrage, then we must claim representation through Separate Electorates. That is our position.

Now regarding the question of the number of seats, it is not possible, of course, for us to state definitely what that number should be, except to state that we will not tolerate any invidious discrimination. We insist upon equality of treatment. But the whole question, in my opinion, is entirely a relative question: it is a question that can be determined only in connection with, and by taking into account, the seats that will be allotted to the other minority communities; but I will make two observations in this connection. The first observation that I will make is this—that we, the Depressed Classes, demand a complete partition between ourselves and the Hindus. That is the first thing. We have been called Hindus for political purposes, but we have never been acknowledged socially by the Hindus as their brethren. They have taken for themselves all the political advantage with our numbers, with our voting strength, have given to them, but in return we have received nothing. All that we have received is a treatment which is worse than the treatment that they themselves have accorded to other communities whom they do not call Hindus. That must be the first thing, therefore, that we want to be done.

The second thing that I will say concerns the question of weightage. Now, this system—I will be plain, to my mind has been abused. I am not against the principle of weightage. I do not accept the principle that in all circumstances every minority must be confined to its population ratio. A minority may be so small that its population ratio may give a representation which may be wholly inadequate for the purpose of its protection. It may be a representation which may be of no consequence at all. If, therefore, you want to protect a minority adequately and really, then in certain circumstances the principle of weightage will have to be conceded. But the distribution of weightage must be subject to some uniform and intelligible principle. In our opinion weightage is to be conceded because a minority is weak, either in numbers, or because its social standing is low, or its educational standing is backward as compared with others, or because its economic strength is not sufficient to place it on a fighting par with other communities.

But I cannot understand, for instance, how weightage can be allowed on the ground of political importance, or loyalty, or services rendered either to the Empire or to the British Government. I think if we adopt that principle, we shall land ourselves in very difficult circumstances from which it will be difficult to extricate ourselves.

Regarding the question of the representation of the Depressed Classes in the Central Legislature. If you have again adult suffrage for the election of members of the Central Legislature, then, of course, the Depressed Classes will claim separate representation in the Legislature, such number of seats being allotted to them in conjunction with the seats allotted to other minorities. But if your representation is to be by a suffrage which is higher or much higher, based on property, and so much higher that the Depressed Classes will probably be entirely left out, then I am afraid the Depressed Classes will have to claim indirect election to the Central Legislature, carried on by electoral colleges composed of members of the Depressed Classes, in the Provincial Legislature, in Municipalities, and in district local boards. That is all that I have to say so far as the Depressed Classes are concerned.

Having said all that I need say let me add one thing in conclusion. This whole question of minority representation is really the crux of the whole situation, and if the majority community desire that all minorities should associate with them in having or in claiming, a constitution which will give India what they call Dominion Status, or what we prefer to call Government by the people, for the people and in the name of the people, then I am afraid that the majority community must see to it that all fears of the minorities are set at rest. Otherwise it may not be possible for us to take what I do not conceal from myself is the risk that most of us are taking in claiming Dominion Status.

9

A Scheme of Political Safeguards for the Protection of Depressed Classes*
31 December 1930

The following are the terms and conditions on which the Depressed Classes will consent to place themselves under a majority rule in a self-governing India:

CONDITION NO. I: EQUAL CITIZENSHIP

The Depressed Classes cannot consent to subject themselves to majority rule in their present state of hereditary bondsmen. Before majority rule is established their emancipation from the system of untouchability must be an accomplished fact. It must not be left to the will of the majority. The Depressed Classes must be made free citizens entitled to all the rights of citizenship in common with other citizens of the State.

To secure the abolition of untouchability and to create the equality of citizenship, it is proposed that the following fundamental right shall be made part of the constitution of India:

All subjects of the State in India are equal below the law and possess equal civic rights. Any existing enactment, regulation, order, custom or interpretation of law by which any penalty, disadvantage, disability is imposed upon or any discrimination is made against any subject of the State on account of untouchability shall, as from the day on which this Constitution comes into operation, cease to have any effect in India.

To abolish the immunities and exemptions now enjoyed by Executive officers by virtue of sections 110 and 111 of the Government of India Act, 1919 and their liability for Executive action be made co-extensive with what it is in the case of a European British subject.

*BAWS 1982, vol. 2: 546–54.

CONDITION NO. II: FREE ENJOYMENT OF EQUAL RIGHTS

It is no use for the Depressed Classes to have a declaration of equal rights. There can be no doubt that the Depressed Classes will have to face the whole force of orthodox society if they try to exercise the equal rights of citizenship. The Depressed Classes therefore feel that if these declarations of rights are not to be mere pious pronouncements but are to be realities of everyday life then they should be protected by adequate pains and penalties from interference in the enjoyment of these declared rights.

The Depressed Classes therefore propose that the following section should be added to Part XI of the Government of India Act, 1919, dealing with Offences, Procedure and Penalties:

Offence of Infringement of Citizenship

Whoever denies to any person except for reasons by law applicable to persons of all classes and regardless of any previous condition of untouchability the full enjoyment of any of the accommodations, advantages, facilities, privileges of inns, educational institutions, roads, paths, streets, tanks, wells and other watering places, public conveyances on land, air or water, theatres or other places of public amusement, resort or convenience whether they are dedicated to or maintained or licensed for the use of the public shall be punished with imprisonment of either description for a term which may extend to five years and shall also be liable to fine.

Obstruction by orthodox individuals is not the only menace to the Depressed Classes in the way of peaceful enjoyment of their rights. The commonest form of obstruction is the social boycott. It is the most formidable weapon in the hands of the orthodox classes with which they beat down any attempt on the part of the Depressed Classes to undertake any activity if it happens to be unpalatable to them. The way it works and the occasions on which it is brought into operation are well described in the Report of the Committee appointed by the Government of Bombay in 1928 to enquire into the educational, economic and social condition of the Depressed Classes (Untouchables) and of the Aboriginal Tribes in the Presidency and to recommend measures for their uplift. The following is an extract from the same.

DEPRESSED CLASSES AND SOCIAL BOYCOTT

Although we have recommended various remedies to secure to the Depressed Classes their rights to all public utilities we fear that there will be difficulties in the way of their exercising them for a long time to come. The first difficulty is the fear of open violence against them by the orthodox classes. It must be noted that the Depressed Classes form a small minority in every village, opposed to which is a great majority of the orthodox who are bent on protecting their interests and dignity from any supposed invasion by the Depressed Classes at any cost. The danger of prosecution by the Police has put a limitation upon the use of violence by the orthodox classes and consequently such cases are rare.

The second difficulty arises from the economic position in which the Depressed Classes are found today. The Depressed Classes have no economic independence in most parts of the Presidency. Some cultivate the lands of the orthodox classes as their tenants at will. Others live on their earnings as farm labourers employed by the orthodox classes and the rest subsist on the food or grain given to them by the orthodox classes in lieu of service rendered to them as village servants. We have heard of numerous instances where the orthodox classes have used their economic power as a weapon against those Depressed Classes in their villages, when the latter have dared to exercise their rights, and have evicted them from their land, and stopped their employment and discontinued their remuneration as village servants. This boycott is often planned on such an extensive scale as to include the prevention of the Depressed Classes from using the commonly used paths and the stoppage of sale of the necessities of life by the village Bania. According to the evidence sometimes small cause suffice for the proclamation of a social boycott against the Depressed Classes. Frequently it follows on the exercise by the Depressed Classes of their right to the use of the common well, but cases have been by no means rare where a stringent boycott has been proclaimed simply because a Depressed Class man has put on the sacred thread, has bought a piece of land, has put on good clothes or ornaments, or has carried a marriage procession with the bridegroom on the horse through the public street.

We do not know of any weapon more effective than this social boycott which could have been invented for the suppression of the Depressed

Classes. The method of open violence pales away before it, for it has the most far-reaching and deadening effects. It is the most dangerous because it passes as a lawful method consistent with the theory of freedom of contact. We agree that this tyranny of the majority must be put down with a firm hand if we are to guarantee the Depressed Classes the freedom of speech and action necessary for their uplift.

In the opinion of the Depressed Classes the only way to overcome this kind of menace to their rights and liberties is to make social boycott an offence punishable by law. They are therefore bound to insist that the following sections should be added to those included in Part XI of the Government of India Act, 1919, dealing with Offences, Procedure and Penalties:

Offence of Boycott Defined

1. A person shall be deemed to boycott another who—
    (a) Refuses to let or use or occupy any house or land, or to deal with, work for hire, or do business with another person, or to render to him or receive for him any service, or refuses to do any of the said things on the terms on which such things should commonly be done in the ordinary course of business, or
    (b) Abstains from such social, professional or business relations as he would, having regard to such existing customs in the Community which are not inconsistent with any fundamental right or other rights of citizenship declared in the Constitution, ordinarily maintain with such person, or
    (c) In any way injures, annoys or interferes with such other person in the exercise of his lawful rights.

Punishment for Boycotting

Whoever, in consequence of any person having done an act which he was legally entitled to do or of his having omitted to do any act which he was legally entitled to omit to do or with intent to cause any person to do any act which he is not legally bound to do or to omit to do any act which he is legally entitled to do, or with intent to cause harm to such person in body, mind, reputation or property, or in his business or means of living, boycotts such person or any person in whom such person is interested, shall be punished with imprisonment of either description for a term which may extend to seven years or with fine or with both.

Provided that no offence shall be deemed to have been committed under this section if the Court is satisfied that the accused person has not acted at the instigation of or in collusion with any other person or in pursuance of or in collusion with any other person or in pursuance of any conspiracy or of any agreement or combination to boycott.

Punishment for Instigating or Promoting a Boycott

Whoever—

1. Publicly makes or publishes or circulates a proposal for, or
2. Makes, publishes or circulates any statement, rumour or report with intent to, or which he has reason to believe to be likely to, cause, or
3. In any other way instigates or promotes the boycotting of any person or class of persons, shall be punished with imprisonment which may extend to five years or with fine or with both.

Explanation: An offence under this section shall be deemed to have been committed although the person affected or likely to be affected by any action of the nature referred to herein is not designated by name or class but only by his acting or abstaining from acting in some specified manner.

Punishment for Threatening a Boycott

Whoever, in consequence of any person having done any act which he was legally entitled to do or of his having omitted to do an act which he was legally entitled to omit to do, or with intent to cause any person to do any act which he is not legally bound to do, or to omit to do any act which he is legally entitled to do, threatens to cause such person or any person in whom such person is interested, to be boycotted shall be punished with imprisonment of either description for a term which may extend to five years or with fine or with both.

Exception—It is not boycott—

1. To do any act in furtherance of a *bona fide* labour dispute.
2. To do any act in the ordinary course of business competition.

N.B. All these offences shall be deemed to be cognizable offences.

CONDITION NO. III: PROTECTION AGAINST DISCRIMINATION

The Depressed Classes entertain grave fears of discrimination either by legislation or by Executive order being made in the future. They cannot therefore consent to subject themselves to majority rule unless it is rendered impossible in law for the Legislature or the Executive to make any invidious discrimination against the Depressed Classes.

It is therefore proposed that the following Statutory provision be made in the constitutional law of India—

It shall not be competent for any Legislature or Executive in India to pass a law or issue an order, rule or regulation so as to violate the rights of the subjects of the State, regardless of any previous condition of untouchability, in all territories subject to the jurisdiction of the dominion of India: -

1. to make and enforce contracts, to sue, be parties, and give evidence, to inherit, purchase, lease, sell, hold and convey real and personal property,
2. to be eligible for entry into the civil and military employ and to all educational institutions except for such conditions end limitations as may be necessary to provide for the due and adequate representation of all classes of the subjects of the State,
3. to be entitled to the full and equal enjoyment of the accommodations, advantages, facilities, educational institutions, privileges of inns, rivers, streams, wells, tanks, roads, paths, streets, public conveyances on land, air and water, theatres, and other places of public resort or amusement except for such conditions and limitations applicable alike to all subjects of every race, class, caste, colour or creed,
4. to be deemed fit for and capable of sharing without distinction the benefits of any religious or charitable trust dedicated to or created, maintained or licensed for the general public or for persons of the same faith and religion,
5. to claim full and equal benefit of all laws and proceedings for the security of person and property as is enjoyed by other subjects regardless of any previous condition of untouchability and be subject to like punishment, pains and penalties and to none other.

Condition No. IV: Adequate Representation in the Legislatures

The Depressed Classes must be given sufficient political power to influence legislative and Executive action for the purpose of securing their welfare. In view of this they demand that the following provisions shall be made in the electoral law so as to give them—

1. Right to adequate representation in the Legislatures of the Country, Provincial and Central.
2. Right to elect their own men as their representatives, (a) by adult suffrage, and (b) by Separate Electorates for the first ten years and thereafter by Joint Electorates and reserved seats, it being understood

that Joint Electorates shall not be forced upon the Depressed Classes against their will unless such Joint Electorates are accompanied by adult suffrage.

N.B. Adequate Representation for the Depressed Classes cannot be defined in quantitative terms until the extent of representation allowed to other communities is known. But it must be understood that the Depressed Classes will not consent to the representation of any other community being settled on better terms than those allowed to them. They will not agree to being placed at a disadvantage in this matter. In any case the Depressed Classes of Bombay and Madras must have weightage over their population ratio of representation irrespective of the extent of representation allowed to other minorities in the Provinces.

CONDITION NO. V: ADEQUATE REPRESENTATION IN THE SERVICES

The Depressed Classes have suffered enormously at the hands of the high caste officers who have monopolized the Public Services, by abusing the Law or by misusing the discretion vested in them in administering it to the prejudice of the Depressed Classes and to the advantage of the caste-Hindus without any regard to justice, equity or good conscience. This mischief can only be avoided by destroying the monopoly of caste-Hindus in the Public Services and by regulating the recruitment to them in such a manner that all communities including the Depressed Classes will have an adequate share in them. For this purpose the Depressed Classes have to make the following proposals for statutory enactment as part of the constitutional law: —

1. There shall be established in India and in each Province in India a Public Service Commission to undertake the recruitment and control of the Public Services.

2. No member of the Public Service Commission shall be removed except by a resolution passed by the Legislature nor shall he be appointed to any office under the Crown after his retirement.

3. It shall be the duty of the Public Service Commission subject to the tests of efficiency as may be prescribed—(a) to recruit the Services in such a manner as will secure due and adequate representation of all communities, and (b) to regulate from time to time priority in employment in accordance with the existing extent

of the representation of the various communities in any particular service concerned.

CONDITION NO. VI: REDRESS AGAINST PREJUDICIAL ACTION OR NEGLECT OF INTERESTS

In view of the fact that the majority rule of the future will be the rule of the orthodox, the Depressed Classes fear that such a majority rule will not be sympathetic to them and that the probability of prejudice to their interests and neglect of their vital needs cannot be overlooked. It must be provided against, particularly because, however adequately represented, the Depressed Classes will be in a minority in all Legislatures. The Depressed Classes think it very necessary that they should have the means of redress given to them in the constitution. It is therefore proposed that the following provision should be made in the constitution of India:

1. In and for each Province and in and for India it shall be the duty and obligation of the Legislature and the Executive or any other Authority established by law to make adequate provision for the education, sanitation, recruitment in Public Services and other matters of social and political advancement of Depressed Classes and to do nothing that will prejudicially affect them.
2. Where in any Province or in India the provisions of this section are violated an appeal shall lie to the Governor-General in Council from any act or decision of any Provincial Authority and to the Secretary of State from any act or decision of a Central Authority affecting the matter.
3. In every such case where it appears to the Governor-General in Council or to the Secretary of State the Provincial Authority or Central Authority does not take steps requisite for the due execution of the provisions of this section then and in every such case, and as far only as the circumstances of each case require, the Governor-General in Council or the Secretary of State acting as an appellate authority may prescribe, for such period as they may deem fit, remedial measures for the due execution of the provisions of this section and of any of its decisions under this section and which shall be binding upon the authority appealed against.

CONDITION NO. VII: SPECIAL DEPARTMENTAL CARE

The helpless, hapless and sapless condition of the Depressed Classes must be entirely attributed to the dogged and determined opposition of the whole mass of the orthodox population which will not allow the Depressed Classes to have equality of status or equality of treatment. It is not enough to say of their economic condition that they are poverty-stricken or that they are a class of landless labourers, although both these statements are statements of fact. It has to be noted that the poverty of the Depressed Classes is due largely to the social prejudices in consequence of which many an occupation for earning a living is closed to them. This is a fact which differentiates the position of the Depressed Classes from that of the ordinary caste labourers and is often a source of trouble between the two. It has also to be borne in mind that the forms of tyranny and oppression practised against the Depressed Classes are very various and the capacity of the Depressed Classes to protect themselves is extremely limited. The facts which obtain in this connection and which are of common occurrence throughout India are well described in the Abstracts of Proceedings of the Board of Revenue of the Government of Madras dated 5th November 1882, No. 723, from which the following is an extract:

134. There are forms of oppression only hitherto hinted at which must be at least cursorily mentioned. To punish disobedience of Pariahs, their masters—
1. Bring false cases in the village court or in the criminal courts.
2. Obtain, on application, from Government, waste lands lying all round the paracheri, so as to impound the Pariahs' cattle or obstruct the way to their temple.
3. Have mirasi names fraudulently entered in the Government account against the paracheri.
4. Pull down the huts and destroy the growth in the backyards.
5. Deny occupancy right in immemorial sub-tenancies.
6. Forcibly cut the Pariahs' crops, and on being resisted charge them with theft and rioting.
7. Under misrepresentations, get them to execute documents by which they are afterwards ruined.
8. Cut off the flow of water from their fields.
9. Without legal notice, have the property of sub-tenants attached for the landlords' arrears of revenue.

135. It will be said there are civil and criminal courts for the redress of any of these injuries. There are the courts indeed; but India does not breed village Hampdens. One must have courage to go to the courts; money to employ legal knowledge and meet legal expenses; and means to live during the case and the appeals. Further most cases depend upon the decision of the first court; and these courts are presided over by officials who are sometimes

corrupt and who generally, for other reasons, sympathize *with the* wealthy and landed classes to which they belong.

136. The influence of these classes with the official world can hardly be exaggerated. It is extreme with natives and great even with Europeans. Every office, from the highest to the lowest, is stocked with their representatives, and there is no proposal affecting their interests but they can bring a score of influence to bear upon it in its course from inception to execution.

There can be no doubt that in view of these circumstances the uplifts of the Depressed Classes will remain a pious hope unless the task is placed in the forefront of all governmental activities and unless equalization of opportunities is realized in practice by a definite policy and determined effort on the part of the Government. To secure this end the proposal of the Depressed Classes is that the Constitutional Law should impose upon, the Government of India a statutory to maintain at all times a department to deal with their problems by the addition of a section in the Government of India Act to the following effect:

1. Simultaneously with the introduction of this Constitution and as part thereof there shall be created in the Government of India a Department to be in-charge of a Minister for the purpose of watching the interests of the Depressed Classes and promoting their welfare.
2. The Minister shall hold office so long as he retains the confidence of the Central Legislature.
3. It shall be the duty of the Minister in the exercise of any powers and duties conferred upon him or transferred to him by law, to take all such steps as may be desirable to secure the preparation, effectively carrying out and co-ordination of measures preventative of acts of social injustice, tyranny or oppression against the Depressed Classes and conducive to their welfare throughout India.
4. It shall be lawful for the Governor-General
   (a) to transfer to the Minister all or any powers or duties in respect of the welfare of the Depressed Classes arising from any enactment relating to education, sanitation, etc.,
   (b) to appoint Depressed Classes welfare bureau in each province to work under the authority of and in co-operation with the Minister.

Condition No. VIII: Depressed Classes and the Cabinet

Just as it is necessary that the Depressed Classes should have the power to influence government action by seats in the Legislature so also it is desirable that the Depressed Classes should have the opportunity to frame the general policy of the Government. This they can do only if they can find a seat in the Cabinet. The Depressed Classes therefore claim that in common with other minorities, their moral rights to be represented in the Cabinet should be recognized. With this purpose in view the Depressed Classes propose that in the Instrument of Instructions an obligation shall be placed upon the Governor and the Governor-General to endeavour to secure the representation of the Depressed Classes in his Cabinet.

10

Report of Sub-Committee No. III (Minorities)*
16 January 1931

One of the chief proposals brought before the Sub-Committee was the inclusion in the constitution of a declaration of fundamental rights safeguarding the cultural and religious life of the various communities and securing to every individual without discrimination as to race, caste, creed or sex, the free exercise of economic, social and civil rights (Dr. Ambedkar called attention to the necessity of including in the constitution sanctions for the enforcement of the fundamental rights, including a right of redress when they are violated).

Whilst it was generally admitted that a system of joint free electorates was in the abstract consistent with democratic principles as generally understood, and would be acceptable to the Depressed Classes after a short transitional period, provided the franchise was based on adult suffrage, the opinion was expressed that, in view of the distribution of the communities in India and of their unequal economic, social and political effectiveness, there was a real danger that under such a system the representation secured by minorities would be totally inadequate, and that this system would therefore give no communal security.

Claims were therefore advanced by various communities that arrangements should be made for representation and for fixed proportions of seats. It was also urged, that the number of seats reserved for a minority community should in no case be less than its proportion in the population. The methods by which this could be secured were mainly three (1) Nomination, (2) Joint Electorates with reservation of seats, and (3) Separate Electorates.

The discussion made it evident that the demand, which remained as the only one, which would be generally acceptable, was Separate Electorates. The general objection to this scheme has been subject to much previous discussion in India. It involves what is very difficult

---

*BAWS 1982, vol. 2: 554–56. (*These are some of the paragraphs of the Report related to the interests of Depressed Classes, which were approved by the Committee of Whole Conference*).

problem for solution, viz. what should be the amount of communal representation in the various Provinces and in the Centre; that, if the whole, or practically the whole, of the seats in a Legislature are to be assigned to communities, there will be no room for the growth of independent political opinion or of true political parties, and t his problem received a serious complication by the demand of the representatives of the Depressed Classes that they should be deducted from the Hindu population and be regarded, for electoral purposes, as a separate community.

There was general agreement with the recommendation of Sub-Committee No. II (Provincial Constitution) that the representation on the Provincial Executives of important minority communities was a matter of the greatest practical importance for the successful working of the new constitution, and it was also agreed that on the same grounds Muhammadans should be represented on the Federal Executive (Dr. Ambedkar would add the words, 'and other important minorities' after the word 'Muhammadans'). On behalf of smaller minorities, a claim was put forward for their representation, either individually or collectively, on the Provincial and Federal Executives, or that, if this should be found impossible in each Cabinet, there should be a Minister specially charged with the duty of protecting minority interests.

As regards the administration, it was agreed that recruitment of both Provincial and Central Services should be entrusted to P.S.Cs., with instruction to recruit the claims or various communities to fair and adequate representation in the Public Services, whilst providing for the maintenance of a proper standard of efficiency.

It has also been made clear that the British Government cannot with any chance of agreement impose upon the communities an electoral principle which, in some feature or other, would, be met by their opposition. It was therefore plain that, failing an agreement, Separate Electorates with all their drawbacks and difficulties, would have to be retained as the basis of the electoral arrangements under the new Constitution. From this the question of proportions would arise. Under these circumstances, the claims of the Depressed Classes will have to be considered adequately.

The Minorities and Depressed Classes were definite in their assertion that they would not consent to any self-governing constitution for India unless their demands were met in a reasonable manner.

11

Demand for Specific and Concrete Provisions for Safeguards of Depressed Classes in the Future Constitution*
19 January 1931

Dr. Ambedkar: Mr. Prime Minister, the Round Table Conference has had to grapple with two most important questions which must arise in any attempt to organize the political life of a community. The problem of responsible government was one of them and the other was that of representative government.

... The franchise and the representation of the different classes in the Legislatures are the two pillars on which a truly representative government can rest. Everybody knows that the Nehru Committee had adopted adult suffrage and that that part of the Constitution framed by it had the support of all political parties in India. When I came to this Conference I had thought that so far as the question of franchise was concerned the battle had already been won. But in the Franchise Committee I was completely disillusioned. I found to my great surprise that all those who had signed the Nehru Report had done so with mental reservations, so much so that it was difficult to persuade even the Indian Liberals to consent to enfranchise 25 per cent of the population for Provincial Legislatures. The franchise for the Central Legislature is no doubt an unknown quantity. But I have no hope that it will be such as to make the Central Legislature more representative of the people than the Provincial Legislatures are going to be. A franchise so limited must necessarily make the future government of India a government of the masses by the classes.

Regarding the question of the distribution of seats among the majority and the various minority communities we all know that there is a deadlock. The deadlock is largely due, in my opinion, to the mischief done in the past. I am sure that if the authorities in India had acted in the past on the principle of justice to all and favour to none, the problem would not have become so difficult of solution. The British Government set different values on different communities according to the political use they made of them and gave to many communities an extraordinary share of political power by denying it to the Depressed Classes in a measure which was their rightful due. In this matter the most aggrieved community is the Depressed Classes, and I was hoping that this Conference would proceed on the principle that what is wrongly settled is never settled, and give to the Depressed Classes their rightful quota of seats by a revaluation of the old values. But this has not happened. The claims of the other minorities have already been acknowledged and defined. All that they stand in need of is alterations and amendments to bring them in conformity with the enlarged structure and increased scope of the new Government. Whatever be the alterations and amendments, no one will dare to furrow out the foundations that have already been laid down. The case of the Depressed Classes is totally different. Their claims have just been heard. They have not even been adjudged and I do not know how many of them will be admitted. To my mind it is not improbable that having regard to the helplessness of their position, the claims of the Depressed Classes for representations may be whitted down to satisfy the ever-increasing scramble by other communities who are manoeuvring not so much for protection as for power.

In view of this I am bound to make my attitude perfectly plain. As the rights of the Depressed Classes in the future Constitution are not defined, any announcement that might be made on behalf of His Majesty's Government regarding the introduction of responsibility in the Centre as well as in the Provinces should make it clear that any advance in that direction must be on condition and subject to an agreement between the communities which would provide effective safeguards for the rights and interests of the Depressed Classes. I must emphasize the gravity of the situation and bring to your notice that no announcement will be acceptable to us unless the position is made perfectly clear in this behalf, and that failing this I and my colleague will be unable to accept the responsibility of participating in the further work of the Conference, and will be compelled to dissociate ourselves from it. Sir, in asking you to do so, I am not asking you to do more than give effect to your pledged word. The British Parliament and those who speak for it, have always stated that they are trustees for the

Depressed Classes and I am sure that what they have been saying is not one of those conventional lies of civilization which we are all led to utter to keep human relations as pleasant as possible. In my opinion it is therefore the bounden duty of any Government to see that that trust is not betrayed and let me tell you, Mr. Prime Minister, that the Depressed Classes would regard it as the greatest betrayal on the part of His Majesty's Government if it were to leave us to the mercy of those who have taken no interest in our welfare and whose prosperity and greatness is founded on our ruination and degradation.

For saying so I will be called a communalist by the nationalists and patriots of India. I am not afraid of that. India is a peculiar country and her nationalists and patriots are a peculiar people. A patriot and a nationalist in India is one who sees with open eyes his fellowmen treated as being less than men. But his humanity does not rise in protest. He knows that men and women for no cause are denied their human rights. But it does not prick his civic sense to helpful action. He finds a whole class of people shut out from public employment. But it does not rouse his sense of justice and fair play. Hundreds of evil practices that injure man and society are perceived by him. But they do not sicken him with disgust. The patriot's one cry is power and more power for him and for his class. I am glad I do not belong to that class of patriots. I belong to that class which takes its stand on democracy and which seeks to destroy monopoly in every shape and form. Our aim is to realize in practice our ideal of one man one value in all walks of life, political, economic and social. It is because representative government is one means to that end that the Depressed Classes attach to it so great a value and it is because of its value to us that I have urged upon you the necessity of making your declaration subject to its fulfillment. You may tell me that the Depressed Classes have your sympathy. My reply is, for a stricken people what is wanted is something more concrete, something more defined. You may despise me for being unduly apprehensive. My reply is it is better to be despised for too anxious apprehensions rather than be ruined by too confident a security.

12

In the Minorities Committee*
8 October 1931

Chairman: When we met last Thursday, by common consent we adjourned for a week in order to enable informal and unofficial consultations to take place, with a view of coming to an agreement. Perhaps our first business is to receive a report from those who conducted the negotiations. May I ask Mr. Gandhi to speak first?

Mr. Gandhi: Prime Minister and friends, it is with deep sorrow and deeper humiliation that I have to announce utter failure on my part to secure an agreed solution of the communal question through informal conversations among and with the representatives of different groups. I apologize to you, Mr. Prime Minister, and the other colleagues for the waste of a precious week. My only consolation lies in the fact that when I accepted the burden of carrying on these talks I knew that there was not much hope of success, and still more in the fact that I am not aware of having spared any effort to reach a solution.

But to say that the conversations have to our utter shame failed is not to say the whole truth. Causes of failure were inherent in the composition of the Indian Delegation. We are almost all not elected representatives of the parties or groups whom we are presumed to represent; we are here by nomination of the Government. Nor are those whose presence was absolutely necessary for an agreed solution to be found here. Further you will allow me to say that this was hardly the time to summon the Minorities Committee. It lacks the sense of reality in that we do not know what it is that we are going to get. If we knew in a definite manner that we were going to get the thing we want, we should hesitate fifty times before we threw it away in a sinful wrangle, as it would be if we are told that the getting of it would depend upon the ability of the present Delegation to produce an agreed solution of the communal tangle. The solution can be the crown of the Swaraj

BAWS 1982, vol. 2: 659–63.

constitution, not its foundation—if only because our differences have hardened, if they have not arisen, by reason of the foreign domination. They have not a shadow of a doubt that the iceberg of communal differences will melt under the warmth of the sun of freedom.

I, therefore, venture to suggest that the Minorities Committee be adjourned *sine die* and that the fundamentals of the constitution be hammered into shape as quickly as may be. Meanwhile, the informal work of discovering a true solution of the communal problem will and must continue: only it must not baulk or be allowed to block the progress of constitution-building. Attention must be diverted from it and concentrated on the main part of the structure.

Lastly, in as much as the only reason for my appearance at these deliberations is that I represent the Indian National Congress, I must clearly set forth its position. In spite of appearances to the contrary, especially in England, the Congress claims to represent the whole nation, and most decidedly the dumb millions, among whom are included the numberless Untouchables, who are more suppressed than depressed, as also in a way the more unfortunate and neglected classes known as Backward Races.

It seems to have been represented that I am opposed to any representation of the Untouchables on the Legislature. This is a travesty of the truth. What I have said, and what I must repeat, is that I am opposed to their special representation. I am convinced that it can do them no good, and may do much harm; but the Congress is wedded to adult franchise. Therefore millions of them can be placed on the Voters' Roll. It is impossible to conceive that with untouchability fast disappearing, nominees of these voters can be boycotted by the others; but what these people need more than election to the Legislatures is protection from social and religious persecution. Custom, which is often more powerful than law, has brought them to a degradation of which every thinking Hindu has need to feel ashamed and to do penance. I should, therefore, have the most drastic legislation rendering criminal all the special persecution to which these fellow-countrymen of mine are subjected by the so-called superior classes. Thank God, the conscience of Hindus has been stirred, and untouchability will soon be a relic of our sinful past.

Dr. Ambedkar: Mr. Prime Minister, last night when we parted at the conclusion of the meeting of the informal Committee we parted although with a sense of failure, at least with one common understanding, and that was that when we meet here today none of us should make any speech or any comment that would cause exasperation. I am sorry to see that Mr. Gandhi should have been guilty of a breach of this understanding. Excuse me, I must have the opportunity to speak. He started by giving what were, according to him, the causes of the failure of the informal Committee. Now, I have my own causes which I think were responsible for the failure of the informal Committee to reach an agreement, but I do not propose to discuss them now. What disturbs me after hearing Mr. Gandhi is that instead of confining himself to his proposition, namely, that the Minorities Committee should adjourn *sine die,* he started casting certain reflections upon the representatives of the different communities who are sitting round this table. He said that the Delegates were nominees of the Government, and that they did not represent the views of their respective communities for whom they stood. We cannot deny the allegation that we are nominees of the Government, but, speaking for myself, I have not the slightest doubt that even if the Depressed Classes of India were given the chance of electing their representatives to this Conference, I would, all the same, find a place here. I say therefore that, whether I am a nominee or not, I fully represent the claims of my community. Let no man be under any mistaken impression as regards that.

The Mahatma has been always claiming that, the Congress stands for the Depressed Classes, and that the Congress represents the Depressed Classes more than I or my colleague can do. To that claim I can only say that it is one of the many false claims which irresponsible people keep on making, although the persons concerned with regard to those claims have been invariably denying them. I have here a telegram which I have just received from a place which I have never visited and from a man whom I have never seen from the President of the Depressed Classes Union, Kumaun, Almora, which I believe is in the United Provinces, and which contains the following resolution:

This Meeting declares its no-confidence in the Congress movement which has been carried on in and outside the country, and condemns the methods adopted by the Congress workers.

I do not care to read further, but I can say this (and I think if Mr. Gandhi will examine his position he will find out the truth), that although there may be people in the Congress who may be showing sympathy towards the Depressed Classes, the Depressed Classes are not in the Congress. That is a proposition which I propose to substantiate. I do not wish to enter into these points of controversy. They seem to be somewhat outside the main proposition. The main proposition which Mr. Gandhi has made is that this Committee should be adjourned *sine die*. With regard to that proposition, I entirely agree with the attitude taken up by Sir Muhammad Shaf. I, for one, cannot consent to this proposition. It seems to me that there are only two alternatives—either that this Minorities Committee should go on tackling the problem and trying to arrive at some satisfactory solution, if that is possible, and then, if that is not possible, the British Government should undertake the solution of that problem. We cannot consent to leave this to the arbitration of third parties whose sense of responsibility may not be the same as must be the sense of responsibility of the British Government.

Prime Minister, permit me to make one thing clear. The Depressed Classes are not anxious, they are not clamorous, they have not started any movement for claiming that there shall be an immediate transfer of power from the British to the Indian people. They have their particular grievances against the British people and I think I have voiced them sufficiently to make it clear that we feel those grievances most genuinely. But, to be true to facts, the position is that the Depressed Classes are not clamouring for transfer of political power. Their position, to put it plainly, is that we are not anxious for the transfer of power; but if the British Government is unable to resist the forces that have been set up in the country which do clamour for transference of political power—and we know the Depressed Classes in their present circumstances are not in a position to resist that—then our submission is that if you make that transfer, that transfer will be accompanied by such conditions and by such provisions that the power shall not fall into the hands of a clique, into the hands of an oligarchy, or into the hands of a group of people, whether Muhammadans or Hindus; but that that solution shall be such that the power shall be shared by all communities in their respective proportions. Taking that view, I do not see how I, for one, can take any serious part in the deliberations of the Federal Structure Committee unless I know where I and my community stand.

Mr. Gandhi: One word more as to the so-called Untouchables.

I can understand the claims advanced by other minorities, but the claims advanced on behalf of the Untouchables, that to me is the 'unkindest cut of all'. It means the perpetual bar-sinister. I would not seal the vital interests of the Untouchables even for the sake of winning the freedom of India. I claim myself in my own person to represent the vast mass of the Untouchables. Here I speak not merely on behalf of the Congress, but I speak on my own behalf, and I claim that I would get, if there was a referendum of the Untouchables, their vote, and that I would top the poll. And I would work from one end of India to the other to tell the Untouchables that Separate Electorates and separate reservation is not the way to remove this bar-sinister, which is the shame, not of them but of orthodox Hinduism.

Let this Committee and let the whole world know that today there is a body of Hindu reformers who are pledged to remove this blot of untouchability. We do not want on our register and on our census Untouchables classified as separate class. Sikhs may remain as such in perpetuity, so may Muhammadans, so may Europeans. Will Untouchables remain Untouchables in perpetuity? I would fear rather that Hinduism died than that untouchability lived. Therefore, with all my regard for Dr. Ambedkar, and for his desire to see the Untouchables uplifted, with all my regard for his ability, I must say in all humility that here the great wrong under which he has laboured and perhaps the bitter experiences that he has undergone have for the moment warped his judgment. It hurts me to have to say this, but I would be untrue to the cause of the Untouchables, which is as dear to me as life itself, if I did not say it. I will not bargain away their rights for the kingdom of the whole world. I am speaking with a due sense of responsibility, and I say that it is not a proper claim which is registered by Dr. Ambedkar when he seeks to speak for the whole of the Untouchables of India. It will create a division in Hinduism which I cannot possibly look forward to with any satisfaction whatsoever. I do not mind Untouchables, if they so desire, being converted to Islam or Christianity. I should tolerate that, but I cannot possibly tolerate what is in store for Hinduism if there are two divisions set forth in the villages. Those who speak of the political rights of Untouchables do not know their India, do not know how Indian society is today constructed, and therefore I want to say with all the emphasis that I can command that if I was the only person to resist this thing I would resist it with my life.

13

Provisions for a Settlement of the Communal Problem*
8 October 1931

CLAIMS OF MINORITY COMMUNITIES

1. No person shall by reason of his origin, religion, caste or creed be prejudiced in any way in regard to public employment, office of power or honour, or with regard to enjoyment of his civic rights and the exercise of any trade or calling.
2. Statutory safeguards shall be incorporated in the constitution with a view to protect against enactments of the Legislature of discriminatory laws affecting any community.
3. Full religious liberty, that is, full liberty of belief, worship observances, propaganda, associations and education, shall be guaranteed to all communities subject to the maintenance of public order and morality. No person shall merely by change of faith lose any civic right or privilege, or be subject to any penalty.
4. The right to establish, manage and control, at their own expense, charitable, religious and social institutions, schools and other educational establishments with the right to exercise their religion therein.
5. The constitution shall embody adequate safeguards for the protection of religion, culture and personal law, and the promotion of education, language, charitable institutions of the minority communities and for their due share in grants-in-aid given by the State and by the self-governing bodies.
6. Enjoyment of civic rights by all citizens shall be guaranteed by making any act or omission calculated to prevent full enjoyment an offence punishable by law.
7. In the formation of Cabinets in the Central Government and Provincial Governments, so far as possible, members belonging to the Mussulman community and other minorities of considerable number shall be included by convention.

*BAWS 1982, vol. 2: 664–6.

8. There shall be Statutory Departments under the Central and Provincial Governments to protect minority communities and to promote their welfare.

9. All communities at present enjoying representation in any Legislature through nomination or election shall have representation in all Legislatures through Separate Electorates and the minorities shall have not less than the proportion set forth in the Annexure but no majority shall be reduced to a minority or even an equality. Provided that after a lapse of ten years it will be open to Muslims in Punjab and Bengal and any minority communities in any other Provinces to accept Joint Electorates, or Joint Electorates with reservation of seats, by the consent of the community concerned. Similarly after the lapse of ten years it will be open to any minority in the Central Legislature to accept Joint Electorates with or without reservation of seats with the consent of the community concerned.

   With regard to the Depressed Classes no change to Joint Electorates and reserved seats shall be made until after 20 years experience of Separate Electorates and until direct adult suffrage for the community has been established.

10. In every Province and in connection with the Central Government a Public Services Commission shall be appointed, and the recruitment to the Public Services, except the proportion, if any, reserved to be filled by nomination by the Governor-General and the Governors, shall be made through such Commission in such a way as to secure a fair representation to the various communities consistently with the considerations of efficiency and the possession of the necessary qualifications. Instructions to the Governor-General and the Governors in the Instrument of Instructions with regard to recruitment shall be embodied to give effect to this principle, and for that purpose, to review periodically the composition of the services.

11. If a Bill is passed which, in the opinion of two-thirds of the members of any Legislature representing a particular community affects their religion or social practice based on religion, or in the case of fundamental rights of the subjects if one-third of the members object, it shall be open to such members to lodge their objection thereto, within a period of one month of the Bill being passed by the House, with the President of the House who shall forward the same to the Governor-General or the Governor, as

the case may be, and he shall thereupon suspend the operation of that Bill for one year, upon the expiry of which period he shall remit the said Bill for further consideration by the Legislature. When such a Bill has been further considered by the Legislature and the Legislature concerned has refused to revise or modify the Bill so as to meet the objection thereto, the Governor-General or the Governor, as the case may be, may give or withhold his assent to it in the exercise of his discretion, provided further, that the validity of such Bill may be challenged in the Supreme Court by any two members of the denomination affected thereby, on the grounds that it contravenes one of their fundamental rights. ...

SPECIAL CLAIMS OF THE DEPRESSED CLASSES

1. The Constitution shall declare invalid any custom or usage by which any penalty or disadvantage or disability is imposed upon or any discrimination is made against any subject of the State in regard to the enjoyment of civic rights on account of Untouchability.
2. Generous treatment in the matter of recruitment to Public Service and the opening of enlistment in the Police and Military Services.
3. The Depressed Classes in the Punjab shall have the benefit of the Punjab Land Alienation Act extended to them.
4. Right of Appeal shall lie to the Governor or Governor-General for redress of prejudicial action or neglect of interest by any Executive Authority.
5. The Depressed Classes shall have representation not less than set forth in the Annexure (for details see *BAWS* 1982, vol. 2: 667–8).

Agreed by—
His Highness the Aga Khan (Muslims)
Dr. Ambedkar (Depressed Classes)
Rao Bahadur Pannir Selvam (Indian Christians)
Sir Henry Gidney (Anglo-Indians)
Sir Hubert Carr (Europeans)

14

Supplementary Memorandum on the Claims of the Depressed Classes for Special Representation*
4 November 1931

In the memorandum that was submitted by us last year dealing with the question of political safeguards for the protection of the Depressed Classes in the Constitution for a self-governing India, and which forms Appendix III to the printed volume of Proceedings of the Minorities Sub-Committee, we had demanded that special representation of the Depressed Classes must form one of such safeguards. But we did not then define the details of the special representation we claimed as being necessary for them. The reason was that the proceedings of the Minorities Sub-Committee came to an end before the question was reached. We now propose to make good the omission by this supplementary memorandum so that the Minorities Sub-Committee, if it comes to consider the question this year, should have the requisite details before it.

EXTENT OF SPECIAL REPRESENTATION

Special Representation in Provincial Legislature
1. In Bengal, Central Provinces, Assam, Bihar and Orissa, Punjab and the United Provinces, the Depressed Classes shall have representation in proportion to their population as estimated by the Simon Commission and the Indian Central Committee.
2. In Madras the Depressed Classes shall have twenty-two per cent representation.
3. In Bombay—
   (a) In the event of Sind continuing to be a part of the Bombay Presidency the Depressed Classes shall have sixteen per cent representation.

(b) In the event of Sind being separated from the Bombay Presidency the Depressed Classes shall enjoy the same degree of representation as the Presidency Muslims, both being equal in population.

Special Representation in the Federal Legislature
In both Houses of the Federal Legislature the Depressed Classes shall have representation in proportion of their population in India.

Reservations
We have fixed this proportion of representation in the Legislatures on the following assumptions—

1. We have assumed that the figures for the population of the Depressed Classes given by the Simon Commission (vol. I, p. 40) and the Indian Central Committee (Report, p. 44) will be acceptable as sufficiently correct to form a basis for distributing seats.
2. We have assumed that the Federal Legislature will comprise the whole of India, in which case the population of the Depressed Classes in Indian States, in Centrally Administered Areas, and in Excluded Territories, besides their population in Governor's Provinces, will form very properly an additional item in calculating the extent of representation of the Depressed Classes in the Federal Legislature.
3. We have assumed that the administrative area of the Provinces of British India will continue to be what they are at present.

But if these assumptions regarding figures of population are challenged as some interested parties threaten to do, and if under a new census over which the Depressed Classes can have no control, the population of the Depressed Classes shows a lower proportion, or if the administrative areas of the Provinces are altered, resulting in disturbing the existing balance of population, the Depressed Classes reserve their right to revise their proportion of representation and even to claim weightage. In the same way, if the All-India Federation does not come into being, they will be willing to submit to readjustment in their proportion of representation calculated on that basis in the Federal Legislature.

METHOD OF REPRESENTATION

The Depressed Classes shall have the right to elect their representatives to the Provincial and Central Legislatures through Separate Electorates of their voters.

For their representation in the Upper House of the Federal or Central Legislature, if it is decided to have indirect election by members of the Provincial Legislatures, the Depressed Classes will agree to abandon their right to Separate Electorates so far as their representation to the Upper House is concerned subject to this: that in any system of proportional representation arrangement shall be made to guarantee to them their quota of seats.

Separate Electorates for the Depressed Classes shall not be liable to be replaced by a system of Joint Electorates and reserved seats, except when the following conditions are fulfilled—

1. A referendum of the voters held at the demand of a majority of their representatives in the Legislatures concerned and resulting in an absolute majority of the members of the Depressed Classes having the franchise.
2. No such referendum shall be resorted to until after twenty years and until universal adult suffrage has been established.

Necessity of Defining the Depressed Classes

The representation of the Depressed Classes has been grossly abused in the past inasmuch as persons other than the Depressed Classes were nominated to represent them in the Provincial Legislatures, and cases are not wanting in which persons not belonging to the Depressed Classes got themselves nominated as representative of the Depressed Classes. This abuse was due to the fact that while the Governor was given the power to nominate persons to represent the Depressed Classes, he was not required to confine his nomination to persons belonging to the Depressed Classes. Since nomination is to be substituted by election under the new constitution, there will be no room for this abuse. But in order to leave no loophole for defeating the purpose of their special representation we claim—

1. That the Depressed Classes shall not only have the right to their own Separate Electorates, but they shall also have the right to be represented by their own men.
2. That in each Province the Depressed Classes shall be strictly defined as meaning persons belonging to communities which are subjected to the system of untouchability of the sort prevalent therein and which are enumerated by name in a schedule prepared for electoral purposes.

Nomenclature

In dealing with this part of the question we would like to point out that the existing nomenclature of Depressed Classes is objected to by members of the Depressed Classes who have given thought to it and also by outsiders who take interest in them. It is degrading and contemptuous, and advantage may be taken of this occasion for drafting the new constitution to alter for official purposes the existing nomenclature. We think that they should be called 'Non-caste-Hindus', 'Protestant Hindus', or 'Non-conformist Hindus', or some such designation, instead of 'Depressed Classes'. We have no authority to press for any particular nomenclature. We can only suggest them, and we believe that if properly explained the Depressed Classes will not hesitate to accept the one most suitable for them.

We have received a large number of telegrams from the Depressed Classes all over India supporting the demands contained in this Memorandum.

15

Note Submitted to the Indian Franchise Committee*
1 May 1932

I have agreed to confine the term Depressed Classes to Untouchables only. In fact, I have myself sought to exclude from the Untouchables all those in whom there cannot be the same consciousness of kind as is shared by those who suffer from the social discrimination that is inherent in the system of untouchability and who are therefore likely to exploit the Untouchables for their own purposes. I have also raised no objection to the utilization of tests 7 and 8 referred to in the Committee's report for the ascertainment of the Untouchable classes. But as I find that different persons seek to apply them in different ways, or put different constructions on them. I feel it necessary to explain my point of view in regard to this matter.

In the first place it is urged in some quarters that whatever tests are applied for ascertaining the Untouchable classes they must be applied uniformly all over India. In this connection, I desire to point out that in a matter of this sort it would hardly be appropriate to apply the same test or tests all over India. India is not a single homogeneous country. It is a continent. The various Provinces are marked by extreme diversity of conditions and there is no tie of race or language. Owing to absence of communication each Province has evolved along its own lines with its own peculiar manners and modes of social life. In such circumstances the degree of uniformity with which most of the tests of untouchability are found to apply all over India is indeed remarkable. For instance, bar against temple entry exists everywhere in India. Even the tests of well-water and pollution by touch apply in every Province, although not with the same rigidity everywhere. But to insist on absolute uniformity in a system like that of untouchability which after all is a matter of social behaviour and which must therefore vary with the circumstances of each Province and also of each individual is simply to trifle with the problem. The Statutory Commission was quite alive

*BAWS 1982, vol. 2: 491–50.

to this possible line of argument and after careful consideration rejected it by recognizing the principle of diversity in the application of tests of untouchability. On page 67 of vol. II which contains its recommendations it observed:

It will plainly be necessary, after the main principles of the new system of representation have been settled, to entrust to some specially appointed body (like the former Franchise Committee) the task of drawing up fresh electoral rules to carry these principles into effect, and one of the tasks of such a body will be to frame for each province a definition of 'Depressed Classes' (which may well vary, sometimes even between parts of the same province), and to determine their numbers as so defined.

Another point which I wish to emphasize is the futility of insisting upon the application of uniform tests of untouchability all over India. It is a fundamental mistake to suppose that differences, in tests of untouchability indicate differences in the conditions of the Untouchables. On a correct analysis of the mental attitude they indicate, it will be found that whether the test is causing pollution by touch or refusal to use common well, the notion underlying both is one and the same. Both are outward registers of the same inward feeling of defilement, odium, aversion and contempt. Why will not a Hindu touch an Untouchable? Why will not a Hindu allow an Untouchable to enter the temple or use the village well? Why will not a Hindu admit an Untouchable in the inn? The answer to each one of these questions is the same. It is that the Untouchable is an unclean person not fit for social intercourse. Again, why will not a Brahmin priest officiate at religious ceremonies performed by an Untouchable? Why will not a barber serve an Untouchable? In these cases also the answer is the same. It is that it is below dignity to do so. If our aim is to demarcate the class of people who suffer from social odium then it matters very little which test we apply. For as I have pointed out each of these tests is indicative of the same social attitude on the part of the touchables towards the Untouchables.

In the second place the view is put forth that in applying the test of causing pollution by touch for ascertaining the Untouchable classes effect must be given to it in its literal sense—and not in its notional sense. In the literal sense Untouchables are only those persons whose touch not only causes pollution and is therefore avoided, or if not avoided is washed off by purification. In the notional sense an Untouchable is a person who is deemed to belong to a class which is commonly held to cause pollution by touch, although contact with such a person may for local circumstances not be avoided or may not necessitate ceremonial purification. According to those who seek to apply the test in its literal sense the conclusion would be the so-called Untouchables should cease to be reckoned as Untouchables wherever conditions have so changed that people do not avoid the touch of an Untouchable, or do not trouble to purify themselves of the pollution caused by their touch. I cannot accept this view which, in my opinion, is based on a misconception. An individual may not be treated as an Untouchable in the literal sense of the term on account of various circumstances. Nonetheless outside the scope of such compelling circumstances he does continue to be regarded as an impure person by reason of his belonging to the Untouchable class. This distinction is well brought out by the Census Superintendent of Bihar and Orissa in his Census Report of 1921 from which the following is an extract. Speaking of the relaxation of caste rules he says:

Such incidents however which we have only noticed amongst the upper and more educated castes that are aspiring to the upper ranks, are to be regarded not as sign portending the collapse of the caste system, but of its adjustment to modern conditions. The same may be said with regard to modifications of the rules about personal contact or the touching of what is eaten or drunk.... In places like Jamshedpur where work is done under modern conditions men of all castes and races work side by side in the mill without any misgivings regarding the caste of their neighbours. But, because the facts of everyday life make it impossible to follow the same practical rules as were followed a hundred years ago, it is not to be supposed that the distinctions of pure and impure, touchable and Untouchable are no longer observed. A high caste-Hindu will not allow an 'Untouchable' to sit on the same seat, to smoke the same *hookah* or to touch his person, his seat, his food or the water that he drinks.

If this is a correct statement of the facts of life then the difference between untouchability in its literal and notional sense is a distinction which makes no difference to the ultimate situation; for as the extract shows untouchability in its notional sense persists even where untouchability in its literal sense has ceased to obtain. This is why I insist that the test of untouchability must be applied in its notional sense.

In the third place the idea is broadcast that untouchability is rapidly vanishing. I wish to utter a word of caution against the acceptance of this view, and to point out the necessity of distinguishing facts from propaganda. In my opinion what is important to be borne in mind in drawing inference from instances showing the occasional comingling of Brahmins and non-Brahmins, touchables and Untouchables is that the system of caste and the system of untouchability form really the steel frame of Hindu society. This division cannot easily be wiped out for the simple reason that it is not based upon rational, economic or racial grounds. On the other hand, the chances are that untouchability will endure far longer into the future than the optimist reformer is likely to admit on account of the fact that it is based on religious dogma. What makes it so difficult, to break the system of untouchability is the religious sanction which it has behind it. At any rate the ordinary Hindu looks upon it as part of his religion and there is no doubt that in adopting towards Untouchables in what is deemed to be an inhuman way of behaviour he does so more from the sense of observing his religion than from any motive of deliberate cruelty. Based on religion the ordinary Hindu only relaxes the rules of untouchability where he cannot observe them. He never abandons them. For abandonment of untouchability to him involves a total abandonment of the basic religious tenets of Hinduism as understood by him and the mass of Hindus. Based on religion untouchability will persist as all religious notions have done. Indian history records the attempts of many a Mahatma to uproot untouchability from the Indian soil. They include such great men as Buddha, Ramanuja and the Vaishnava saints of modern times. It would be hazardous to assume that a system which has withstood all this onslaught will collapse. The Hindu looks upon the observance of untouchability as an act of religious merit, and non-observance of it as sin. My view therefore is that so long as this notion prevails untouchability will prevail....

16

Poona Pact Correspondence between Gandhiji and British*
August–September 1932

Before I resume the narrative and state what decision the Prime Minister gave, I must describe the strange phenomenon which I, as a member of the Franchise Committee, witnessed. After the close of the second session of the Round Table Conference, the Prime Minister thought it advisable to have the question of franchise for the new constitution examined by a Committee. Accordingly, in December 1931 he appointed a Committee with the late Lord Lothian as its Chairman. Its main term of reference was to devise a system of franchise whereby, to use the language of the Prime Minister's letter of instructions to the Chairman,

The Legislatures to which responsibility is to be entrusted should be representative of the general mass of the population, and that no important section of the community may lack the means of expressing its needs and its opinions.

The Committee started its work early in January 1932. For doing its work the Committee took the help of the Provincial Governments and of the Provincial Franchise Committees consisting of non-officials specially constituted for that purpose province by province. The Committee issued questionnaires. They were replied to by the Provincial Governments, by the Provincial Franchise Committees and by individuals. Witnesses were examined by the Committee sitting with each Provincial Franchise Committee. The Provincial Governments and the Provincial Committees submitted their reports separately to the Committee. They were discussed by the Committee with the Provincial Government and the Provincial Committee before it came to its own conclusion. Besides the general tasks assigned to the Lothian

Committee, it had a special task with which it was charged by the Prime Minister. It had relation to the political demands of the Untouchables which the Prime Minister had referred to in the following terms in his letter of instruction to the Chairman—

It is evident from the discussions which have occurred in various connections in the Conference that the new constitution must make adequate provision for the representation of the Depressed Classes, and that the method of representation by nomination is no longer regarded as appropriate. As you are aware, there is a difference of opinion whether the system of Separate Electorates should be instituted for the Depressed Classes and your committee's investigations should contribute towards the decision of this question by indicating the extent to which the Depressed Classes would be likely, through such general extension of the franchise as you may recommend, to secure the right to vote in ordinary electorates. On the other hand, should it be decided eventually to constitute Separate Electorates for the Depressed Classes, either generally or in those provinces in which they form a distinct and separable element in the population, your Committee's inquiry into the general problem of extending the franchise should place you in possession of facts which would facilitate the devising of a method of separate representation for the Depressed Classes.

Following upon these instructions, it became the task of the Committee to come to some conclusion as to the total population of the Untouchables in British India.

To the question what is the population of the Untouchables the replies received were enough to stagger anybody. Witness after witness came forward to say that the Untouchables in his Province were infinitesimally small. There were not wanting witnesses who said that there were no Untouchables at all!! It was a most extraordinary sight to see Hindu witnesses perjuring themselves regardless of truth by denying the existence of the Untouchables or by reducing their number to a negligible figure. The members of the Provincial Franchise Committee were also a party to this plan. Strange to say that some of the Hindu members of the Lothian Committee were in the game. This move of denying the very existence of the Untouchables or reducing their number almost to nil was particularly rampant in certain Provinces. How the Hindus were prepared to economize truth, even to a vanishing point, will be evident from the following figures. In the United Provinces, the Census Commissioner in 1931 had estimated the total population of the Untouchables at 12.6 millions, the Provincial Government at

6.8 millions but the Provincial Franchise Committee at .6 millions only!! In Bengal, the Census gave the figures of 10.8 millions, Provincial Government fixed it as 11.2 millions but the Provincial Franchise Committee at .07 millions only!

Before the Round Table Conference no Hindu bothered about the exact population of the Untouchables and were quite satisfied with the accuracy of the Census figures which gave the total of the Untouchables at about 70 to 80 millions. Why did then the Hindus start suddenly to challenge this figure when the question was taken up by the Lothian Committee? The answer is very clear. Before the time of the Lothian Committee the population of the Untouchables had no value. But after the Round Table Conference the Hindus had come to know that the Untouchables were demanding separate allotment of their share of representation, that such share must come out of the lump which the Hindus had been enjoying in the past and that the measure of the share must depend upon the population of the Untouchables. The Hindus had realized that to admit the existence of the Untouchables was detrimental to their interest. They did not mind sacrificing truth and decency and decided to adopt the safest course, namely, to deny that there are any Untouchables in India at all, and thereby knock out the bottom of the political demands of the Untouchables and leave no room for argument. This shows how the Hindus can conspire in a cold, calculated manner against the Untouchables out of pure selfishness and do indirectly what they cannot do directly.

To resume the thread. Having been disgusted with the Round Table Conference where there were critics but no devotees, Mr. Gandhi was the first to return to India. On account of a statement which he is alleged to have made in an interview he gave to a newspaper correspondent in Rome wherein he threatened to revive his campaign of civil disobedience, Mr. Gandhi on his arrival was arrested and put in jail. Though in jail, not Swaraj but the Untouchables were on his brain. He feared that, notwithstanding his threat to resist it with his life, the Prime Minister as a sole arbitrator might accept the claims made on behalf of the Untouchables at the Round Table Conference. Long before any decision was given by the Prime Minister, Mr. Gandhi on 11th March 1932 addressed from jail a letter to Sir Samuel Hoare, the then Secretary of State for India, reminding him of his opposition to the claim of the Untouchables. The following is the text of that letter:

Dear Sir Samuel,

You will perhaps recollect that at the end of my speech at the Round Table Conference when the Minorities' claim was presented, I had said that I should resist with my life the grant of Separate Electorates to the Depressed Classes. This was not said in the heat of the moment nor by way of rhetoric. It was meant to be a serious statement. In pursuance of that statement, I had hoped on my return to India to mobilize public opinion against Separate Electorates, at any rate, for the Depressed Classes. But it was not to be.

From the newspapers, I am permitted to read, I observe that any moment His Majesty's Government may declare their decision. At first I had thought, if the decision was found to create Separate Electorates for the Depressed Classes, I should take such steps as I might then consider necessary to give effect to my vow. But I feel it would be unfair to the British Government for me to act without giving previous notice. Naturally, they could not attach the significance I give to my statement.

I need hardly reiterate all the objections I have to the creation of Separate Electorates for the Depressed Classes. I feel as if I was one of them. Their case stands on a wholly different footing from that of others. I am not against their representation in the Legislatures. I should favour everyone of their adults, male and female, being registered as voters irrespective of education or property qualification, even though the franchise test may be stricter for others. But I hold that Separate Electorate is harmful for them and for Hinduism, whatever it may be from the purely political standpoint. To appreciate the harm that Separate Electorate would do them, one has to know how they are distributed amongst the so-called caste-Hindus and how dependent they are on the latter. So far as Hinduism is concerned, Separate Electorates would simply vivisect and disrupt it.

For me the question of these classes is predominantly moral and religious. The political aspect, important though it is, dwindles into insignificance compared to the moral and religious issue.

You will have to appreciate my feelings in this matter by remembering that I have been interested in the condition of these classes from my boyhood and have more than once staked my all for their sake. I say this not to pride myself in any way. For, I feel that no penance that the Hindus may do can in any way compensate for the calculated degradation to which they have consigned the Depressed Classes for centuries.

But I know that Separate Electorate is neither a penance nor any remedy for the crushing degradation they have groaned under. I, therefore, respectfully inform His Majesty's Government that in the event of their decision creating Separate Electorate for the Depressed Classes, I must fast unto death.

I am painfully conscious of the fact that such a step, whilst I am a prisoner, must cause grave embarrassment to His Majesty's Government, and that it will be regarded by many as highly improper on the part of one holding my position to introduce into the political field methods which they would describe as hysterical if not much worse. All I can urge in defence is that for me the contemplated step is not a method, it is part of my being. It is the call of conscience which I dare not disobey, even though it may cost whatever reputation for sanity I may possess. So far as I can see now my discharge from imprisonment would not make the duty of fasting any the less imperative. I am hoping, however, all my fears are wholly unjustified and the British Government have no intention whatever of creating Separate Electorate for the Depressed Classes.'

The following reply was sent to Mr. Gandhi by the Secretary of State:

India Office, Whitehall,
13 April 1932

Dear Mr. Gandhi,

I write this in answer to your letter of 11th March, and I say at once I realize fully the strength of your feeling upon the question of Separate Electorates for the Depressed Classes. I can only say that we intend to give any decision that may be necessary solely and only upon the merits of the case. As you are aware, Lord Lothian's Committee has not yet completed its tour and it must be some weeks before we can receive any conclusions at which it may have arrived. When we receive that report we shall have to give most careful consideration to its recommendations, and we shall not give a decision until we have taken into account, in addition to the view expressed by the Committee, the views that you and those who think with you have so forcibly expressed. I feel sure if you were in our position you would be taking exactly the same action we intend to take. You would admit the Committee's report, you would then give it your fullest consideration, and before arriving at a final decision you would take into account the views that have been expressed on both sides of the controversy. More than this I cannot say. Indeed I do not imagine you would expect me to say more.

After giving this warning, Mr. Gandhi slept over the matter thinking that a repetition of his threat to fast unto death was sufficient to paralyse the British Government and prevent them from accepting the claim of the Untouchables for special representation. On the 17th August 1932 the decision of the Prime Minister on the communal question was announced.

That part of the decision which relates to the Untouchables is produced below:

COMMUNAL DECISION BY HIS MAJESTY'S GOVERNMENT 1932

In the statement made by the Prime Minister on 1st December last on behalf of His Majesty's Government at the close of the second session of the Round Table Conference, which was immediately afterwards endorsed by both Houses of Parliament, it was made plain that if the communities in India were unable to reach a settlement acceptable to all parties on the communal questions which the Conference had failed to solve, His Majesty's Government were determined that India's constitutional advance should not on that account be frustrated, and that they would remove this obstacle by devising and applying themselves a provisional scheme.

On the 19th March last His Majesty's Government, having been informed that the continued failure of the communities to reach agreement was blocking the progress of the plans for the framing of a new Constitution, stated that they were engaged upon a careful re-examination of the difficult and controversial questions which arise. They are now satisfied that without a decision of at least some aspects of the problems connected with the position of minorities under the new Constitution, no further progress can be made with the framing of the Constitution.

His Majesty's Government have accordingly decided that they will include provisions to give effect to the scheme set out below in the proposals relating to the Indian Constitution to be laid in due course before Parliament. The scope of this scheme is purposely confined to the arrangements to be made for the representation of the British Indian communities in the Provincial Legislatures, consideration of representation in the Legislature at the Centre being deferred for the reason given in paragraph 20 below. The decision to limit the scope of the scheme implies no failure to realize that the framing of the Constitution will necessitate the decision of a number of other problems of great importance to minorities, but has been taken in the hope that once a pronouncement has been made upon the basic questions of method and proportions of representation the communities themselves may find it possible to arrive at *modus vivendi* on other communal problems, which have not received the examination they require.

His Majesty's Government wish it to be most clearly understood that they themselves can be no parties to any negotiations which may be initiated with a view to the revision of their decision, and will not be prepared to give consideration to any representation aimed at securing the modification of it which is not supported by all the parties affected. But they are most desirous to close no door to an agreed settlement should such happily be forthcoming. If, therefore, before a new Government of India Act has passed into law, they are satisfied that the communities who are concerned are mutually agreed upon a practicable alternative scheme, either in respect of any one or more of the Governors' Provinces or in respect of the whole of the British India, they will be prepared to recommend to Parliament that that alternative should be substituted for the provisions now outlined....

Members of the 'Depressed Classes' qualified to vote will vote in a general constituency. In view of the fact that for a considerable period these classes would be unlikely, by this means alone, to secure any adequate representation in the Legislature, a number of special seats will be assigned to them as shown in the table. These seats will be filled by election from special constituencies in which only members of the 'Depressed Classes' electorally qualified will be entitled to vote. Any person voting in such a special constituency will, as stated above, be also entitled to vote in a general constituency. It is intended that these constituencies should be formed in selected areas where the Depressed Classes are most numerous, and that, except in Madras, they should not cover the whole area of the Province.

In Bengal it seems possible that in some general constituencies a majority of the voters will belong to the Depressed Classes. Accordingly, pending further investigation, no number has been fixed for the members to be returned from the special Depressed Class constituencies in that Province. It is intended to secure that the Depressed Classes should obtain not less than 10 seats in the Bengal Legislature.

The precise definition in each Province of those who (if electorally qualified) will be entitled to vote in the special Depressed Class constituencies has not yet been finally determined. It will be based as a rule on the general principles advocated in the Franchise Committee's Report. Modification may, however, be found necessary in some

Provinces in Northern India where the application of the general criteria of untouchability might result in a definition unsuitable 'in some respects to the special conditions of' the Province.

His Majesty's Government do not consider that these special Depressed Classes constituencies will be required for more than limited time. They intend that the Constitution shall provide that they shall come to an end after 20 years if they have not previously been abolished under the general powers of electoral revision referred to in paragraph 6.

Mr. Gandhi found that his threat had failed to have any effect. He did not care that he was a signatory to the requisition asking the Prime Minister to arbitrate. He forgot that as a signatory he was bound to accept the award. He started to undo what the Prime Minister had done. He first tried to get the terms of the Communal Award revised. Accordingly, he addressed the following letter to the Prime Minister:

Yeravda Central Prison
18 August 1932

Dear Friend,

There can be no doubt that Sir Samuel Hoare has showed you and the Cabinet my letter to him of 11th March on the question of the representation of the Depressed Classes. That letter should be treated as part of this letter and be read together with this.

I have read the British Government's decision on the representation of minorities and have slept over it. In pursuance of my letter to Sir Samuel Hoare and my declaration at the meeting of the Minorities Committee of the Round Table Conference on 13th November, 1931, at St. James' Palace, I have to resist your decision with my life. The only way I can do so is by declaring a perpetual fast unto death from food of any kind save water with or without salt and soda. This fast will cease if during its progress the British Government, of its own motion or under pressure of public opinion, revise their decision and withdraw their scheme of communal electorates for the Depressed Classes, whose representatives should be elected by the general electorate under the common franchise, no matter how wide it is.

The proposed fast will come into operation in the ordinary course from the noon of 20th September next, unless the said decision is meanwhile revised in the manner suggested above.

I am asking the authorities here to cable the text of this letter to you so as to give you ample notice. But in any case, I am leaving sufficient time for this letter to reach you in time by the slowest route.

I also ask that this letter and my letter to Sir Samuel Hoare already referred to be published at the earliest possible moment. On my part, I have scrupulously observed the rule of the jail and have communicated my desire or the contents of the two letters to no one, save my two companions, Sardar Vallabhbhai Patel and Mr. Mahadev Desai. But I want, if you make it possible, public opinion to be affected by my letters. Hence my request for their early publication.

I regret the decision I have taken. But as a man of religion that I hold myself to be, I have no other course left open to me. As I have said in my letter to Sir Samuel Hoare, even if His Majesty's Government decided to release me in order to save themselves from embarrassment, my fast will have to continue. For, I cannot now hope to resist the decision by any other means; and I have no desire whatsoever to compass my release by any means other than honourable'.

It may be that my judgment is warped and that I am wholly in error in regarding Separate Electorates for the Depressed Classes as harmful to them or to Hinduism. If so, I am not likely to be in the right with reference to other parts of my philosophy of life. In that case, my death by fasting will be at once a penance for my error and a lifting of a weight from off these numberless men and women who have childlike faith in my wisdom. Whereas if my judgment is right, as I have little doubt it is, the contemplated step is but due to the fulfillment of the scheme of life which I have tried for more than a quarter of a century, apparently not without considerable success'.

I remain,
Your faithful friend,
M. K. Gandhi.

The Prime Minister replied as under:

10, Downing Street,
8 September 1932

Dear Mr. Gandhi

I have received your letter with much surprise and, let me add with very sincere regret. Moreover, I cannot help thinking that you have written it under a misunderstanding as to what the decision of His Majesty's Government as regards the Depressed Classes really implies. We have always understood you were irrevocably opposed to the permanent segregation of the Depressed Classes from the Hindu community. You made your position very clear on the Minorities Committee of the Round Table Conference and you expressed it again in the letter you wrote to Sir Samuel Hoare on, 11th March. We also knew your view was shared by the great body of Hindu opinion, and we, therefore, took it into most careful account when we were considering the question of representation of the Depressed Classes.

Whilst, in view of the numerous appeals we have received from Depressed Class Organizations and the generally admitted social disabilities under which they labour and which you have often recognized, we felt it our duty to safeguard what we believed to be the right of the Depressed Classes to a fair proportion of representation in the Legislatures we were equally careful to do nothing that would split off their community from the Hindu world. You yourself stated in your letter of March 11, that you were not against their representation in the Legislatures.

Under the Government scheme the Depressed Classes will remain part of the Hindu community, and will vote with the Hindu electorate on an equal footing but for the first twenty years, while still remaining electorally part of the Hindu community, they will receive through a limited number of special constituencies, means of safeguarding their rights and interests that, we are convinced, is necessary under present conditions.

Where these constituencies are created, members of the Depressed Classes will not be deprived of their votes in the general Hindu constituencies, but will have two votes in order that their membership of the Hindu community should remain unimpaired.

We have deliberately decided against the creation of what you describe as a communal electorate for the Depressed Classes and included all Depressed Class voters in the general or Hindu constituencies so that the higher caste candidates should have to solicit their votes or Depressed Class candidates should have to solicit the votes of the higher castes at elections. Thus, in every way was the unity of Hindu society preserved.

We felt, however, that during the early period of responsible Government, when power in the Provinces would pass to whoever possessed a majority in the Legislatures, it was essential that the Depressed Classes whom you have, yourself described in your letter to Sir Samuel Hoare as having been consigned by caste-Hindus to calculated degradation for centuries, should return a certain number of members of their own choosing to Legislatures of seven of the nine provinces to voice their grievances and their ideals and prevent decisions going against them without the Legislature and the Government listening to their case—in a word, to place them in a position to speak for themselves, which every fair-minded person must agree to be necessary. We did not consider the method of electing special representatives by reservation of seats in the existing conditions, under any system of franchise, which is practicable, members who could genuinely represent them and be responsible for them, because in practically all—cases, such members would be elected by a majority consisting of higher caste-Hindus.

The special advantage initially given under our scheme to the Depressed Classes by means of a limited number of special constituencies, in addition to their normal electoral rights in the general Hindu constituencies, is wholly different in conception and effect from the method of representation adopted for a minority such as the Moslems by means of separate communal electorates. For example, a Moslem cannot vote or be a candidate in a general constituency, whereas any electorally qualified member of the Depressed Classes can vote in and stand for the general constituency.

The number of territorial seats allotted to Moslems is naturally conditioned by the fact that it is impossible for them to gain any further territorial seats and in most provinces they enjoy weightage in excess of their population ratio; the number of special seats to be tilled from special Depressed Classes constituencies will be seen to be small and has been fixed not to provide a quota numerically appropriate for the total representation of the whole of the Depressed Class population, but solely to secure a minimum number of spokesmen for the Depressed Classes in the Legislatures who are chosen exclusively by the Depressed Classes. The proportion of their special seats is everywhere much below the population percentage of the Depressed Classes.

As I understand your attitude, you propose to adopt the extreme course of starving yourself to death not in order to secure that the Depressed Classes should have Joint Electorate with other Hindus, because that is already provided, nor to maintain the unity of Hindus, which is also provided, but solely to prevent the Depressed Classes, who admittedly suffer from terrible disabilities today, from being able to secure a limited number of representatives of their own choosing to speak on their behalf in the Legislatures which will have a dominating influence over their future.

In the light of these very fair and cautious proposals, I am quite unable to understand the reason of the decision you have taken and can only think you have made it under a misapprehension of the actual facts.

In response to a very general request from Indians after they had failed to produce a settlement themselves the Government much against its will, undertook to give a decision on the minorities question. They have now given it, and they cannot be expected to alter it except on the condition they have stated. I am afraid, therefore, that my answer to you must be that the Government's decision stands and that only agreement of the communities themselves can substitute other electoral arrangements for those that Government have devised in a sincere endeavour to weigh the conflicting claims on their just merits.

You ask that this correspondence, including your letter to Sir Samuel Hoare of March 11th, should be published. As it would seem to me unfair if your present internment were to deprive you of the opportunity of explaining to the public the reason why you intend to fast, I readily accede to the request, if on reconsideration you repeat it. Let me, however, once again urge you to consider the actual details of Government's decision and ask yourself seriously the question whether it really justifies you in taking the action you contemplate.

I am,
Yours very sincerely,
J. Ramsay MacDonald'

Finding that the Prime Minister would not yield he sent him the following letter informing him that he was determined to carry out his threat of fast unto death:

Yeravda Central Prison,
9 September 1932

Dear Friend,

I have to thank you for your frank and full letter telegraphed and received this day. I am sorry, however, that you put upon the contemplated step an interpretation that never crossed my mind. I have claimed to speak on behalf of the very class, to sacrifice whose interests you impute to me a desire to fast myself to death. I had hoped that the extreme step itself would effectively prevent any such selfish interpretation. Without arguing, I affirm that for me this matter is one of pure religion. The mere fact of the Depressed Classes having double votes does not protect them or Hindu society in general from being disrupted. In the establishment of Separate Electorate at all for the Depressed Classes I sense the injection of poison that is calculated to destroy Hinduism and do no good whatever to the Depressed Classes. You will please permit me to say that no matter how sympathetic you may be, you cannot come to a correct decision on a matter of such vital and religious importance to the parties concerned.

I should not be against even over-representation of the Depressed Classes. What I am against is their statutory separation even in a limited form, from the Hindu fold, so long as they choose to belong to it. Do you realize that if your decision stands and the constitution comes into being, you arrest the marvellous growth of the work of Hindu reformers, who have dedicated themselves to the uplift of their suppressed brethren in every walk of life ?

I have, therefore, been compelled reluctantly to adhere to the decision conveyed to you. As your letter may give rise to a misunderstanding, I wish to state that the fact of my having isolated for special treatment the Depressed Classes question from other parts of your decision does not in any way mean that I approve of or am reconciled to other parts of the decision. In my opinion, many other parts are open to very grave objection. Only, I do not consider them to be any warrant for calling from me such self immolation as my conscience has promoted me to in the matter of the Depressed Classes.

I remain,
Your faithful friend,
M.K. Gandhi.

Accordingly, on the 20th September 1932, Mr. Gandhi commenced his 'fast unto death' as a protest against the grant of Separate Electorates to the Untouchables. ...

17

Statement on Gandhiji's Fast*
19 September 1932

I need hardly say that I was astounded to read the correspondence between Mahatma Gandhi, Sir Samuel Hoare and the Prime Minister, which was published recently in the papers in which he has expressed his determination to starve himself unto death till the British Government of its own accord or under pressure of public opinion revise their opinion and withdraw their scheme of communal representation for the Depressed Classes. The unenvinable position, in which I have been placed by the Mahatma's vow of self-immolation, can easily be imagined.

It passes my comprehension why Mr. Gandhi should stake his life on an issue arising out of the communal question which he, at the Round Table Conference, said was one of comparatively small importance. Indeed, to adopt the language of those of Mr. Gandhi's way of thinking, the communal question was only an appendix to the book of India's Constitution and not the main chapter. It would have been justifiable, if Mr. Gandhi had resorted to this extreme step for obtaining independence for the country on which he was so insistent all through the R.T.C. debates. It is also a painful surprise that Mr. Gandhi should single out special representation for the Depressed Classes in the Communal Award as an excuse for his self-immolation. Separate Electorates are granted not only to the Depressed Classes, but to the Indian Christians, Anglo-Indians, Europeans, as well as to the Mahomedans and the Sikhs. Also Separate Electorates are granted to landlords, labourers and traders. Mr. Gandhi had declared his opposition to the special representation of every other class and creed except the Mahomedans and the Sikhs. All the same, Mr. Gandhi chooses to let everybody else except the Depressed Classes retain the special electorates given to them.

The fears expressed by Mr. Gandhi about the consequence of the arrangements for the representation of the Depressed Classes are, in my opinion, purely imaginary. If the nation is not going to be split up by Separate Electorates to the Mahomedans and the Sikhs, the Hindu Society cannot be said to be split up if the Depressed Classes are given Separate Electorates. His conscience is not aroused if the nation is split by the arrangements of special electorates for classes and communities other than the Depressed Classes.

I am sure, many have felt that if there was any class which deserved to be given special political rights in order to protect itself against the tyranny of the majority under the Swaraj Constitution it was the Depressed Classes. Here is a class which is undoubtedly not in a position to sustain itself in the struggle for existence. The religion to which they are tied, instead of providing for them an honourable place, brands them as lepers, not fit for ordinary intercourse. Economically, it is a class entirely dependent upon the high-caste-Hindus for earning its daily bread with no independent way of living open to it. Nor are all ways closed by reason of the social prejudices of the Hindus but there is a definite attempt all throughout the Hindu Society to bolt every possible door so as not to allow the Depressed Classes any opportunity to rise in the scale of life. Indeed it would not be an exaggeration to say that in every village the caste-Hindus, however, divided among themselves, are always in a standing conspiracy to put down in a merciless manner any attempt on the part of the Depressed Classes who form a small and scattered body of an ordinary Indian citizen.

In these circumstances, it would be granted by all fair minded persons that as the only path for a community so handicapped to succeed in the struggle for life against organized tyranny, some share of political power in order that it may protect itself is a paramount necessity.

I should have thought that a well wisher of the Depressed Classes would have fought tooth and nail for securing to them as much political power as might be possible in the new constitution. But the Mahatma's ways of thinking are strange and are certainly beyond my comprehension. He not only does endeavour to augment the scanty political power which the Depressed Classes have got under the Communal Award, but on the contrary he has staked his very life in order to deprive them of little they have got. This is not the first attempt on the part of the Mahatma to completely dish the Depressed Classes out of political existence. Long before, there was the Minorities Pact. The Mahatma tried to enter into an agreement with the Muslims and the Congress.

He offered to the Muslims all the fourteen claims which they had put forth on their behalf, and in return asked them to join with him in resisting the claims for social representation made by me on behalf of the Depressed Classes.

It must be said to the credit of the Muslim delegates, that they refused to be a party to such a black act and saved the Depressed Classes from what might as well have developed into a calamity for them as a result of the combined opposition of the Mahomedans and Mr. Gandhi.

I am unable to understand the ground of hostility of Mr. Gandhi to the Communal Award. He says that the Communal Award has separated the Depressed Classes from the Hindu community. On the other hand, Dr. Moonje, a much stronger protagonist of the Hindu caste and a militant advocate of its interests, takes a totally different view of the matter. In the speeches which he has been delivering since his arrival from London, Dr. Moonje has been insisting that the Communal Award does not create any separation between the Depressed Classes and the Hindus. I am sure that Dr. Moonje is right in his interpretation of the Communal Award although, I am not sure that the credit of it can legitimately go to Dr. Moonje. It is therefore surprising that Mahatma Gandhi who is a nationalist and not known to be a communalist should read the Communal Award, in so far as it relates to the Depressed Classes, in a manner quite contrary to that of a communalist like Dr. Moonje. If Dr. Moonje does not sense any separation of the Depressed Classes from the Hindus in the Communal Award the Mahatma ought to feel quite satisfied on that score.

In my opinion the Communal Award should not only satisfy the Hindus, but also satisfy those individuals among the Depressed Classes such as Rao Bahadur Rajah, Mr. Baloo or Mr. Gavai, who are in favour of Joint Electorates. Mr. Rajah's fulminations in the Assembly have amused me considerably. An intense supporter of Separate Electorates and the bitterest and the most vehement critic of caste-Hindu tyranny now professes faith in the Joint Electorates and love for the Hindus. How much of that is due to his natural desire to resuscitate himself from the oblivion in which he was cast by his being kept out of the Round Table Conference and how much of it is to his honest change of faith, I do not propose to discuss.

The points on which Mr. Rajah is harping by way of criticism on the Communal Award are two. One is that the Depressed Classes have gained lesser number of seats than they are entitled to on the population basis, and the other is that the Depressed Classes have been separated from the Hindu fold.

I agree to his first grievance, but when the Rao Bahadur begins to accuse those who represented the Depressed Classes at the R.T.C. for having sold their rights, I am bound to point out what Mr. Rajah did as a member of the Indian Central Committee. In that committee's report, the Depressed Classes were given in Madras 10 seats out of 150, in Bombay 8 seats out of 14, in Bengal 8 seats out of 200, in Uttar Pradesh 8 seats out of 182, in the Punjab 6 seats out of 150, in Bihar and Orissa 6 out of 150, in C. P. 8 out of 125 and in Assam 9 seats for the Depressed Classes and the indigenous and primitive races out of 75. I do not wish to overburden this statement by pointing out how this distribution compares with the population ratio. But there can be no doubt that this meant a terrible under-representation of the Depressed Classes. To this distribution of seats Mr. Rajah was a party. Surely, Mr. Rajah, before he criticises the Communal Award and accuses others, should refresh his memory of what he accepted as member of the Indian Central Committee on behalf of the Depressed Classes without any protest. If the population ratio of representation was to him a natural right of Depressed Classes and its full realisation was a necessity for their protection why did not Mr. Rajah insist upon it in the Central Committee when he had an opportunity to do so?

As to his contention that in the Communal Award, the Depressed Classes have been separated from the caste-Hindus, it is a view to which I cannot subscribe. If Mr. Rajah has any conscientious objection to Separate Electorates, there is no compulsion on him to stand as a candidate in the Separate Electorates. The opportunity to stand as a candidate in the General electorate as well as the right to vote in it are there; and Mr. Rajah is free to avail himself of the same. Mr. Rajah is crying at the top of his voice to assure to the Depressed Classes that there is a complete change of heart on the part of the caste-Hindus towards the Depressed Classes. He will have the opportunity to prove that fact to the satisfaction of the Depressed Classes who are not prepared to take his word by getting himself elected in the general constituency. The Hindus, who profess love and sympathy for the Depressed Classes will have also an opportunity to prove their bona fides by electing Mr. Rajah to the Legislature.

The Communal Award therefore in my opinion satisfied both those who want Separate Electorates and those who want Joint Electorates. In this sense, it is already a compromise and should be accepted as it is. As to the Mahatma, I do not know what he wants. It is assumed that although Mahatma Gandhi is opposed to the system of Separate Electorates, he is not opposed to the system of Joint Electorates and reserved seats. That is a gross error, whatever his views are today, while in London he was totally opposed to any system of special representation for the Depressed Classes whether by Joint Electorates or by Separate Electorates. Beyond the right to vote in a general electorate based upon Adult Suffrage, he was not prepared to concede anything to the Depressed Classes by way of securing their representation in the Legislatures. This was the position he had taken at first. Towards the end of the R. T. C. he suggested to me a scheme, which he said he was prepared to consider. The scheme was purely conventional without any constitutional sanction behind it and without any single seat being reserved for the Depressed Classes in the electoral law.

The Scheme was as follows:

Depressed Class candidates might stand in the general electorate as against other high caste-Hindu candidates. If any Depressed Class candidate was defeated in the election, he should file an election petition and obtain the verdict that he was defeated because he was an Untouchable. If such a decision was obtained, the Mahatma said he would undertake to induce some Hindu members to resign and thus create a vacancy. There would be then another election in which the defeated Depressed Class candidate or any other Depressed Class candidate might again try his luck against the Hindu candidates. Should he be defeated again, he should get a similar verdict that he was defeated because he was an Untouchable and so on. I am disclosing these facts as some people are even now under the impression that the Joint Electorates and reserved seats would satisfy the conscience of the Mahatma. This will show why I insist that there is no use discussing the question until the actual proposals of the Mahatma are put forth.

I must, however, point out that I cannot accept the assurances of the Mahatma that he and his Congress will do the needful for the conventions and understandings. The Mahatma is not an immortal person and the Congress assuming it is not a malevolent force, is not to have an abiding existence. There have been many Mahatmas in India, whose sole object was to remove untouchability and to elevate and absorb the Depressed Classes, but every one of them has failed in his mission. Mahatmas have come and Mahatmas have gone, but the Untouchables have remained as Untouchables.

I have enough experience of the pace of reform and the faith of Hindu reformers in the conflicts that have taken place at Mahad and Nasik to say that no well-wisher of the Depressed Classes will ever consent to allow the uplift of the Depressed Classes to rest upon such treacherous shoulders. Reformers who in moments of crises prefer to sacrifice their principles rather than hurt the feelings of their kindred can be of no use to the Depressed Classes.

I am, therefore, bound to insist upon a statutory guarantee for the protection of any people. If Mr. Gandhi wishes to have the Communal Award altered, it is for him to put forth his proposals and to prove that they give a better guarantee than has been given to us under the Award.

I hope that the Mahatma will desist from carrying out the extreme step contemplated by him. We mean no harm to the Hindu society when we demand Separate Electorates. If we choose Separate Electorates, we do so in order to avoid the total dependence on the sweet will of the caste-Hindus in matters affecting our destiny. Like the Mahatma we also claim our right to err, and we expect him not to deprive us of that right. His determination to fast himself unto death is worthy of a far better cause. I could have understood the propriety of the Mahatma contemplating such extreme step for stopping riots between Hindus and Mohammedans or between the Depressed Classes and the Hindus or any other national cause. It certainly cannot improve the lot of the Depressed Classes. Whether he knows it or not, the Mahatma's act will result in nothing but terrorism by his followers against the Depressed Classes all over the country.

Coercion of this sort will not win the Depressed Classes to the Hindu fold if they are determined to go out. And if the Mahatma chooses to ask the Depressed Classes to make a choice between Hindu faith and possession of political power, I am quite sure that the Depressed Classes will choose political power and save the Mahatma from self-immolation. If Mr. Gandhi coolly reflects on the consequences of his act, I very much doubt whether he will find this victory worth having. It is still more important to note that the Mahatma is a reactionary and uncontrollable force and is fostering the spirit of hatred between the Hindu community and the Depressed Classes by resorting to this method and thereby widening the existing gulf between the two. When I opposed Mr. Gandhi at the R.T.C. there was a hue and cry against me in the country and there was a conspiracy in the so-called nationalist press to represent me as a traitor to the nationalist cause, to suppress correspondence coming from my side and to boost the propaganda against my party by publishing exaggerated reports of meetings and conferences, many of which were never held. Silver bullets were freely used for creating divisions in the ranks of the Depressed Classes. There have been also a few clashes ending in violence.

If the Mahatma does not want all this to be repeated on a larger scale, let him, for God's sake, reconsider his decision and avert the disastrous consequences. I believe the Mahatma does not want this. But if he does not desist, in spite of his wishes, these consequences are sure to follow as night follows the day.

Before concluding this statement, I desire to assure the public that although I am entitled to say that I regard the matter as closed, I am prepared to consider the proposals of the Mahatma. I however, trust the Mahatma will not drive me to the necessity of making a choice between his life and the rights of my people. For I can never consent to deliver my people bound hand and foot to the caste-Hindus for generations to come.

Part III

Extending the Representation
Employment and Education, 1934–46

Introduction

The proceedings of the second RTC and its culmination in the Poona Pact had a detrimental impact on Ambedkar's future course of action to safeguard the interests of the SCs. Though, Ambedkar made some references to the Pact afterwards, he avoided any overturn comment on it immediately. However, it was in April 1934, he said, 'Nothing could be better if the agreement accepted the principle that the decision in the matter of electorates is to rest with the Minority in each constituency'. On 4 February 1940, he came openly against the Pact saying that 'Safeguards under Poona Pact are inadequate.' It was again after a gap of two years that Ambedkar raised the issue of safeguarding the interests of the SCs in a comprehensive way while submitting a Memorandum to the Governor General on 29 November 1942. And from this period till the formation of the Constituent Assembly, he intervened in the following ways:

1. Joint v/s Separate Electorates—Dr. Ambedkar's Via Media (Statement to *The Times of India*): 28 April 1934.
2. Grievances of the Scheduled Castes (Memorandum Submitted to His Excellency Governor-General of India as Member of the Executive Council): 29 October 1942.
3. Problem of the Untouchables of India (Paper written for the Institute of Pacific Studies): 1 September 1943.
4. Communal Deadlock and How to Solve it (While the Demand for Pakistan was Rising): 6 May 1945.
5. Proposal for the Representation of Scheduled Castes in the Executive Council (To Lord Wavell on the Transfer of Power to Indians): 7 June 1945.
6. Memorandum Submitted to the Cabinet Mission by the All India Scheduled Castes Federation(On the future Constitution of India): 5 April 1946.
7. Letter to PM Attlee to Restore Separate Electorates: 12 August 1946.
8. Cabinet Mission and the Untouchables—How the Cabinet Mission Have Ignored Untouchables: 14 October 1946.

The Cripps Mission came to India on 22 March 1942 to negotiate with Indian political parties to find a solution of the constitutional crisis arising out of resignation by the Congress Ministries and secure their co-operation in the war efforts of the Second World War. It proposed for constituting a Constituent Assembly and it became a contentious issue for the SCs, who did not have adequate representation in the Legislatures. It was perhaps for the first time that all sections of the society whether Hindus or Muslims or Sikhs or SCs opposed the proposals of the Cripps Mission, though all of them for different reasons.

It was in this light that Ambedkar submitted a Memorandum to the Governor General as Member of his Council to put forward the grievances of the SCs (*BAWS* 1991, vol. 10: 404–42). The Memorandum was divided into four parts where the first part deals with the political grievances, second with the educational grievances, third with grievances of neglect of publicity and role in government contacts, and the fourth with the duty of the government towards distressed people. The political grievances have been further divided into four parts—inadequate representation in the Central Legislature; inadequate representation in the Central Executive; absence of representation in the Public Services; and absence of representation on the Federal Public Services Commission.

Ambedkar pointed out low representation in Public Services for the minorities and absence of it in case of SCs. And it was due to two factors—absence of declaration of SCs to be minority, and non-fixation of a particular quota for them. It brought out that in case of other minorities the Public Services were made a matter of obligation, whereas, in case of SCs, it had been a matter of discretion of the government functionaries.

On the education front, emphasis was more on solutions than on describing the evolution of educational policy of the British and its neglect of application to SCs. Bringing out the significance of education Ambedkar opined that howsoever numerous the SCs might get ministerial posts will have no consequence for their community but to have occupied the Executive posts and it could be achieved by high degree of education. He emphasized for education more in the field of science and technology than elsewhere. The solutions offered had been like granting scholarships to SC students taking science and technology courses, grants to study abroad, reserving a fixed number of seats for the SC students, spending equal amount as that the University of Aligarh and University of Banaras—the institutions of Muslims and Hindus, appointing two members of SCs on the Central Advisory Board of Education to make the board interested for them and providing technical knowledge to the unskilled labour of SCs. Thus we find that while representing the DC before Simon Commission, Ambedkar did focus on primary education, whereas here the focus was on technical and advanced education during this period. Here two important issues which were not touched earlier were taken up. First, neglect in the matter of publicity of SC programmes and second, share in government contracts. It was pointed out that though the government contract was provided to a person offering lowest price but for the SC contractors the rate of tender could be fixed 5 per cent low as compared to others so that they also get opportunity.

During the same period, the Institute of Pacific Studies requested Ambedkar to write on the problems and solutions of the SCs question (*BAWS* 1990, vol. 9: 396–433). Apart from re-emphasizing the questions raised in the memorandum to the Governor General another important issue of forming separate settlements for the SCs was raised in the paper.

On another occasion, addressing session of the Scheduled Castes Federation of India (*BAWS* 1979, vol. 1: 355–79), Ambedkar maintained that the majority in India is communal majority that is fixed and unchanging, not a political majority, which keeps changing with time and space. During the address he also referred to the question of SCs as part of minority community problem. Coming down heavily on the existing state of affairs, it was suggested that for representation in the Public Services, there was already administrative practice to give representation to the minorities as per Resolutions of 1934 and 1943 which needs to be converted into statutory obligation through a schedule in the Constitution. To make Executive representative and efficient, he suggested:

1. The quantum of representation in the Executive should be as per their population and it should be constituted in a way that it has a mandate not only from the majority but also from the minorities in the Legislature.
2. The Executive should be non-parliamentary in the sense that it is not removable before the term of the Legislature.
3. The positions in the Executive should be so filled that the prime minister represents not the majority but the whole House and the persons representing a particular minority community should

have the confidence of the members of his community members in the Legislature.

4. The prime minister and the cabinet should be so elected by a single transferable vote and the representatives of the cabinet of minority community should be elected by the members of the minority communities of the Legislature.

The representation in the Legislature should be so distributed that the quantum of representation gives relative majority to the majority community and not the absolute majority. The relative majority could be such that—the majority community does not establish its rule with the help of smallest minorities; the minorities combined together could form government, and the weight taken from the majority should be distributed among the minorities, the minority that has a better social, educational and economic standing gets a lesser amount of weightage than the one which stands lower to it. So far as the nature of electorates is concerned, Separate Electorates give minority an absolute guarantee but a system of Joint Electorates that gives equal protection to the minorities should not be overlooked. However, Ambedkar came out with another solution where there is four-member constituency, with a right to minorities to have a double vote and requiring a minimum percentage of minority votes to get elected as an alternative.

The Governor General of India, Lord Wavell, had asked for Indianization of the Executive Council vis-à-vis full self-government to the Indian people.

The political parties in India condemned the Wavell's Plan as it offered nothing materially different from the Cripps Plan. In the meantime, the British government sent a three member delegation of cabinet ministers known as Cabinet Mission Plan on 23 March 1946. The Cabinet Mission met various leaders and Ambedkar presented a memorandum (*BAWS* 2003, vol. 17, no. 2: 171–81) on behalf of the All India Scheduled Castes Federation on 5 April 1946. In the memorandum it was categorically mentioned that the SCs will not accept any constitution which does not contain their long-standing demands like, Separate Electorates, adequate representation in the Public Services and Public Service Commissions at the federal and provincial levels, provision of adequate sum in the annual budgets of the provincial and Central governments for the higher education of SCs, and provision of new and separate settlements.

Reiterating the demand for the separate settlements, it was argued that the existing village system has—(1) perennial untouchability, (2) not allowing Untouchables to live inside the village, (3) no independent means of livelihood for them, (4) forced labour imposed upon them, (5) made their lives, a life of degradation, dishonour and ignominy from generation to generation, and (6) most formidable weapon of social boycott if any progress is made to them against the wishes of the caste-Hindus. To solve such a multidimensional problem of SCs the separate settlements are imperative and to this effect, measures be taken by the Constitution, including—(1) transfer of the SCs from their present habitations and form separate villages away and independent of Hindu villages, (2) establishing a Settlement Commission, (3) handing over all cultivable and unoccupied government land to the Commission for the purpose of making new settlements, (4) giving right to the Commission to purchase land from private owners for fulfillment of the scheme, and (5) making it obligatory for the Central government to provide a sum of Rupees five crores per annum to the Commission to carry out its duties.

The Cabinet Mission submitted its report for a solution of the political problems of India. The minority communities including the SCs leaders criticized the Cabinet Mission proposals for not giving adequate attention to their demands. The SCs were not even recognized as minorities and the demand of Separate Electorates was set aside. In response, Ambedkar wrote a letter to the Prime Minister Attlee to reconsider government position regarding the SCs.

In October 1946, Ambedkar went to meet Attlee and Churchill and with a memorandum (*BAWS* 1991, vol. 10: 512–14), he brought the following facts to light and asked for their consideration—the Untouchables denied right to send their representative in the Central Executive as one of them appointed by the Congress and the other by the Muslim League; the Cabinet had to have two members of SCs as per Shimla Agreement in 1945 but denied in 1946 by the Mission; and no departure from the policy accepted in 1932 on Separate Electorates.

This phase of Ambedkar's efforts show that the following issues were brought forth in eight major interventions viz. memorandum to the Governor General, paper to the Institute of Pacific Studies, memorandum to the Cabinet Mission Plan, letters to Prime Minister Attlee and Churchill:

1. The representation in the Legislatures, Executive and the Public Services was demanded in accordance with the population.
2. Reiterating the demand of Separate Electorates.
3. Severe criticism of the British for not giving proper attention to the interests of the SCs.
4. Comprehensive plan to address the issue of education of SCs.
5. To have separate settlements for the SCs and sufficient fund allocation for the same from the government in its budget.
6. Declaring Untouchables as minority which was denied due to Poona Pact.
7. Instituting a machinery to examine whether the safeguards for minorities framed by the Constituent Assembly are adequate and real.
8. Circumscribing the power of the future Indian Legislature to do away with minority safeguards by bare majority.

To sum up, this period of Ambedkar's interventions could be termed articulations of solutions than the problem. Here, the solutions are more descriptive and intense than the previous phases of his efforts. And this period could be seen as the grounding to the inclusive policies which are covered by the Reservation Policy at present, whether it is the sphere of education or the employment. A few other solutions such as separate settlements and re-emphasizing on the Separate Electorates and asking for share in the government contracts carried out by private contractors were also suggested.

So far as the achievement of this phase is concerned, there were two major achievements—the British passed a resolution to give adequate representation to the SCs in the Public Services in 1942, and Ambedkar was appointed as the Member of the Executive Council of the Governor General.

18

Joint v/s Separate Electorates
Dr. Ambedkar's Via Media*
28 April 1934

... The exchange of views and compliments between Pandit Madan Mohan Malaviya and Mr. Jinnah has once more revealed that there is no hope in the immediate future of the Hindus and Muslims agreeing to replace the Communal Decision of His Majesty's Government by a settlement based on mutual agreement. Pandit Malaviya has left the field by saying that for the present the two communities must work separately. I do not know how many will look with satisfaction at the prospect of the two communities working separately. To me at any rate it appears that working in separation must inevitably end in working in antagonism.

I am neither a Hindu nor a Muslim, and I make this proposal not as a partisan but as a student of the problem.

Before I set forth the proposal, I should like to promise that the expression 'minority' has been loosely used in the communal controversy and what is worse is that it is used without any reference to the Province or to the constituency in a Province in relation to which alone it can have any meaning in politics. In my view a community is a minority and is entitled to get protection as a 'minority' only if it is a minority in the Province, or strictly speaking if it is a 'minority' in the constituency. Except in relation to the Province or to the constituency a 'minority' has no political significance.

A SUGGESTION

Starting from this basic point, on which I should like to lay the utmost emphasis I can, my proposal is to separate the two questions that are covered in the Communal Award, namely the question of seats and the question of electorates. These two questions are separate questions and the considerations that have to be taken into account for their solution are quite different. Having separated the two questions, my advice to Hindus and to Muslims is to accept that part of the Communal Award which deals with the number of seats if not permanently, *Pro tern*, leaving it to be decided on some more equitable principle at some future stage. But with regard to the question of electorates let the Communal Award be modified by the acceptance by Hindus and Muslims of this simple proposition, that the question of electorates is a matter for the minority in the Province or strictly for a minority in a particular constituency of the Province whether the election before the Central or Provincial Legislature and the majority should abide by the decision of the minority.

MINORITY MUST DECIDE

If the minority wants Separate Electorates the majority should have nothing to say against it; equally if the minority wants Joint Electorates, the majority should be bound to accept their decision.

The proposal could be applied even in cases where there are many minorities and where they are not of a common mind on the issue of electorates. In such cases the minority which wants a Separate Electorate will have a separate register for itself, while the minority wishing to have a Joint Electorate will have a common register with the majority. Nothing could be better if the agreement accepted the principle that the decision in the matter of electorates is to rest with the minority in each constituency. But if that cannot be achieved, it would be some advance if an agreement could be arrived at on the basis that the decision as to the electorates is to be left to the minority in the Province.

By such an agreement the Muslim minorities in the Hindu majority Provinces like Bombay, Madras, the Central Provinces, the United Provinces, etc. will get Separate Electorates if they choose to have them. On the other hand, in the Muslim majority Provinces like the Punjab, Sind, Bengal and the N. W. F. Provinces the Hindus will have Joint Electorates if they ask for them. The whole point of the proposal is to leave the question of the electorates to the decision of the minority. Separate or Joint Electorates are devised for the protection of the minority and the minority is the best judge as to which of these two will protect it best.

If the proposal is faulty in principle, it would, of course, deserve no consideration at the hands of either Mr. Jinnah or Pandit Madan Mohan Malaviya. But if the proposal is just and fair, as I believe it is, I hope Mr. Jinnah will have the courage to pass it upon his co-religionists and Pandit Malaviya the wisdom to accept.

A MIDDLE STAGE

The proposal does not, of course, help in one sweep to realize the goal of the Congress and the Hindu Mahasabha to have Joint Electorates instituted in all the Provinces of India between Hindus and Muslims. But the proposal has the merit of establishing a middle stage between the extreme Congress and Hindu Mahasabha stand on Joint Electorates throughout and the extreme Muslim demand of Separate Electorates throughout. From this middle stage, at which there will prevail a mixed system of Joint Electorates in some Provinces and Separate Electorates in the rest, the journey to the final stage of Joint Electorates throughout will be rendered very easy. It is only the impatient idealists among the protagonists of Joint Electorates who will disapprove of the proposal....

The structure of the electorate is not an exclusive concern of the minority. It is a problem in constitution-making in which the whole nation has a stake. A national problem cannot be converted into a special preserve for the exclusive judgment of this or that part of it, by the mere assertion of some claim for protection supposed to be connected with it. Since uniformity on any question is impossible, the judgment of the majority has come to do duty as the nearest possible substitute to the will of the people, in a world of inevitable divergence in political tenets.

To elevate the minority, only because it is a minority, to a pinnacle of power and prestige superior to that held by the majority, is the way to cut at the root of the very fundamental principle of democratic government. Political thought marches from precedent to precedent. An objectionable principle, once given quarter tends to surround itself with a sort of vested interest. With power secured from mere sufferance, it defies all attempts made to dislodge it. It is for this reason that temporary compromises, tolerated with the hope of being soon dispensed with, end by becoming formidable obstacles to progress.

No consideration can justify the setting up of a tyranny of the minority, or the relegation of the will of the majority to a status inferior to that of minority.

19

Grievances of the Scheduled Castes*
29 October 1942

INTRODUCTION

This memorandum sets out the grievances of the Scheduled Castes in British India and suggests the measures that are necessary for redressing them. In listing the grievances I have taken note of such grievances only as the Central Government alone can remedy.

The grievances listed in this memorandum are divided into three categories (1) Political, (2) Educational and (3) Other Grievances, and are discussed separately. Part I deals with Political grievances, Part II with Educational grievances, and Part III with Other grievances. To this I have added Part IV in which I have ventured to speak of the duty which every Government must assume towards those who are living in a life of perpetual distress, in the hope that the Government of India will recognize it and do what they are bound to do to the Scheduled Castes.

I have thought it advisable to give below a table divided into parts. This table, it will be seen serves two purposes. It gives at the start the contents of this memorandum, and secondly it helps to convey at the outset a general idea of what these grievances are:

Part I. Political Grievances
1. Inadequate Representation in the Central Legislature
2. Inadequate Representation in the Central Executive
3. Absence of Representation in the Public Services
4. Absence of Representation on the Federal Public Services Commission
Part II. Educational Grievances
1. Want of Aid for University and for Advanced Education
2. Want of Facilities for Technical Training

*BAWS 1991, vol. 10: 404–42.

Part III. Other Grievances
1. Untouchables and Government Publicity
2. Untouchables and Government Contracts
Part IV. Duty of Government Towards Distressed People

PART I. POLITICAL GRIEVANCES

Inadequate Representation in the Central Legislature

As at present constituted the Central Assembly consists of 141 members. Of these 102 are elected and 39 nominated. Of the nominated members 19 are Non-Officials and 20 are Officials. Of this total of 141 there are two who belong to the Scheduled Castes. Consider as against this the population of the Scheduled Castes. The census in India has become a political affair; and the Hindus, Muslims and the Sikhs have been attempting to cook up the census so as to show a rise in their numbers. This is done mostly at the cost of the Untouchables. It is therefore difficult to get a correct figure of their population. Whatever estimate the census gives, it is bound to be an underestimate. However, taking the figure of 40 millions which is the figure given in the census of 1940 there can be no doubt that the representation of the Scheduled Castes in the Central Legislature is ridiculously low.

To make the position clear, I give below two tables which have a bearing on this question:

Table 1   Population in British India

Communities	Total of Each Community in 1941	Order of Importance in Terms of Population	Percentage to Total Population
Total	295,808,722	....	....
Hindus	150,890,146	1	50.0
Muslims	79,398,503	2	23.6
Scheduled Castes	39,920,807	3	13.5
Tribal	16,713,256	4	5.7
Sikhs	4,165,097	5	1.3
Indian Christians	3,245,706	6	1.0
Europeans	122.7S8	7	....
Anglo-Indians	113,936	8	....
Parsis	101,968	9	....

Note: In this table only the population of those communities whose position is relevant to the purpose of this Memorandum is given.

Table 2   Communal Composition of the Central Assembly

Community	Elected Members		Nominated Non-Official Members		Nominated Official Members		Total including Official Members		Total excluding Official Members	
	No.	Per cent	No.	Per cent	No.	Per cent	No.	Per cent	No.	Per cent
Hindu	56	54.9	4	21	8	–	68	48.5	60	49.5
Muslims	34	33.5	7	37	3	–	44	31	41	33.8
Sikhs	2	–	2	10.5	–	–	4	2.8	4	3.3
Parsis	1	–	2	10.5	1	–	4	2.8	3	2.4
Europeans	8	7.8	1	–	7	–	16	11.3	9	7.4
Indian Christians	–	–	1	–	–	–	1	–	1	...
Anglo-Indians	–	–	1	–	–	–	1	–	1	...
Scheduled Castes	–	–	1	–	1	–	2	1.4	1	–
Vacant	1	–	–	–	–	–	1	–	1	–
Total	102	–	19	–	20	–	141	–	121	–

This table throws a flood of light on the extent of representation which the different communities in the Central Legislature have at present. Figures in column 5 give the total representation each community has, with the percentage ratio for some of them. I do not, however, wish to lay stress on them. They include figure for Nominated Officials. They are intended primarily to represent Government and not the communities to whom they belong. Secondly, the communal composition of the Nominated Official Block is variable and not fixed. But I do wish to invite attention to figures in other columns. I will begin with column 6. It gives the total extent of the representation which different communities have secured through election as well as nomination. More striking are the figures given in column 3. It shows that the Hindus have been allowed 54.9% by election. In addition they are given 21% out of the quota reserved for nomination. The Muslims have got 33.5% by election. This is great deal in excess of what they are entitled to on the basis of their population. In addition they are allowed the benefit of 37% out of the quota reserved for nomination. The same is the case with the Sikhs and the Parsis. Both of them have representation through election much beyond what their numbers would justify. Yet each is allowed to have the benefit of 10.5% out of the quota for nomination. As against this, there is the naked fact that the Scheduled Castes who number 40 millions and who form the third largest community in India have no seat by election, and only one by nomination.

Given these facts two comments become quite in order. In the first place, the Legislature is quite an unbalanced body. It suffers from both the evils from over-representation of some communities and under-representation of other communities. The evil exists in its most aggravated form. For the over-representation is of communities which are strong and powerful and the under-representation is of communities which are weak and poor. The second comment relates to the wrong use of the power of nomination. The power of nomination was reserved under the Constitution to rectify the inequalities of representation. To put it in a different language, it was intended to give these communities, which did not secure enough representation by election, sufficient representation through nomination.

There is no principle which seems to govern either the election or the nomination in so far as they relate to the composition of the Central Legislature. If at all there is any principle, it is to give Peter more than Paul and then to rob Paul who has almost nothing to enrich Peter who has almost everything.

There is no justification for so grave a wrong done to the Scheduled Castes in the matter of representation. In a Legislature in which the Muslims and the Hindus are waging a war against each other for rights and privileges and in which both are careful not to lose anything to a third party like the Scheduled Castes what support can a single representative of the Scheduled Caste in a House of 141 get in his right for the rights of the Scheduled Castes? It was the view of the Southborough Committee, on the recommendations of which the present structure of the Central Legislature is reared, that the nominated officials may be expected to bear in mind the interests of the Scheduled Castes. It is a matter of some considerable interest that the then Government of India refused to accept this view. In their Dispatch on the Report of the Southborough Committee, the Government of India said:—

But that arrangement is not, in our opinion, what the (Montague-Chelmsford) Report on Reforms aims at. The authors stated that the Depressed Classes should also learn the lesson of self-protection. It is surely fanciful to hope that this result can be expected from including a single member of the community in an assembly where there are 60 to 90 caste-Hindus. To make good the principles of paras 151, 152 and 155 of the Report we must treat the outcastes more generously....

Unfortunately no generosity was shown by the Government of India to the Scheduled Castes in making its proposal for the composition of the Central Legislative Assembly. They gave them one seat by nomination, and it has continued to be one since 1921.

The result of this meagre representation has been quite deplorable. A single representative of the Scheduled Castes in an Assembly of 141 cannot but feel the utter helplessness of his position. He has to contend against a vast volume of anti-Scheduled Caste prejudices arising from the Hindu side of the House. He cannot depend upon the support either of the Muslim block who are lighting their battle to advance their interests. Nor can he depend upon the Official Block which has been more careful to preserve its good relations with the major Hindu and Muslim blocks than to support the just interests of the Scheduled Castes. It is not even possible for the single and solitary representative of the Scheduled Castes in the assembly to ventilate the grievances of the Scheduled Castes. I am informed that under the rules made by the President of the Legislative Assembly, the President gives the first chance to speak to those Hon'ble members who belong to a recognized party. I also understand that the President does not recognize a party unless it has the minimum strength of ten members. This means that ordinarily the representative of the Scheduled Castes has no chance of speaking in the House unless he chooses to join a party. For a representative of the Scheduled Castes to be faced with this kind of situation is not a very happy thing. To join a party means for him to subordinate the interests of the Scheduled Castes to that of a party, the principles and interests of which may be quite inconsistent with the principles and interests of the Scheduled Castes. On the other hand, not to join a party means to lose altogether the right to speak. If one may refer to what happened in the Assembly session (September 1942) in the debate that took place on the present political situation in India, the Hon'ble Rao Bahadur N. Sivaraj, the representative of the Scheduled Castes in the Central Assembly, found it difficult to obtain a chance to speak on behalf of the Scheduled Castes, although 5 or 6 Muslim members could easily speak for the Muslims.

It is, therefore, greatly necessary that the representation of the Scheduled Castes in the Assembly should be augmented. Of course this can be done only when vacancies occur in nominated non-official seats. When they do occur, justice requires that such vacancies should go to increase the representation of the Scheduled Castes in the Assembly.

Inadequate Representation in the Central Executive

The Government of India has been very tardy in recognizing the right of the Scheduled Castes for representation in the Central Executive. This has been a very sore point with the Scheduled Castes. For they hold that whatever may have been their political status in the past, since the Round Table Conference their political status had become equal to the status of that of the Muslims, and if the Muslims have a right to representation in the Central Executive, so have the Scheduled Castes. There is no doubt that their contention is well founded. At the Round Table Conference it was the demand of the Scheduled Castes, and not merely of the Muslims, that provision for the adequate representation of the Scheduled Castes should be made by law. The Hindu point of view was not opposed to this demand. All that the Hindus said was that it should be left to convention. Ultimately a compromise was arrived at and it was agreed that the Instrument of Instructions to the Governors of the Provinces and the Governor-General of India should contain a specific clause imposing upon them the obligation to endeavour to include representatives of important minority communities. Although the communities were not specified, there could be no doubt that the phrase 'important minorities' was intended to include the Scheduled Castes. At long last the Government of India has recognized this obligation to give representation to the Scheduled Castes in the Cabinet.

It must, however, be said that the recognition of their right has lost much of its virtue by reason of the delay and has not removed this grievance. For the Scheduled Castes feel that their representation in the cabinet is very inadequate. In a Cabinet of 15, there is only 1 Member of the Scheduled Castes while the Muslims have 3 Members. The grievances arise by reason of the great contrast between the representation granted to the various communities and their needs and their numbers. If population alone was the criterion there is no doubt that the Scheduled Castes are very near to the Muslims in the matter of population. It is therefore only fair to say that if the

Muslims have three, the Scheduled Castes should at least have two in a Cabinet of fifteen. As it is, the communal formation of the Cabinet seems to be governed by no principle. The Sikhs who number only millions and the Untouchables who number 40 millions are placed on the same footing.

The position of the Scheduled Castes in Indian politics needs a great deal of stabilization, and there can be no doubt that the only effective remedy of stabilizing their position in Indian politics is to give them representation in the Cabinet which is demanded by their numbers and their needs. I am sure I am not disclosing any secrets when I say that in the course of the interview that I had with Sir Stafford Cripps when he came to India he told me that one of the principal objects of His Majesty's Government was to stabilize the position of the Scheduled Castes by their inclusion in the Central Executive which was to be formed during the interim period, so that the Constituent Assembly which under his proposals was to meet to draft the new constitution would find their positions established beyond challenge. I request that this policy should be given effect to when the next step in the direction of the Indianization of the Executive Council takes place.

Absence of Representation in the Public Services

No greater injustice has been done to the Scheduled Castes than in the matter of their employment in Public Services. Having regard to the scope of this Memorandum I can deal only with those Services with which the Central Government is particularly concerned. They fall into two classes:—

1. The I.C.S.
2. The Central Services—
   (i) Those recruited on an all-India basis, and
   (ii) those recruited locally.

Any one who examines the communal composition of these services can have no manner of doubt that the Scheduled Castes have been rigorously excluded from both those Services. To give an idea of the rigorous exclusion of the Scheduled Castes from these Services, I like to present the following facts. I will first take the position as it stands in the Indian Civil Service. The communal composition of the I.C.S. as it stands at present (1942) is as follows:—

Communal Composition of the I.C.S.

Community	Number in the I.C.S.
Europeans	488
Hindus	363
Muslims	109
Indian Christians	23
Anglo-Indians	9
Parsis	9
Sikhs	11
Scheduled Castes	1
Others	43
Total	1056

Out of 1,056 men in the I.C.S. there is only 1 from the Scheduled Castes. Such is the state of affairs so far as the I.C.S. is concerned.

In the matter of their recruitment to the central services the condition of the Scheduled Castes is equally bad. I do not propose to quote any figures. It is quite unnecessary to overburden this Memorandum with facts. For there is a clear admission on the part of the Home Department of the Government of India relating to this question. In one of their Office Memoranda relating to the recruitment of the different communities the Home Department say: 'This Department are much concerned at the almost total lack of progress in the recruitment of the members of the Depressed Classes as revealed by the information available.'

The Memorandum from which the above statement is quoted is No. 4/5/38 Ests (s) and is dated 1st June 1939 and records a state of affairs as it existed on that date.

How is it that other communities have found a place in the services controlled by the Government of India? What are the reasons for the exclusion of the Scheduled Castes? As will be seen the reasons are to be found in the difference in the principles and methods for securing communal representation which the Government of India has adopted towards the Scheduled Castes and the other minority communities in India.

The principle of communal representation in the services centrally controlled came into operation in 1925 when the Government of India accepted a Resolution of Mr. Nair on the need of Communal

Representation in Public Services moved in the Central Assembly on 10th March 1923 in which he complained that the Public Service was entirely monopolized by the Hindus, and particularly by the Brahmins, and that the other communities had found it extremely difficult to secure a footing. In pursuance of this Resolution the method adopted by the Government of India was to reserve one-third of all permanent vacancies for direct recruitment for the redress of communal inequalities.

This method of giving effect to the policy of Communal Representation in Public Services did not satisfy the non-Hindu communities. The matter was taken up at the Round Table Conference and a demand was made for devising a more effective method of gaining the object. This demand was accepted by the Secretary of State and by the Government of India and given effect to in Home Department Resolution No. F. 14–17–8–33 of 4th July 1934.

It is this resolution which is now in operation and constitutes the Magna Charta securing justice to all communities in the Public Services of the country. A reference to the provisions of this Resolution is very necessary. It will show why the other minority communities have been so well represented in the Public Services and why the Scheduled Castes have not been represented at all. The Resolution has two fundamental provisions and which, as compared with the old resolution of 1923, are quite new:

1. It declares what communities are to be treated as minorities for the purposes of recruitment to Public Services;
2. It defines a fixed proportion of annual vacancies which are to be allotted to the communities declared as minorities.

These are the provisions laid down by the Resolution of 1934 for securing representation to the various communities. Coming to particulars the Resolution in the first place defines the following communities as minorities:

(1) Muslims, (2) Anglo-Indians, (3) Indian Christians, (4) Sikhs, (5) Parsis.

In the second place, the Resolution fixes the following proportion of annual vacancies to be filled by members belonging to the above mentioned minorities.

What is the provision which this resolution makes to safeguard the position of the Scheduled Castes? I give below the two relevant provisions of the Resolution. In paragraph 3 the Resolution states that:—

Proportions Fixed by the Resolution of 4th July 1934

Minorities	Services			
	I.C.S. Central and Subordinate Services Recruited on All-India Basis	Railways and Customs	Posts and Telegraphs	Appraising Department and Preventive Services
Muslims	25%	25%	25%	This service is excluded from the operation of the Resolution, apparently to reserve recruitment for Anglo-Indians only on the ground that the Service requires special qualifications.
Anglo-Indians		8%	5%	
Indian Christians	8.1/3	6%	3½ %	
Sikhs	–	–	–	
Parsis	–	–	–	

Note: Para 7 (iii) of the said Resolution says—If communities obtain less than their reserved percentage and duly qualified candidates are not available, the residue of 8.1/3% will be available for Muslims.

No useful purpose will be served by reserving for them (Depressed Classes) a definite percentage of vacancies out of the number available for Hindus as a whole, but they hope to ensure that duly qualified candidates from the Depressed Classes are not deprived of fair opportunities of appointment.

The way in which Government hoped to ensure to the Scheduled Castes a fair share of representation in the Public Services is specified in para 7 (1) (vi) of the Resolution, which reads as follows:—

In order to secure fair representation for the Depressed Classes duly qualified members of these classes may be nominated to a Public Service even though recruitment to that service is being made by competition.

A perusal of these proposals brings out two facts:—
1. The Resolution does not declare the Scheduled Castes to be a minority.

2. The Resolution does not allot to the Scheduled Castes any fixed
   proportion of the annual vacancies.

It goes without saying that there is a striking contrast between the provisions
made by the Government of India for securing the recruitment of the Scheduled
Castes and for the other minor communities to the Public Services. This contrast
can be expressed in one sentence. The recruitment of the other communities
is owing to the Resolution, not left to be a matter of discretion. It has been
made a matter of obligation. The recruiting authority must fill in vacancy by
recruiting a person, belonging to the community for which the vacancy is
reserved. The recruitment of the Scheduled Castes on the other hand has been
made a mere matter of discretion. The recruiting authority may fill an unreserved
vacancy by appointing a person from the Scheduled Castes.

It is owing to this difference between must and may that the
Muslims and other communities have been so well represented in the
Public Services and the Scheduled Castes so completely excluded. No
better result is possible so long as the Government of India leaves the
matter of recruitment of the Scheduled Castes in Public Services to
the discretion and goodwill of the appointing officers. These officers
are Europeans, Hindus or Muslims. The European is blissfully ignorant
of the Scheduled Castes, and he has never made the protection of the
interests of the Scheduled Castes his special concern. So long as his
general authority is maintained he is prepared to follow the advice of
his Hindu or Muslim subordinates. The Muslims are naturally striving
to strengthen their own position. They are concerned to see that as
many vacancies as possible should go to the Muslims: at any rate all
those which are reserved to them. The Hindus who had so far the
monopoly in the Public Service and who never know how to share the
good things of life with others want to keep the balance to themselves.
With their self-interest combined with their age-old prejudices against
the Scheduled Castes the Hindus will never be fair to them. It is a sheer
delusion to leave to the discretion of such officers the question of the
recruitment of the Scheduled Castes and to hope that the Scheduled
Castes will as a result of it secure a fair share of representation.

The question of entry into the Public Service is an important question
for all minority communities. But to the Scheduled Castes it is a vital
question, a question of life and death. There are many reasons why this
must be so. In the first place, it is a question of opening up a career for
young men from the Scheduled Castes. This is an aspect of the question
which the Scheduled Castes, and even the Government of India,

cannot ignore. Trade and Industry, as openings for a career, are all blocked to young men of the Scheduled Castes. It is only in Government service that they can find a career. While this is an important aspect, it is not the only aspect which makes this question so vital. For there is another aspect which is calculated to invest it with such importance. That aspect relates to the effect which the bestowal of Government patronage has in encouraging the spread of education in a community. The case of the Hindu community is quite in point. The rapid progress which the Hindu community has made is of course very striking. But it is very seldom realized that the reason why education has taken such deep root in the Hindu society is entirely due to the assurance that education opens up a career by entry in Government service. Such assurance of career is absolutely necessary in the case of the Scheduled Castes who are so backward in education. There is a third argument far more weighty that the two which have been referred to above. It relates to the interest of the general population of the Scheduled Caste people as distinguished from the interests of the educated classes from the Scheduled Castes. This will be clear if it is realized how important public administration is from the point of view of public welfare. In the first place, power of administration now-a-days includes the power to legislate. No Statute in modern days is complete and exhaustive. Most allow the administration the statutory power to make rules to carry into effect the purposes of the Act. Secondly, whether the law is beneficial or not depends upon how efficaciously and how justly it is carried out. Good administration is therefore far more important than good laws. Good laws may prove of no avail if the administration is bad. Administration is therefore a vital question for the Scheduled Castes who are more interested in good administration than in good laws. Is the present administration good administration? What do the Scheduled Castes think of the present day administration? There can be no doubt that the view universally held is that the whole administration is hostile, unjust, and perverse in its attitude towards the Scheduled Castes all over India. Indeed much of the suffering and harassment of the Scheduled Caste population arises from the fact that the discretion vested in public servants is in almost all cases exercised against the interests of the Scheduled Castes and with the object of keeping them down. This is as it must be given the mentality of the Hindu and Muslim officers, towards the Scheduled Castes. This will continue to be so as long as the personnel of the administration is drawn from classes who have been opposed to the Scheduled Castes and who believe in their suppression. There cannot be a more powerful argument than that of the advantage and welfare of the general population of the Scheduled Castes to show that the entry of the Scheduled Castes in the Public Service must be regarded as a most vital consideration.

Certain facts are beyond doubt. The source of mischief is evident. How vital is the service interest of the Scheduled Castes is also clear. How serious is the mischief done to this vital interest by the discrimination which Government has in its resolution of 4th July, 1934 made against the Scheduled Castes as compared with the other communities nobody can dispute. How disastrous have been the consequences to the Scheduled Castes will be apparent from the figures given in the following table relating to the communal composition to the I.C.S.:

Table 3   Communal Proportion in the I.C.S. in 1942

Community	Total	Percentage of Total of 1056 including Europeans	Percentage of Total of 568 excluding Europeans
Europeans	488	42.4	–
Hindus	363	34.4	63.2
Muslims	109	10.3	19.2
Indian Christians	23	2.2	4.0
Anglo-Indians	9	.9	1.5
Parsis	9	.9	1.5
Sikhs	11	1.0	2.0
Scheduled Castes	1	Nil	Nil
Others	43	3.9	8.0
Total	1056	–	–

Table 4   I.C.S. Through Competition and Nomination

Communities	Through Competition	Through Nomination	Total
Europeans	336	152	488
Hindus	332	31	363
Muslims	35	74	109
Indian Christians	19	4	23
Anglo-Indians	8	1	9
Parsis	8	1	9
Sikhs	5	6	11
Scheduled Castes	–	1	1
Others	28	15	43
Total	771	285	1,056

Table 5   Population Ratio as Compared with Ratio in the I.C.S.

Communities	Actual Ratio in I.C.S Excluding Europeans	Population Ratio	Excess + Deficiencies of Service Ratio as Compared with Population Ratio
Hindus	63.2	50.0	+ 13.2
Muslims	19.2	23.6	−4.4
Indian Christians	4.0	1.0	+ 3.0
Anglo-Indians	1.5	.03	+ 1.47
Parsis	1.5	0.3	+ 1.47
Sikhs	2.0	1.3	+ 0.7
Scheduled Castes		13.5	−13.5
Others	8.0		

From these tables the following conclusions stand out as incontrovertible facts:

1. All communities have made a fair degree of progress towards getting their apportioned share of representation in the I.C.S. The only exception is the unfortunate community of the Scheduled Castes who have made no progress at all.

2. Some communities have secured a degree of representation in the I.C.S. much in excess of their population ratio. This is noticeable in the case of the Hindus. Excluding the share of the Europeans which is 50% and which must be excluded for comparing the relative position of the Indians the Hindus have got 63% of the I.C.S. appointments when the ratio of their population to the total population is only 50%. They are enjoying an excess of 13%.

3. Nomination was intended only to correct the inequities of competition. Yet some communities have been given the benefit of nomination although they have been able to secure a very large proportion of the I.C.S. appointments by competition and who do not need and cannot claim the benefit of nomination. This is undoubtedly the case with the Hindus. Between 1920–1942 the Hindus were able to secure 332 out of 435 seats that were filled by Indians by competition, and yet they were given 31 seats by nomination. The Muslims got only 35 appointments to the I.C.S. by competition between 1920–1942. But they were given 74 by nomination. The Sikhs have got only 5 by competition. But they got 6 by nomination. The Scheduled Castes who got none by competition get only one by nomination. All this shows how the position of the Scheduled Castes has remained deplorable and how

Government which is striving to be considerate to other communities by not even trying to be correct towards the Scheduled Castes, is responsible for this result.

The condition of the Scheduled Castes is not only deplorable, but it is also intolerable. This is the result of the present policy of the Government of India under which the quantum of recruitment of the Scheduled Castes in the Public Services instead of fixed by rule as is done in the case of the other minorities is left to the discretion of the appointing authorities. The appointing authorities are mostly caste-Hindus and it is not possible to expect them to give the benefit of this discretion to the Scheduled Castes. I have no doubt that the interests of the Scheduled Castes will continue to be neglected and sacrificed to serve the interests of other communities so long as the present system continues. The Government of India should without further delay equalize the position of the Scheduled Castes and—

1. declare that they are a minority for the purpose of services like the other communities.
2. fix 13.5 % as the proportion of annual vacancies in the I.C.S. and both in the Central Services that are recruited on an all India basis and that are recruited locally as the share to which they are entitled and which in equity and justice should be reserved for them.

Unless this is done the Scheduled Castes will never get their due share in Public Services.

The difficulty lies in the Scheduled Castes not being declared a minority. It is essential that this obstacle in their way be removed. The reason is that under the resolution of 4th July 1934 it is only when a community is declared to be a minority that it becomes entitled to the benefit of reservation in the Public Services. A community as such does not get any such benefit. It is difficult to see what objection there can be to a declaration that the Scheduled Castes are a minority. The term minority is a political term and whatever may be its *de jure* definition its *de facto* definition can never be in doubt. The matter is settled by the terms of Communal Award so that any community which is covered by the Communal Award of His Majesty's Government must be held to be a minority. Indeed that is the basis on which the Government of India could declare that the Muslims, Sikhs, Indian Christians, and Anglo-Indians are minorities. If these communities are minorities and they are minorities because they are covered by the Communal Award— then it is difficult to see how the claim of the Scheduled Castes to be declared a minority be denied. For, they too are covered by the same Award. Secondly, if Government is bound to declare them a minority then it follows as a natural consequence that Government is bound to define their share in the services and make it available by the same means and methods by which the share of other communities has been secured to them. Nor can anybody oppose the quantum of share to which they are entitled as the legitimate share of the Scheduled Castes. It has been shown that their population in British India is 13.6% and nothing more than a share of 13.6% in the services is claimed for them. This cannot injure the Hindus, for their population is 50% and they are getting 63% which is 13% more than is their due.

The opposition to this claim of the Scheduled Castes comes from very strange and unexpected quarters. It should come from the Hindus. But it cannot. The mutual rights of the Scheduled Castes and the Hindus are defined by the Poona Pact which was made in 1932. It is an agreement by which the Hindus have accepted that the Scheduled Castes are a minority and that they are entitled to adequate share in the Public Services of the Country. It is true that the term 'adequate' was not given a quantitative expression. That is because it was done in a hurry to save Mr. Gandhi from the hands of death. But there can be no doubt that 'adequate' was never intended to be anything less than the population ratio. The Hindus therefore cannot oppose the claim of the Scheduled Castes and, as a matter of fact, they do not. The party opposing the claim of the Scheduled Castes is the Government of India and nobody else. In the debate on the question that took place in the Central Legislative Assembly on March 1942 on a cut motion by Rao Bahadur N. Sivaraj, M.L.A. the claim of the Scheduled Castes for being declared a minority and for defining their share in services which was the subject matter of the Motion was supported by the Muslims, by the Europeans, Anglo-Indians and Sikhs. Except for one solitary individual, the Hindus did not oppose it. It was, however, opposed by the spokesmen of the Government of India. This is the most tragic part of the story. The Government of India have said that they were trustees for the welfare of the Scheduled Castes. As trustees, they should be more ready to safeguard the rights of the Scheduled Castes than to safeguard the rights of the other minorities. There would have been some excuse for the Government of India hesitating to allot to the Scheduled Castes their rights in the matter of recruitment to the Public Services if there was any obstacle placed in their way by the Hindus. But there is no such excuse. Would it be wrong if it was said that the enemies of the Scheduled Castes are not the Hindus and that their real enemy is the Government of India?

What is the reason which the Government of India gives for opposing the claim of the Scheduled Castes ? So far as the speech of the Hon'ble the Home Member made on the motion moved by the Hon'ble Rao Bahadur N. Sivaraj M.L.A., is an indication, the reason is that there are not enough educated men among the Scheduled Castes. It must be said that this is by no means a convincing reason. In the first place, this is the old reason given in 1934 in paragraph 3 of the Resolution. It takes no account of the progress that has been made during the last 8 years. In the second place, the statement was not true even for 1934. For 1942 it will be gross misstatement. As a matter of fact a census of college students of the Scheduled Castes was taken privately in about 1939–40, and the total number of graduates among the Scheduled Castes were found to number about 400 to 500. In the third place, this fact even if it were true cannot be a bar against declaring the Scheduled Castes a minority and against fixing their proportion. For if the Scheduled Castes candidates with minimum qualification fall short in any one year of the annual proportion of vacancies reserved for them nobody will be hurt because the unused vacancies will go to the Hindus. The difficulty anticipated by the Home Member cannot be said to arise only in the case of the Scheduled Castes. The condition of other minorities is not free from giving rise to the same difficulty. In fact when the government issued the resolution in 1934 they felt that such a difficulty might arise in their case also. But this did not stop Government from declaring them to be minorities and fixing their proportion. Government did declare them to be minorities and also fixed their proportion, and for the difficulty that duly qualified candidates may in any given year be less than the vacancies reserved. Government provided by paragraph 7 (1) (iii) of the resolution that the residue of the vacancies will be available for the Muslims.

Surely the difficulties which can be overcome successfully in the case of the other minorities cannot be allowed to stand in the way of the Scheduled Castes. If Government does that, it will be guilty of unjustly-defeating the just claims of the Scheduled Castes. It will be accused of using grounds which are not reasons but which are only excuses for sustaining its opposition to the claims of the Scheduled Castes.

Besides the two remedies suggested, namely (1) declaring them a minority and (2) fixing their proportion in the annual vacancies, it

will be necessary to sanction other remedies to the Scheduled Castes for securing to them their fair share in the services. They are:
1. Raising the Age bar.
2. Reduction in examination fees.
3. Appointment of a Scheduled Caste officer to see that the provisions made in the interests of the Scheduled Castes in this behalf are carried by all Departments concerned....

Absence of Representation on the Federal Public Service Commission

There are four members who at present constitute the Federal Public Service Commission. Of these, two are Europeans, one is a Hindu and one is a Mohamedan. The Scheduled Castes have been left out in framing the composition of the Federal Public Service Commission. There is no ground why they should be denied representation on the Federal Public Service Commission. There are three main sections of the people in India. Of these the Scheduled Castes form the third main section. The population of this section is measured in millions. Their interest in the service question is quite as important as those of the other two main sections of the population. The danger to their interests is no less real than to the interests of the other two sections. And the necessity of warding off that danger is much greater than it is in the case of the other two. Judged by any test it is difficult to justify the refusal to give representation to the Scheduled Castes on the Federal Public Service Commission. The Federal Public Service Commission has definitely been given a communal character. There can be only two conceivable reasons for doing this. In the first place it may be because it is desirable to have representatives of large sections of the people on the Commission. The second reason one can conceive of for giving communal composition to the Commission is to set off the communal bias of one community by the communal bias of the other community. Whichever way one looks at it, the omission to give representation to the Scheduled Castes on the Federal Public Service Commission is sheer injustice. The Scheduled Castes cannot have any confidence in a Public Service Commission which is infected by the point of view of the Hindus and the Muslims who with all their quarrels can very easily unite to distribute the loaves and fishes among themselves and to keep out the Scheduled Castes from getting their due share. It is difficult to prove that the Commission has been unjust to the Scheduled Castes though the fact remains that not a single Scheduled Caste candidate has so far been certified by the Commission to be fit. For no Commission can be convicted of partiality. It is open to every Commission to take shelter under that most elusive term 'unsuitable'. That term far from giving an explanation is intended to cover a multitude of sins. Justice requires that the Scheduled Castes should get representation on the Federal Public Service Commission which is their due.

PART II. EDUCATIONAL GRIEVANCES

Want of Assistance for Advanced Education
Looking at the growth of Advanced Education among the Scheduled Caste boys, the following conclusions are deducible:—
1. That education in Arts and Law is progressing satisfactorily.
2. That education in Science and Engineering has made no progress.
3. That Advanced Education in foreign Universities is a very far cry.

This sad situation needs to be properly appreciated. As was said in discussing the question of the entry of the Scheduled Castes in the Public Services the welfare of the Scheduled Castes depends entirely upon a sympathetic Public Service and that the Public Service if it is to be sympathetic must be representative of the different elements in the national life of the country, and particularly of the Scheduled Castes. To this it must be added that the representation of the Scheduled Castes if it is confined to ministerial posts will be of no consequence no matter how numerous are the posts they are permitted to occupy. This may be good from the standpoint of providing a career for educated young men. It cannot affect the condition of the Scheduled Castes. The status and condition of the Scheduled Castes will be improved only when the representatives of the Scheduled Castes come to occupy Executive posts as distinguished from ministerial posts. Executive posts are strategic posts, posts from which a new direction can be given to the affairs of the State. The attainment of Executive post it is obvious requires a high degree of education. Such posts will not be open except to those who have acquired advanced education.

Education in Arts and Law cannot be of much value to the Scheduled Castes either to the graduates themselves or to the people. It has not been of very high value even to Hindus. What will help the Scheduled

Castes is education of an advanced type in Science and Technology. But it is obvious that education in Science and Technology is beyond the means of the Scheduled Castes and this is why so many of them send their children to take up courses in Arts and Law. Without Government assistance, the field of Advanced Education in Science and Technology will never become open to the Scheduled Castes, and it is only just and proper that the Central Government should come forward to aid them in this connection.

This problem will be solved if the following proposals are accepted by the Government of India:

1. An annual grant of Rs. 2 lakhs for scholarships for Scheduled Caste students taking science and Technology courses tenable at the Universities or other Scientific and Technical Training Institutions in India.

2. An annual grant of one lakh of rupees to be spent on scholarships for the education of Scheduled Caste students of Science and Technology in foreign Universities in England, the Dominions, in Europe and in America.

There is nothing to prevent the Government of India from undertaking this responsibility. Education it is true is not a Central subject for legislative purposes. Still, Section 150 (2) of the Government of India Act says that the Central Government may make grants for any purpose, notwithstanding that the purpose is not one with respect to which the Central Legislature may make laws. This power has been used by the Government of India to support Educational Institutions....

The scheme if it is given effect to will revolutionize the condition and status of the Scheduled Castes. The Scheduled Castes lay great store by it. They would even be prepared for the scheme being made a loan system rather than a system of grants. The Scheduled Caste boys who receive these scholarships shall be glad to take advantage of it even if they are required to refund the sums received by them when they are employed or they may be made to serve the Government for a term under a lower scale of salary. There can be no objection to Government accepting these proposals.

For the purpose of assisting Advanced Scientific and Technical Education among the Scheduled Caste students I am making two other proposals. One is to make:

PROVISION FOR SCHEDULED CASTE STUDENTS IN THE SCHOOL OF MINES

The Government of India has under its control the Indian School of Mines which is located at Dhanbad. The school provides high grade instructions in Mine Engineering and in Geology. The training given in the Indian School of Mines is calculated to train men who can serve in the coal mining industry and other mineral industries in India. The number of students that are at present taking instructions in the Indian School of Mines are about 97. The school is open to students from all parts of India. From enquiries made it is established that out of the 97 students there is not a single one from the Scheduled Castes. It is very necessary that some special measures should be taken by the Government of India to see that the students belonging to the Scheduled Castes are in a position to take advantage of the Indian School of Mines. To achieve this object it will be necessary:

1. To reserve a certain number of seats for the Scheduled Caste boys having the minimum standard of education required for admission.
2. The grant of free-ships.
3. The grant of scholarships.

It will not be too much to claim that one-tenth of the total number of admissions should be reserved for the Scheduled Castes. This is a matter which falls within the scope of the Labour Department. But it is a question which concerns also the Finance Department in as much as the free-ships and scholarships would mean the loss of revenue to the State. But the loss on account of these measures will not be very great. The annual fee on an average which a student has to incur in the School of Mines is about 60 rupees a month which would mean a monthly expense of Rs. 60 per student.

The other proposal which I wish to make is to give *representation to the Scheduled Castes on the Central Advisory Board of Education.*

The constitution of the Board consists of—

1. The Honourable Member in charge of the Department of Education, Health and Lands (Chairman);
2. The Educational Commissioner with the Government of India;
3. Ten nominees of the Government of India, of whom one at least shall be a woman;
4. One member of the Council of State elected by the Council of State;
5. Two members of the Legislative Assembly elected by the Legislative Assembly.

6. Three members of the Inter-University Board, India, nominated by the Inter-University Board of India.

7. A representative of each local Government, who shall be either the Minister in charge of Education (or his deputy) or the Director of Public Instruction (or his deputy) or such other person as the Provincial Government may nominate in this behalf.

The functions of the Board are:—

(a) To advise on any educational question which may be referred to it by the Government of India or by local Government.

(b) To call for information and advice regarding educational developments of special interest and value to India; to examine this information and to circulate it with recommendations to the Government of India and to local Governments.

From the functions of the Board it is quite clear that the board can study the educational problem of the Scheduled Castes as that of special interest and frame recommendations and advice Central and Provincial Governments in that connection. Such a thing can be of immense importance in focusing the attention of the Governments and the Universities on the spread of higher education among the Scheduled Castes.

It is, however, necessary in the first place to get the Board interested in the educational problem of special classes like the Scheduled Castes. This can be done only by giving representation to members of the Scheduled Castes on the Board. It is therefore suggested that two representatives of the Scheduled Castes should be nominated on the board.

Want of Facilities for Technical Training Technical Education

From the point of raising the economic condition, technical education for the Scheduled Castes is more important than literary education. But technical education is also very costly and it is not possible for children of the Scheduled Castes to take technical education, and without technical education their economic condition will not be improved. Owing to the social system of the Hindus, the Scheduled Castes occupy economically a very low place in the Indian economy. In times of prosperity he is last to be employed, and in times of depression he is first to be discharged. This, of course, is a result of the social prejudices of the Hindus which operate against him. But there is also the other difficulty which stands in his way and that is he is generally an unskilled labourer with no technical knowledge.

It seems to me that the Government of India can do a great deal to improve his lot by enabling him to acquire technical skill which he does not now possess and this can be easily done by introducing a system of apprenticeship for the Scheduled Caste boys in undertakings run or controlled by the Government of India, in which the possibilities of giving such technical training do exist.

I am referring only to two:—

(1) Apprenticeships in Government Printing Presses:
There are a number of Printing Presses which are maintained by the Government of India. There are so many skilled occupations which are open to persons trained in a printing press—compositors, printers, binders, etc. There is no reason why the Government of India should not have a scheme whereby suitable boys from the Scheduled Castes may be taken as apprentices to learn the various occupations which are related to the printing trade.

(2) Apprenticeships in Railway Workshops:
The Railways in India, most of which are owned by the Government of India, also maintain workshops where fitters, carpenters and other technicians are employed, and I do not know whether the Railway Department have schemes of taking apprentices to be trained as technicians to be subsequently employed on the Railways. But even if such a scheme was not in existence it is necessary to have one for the benefit of the Scheduled Castes.

I therefore suggest the scheme of apprenticeship whereby / annually a good number of boys from the Scheduled Castes should be given training in the printing press and the Railway Workshops. The cost of it cannot be very great.

PART III. OTHER GRIEVANCES

Neglect in the Matter of Publicity
It is quite well known that the Government of India engages itself very largely in giving publicity to the sayings and doings of different individuals and parties who represent the main forces operating in India. As an illustration of this I would refer to the Volume called 'India and the Aggressor' (*The Trend of Indian Opinion Between* 1935–40) issued by the Bureau of Public Information of the Government of

India. The name of the Volume is very misleading. It has nothing to do with the Aggressor. It is a collection of sayings and doings of the Political Parties and Politicians in the country and presents a full resume of the views of the majority and minority in India.

Now the most annoying part of this volume is the complete neglect of the sayings and doings of the Scheduled Castes. Out of the 940 pages, 158 pages are given to the Congress, 85 pages are allotted to the Muslims. The Hindu Mahasabha and the Hindu League are given about 10 pages. The Liberal Federation has received 16 pages. The Sikhs are spread over 6 pages, Indian Christians over 2 pages and the Scheduled Castes are disposed of in about 3 pages and what is surprising is that in these 3 pages devoted to the Scheduled Castes the material which is included is of a trifling character. It omits altogether to take notice of some of the most important events that have taken place during this period and important pronouncements made by leading individuals from the Scheduled Castes. I may mention only one such event viz., the movement for conversion. Beyond question it was a movement which shook the Hindu Society to its very foundations and attracted the notice of the whole world. To emphasize the trumpery sort of publicity given to the Scheduled Castes in this volume it is enough to say that the St. Mary's College, Kurseong, once undertook to give publicity to the cause of the Scheduled Castes and has as a result published material covering the same period and which fills a Volume of 507 pages. So vast have been the forces and movements affecting and emanating from the Scheduled Castes during this period of 1935–40. As to myself, I must have made many pronouncements touching the Scheduled Castes. Not one of them however finds a place in this Volume.

It is true that this Volume is intended for official use only. But in my opinion this fact does not alter the great value which the compilation must necessarily have. It goes without saying that it is the mind of the Official which is, to a large degree, responsible for determining the direction which the affairs of the State will take. It also determines the value which he ought to give to issues in which communal interests are involved. It also goes without saying that the attitude and the mind of the Official is bound to be determined by the kind of material which is presented to him and on which he feeds in a Volume like this. Further, the degree of publicity given to a cause by Government in a Government publication may be treated by him as the value which government attaches to it and as a direction for him for evaluating the needs and claims of different communities. Looked at from this point of view this Volume is sure to give to the Officers working in the Central Secretariat as well as in the Provincial Governments and even to the Secretary of State the impression that the Government of India regards the Scheduled Castes as a negligible force not worth bothering about. That this is the effect which this volume has produced is evident from the speech delivered in Parliament by the Secretary of State where the references to the Muslims are emphatic and positive while the references to the Scheduled Castes are just of a parenthetical character. It is a grievous wrong done to the Scheduled Castes whose cause has received a setback at a most critical period in their struggle by reason of this unbalanced presentation of their case on the part of Government. I would press that the Bureau of Public Information be asked to prepare a supplement to the Volume which it has issued giving full space to movements carried on by the Scheduled Castes and the pronouncements their leaders have made.

Of course, Government may say that it is not bound to do publicity work for parties and communities, and that the parties and communities may do their own publicity. But that is not the case here. The Government of India, as I have shown, does engage itself very much in this work of publicity. And when a Government does it, it is bound to treat all parties on equal footing in the matter of publicity and give a true and correct picture of the movements and forces operating in the country.

Closed-door in Government Contracts

A good part of Government needs in Public Works is carried out not departmentally but by contracts. This is so in normal times. In war times the work done for Government by the contract system has expanded several hundred fold. I can speak only of the Central Public Works Department. The list of approved contractors maintained by the Central Public Works Department is 1,171. Of these, I am told, there is only one contractor belonging to the Scheduled Castes. The rest of them are Hindus, Sikhs and Muslims. It should be possible for Government to arrange things in such a manner as to make its contract system allow an open door to members of all communities to profit by it. There are many persons of the Scheduled Castes who could be trusted to carry out a Government contract. Already many members of the Scheduled Castes are working as employees of Hindus, Muslim or Sikh contractors. The result is that the Hindu, Muslim or Sikh contractors are taking profit while the Scheduled Caste men are working on a mere wage.

There is not much difficulty in getting a certain number of men from the Scheduled Castes put on the list of approved contractors. But what is important is to enable them to get a contract. There are two rules in the matter of Government contracts:—

1. That a contract is to be given generally to a contractor whose tender is the lowest;

2. That Government is not bound to accept the lowest tender.

It is therefore, a matter of discretion which is exercised by the Officer in charge whether a contract will go to a particular contractor or not. This discretion is not likely to be exercised in favour of a Scheduled Caste contractor. His tender may be the lowest but owing to communal prejudice he may not accept it and rely on the second rule 'that he is not bound to accept the lowest'. If his tender is higher than the lowest, he will not accept it although he is free to do so. He will rely on the first of the two rules. Either way he will have his justification for rejecting the tender of the Scheduled Caste contractors.

There is of course, no remedy against communal bias. The only thing that strikes me that we can do is to amend the rule by saying that a tender of a Scheduled Caste contractor, if it is not higher than the lowest by 5 per cent, shall be deemed to be the lowest. This, of course, involves financial loss and the Finance Department will have to agree to it. I cannot give any idea of the approximate cost of such a concession. I am sure it will not be so heavy as to break the camel's back.

Part IV. Duty of Government Towards Distressed People

Some of the proposals submitted in this Memorandum on behalf of the Scheduled Castes, particularly those which are put forth to remove political grievances, do not involve any financial burden on the public treasury. They are really not proposals so much as political demands which, by reason of their logic and their justice, Government must grant. The difficulty arises only with regard to the acceptance of those proposals which involve a financial burden upon the revenues of the Central Government. Financial burden there is. But, it will not do to reject them merely on that account. For there can be no doubt that Government has a duty towards the Scheduled Castes, and if they accept their duty in this behalf they are bound to discharge it even if it involves a certain amount of financial burden on the public purse.

The policy of the British Government towards the Scheduled Castes has been one of complete and continuous neglect. It began from the very beginning when the British Government realized that its duty was not merely to maintain law and order, and extended to giving the people education and looking after their welfare. This will be clear from the following quotations from *the report of the Board of Education of the Bombay Presidency for the year 1850–51:—*

... Question as to Educating Low Castes

Paragraph 21. The practical conclusion to be drawn from these facts which years of experience have forced upon our notice, is that a very wide door should be opened to the children of the poor higher castes, who are willing to receive education at our hands. But here, again, another embarrassing question arises, which it is right to notice. If the children of the poor are admitted freely to Government Institutions what is there to prevent all the despised castes—the Dheds, Mahars, etc., from flocking in numbers to their walls?

Social Prejudices of the Hindus

Paragraph 22. There is little doubt that if a class of these latter were to be formed in Bombay they might be trained, under the guiding influence of such Professors and masters as are in the service of the Board, into men of superior intelligence to any in the community: and with such qualifications, as they would then possess, there would be nothing to prevent their aspiring to the highest offices open to Native talent—to Judgeships, the Grand Jury, Her Majesty's Commission of the Peace. Many benevolent men think it is the height of illiberality and weakness in the British Government to succumb to the prejudices which such appointments would excite into disgust amongst the Hindu community, and that an open attack should be made upon the barriers of caste.

Wise Observations of the Honourable Mount Stuart Elphinstone Cited

Paragraph 23. But herewith wise reflections of Mr. Elephinstone, the most liberal and large minded administrator who has appeared this side of India, point out the true rule of action. 'It is observed,' he says, 'that the missionaries find the lowest caste the best pupils; but we must be careful how we offer any special encouragement to men of that description; they are not only the most despised, but among the least numerous of the great divisions of society and it is to be feared that if our system of education first took root among them, it would never spread further, and we might find ourselves at the head of a new class, superior to the rest in useful knowledge, but hated and despised by the castes to whom these new attainments would always induce us to prefer them. Such a state of things would be desirable, if we were contented to rest our power on our army or on the attachment of a part of the population but is inconsistent with every attempt to found it on a more extended basis.'

Such is the antagonism towards the Scheduled Castes with which began Government's policy of giving education to Indians. This policy was firmly applied. There is a case on record of a Mahar (Untouchable) boy who in 1856 petitioned to the Government of India for being admitted to a Government school in the Dharwar District. The following is the text of the resolution issued by the Government:

The question discussed in the correspondence is one of very great practical difficulty.

1. There can be no doubt that the Mahar petitioner has abstract justice in his side; and Government trust that the prejudices which at present prevent him from availing himself of existing means of education in Dharwar may be ere long removed.

2. But Government is obliged to keep in mind that to interfere in prejudices of ages in a summary manner, for the sake of one or few individuals, would probably do a great damage to the cause of education. The disadvantage under which the petitioner labours is not one which has originated with this Government, and it is one which Government cannot summarily remove by interfering in his favour as he begs them to do.

In 1882 Government of India appointed the Hunter Commission to examine the Educational Policy. This Commission made a number of important proposals to spread education among Muslims. With regard to the Untouchables it did nothing. All that it did was to express an opinion that 'Government should accept the principle that nobody be refused admission to Government College or School merely on the ground of caste,' but qualified it by saying that the principle should 'be applied with due caution.'

This antagonism when it passed away, its place was taken up by negligence and indifference. This negligence and indifference made its appearance not merely in the field of education. It also made its appearance in other fields, particularly in the Army. The whole Army of the East India Company consisted of the Depressed Classes. Indeed but for the Depressed Classes Army the British would never have been able to conquer India. The Untouchables continued to fill the Army till

1892. In 1892 their recruitment in the army was stopped all of a sudden and they were thrown in the street in utter distress with no education and no means to pursue other ways of honourable living.

Who can raise the Scheduled Castes from the distress in which they are now grovelling? It is certain they cannot do it by their own effort. Their resources are too scanty to afford them the means to raise themselves. They cannot depend upon the charity of the Hindus. The charity of the Hindus is beyond question communal in its scope and its benefits are confined to those who belong to the community of the donor. The Hindu donors are either businessmen or high State officials. The tragedy is that they make their money out of the general public. But when it comes to a question of doing charity they forget the public and remember their own caste and their community. The Scheduled Castes have neither of these sources available to them and they are rigorously excluded from the charity founded by both. The only source therefore on which they can rely is financial aid from Government. I venture to say that it is the duty of the Central Government to come to the rescue of people who are in distress by no fault of theirs as is the case with the Scheduled Castes. The Central Government is bound to take steps to assist the Scheduled Castes to concede their just claims and to compete on more equal terms with their competitors. There is nothing extraordinary in asking the Central Government to pay special attention to improve the condition of the Scheduled Castes....

20

Problem of the Untouchables of India*
1 September 1943

THE POLITICAL DEMANDS OF THE UNTOUCHABLES

The problem of the Untouchables is an enormous problem. As a matter of fact I have been for some time engaged on a work dealing with this problem which will run into several hundred pages. All that I can do within the limits of this paper is to set out in a brief compass what the nature of the problem is and the solution which the Untouchables have themselves propounded. It seems to me that I cannot do better than begin by drawing attention to the following Resolutions which were passed at the All-India Scheduled Castes Conference held in the city of Nagpur on the 18th and 19th July 1942:—

Resolution No. II: Consent Essential to Constitution
This Conference declares that no constitution will be acceptable to the Scheduled Castes unless,
1. It has the consent of the Scheduled Castes.
2. It recognises the fact that the Scheduled Castes are distinct and separate from the Hindus and constitute an important element in the national life of India.
3. Contains within itself provisions which will give to the Scheduled Castes a real sense of security under the new constitution and which are set out in the following resolutions.

Resolution No. III: Essential Provisions in the New Constitution
For creating this sense of security in the Scheduled Castes; this Conference demands that the following provisions shall be made in the new Constitution:
1. That in the budget of every provincial Government an annual sum as may be determined upon by agreement be set apart for promoting the primary education among the children of the Scheduled Castes and another annual

*BAWS 1990, vol. 9: 396–433.

sum for promoting advanced education among them, and such sums shall be declared to be the first charge on the revenues of the Province.

2. That provision shall be made by law for securing representation to the Scheduled Castes in all Executive Governments—Central and Provincial—the proportion of which shall be determined in accordance with their number, their needs and their importance.

3. That provision shall be made by law for securing representation to the Scheduled Castes in the Public Services the proportion of which shall be fixed in accordance with their number, their needs and their importance. This Conference further insists that in the case of security services such as Judiciary, Police and Revenue, provision shall be made that the proportion fixed for the Scheduled Castes shall, subject to the rule of minimum qualification, be realized within a period of ten years.

4. That provision shall be made by law for guaranteeing to the Scheduled Castes representation in all Legislatures and Local bodies in accordance with their number, needs and importance.

5. That provision shall be made by law whereby the representation of the Scheduled Castes in all Legislatures and Local Bodies shall be by the method of Separate Electorates.

6. That provision shall be made by law for the representation of the Scheduled Castes on all Public Service Commissions, Central and Provincial.

Resolution No. IV: Separate Settlements

It is the considered opinion of this conference,

1. That so long as the Scheduled Castes continue to live on the outskirts of the Hindu village, with no source of livelihood and in small number as compared to Hindus, they will continue to remain Untouchables and subject to the tyranny and oppression of the Hindus and will not be able to enjoy free and full life.

2. That for the better protection of the Scheduled Castes from the tyranny and oppression of the caste-Hindus, which may take a worse form under Swaraj which cannot but be a Hindu Raj.

3. To enable the Scheduled Castes to develop to their fullest manhood, to give them economical and social security as also to pave the way for the removal of untouchability.

This Conference has after long and mature deliberation come to the conclusion that a radical change must be made in the village system now prevalent in India and which is the parent of all the ills from which the Scheduled Castes are suffering for so many centuries at the hands of the Hindus. Realizing the necessity of these changes this conference holds that along with the Constitutional changes in the system of Government there must be a change in the village system now prevalent, made along the following lines:

1. The constitution should provide for the transfer of the Scheduled Castes from their present habitation and form separate Scheduled Caste villages away from and independent of Hindu village.
2. For the settlement of the Scheduled Castes in new villages a provision shall be made by the constitution for the establishment of a Settlement Commission.
3. All Government land which is cultivable and which is not occupied shall be handed over to the Commission to be held in trust for the purpose of making new settlements of the Scheduled Castes.
4. The Commission shall be empowered to purchase new land under the Land Acquisition Act from private owners to complete the scheme of settlement of Scheduled Castes.
5. The constitution shall provide that the Central Government shall grant to the Settlement Commission a minimum sum of Rupees five crores per annum to enable the Commission to carry out their duty in this behalf.

HINDU OPPOSITION

The demands set forth in those resolutions fall into three categories (1) Political, (2) Educational and (3) Economic and Social.

Taking the political demands first it is obvious that they ask for three safeguards:—

1. That the Legislature shall not be merely representative of the people but it shall be representative separately of both categories Hindus as well as Untouchables.
2. That the Executive shall not be merely responsible to the Legislature, which means to the Hindus, but shall also be responsible both to the Hindus as well as to the Untouchables.
3. That the administration shall not be merely efficient but shall also be worthy of trust by all sections of the people and also of the Untouchables and shall contain sufficient number of representatives of the Untouchables holding key positions so that the Untouchables may have confidence in it.

These political demands of the Untouchables have been the subject matter of great controversy between the Untouchables and the Hindus. Mr. Gandhi, the friend of the Untouchables, preferred to fast unto death rather than consent to them and although he yielded he is not reconciled to the justice underlying these demands. It will be well if I set out at this stage what the Hindu or the Congress Scheme of representative Government is. It is as follows:—

1. The Legislature to be elected by Constituencies which are to be purely territorial.
2. The Executive to be drawn solely from the majority party in the Legislature.
3. The Administration to be run by a Public Service based entirely upon considerations of efficiency.

The Hindus of the Congress describe their own pet scheme as a National Scheme and call the scheme put forth by the Untouchables as the Communal Scheme. As I will show, there is no substance in this distinction. It is a case of damning what you do not like by the easy method of giving it a bad and a repelling name. Such tactics can't give strength to a case which is inherently weak. To expose its weakness let me examine the merits of the so-called National Scheme. Before proceeding it might be desirable to note the points of agreement and the points of difference between the two. Both have the same object, inasmuch as both stand for a representative Legislature. The point of difference lies in the method of devising a scheme which will make the Legislature a truly representative Legislature. The so-called national scheme insists upon the territorial constituency as being both proper and sufficient for producing a representative Legislature in India. What is called the Communal Scheme denies that a territorial constitution can produce a truly representative Legislature in India in view of the peculiar social structure of the Indian Society as it exists today. The issue can a purely territorial constituency produce a really representative Legislature in India? It is round this issue that the controversy has centered.

The so-called National Scheme of the Hindus generally appeals to the Westerner and he prefers it to the so-called Communal Scheme. This is largely because the Westerner knows and is accustomed only to the system of territorial constituency. But there can be no doubt that this so-called National Scheme is on merits quite unsound and on motives worse than communal.

That it is unsound will be quite obvious to any one who will stop to examine the assumptions which are involved in the alleged efficacy and sufficiency of the territorial constituency. What are these assumptions? To mention only those which are most important,

1. It assumes that the majority of voters in a constituency represents the will of the constituency as a whole.
2. That it is enough to take stock of the general will of the constituency as expressed by the majority and that the will of any particular section however much it may be in conflict with the will of the majority may be ignored without remorse and without being guilty of any inequity.
3. That the representative who is elected by the voters will represent the wishes and interests of the voters and that there is not the danger of the representative allowing the interest of his class to dominate and override the interests and wishes of the voter who elects him.

Every one of these assumptions is a false assumption unjustified by any theory and, unsupported by experience. The history of Parliamentary Government furnishes abundant proof in support of this assertion and even the history of England tells the same tale. It is wrong to suppose that the majority in all circumstances can be trusted to represent the will of all sections of people in the constituency. As a matter of fact it can never do so to any satisfactory degree. If at all, it can only give a very pale reflection of the general will and even that capacity for pale reflection must depend upon how numerous and varied are the interests which are consciously shared by the different sections of the constituency and how full and free is the interplay between them. It is obvious that where, as in India, there are no interests which are shared, where there is no full and free interplay and where there are no common cycles of participation for the different sections, one section large or small cannot represent the will of the other. The will of the majority is the will of the majority and nothing more and no amount of logical ingenuity can alter the fact and to give effect to it is to allow full play to the tyranny of the majority.

Again it is wrong to suppose that the representative elected to the Legislature will represent the wishes of the voters who elect him and forget or subordinate the interests of the class to which he belongs. The case of the representative is a case of divided loyalties. He is confronted with two—rather with three—conflicting duties (1) a duty to himself, (2) a duty to the class to which he belongs, and (3) a duty to the voters who have elected him. Omitting the first from our consideration it is common experience that the representative prefers the interests of his class to that of his voters. And why should any one expect him to act otherwise? It is in the nature of things that a man's self should be nearer to him than his constituency. There is a homely saying that man's skin sits closer to him than his shirt. To the members of the Legislature it is true more often than not that his class is his skin and the constituency is a shirt which it is unnecessary to say is one degree removed than the skin.

The Hindu therefore in relying upon the territorial constituency is seeking to base the political structure of India upon foundations which all political architects have declared to be unsound. The territorial constituency has long since been regarded even in European countries as a discredited piece of political mechanism. In great many European countries the representative system based on territorial constituency has been wound up and replaced by other systems of Government largely because the territorial system of representation produced neither good Government nor efficient Government. In other countries where representative institutions have survived there is an acute discontent with the result produced by the system of territorial constituencies. The proposals for occupational and functional representation, the proposals for referendum and recall all furnish proof, if proof is really wanted, that there is a great body of enlightened and intelligent opinion which is definitely against the system of territorial constituency.

In these circumstances the question as to why the Hindu insists upon a political mechanism which is discredited everywhere excites a certain amount of curiosity. The reason he gives is that it is the only mechanism which is consistent with nationalism. I am not convinced that this is the real explanation. The real explanation to my mind is very different. The Hindu prefers the territorial constituency because he knows that it will enable him to collect and concentrate all political power in the hands of the Hindus, and who can deny that his calculation is incorrect? In a purely territorial constituency the contest, the Hindu knows, will be between a huge majority of Hindu voters and a small minority of Untouchable voters. Given this fact the Hindu majority—if it is a purely territorial constituency—is bound to win in all constituencies. But the Hindus besides relying upon their majority can also rely upon other factors which cannot but work to strengthen that majority. Those factors have their origin in the peculiar nature of the Hindu Society. The Hindu Social system which places communities one above the other is a factor which is bound to have its effect on the result of voting. By the Hindu Social system the Communities are placed in an ascending scale of reverence and a descending scale of contempt. It needs no prophet to predict what effect these social attitudes will have on voting. No caste-Hindu will cast a vote in favour of an Untouchable candidate, for to him he is too contemptible a person to go to the Legislature. On the other hand there will be found many voters among the Untouchables who would willingly cast their votes for a Hindu candidate in preference to an Untouchable candidate. That is because he is taught to revere the former more than himself or his Untouchable kinsmen. I am not mentioning the other means which are often resorted to for catching votes of the poor, illiterate, unconscious, unorganized body of voters which the Untouchables are. A combination of all these circumstances is bound to work in the direction of augmenting the representation of the Hindus. Under a system of purely territorial constituencies it is quite certain the Hindus will have assured to them a majority. They can draw for their majority upon themselves as well as upon the Untouchables. It is equally certain that the Untouchables will lose all seats. They must; firstly because they are a minority, and secondly because the Hindus can successfully exploit the weaknesses of the Untouchables which makes them offer their votes to the Hindus as one offers burnt meat to his gods.

Understood in the light of these forces which are sure to make the territorial constituency profitable to the Hindus by enabling them to loot the political power which the Untouchable would become possessed of if the Communal Scheme came into operation, there can be no doubt that the National Scheme is from the result side, if not from the motive side, worse than the Communal Scheme.

Joint v/s Separate Electorates

The Hindus have after a long struggle accepted the view that a purely territorial constituency will not do in a country like India. In a sense the previous discussion regarding the controversy between territorial constituency and communal constituency as two rival methods of bringing about a truly representative Legislature was unnecessary. But I stated the case for and against because I felt that the foreigners who are not aware of Indian political conditions ought to know the basic conceptions underlying that controversy. Unfortunately, however, the fact is that although the Hindus have accepted the basic argument in favour of communal scheme of representation they have not accepted all what the Untouchables are demanding. The Untouchables demand that their representation shall be by Separate Electorates. A Separate Electorate means an electorate composed exclusively of Untouchable voters who are to elect an Untouchable as their representative to the Legislature. The Hindus agree that certain number of seats are to be reserved for Untouchables to be filled only by Untouchables. But they insist that the Untouchable who is to be the representative of the Untouchables in the Legislature should be elected by a mixed electorate consisting both of the Hindus as well as of the Untouchables and not by an electorate exclusively of the Untouchables. In other words there is still a controversy over the question of joint versus Separate Electorates. Here again I want to set out the pros and cons of this controversy. The objection to Separate Electorate raised by the Hindus is that Separate Electorate means the fragmentation of the nation. The reply is obvious. First of all, there is no nation of Indians in the real sense of the word. The nation does not exist, it is to be created, and I think it will be admitted that the suppression of a distinct and a separate community is not the method of creating a nation. Secondly, it is conceded—as the Hindus have done—that Untouchables should be represented in that Legislature by Untouchable then it cannot be denied that the Untouchable must be a true representative of the Untouchable voters. If this is a correct position then Separate Electorate is the only mechanism by which real representation can be guaranteed to the Untouchables. The Hindu argument against Separate Electorate is insubstantial and unsupportable. The premises on which the political demands of the Untouchables are based are admitted by the Hindus. Separate Electorate is only a consequence which logically follows from those premises. How can you admit the premise and deny the conclusion? Special electorates are devised as a means of protecting the minorities. Why not permit a minority like the Untouchables to determine what kind of electorate is necessary for its protection? If the Untouchables decide to have Separate Electorates why should their choice not prevail? These are questions to which the Hindus can give no answer. The reason is that the real objection to Separate Electorates by the Hindus is different from this ostensible objection raised in the name of a nation. The real objection is that Separate Electorate does not permit the Hindus to capture the seats reserved for the Untouchables.

Name of the Constituency	Total number of seats for Hindus	Seat reserved for the Untouchables	Total No. of Hindu voters	Total No. of Untouchable voters	Ratio of Hindu voters to Untouchable voters
1. Madras City South	2	1	40,626	2,577	16 to 1
2. Chicacole	2	1	83,456	5,125	16 to 1
3. Vijayanagram	2	1	47,594	996	49 to 1
4. Amalapuram	1	1	52,805	7,760	7 to 1
5. Ellore	1	1	51,795	5,155	9 to 1
6. Bandar	1	1	84,191	8,723	10 to 1
7. Tenali	2	1	1,32,107	5,732	24 to 1

On the other hand the Joint Electorate does. Let me illustrate the point by a few examples of how joint and Separate Electorate would work in the constituency. Take the following constituencies from the Madras Presidency.

The figures of the voting strength given in the above table for the seven constituencies taken at random in the Madras Presidency are illuminating. A scrutiny of the above figures is sufficient to show any disinterested person that if there is a Separate Electorate for the Untouchables in these seven constituencies they would be in a position to elect a man in whom they had complete confidence and who would be independent to fight the battle of the Untouchables on the floor of the Legislature against the representatives of the Hindus. If, on the other hand, there is a Joint Electorate in these constituencies the representative of the Untouchables would be only a nominal representative and not a real representative, for no Untouchable who did not agree to be a nominee of the Hindus and a tool in their hands could be elected in a Joint Electorate in which the Untouchable voter was outnumbered in ratio of 1 to 24 or in some cases 1 to 49. The Joint Electorate is from the point of the Hindus to use a familiar phrase a 'rotten borough' in which the Hindus get the right to nominate an Untouchable to set nominally as a representative of the Untouchables but really as a tool of the Hindus. It will be noticed that the Hindu in opposing the so-called Communal Scheme of the Untouchables with his so-called National Scheme is not fighting for a principle nor is he fighting for the nation. He is simply fighting for his own interests. He is fighting to have in his hands the undivided control over political power. His first line of defence is not to allow any shares to be drawn up so that like the Manager of the Hindu joint family he can use the whole for his benefit. That is why he fought for purely territorial constituencies. Failing that he takes his second line of defence. He wants that if he is made to concede power he must not lose control over it. This is secured by Joint Electorates and frustrated by Separate Electorates. That is why the Hindu objects to Separate Electorates and insists on Joint Electorates.

The end of the so-called National Scheme may not be communal but the result undoubtedly is.

The Executive

The second political demand of the Untouchables is that they must not only be represented in the Legislature but they must also be represented in the Executive. This demand is also opposed by the Hindus. The argument of the Hindus takes two forms. One is that the Executive must represent the majority of the Legislature and secondly the men in the Executive must be competent to hold places in the Executive. I propose to deal with the second argument first.

It is an argument which is fundamentally sound. But it is equally necessary to realize that in a representative Government this argument cannot be carried too far. For as Professor Dicey has argued, 'It has never been a primary object of constitutional arrangement to get together the best possible parliament in intellectual capacity. Indeed, it would be inconsistent with the idea of representative Government to attempt to form a parliament far superior in intelligence to the mass of the nation.'

The stress upon competency is needless. Nobody has said that ignorant people should be made Ministers simply because they are Untouchables. Given the right to representation in the cabinet the Untouchables, there is no doubt, will elect the most competent people amongst them—there are a number of them in every province—to fill those places. Again why apply this limiting condition to the Untouchables only? Like the Untouchables the Muslims are also claiming the right to be represented in the cabinet. Why have the Hindus not insisted upon such a limiting condition against the Muslims' claim? This shows that the objection of the Hindus is not based on reason. It is an excuse.

Coming to the second argument the Hindus are simply misusing the words majority and minority. They seem to forget that majority, and minority are political categories. As political categories there is no fixed majority or a fixed minority. Political majorities and political minorities are fluid bodies and what is a majority today may become a minority tomorrow, and what is a minority today may become a majority tomorrow. The difference between the Hindus and the Untouchables cannot be said to be a difference of this sort. There is no endosmosis between the Untouchables and Hindus as there is between the majority and minority. There is another characteristic of a majority and minority relationship which would make them inapplicable to the relationship which subsists between the Hindus and the Untouchables. The majority and minority are divided by a difference only—difference in the point of views. They are not separated by a fundamental and deadly antagonism as the Hindus are from the Untouchables. There is a third characteristic of majority and minority relationship which is not to be found in the relationship that subsists between the Hindus and the Untouchables. A minority grows into a minority and a majority in becoming a majority absorbs so much of the sentiment of the minority that the minority is satisfied with the result and does not feel the urge of fighting out the issue with the majority. Now all these considerations are quite foreign to the relationship between the Hindu majority and the Untouchable minority. They are fixed as permanent communities. They are not merely different but they are antagonistic. To speak of them as majority and minority would be as true and as useful as it would be to speak of the Germans being a majority and the French being a minority.

Public Services

The Untouchables demand that a certain proportion of posts in the Public Services of the country shall be reserved for them, subject to the rule of minimum qualification. The Hindus object to this demand as they do to the other demands of the Untouchables. The stand they take is that the interests of the State require that capacity, efficiency and character should be the only consideration and that caste and creed should have no place in making appointment to public offices. There is no dispute regarding character as a necessary qualification. Nor is there any dispute regarding capacity and efficiency. The only point of dispute, and it is a very important point, is whether caste and creed should form a consideration which must be taken into account in the recruitment for Public Services. Relying upon the educational qualification as the only test of efficiency, the Hindus insist that public offices should be filled on the basis of competitive examinations open to persons of all castes and creeds. They argue that such a system serves both purposes. It serves the purpose of efficiency. Secondly it does not prohibit the entry of the Untouchables in the Public Services of the country.

The Hindus seek to give to their opposition to the demand of the Untouchable an appearance of fairness by relying upon efficiency and competitive examination. Here again the argument is quite beside the point. The question is not whether the competitive system of examination is or is not the proper method of getting efficient persons in Public Services. The question is whether the competitive system simply because it is open to all castes and creeds will enable the Untouchables to get a footing in the Public Service. That depends upon the educational system of the State. Is it sufficiently democratic? Are the facilities for education sufficiently widespread and sufficiently used to permit persons from all classes to come forth to compete? Otherwise, even with the system of open competition large classes are sure to be left out in the cold. This basic condition is conspicuous by its absence in India. Higher education in India is the monopoly of Hindus and particularly of high caste-Hindus. By reason of Untouchability the Untouchables are denied the opportunity for Education. By reason of their poverty higher education necessary for higher posts in the Public Service—and higher posts in the Public Service are the only things that matter because they have a strategic value—is not within their reach. The State will not take the financial responsibility of giving them higher education—they are demanding it by their resolution—and the Hindus will not extend the benefit of their charities to the Untouchables—Hindu charity being shamefully communal—so that to ask the Untouchables to rely upon the results of competitive examination for entry into the Public Services is to practise a fraud upon them. The position taken up by the Untouchables is in no sense unreasonable. They admit the necessity for maintaining efficiency. That is why in their resolution they themselves say that their demand shall be subject to the rule of minimum qualification. In other words what the Untouchables demand is that a minimum qualification should be prescribed for every post in the Public Service and if two persons apply for such a post and the Untouchable has the minimum qualification he should be preferred to a Hindu even though the Hindu may have a qualification higher than the minimum qualification. It, of course, does mean that the basis for appointment should be minimum qualification and not the highest qualification. This may sound queer to those who do not mind if their test of efficiency gives certain communities a monopoly in Public Service. But did not Campbell-Bannerman say that self-government was better than good government? What else are the Untouchables demanding? They are prepared to recognize the need of having an efficient Government. That is why they are ready to accept the requirement of minimum qualifications for entry in the Public Services of the country. What the Untouchables are not prepared to do is to forego self-government for good government. Good government based on highest qualification will be a communal government, for the Hindus alone can claim qualifications higher than minimum qualifications. This is what they do not want. What they say is that minimum qualifications are enough for efficient government and since it makes self-government possible, minimum qualification should be the rule for entry in Public Service. It ensures self-government as well as efficient government.

SEPARATE SETTLEMENTS

Resolution No. IV referred to in the foregoing part of this paper is to my mind quite self-explanatory and not much detailed comment is necessary to explain its purport. Nor is it possible in the compass of this short paper to deal with it in more than general terms. The demand for separate settlements is the result of what might be called 'The New Life Movement' among the Untouchables. The object of the movement is to free the Untouchables from the thralldom of the Hindus. So long as the present arrangement continues it is impossible for the Untouchables either to free themselves from the yoke of the Hindus or to get rid of their untouchability. It is the close-knit association of the Untouchables with the Hindus living in the same villages which marks them out as Untouchables and which enables the Hindus to identify them as being Untouchables. India is admittedly a land of villages and so long as the village system provides an easy method of marking out and identifying the Untouchable, the Untouchable has no escape from untouchability. It is the village system which perpetuates untouchability and the Untouchables therefore demand that it should be broken and the Untouchables who are as a matter of fact socially separate should be made separate geographically and territorially also, and be grouped into separate villages exclusively of Untouchables in which the distinction of the high and the low and of Touchable and Untouchable will find no place.

The second reason for demanding separate settlements arises out of the economic position of the Untouchables in the village. That their condition is most pitiable no one will deny. They are a body of landless labourers who are entirely dependent upon such employment as the Hindus may choose to give them and on such wages as the Hindus may find it profitable to pay. In the villages in which they live they cannot engage in any trade or occupation, for owing to untouchability no Hindu will deal with them. It is therefore obvious that there is no way of earning a living which is open to the Untouchables so long as they live as a dependent part of the Hindu village. This economic dependence has also other consequences besides the condition of poverty and degradation which proceeds from it. The Hindu has a code of life, which is part of his religion. This code of life gives him many privileges and heaps upon the Untouchable many indignities which are incompatible with the sanctity of human life. By the New Life Movement which has taken hold of the Untouchables, the Untouchables all over India are fighting against the indignities and injustices which the Hindus in the name of their religion have heaped upon them. A perpetual war is going on every day in every village between the Hindus and the Untouchables. It does not see the light of the day. The Hindu Press is not prepared to advertise it lest it should injure the cause of their freedom in the eyes of the world. The silent struggle is however a fact. Under the village system the Untouchable has found himself greatly handicapped in his struggle for free and honourable life. It is a contest between the economically and socially strong Hindus and an economically poor and socially small group of Untouchables. That the Hindus most often succeed in pulling down Untouchables is largely due to many causes. The Hindu has the Police and the Magistracy on his side. In a quarrel between the Untouchables and the Hindus the Untouchables will never get protection from the Police or justice from the Magistrate. The Police and the Magistracy are Hindus, and they love their class more than their duty. But the chief weapon in the armoury of the Hindus is economic power which they possess over the poor Untouchables living in the village. The economic processes by which the Hindus can hold down the Untouchables in their struggle for equality are well described in the Report made by a Committee appointed by the Government of Bombay in 1928 to investigate into the grievances of the Depressed Classes and from which the following extracts are made. It illuminates the situation in a manner so simple that even foreigners who do not know the mysteries of the Hindu social system may understand what tyranny the Hindus can practise upon the Untouchables. The committee said:

Although we have recommended various remedies to secure to the Depressed Classes their rights to all public utilities we fear that there will be difficulties in the way of their exercising them for a long time to come. The first difficulty is the fear of open violence against them by the orthodox classes. It must be noted that the Depressed Classes form a small minority in every village, opposed to which is a great majority of the orthodox who are bent on protecting their interests and dignity from any supposed invasion by the Depressed Classes at any cost. The danger of prosecution by the Police has put a limitation upon the use of violence by the orthodox classes and consequently such cases are rare.

The second difficulty arises from the economic position in which the Depressed Classes are found today. The Depressed Classes have no economic independence in most parts of the Presidency. Some cultivate the lands of the orthodox classes as their tenants at will. Others live on their earnings as farm labourers employed by the orthodox classes and the rest subsist on the food or grain given to them by the orthodox classes in lieu of service rendered to them as village servants. We have heard of numerous instances where the orthodox classes have used their economic power as a weapon against those Depressed Classes in their villages, when the latter have dared to exercise their rights, and have evicted them from their land, and stopped their employment and discontinued their remuneration as village servants. This boycott is often planned on such an extensive scale as to include the prevention of the Depressed Classes from using the commonly used paths and the stoppage of sale of the necessaries of life by the village Bania. According to the evidence, sometimes small causes suffice for the proclamation of a social boycott against the Depressed Classes. Frequently it follows on the exercise by the Depressed Classes of their right to the use of the common well, but cases have been by no means rare where a stringent boycott has been proclaimed simply because a Depressed Class man has put on the sacred thread, has bought a piece of land, has put on good clothes or ornaments, or has carried a marriage procession with the bride-groom on the horse through the public street.

This demand for separate settlements is a new demand which has been put forth by the Untouchables for the first time. It is not possible to say as yet as to what attitude the Hindus will take to this demand. But there is no doubt that this is the most vital demand made by the Untouchables, and I am sure that whatever may happen with regard to the other demands they are not likely to yield on this. The Hindus are prone to think that they and the Untouchables are joined together by the will of God as the Bible says the husband is joined to his wife and they will say in the language of the Bible that those whom God is pleased to join let no man put asunder. The Untouchables are determined to repudiate any such view of their relations with the Hindus. They want the link to be broken and a complete divorce from the Hindus effected without delay.

The only questions that arise are those of the cost it will involve and time it will take. As to cost, the Untouchables say it should be financed by Government. It will no doubt fall for the most part on the Hindus. But there is no reason why the Hindus should not bear the same. The Hindus own everything. They own the land in this country. They control trade, and they also own the State. Every source of revenue and profit is controlled by them. Other communities and particularly the Untouchables are just hewers of wood and drawers of water. The social system helps the Hindus to have a monopoly of everything. There is no reason why they should not be asked to pay the cost of this scheme when they practically own the country.

As to time, it matters very little even if the transplantation of the Untouchables to new settlements takes 20 years. Those who have been the bounden slaves of the Hindus for a thousand years may well be happy with the prospect of getting their freedom by the end of 20 years.

CASTE AND CONSTITUTION

It might well be asked why should such questions as are raised by these demands of the Untouchables find a place in the Constitution? Nowhere in the world have the makers of constitution been compelled to deal with such matters. This is an important question and I admit that an answer is required on the part of those who raise such questions and insist that they are of constitutional importance. The answer to this question is to my mind quite obvious. It is the character of the Indian Society which invests this question with constitutional importance. It is the caste system and the religious system of the Hindus which is solely responsible for this. This short statement may not suffice to give an adequate explanation to foreigners of the social and political repercussions of the Hindu caste and religious systems. But it is equally true that in the brief compass of this paper it is impossible to deal exhaustively with the repercussion of the caste system on the constitution. I would refer for a full and complete exposition of the subject to my book on the *Annihilation of Castes* which I wrote some time ago. For I believe it will shed sufficient light on the social and economical ramification of the caste and religious system of the Hindus. In this Paper I will content myself with making the following general observations in framing a constitution the social structure must always be kept in mind. The political structure must be related to the social structure. The operation of the social forces is not confined to the social field. They pervade the political field also. This is the viewpoint of the Untouchables and I am sure this is incontrovertible. The Hindus are quite conscious of this argument and also of its strength. But what they do is to deny that the structure of the Hindu society is in any way different from the structure of European society. They attempt to meet the argument by saying that there is no difference between the caste system of the Hindus and the class system in Western society. This is of course palpably false and, discloses a gross ignorance both of the caste system as well as of the class system. The caste system is a system which is infested with the spirit of isolation and in fact it makes isolation of one caste from another a matter of virtue. There is isolation in the class system but it does not make isolation a virtue nor does it prohibit social intercourse. The class system it is true produces groups. But they are not akin to caste groups. The groups in the class system are only non-social while the castes in the caste system are in their mutual relations definitely and positively anti-social. If this analysis is true then there can be no denying the fact that the social structure of Hindu society is different and consequently its political structure must be different. What the Untouchables are asking, to put it in general terms is a proper correlation of means to ends. End may be the same. But because the end is the same it does not follow that the means must also be the same. Indeed ends may remain the same and yet means must vary according to time and circumstances. Those who are true to their ends must admit this fact and must agree to adopt different means if they wish that the end they have in view is not stultified.

In this connection there is another thing which I would like to mention. As I have said, it is the caste basis of Hindu Society which requires that its political structure should be different and suited to its social structure. There are people who admit this but argue that caste can be abolished from Hindu society. I deny that. Those who advocate such a view think that caste is an institution like a club or a municipality or a County Council. This is a gross error. Caste is religion, and religion is anything but an institution. It may be institutionalized but it is not the same as the institution in which it is embedded. Religion is an influence or force suffused through the life of each individual moulding his character, determining his actions and reactions, his likes and dislikes. These likes and dislikes, actions and reactions are not institutions which can be lopped off. They are forces and influences which can be dealt with by controlling them or counteracting them. If the social forces are to be prevented from contaminating politics and perverting it to the aggrandizement of the few and the degradation of the many then it follows that the political structure must be so framed that it will contain mechanisms which will bottle the prejudices and nullify the injustice which the social forces are likely to cause if they were let loose.

So far I have explained in a general way why the peculiar social structure of the Hindu Society calls for a peculiar political structure and why the marker of the Indian Constitution cannot escape problems which did not plague the makers of Constitution in other countries. Let me now take the specific question, namely why it is necessary that in the Indian Constitution the Communal Scheme must find its place and why in the Public Services for the Untouchables it should be specified and should be assigned to them as their separate possession. The justification for these demands is easy and obvious. It arises from the undeniable fact that what divides the Untouchables from the Hindus is not mere matter of difference on non-essentials. It is a case of fundamental antagonism and antipathy. No evidence of this antipathy and antagonism is necessary. The system of untouchability is enough evidence of the inherent antagonism between the Hindus and the Untouchables. Given this antagonism it is simply impossible to ask the Untouchables to depend upon and trust the Hindus to do them justice when the Hindu gets their freedom and independence from the British. Who can say that the Untouchable is not right in saying that he will not trust the Hindu? The Hindu is as alien to him as a European is and what is worse the European alien is neutral but the Hindu is most shamefully partial to his own class and antagonistic to the Untouchables. There can be no doubt that the Hindus have all these ages despised, disregarded and disowned the Untouchables as belonging to a different and contemptible strata of Society if not to a different race. By their own code of conduct the Hindus behave as the most exclusive class steeped in their own prejudices and never sharing the aspirations of the Untouchables with whom they have nothing to do and whose interests are opposed to theirs. Why should the Untouchables entrust their fate to such people? How could the Untouchables be legitimately asked to leave their interest into the hands of a people who as a matter of fact are opposed to them in their motives and interests, who do not sympathize with the living forces operating among the Untouchables, who are themselves not charged with their wants, cravings and desires, who are inimical to their aspirations, who in all certainty will deny justice to them and discriminate against them and who by reason of the sanction of their religion have not been and will not be ashamed to practise against the Untouchables any kind of inhumanity. The only safety against such people is to have the political rights which the Untouchables claim as safeguards against the tyranny of the Hindu majority defined in the Constitution. Are the Untouchables extravagant in demanding this safety?

21

Communal Deadlock and How to Solve it*
6 May 1945

Mr. President,
I am indeed very grateful for your kind invitation to address the Annual Session of the All-India Scheduled Castes Federation. ...

Ordinarily, at a gathering such as this I would have spoken—and our people would expect me to speak—on any one of the social and political problems of the Scheduled Castes. But I do not propose to engage myself in a discourse on so sectarian a subject. Instead, I propose to speak on a topic, which is general and has a wider appeal, namely the shape and form of the future Constitution of India.

It may be as well for me to explain the reasons for my decision. For the moment, the responsibility for leading the movement of the Scheduled Castes and facing its day-to-day problems does not lie on my shoulders. On account of my office I am out of it and I have no desire to take it up. That is one reason why I do not propose to take up a sectarian subject which is related only to the Scheduled Castes. ...

PROPOSALS FOR SOLUTION OF THE COMMUNAL PROBLEM

Having made my position clear on certain preliminary points, I will now proceed to deal with the subject. The Communal Problem raises three questions:
1. The question of representation in the Legislature;
2. The question of representation in the Executive; and
3. The question of representation in the Services.

Representation in Public Services
To take the last question first or, this. This can hardly be said to be a subject of controversy. The principle that all communities should be represented in the Public Services in a prescribed proportion and no

single community should be allowed to have a monopoly has been accepted by the Government of India. This principle has been embodied in the Government of India Resolutions of 1934 and 1943 and rules to carry it out have been laid down. It has even prescribed that any appointment made contrary to the rules shall be deemed to be null and void. All that is necessary is to convert administrative practice into statutory obligation. This can be done by adding a Schedule to the Government of India Act, which will include the provisions contained in these Resolutions and similar provisions for the different provinces and make the Schedule a part of the Law of the Constitution.

Representation in the Executive

This question raises three points:
1. The quantum of representation in the Executive;
2. The nature of the Executive;
3. The method of filling the places in the Executive.

Quantum of Representation

For the solution of this question, the principle which should be adopted is that the representation of the Hindus, the Muslims and the Scheduled Castes should be equal to the quantum of their representation in this Legislature.

With regard to the other minorities such as the Sikhs, Indian Christians and Anglo-Indians, it is difficult to give them representation in the Executive in strict proportion to their representation in the Legislature. This difficulty arises largely from the smallness of their numbers. If they are to get representation in the Executive exact proportion to their numbers, the Executive would have to be enlarged by a fantastic degree. All that can be done, therefore, is to reserve a seat or two for them in the Cabinet for their representation and to establish a convention that they will get a fair portion of representation in the corps of Parliamentary Secretaries ... when the new Constitution comes into existence.

Nature of the Executive

In the Constitution of the Executive, I would propose the adoption of following principles:
1. It must be recognized that in a country like India where there is a perpetual antipathy between the majority and the minorities and

on which account the danger of communal discrimination by majority against minorities forms an ever-present menace to the minorities, the Executive power assumes far greater importance than the legislative power.

2. In view of (1) above, the system under which party which has secured a majority at the poll is deemed entitled to form a Government on the presumption that it has the confidence of this majority is untenable in Indian conditions. The majority in India is a communal majority and not a political majority. That being the difference, the presumption that arises in England cannot be regarded as a valid presumption in the conditions of India.

3. The Executive should cease to be a Committee of the majority party in the Legislature. It should be so constituted that it will have its mandate not only from the majority but also from the minorities in the Legislature.

4. The Executive should be non-Parliamentary in the sense that it shall not be removeable before the term of the Legislature.

5. The Executive should be Parliamentary in the sense that the members of the Executive shall be chosen from the members of the Legislature and shall have the right to sit in the House, speak, vote and answer questions.

METHOD OF FILLING PLACES

In this connection, I would propose the adoption of the following principles:

1. The Prime Minister as the Executive head of the Government should have the confidence of the whole House.

2. The person representing a particular minority in the Cabinet should have the confidence of the members of his community in the Legislature.

3. A member of the Cabinet shall not be liable to be removed except on impeachment by the House on the ground of corruption or treason.

Following those principles, my proposal is that the Prime Minister and the members of the Cabinet from the majority community should be elected by the whole House by a single transferable vote and that the representatives of the different minorities in the Cabinet should

be elected by a single translatable vote of the members of each minority
community in the Legislature.

Representation in the Legislature
This is the most difficult question. All other questions depend upon
the solution of this question. It raises two points:
1. The quantum of representation; and
2. The nature of the electorate....

PRINCIPLES UNDERLYING THE PROPOSALS

I may now proceed to state the principles on which this distribution
has been made. They are:
1. Majority rule is untenable in theory and unjustifiable in practice.
   A majority community may be conceded a relative majority of
   representation but it can never claim an absolute majority.
2. The relative majority of representation given to a majority community
   in the Legislature should not be so large as to enable the majority to
   establish its rule with the help of the smallest minorities.
3. The distribution of seats should be so made that a combination of
   the majority and one of the major minorities should not give the
   combine such a majority as to make them impervious to the interest
   of the minorities.
4. The distribution should be so made that if all the minorities
   combine they could, without depending on the majority, form a
   government of their own.
5. The weightage taken from the majority should be distributed among
   the minorities in inverse proportion to their social standing, economic
   position and educational condition so that a minority which is large
   and which has a better social, educational and economic standing
   gets a lesser amount of weightage than a minority whose numbers
   are less and whose educational, economic and social position is
   inferior to that of the others.

If I may say so, the representation is a balanced representation. No
one community is placed in a position to dominate others by reason
of its numbers. The Muslim objection to the Hindu majority and the
Hindu and Sikh objections to the Muslim majority are completely
eliminated, both in the Centre as well as in the Provinces.

Nature of the Electorate

With regard to the question of electorates the following propositions should be accepted:

1. Joint Electorate or Separate Electorate is a matter of machinery for achieving a given purpose. It is not a matter of principle.
2. The purpose is to enable a minority to select candidates to the Legislature who will be real and not nominal representatives of the minority.
3. While Separate Electorate gives an absolute guarantee to the minority, that its representatives will be no others except those who enjoy its confidence, a system of Joint Electorates which will give equal protection to the minorities should not be overlooked.
4. A four-member constituency, with a right to the minorities to have a double vote and requiring a minimum percentage of minority votes, may be considered as a possible substitute.

Matters Not Covered

Question of Special Safeguards

There are other demands made on behalf of particular minorities such as:

1. Provision of a Statutory Officer to report on the condition of minorities.
2. Statutory provision of State aid for education, and
3. Statutory provision for land settlement. But they are not of a communal character, I do not therefore wish to enlarge upon them here.

Aboriginal Tribes

It will be obvious that my proposals do not cover the Aboriginal Tribes although they are larger in number than the Sikhs, Anglo-Indians, Indian Christians and Parsees. I may state the reasons why I have omitted them from my scheme. The Aboriginal Tribes have not as yet developed any political sense to make the best use of their political opportunities and they may easily become mere instruments in the hands either of a majority or a minority and thereby disturb the balance without doing any good to themselves. In the present stage of their development it seems to me that the proper thing to do for these backward communities is to establish a Statutory Commission to administer what are now called the 'excluded areas' on the same basis as was done in the case of the South African Constitution. Every Province in which these excluded areas are situated should be compelled to make an annual contribution of an amount for the administration of these areas.

Indian States

It will also be noticed that my proposals do not include the Indian States. I am not opposed to the inclusion of the Indian States, provided the terms and conditions of inclusion are such—

1. that the dichotomy of divided sovereignty between British India and Indian States is completely done away with,
2. that the judicial and political boundaries which separate British India from Indian States will disappear, that there will be no such entities as British India or Indian States and in their place there will be only one entity namely India, and
3. that the terms and conditions of inclusion do not prevent India from having full and plenary powers of a Dominion. I have worked out a scheme for the fusion of the Indian States and British India, which will permit the realization of these objects. I do not wish to overburden this address with the details of the plan. For the moment, it is better if British India marches to her goal without complicating its progress by an entanglement with the Indian States....

A WORD TO HINDUS

Much of the difficulty over the Communal Question is due to the insistences of the Hindus that the rule of majority is sacrosanct and that it must be maintained at all costs. The Hindu does not seem to be aware of the fact that there is another rule, which is also operative in fields where important disputes between individual and nations arise and that rule is a rule of unanimity. If he will take the trouble to examine the position he will realize that such a rule is not a fiction, but it does exist. Let him take the Jury System. In the jury trial the principle is unanimity. The decision is binding upon the judge only if the verdict of the jury is unanimous. Let him take another illustration that of the League of Nations. What was the rule for decisions in the League of Nations? The rule was a rule of unanimity. It is obvious that if the principle of unanimity was accepted by the Hindus as a rule of decision in the Legislature and in the Executive there would be no such thing as a Communal Problem in India.

One may well ask the Hindu that if he is not prepared to concede constitutional safeguards to the minorities, is he prepared to agree to the rule of unanimity? Unfortunately he is not prepared to accept either.

About the rule of majority the Hindu is not prepared to admit any limitations. The majority he wants is an absolute majority. He will not be satisfied with relative majority. He should consider whether his insistence on absolute majority is fair proposition, which political philosophers can accept. He is not aware that even the constitution of the United States does not lend support to the absolutistic rule of majority rule on which the Hindu has been insisting upon.

Let me illustrate the point from the constitution of the United States. Take the clause embodying Fundamental Rights. What does that clause mean? It means that matters included in Fundamental Rights are of such supreme concern that a mere majority rule is not enough to interfere with them. Take another illustration also from the Constitution of the United States. The Constitution says that no part of the Constitution shall be altered unless the proposition is carried by three-fourths majority and ratified by the States. What does this show? It shows that the United States Constitution recognizes for certain purposes, mere majority rule is not competent.

All these cases are of course familiar to many a Hindu. The pity of it is, he does not read from them the correct lesson. If he did, he would realize that the rule of the majority rule is not as sacrosanct a principle as he thinks it is. The majority rule is not accepted as a principle but is tolerated as a rule. I might also state why it is tolerated. It is tolerated for two reasons; (1) because the majority is always a political majority and (2) because the decision of a political majority accepts and absorbs so much of the point of view of the minority that the minority does not care to rebel against the decision.

In India, the majority is not a political majority. In India the majority is born; it is not made. That is the difference between a communal majority and a political majority. A political majority is not a fixed or a permanent majority. It is a majority which is always made, unmade and remade. A communal majority is a permanent majority fixed in its attitude. One can destroy it, but one cannot transform it. If there is so much objection in a political majority, how very fatal must be the objection to a communal majority?

It may be open to the Hindus to ask Mr. Jinnah, why in 1930 when he formulated his fourteen points he insisted upon the principle of majority rule to such an extent that one of the fourteen points stipulated that in granting weightage limits should be placed whereby a majority shall not be reduced to a minority or equality. It may be open to the Hindus to ask Mr. Jinnah if he is in favour of a Muslim majority in Muslim Provinces, why he is opposed to a Hindu majority in the Centre? The Hindu must however realize that these posers may lead to the conclusion that Mr. Jinnah's position is inconsistent. They cannot lead to the affirmation of the principle of majority rule.

The abandonment of the principle of majority rule in politics cannot affect the Hindus very much in other walks of life. As an element in social life they will remain a majority. They will have the monopoly of trade and business which they enjoy. They will have the monopoly of the property which they have. My proposals do not ask the Hindus to accept the principle of unanimity. My proposals do not ask the Hindus to abandon the principle of majority rule. All I am asking them is to be satisfied with a relative majority. Is it too much for them to concede this?

Without marking any such sacrifice the Hindu majority is not justified in representing to the outside world that the minorities are holding up India's Freedom. This false propaganda will not pay. For the minorities are doing nothing of the kind. They are prepared to accept freedom and the dangers in which they likely to be involved; provided they are granted satisfactory safeguards. This gesture of the minorities is not to be treated as a matter for which Hindus need not be grateful. It may well be contrasted with what happened in Ireland. Mr. Redmond, the leader of the Irish Nationalists once told Carson, the leader of Ulster, 'Consent to United Ireland, ask for any safeguard and they shall be granted to you'. He is reported to have turned round and said: 'Damn your safeguards; we don't want to be ruled by you'. The minorities in India have not said that. They are ready to be satisfied with safeguards. I ask the Hindus is this not worth a mass? I am sure it is.

Conclusion

These are some of the proposals I have had in mind for the solution of the Communal Problem. They do not commit the All-India Scheduled Castes Federation. They do not even commit me. In putting them forth, I am doing nothing more than exploring a new way. My emphasis is more on the principle, I have enunciated, than on the actual proposals. If the principles are accepted then I am sure the solution of the Communal Question will not be as baffling as it has been in the past.

The problem of solving the Indian deadlock is not easy. I remember reading a historian describing the condition of Germany before the Confederation of 1867 as one of 'Divinely Ordained Confusion'. Whether that was true of Germany or not, it seems to me that they form a very accurate description of the present conditions of India. Germany did get out of this confusion, if not at one stroke at least by successive stages until just before the war she became a unified people, unified in mind, unified in outlook and unified by belief in a common destiny. India has not so far succeeded in evolving order out of her confusion. It is not that she had no opportunities to do so. In fact, there have been quite a number. The first opportunity came in 1927, when Lord Birkenhead gave a challenge to Indians asking them to produce a constitution for India. That challenge was taken up. A committee was formed to frame a constitution. A constitution was produced and was known as 'The Nehru Constitution'. It was, however, not accepted by Indians and was buried without remorse. A second opportunity presented itself to *Indians in 1930,* when they assembled at the Round Table Conference. There again Indians failed to play their part and write out their own Constitution. A third attempt is the one recently made by the Sapru Committee. The proposals of this committee too have fallen flat.

There is neither enthusiasm nor optimism left to indulge in another attempt. One is perused by a sense of fatality, which suggests that as every attempt is doomed to failure, none need be made. At the same time I feel that no Indian ought to be so down hearted or so callous as to let the deadlock stink, as though it was a dead dog, and say that he is prepared to do nothing more than be a mere witness to the political dog-fight that is going on in this country. The failures of the past need not daunt anybody. They do not daunt me. For, I have a feeling that though it is true that all attempts to reach an agreement on the communal question have failed, the failures have been due not so much to any inherent fault of the Indians as they have been due to a wrong approach. I feel confident that my proposals, if considered dispassionately, should be found acceptable. They constitute a new approach and as such I commend them to my countrymen.

Before I conclude, I must, however, warn my critics that they may be able to amend my proposals in some respects; but it will not be easy to reject them. If they do reject them, the first thing they shall have to do is to controvert the principles on which they are based.

22

Proposal for the Representation of Scheduled Castes in the Executive Council*
7 June 1945

New Delhi

Dear Lord Wavell,

I am grateful to you for asking me in my capacity as the leader of the Scheduled Castes to be a member of the Conference which you propose to call in furtherance of your proposal for the Indianization of the Executive Council. I told you, for reasons which I need not repeat here, that I am unable to accept your offer. Thereupon you desired me to name a substitute. Though I have expressed my disapproval with your proposals, I do not wish to deny you such help as you may derive from the presence of a Scheduled Castes representative in your Conference. I am, therefore, prepared to suggest a substitute. Judging on the suitability of various names that occur to me, I cannot think of any other name than that of Rao Bahadur N. Sivaraj, B.A., B.L. He is the President of the All India Scheduled Castes Federation and is also a member of the Central Legislative Assembly and of the National Defence Council. If you like, you may invite him to the Conference as a representative of the Scheduled Castes.

There is one other matter to which I feel I must draw your attention right now. It relates to the extreme inadequacy of the representation given to the Scheduled Castes in His Majesty's Government's proposals for the reconstitution of the Executive Council. Five seats to 90 millions of Muslims, one seat to 50 millions of Untouchables and 1 seat to 6 millions of Sikhs is a strange and sinister kind of political arithmetic which is revolting to my ideas of justice and common sense. I cannot be a party to it. Measured by their needs, the Untouchables should get as much representation as the Muslims, if not more. Leaving needs

*BAWS 2003, vol. 17, no. 2: 167–70.

aside and taking only numbers the Untouchables should get at least three. Instead, they are offered just one in a Council of fifteen. This is an intolerable position.

This is a matter to which I drew your attention at the meeting of the Executive Council held on the 5th June when you explained His Majesty's Government's proposals to the Council. At the meeting of the 6th morning you replied to the criticisms offered by Members of Council the previous evening on the merits of the proposals. I naturally expected that you would also deal with the point I had raised. But to my great surprise you completely ignored it and made no reference to it whatever. It could not be that I was not emphatic enough. For I was more than emphatic. The conclusion I draw from your omission to refer to it is that either you did not think the matter to be of sufficient importance to deserve your notice or that you thought that I had no intention beyond lodging a protest. It is to remove this impression and to tell you in quite unmistakable terms that I propose to take definite action if His Majesty's Government fail to redress the wrong. Therefore I feel the necessity of writing this letter.

I would not have felt as hurt as I do if such a proposal had come from the Congress or the Hindu Mahasabha. But it is a decision by His Majesty's Government. Even the general Hindu opinion is in favour of increased representation to the Scheduled Castes both in the Legislature and in the Executive. To take the proposals of the Sapru Committee as an indication of general Hindu opinion, the proposal of His Majesty's Government must be admitted to be retrograde. For this is what the Sapru Committee has said:—

the representation given to the Sikhs and Scheduled Castes in the Government of India Act is manifestly inadequate and unjust and should be substantially raised. The quantum of increased representation to be given to them should be left to the Constitution making Body.

Subject to the provisions of clause (b) the Executive of the Union shall be a composite cabinet in the sense that the following communities shall be represented on it, *viz.*—

  (i) Hindus, other than Scheduled Castes
 (ii) Muslims
(iii) Scheduled Castes
 (iv) Sikhs
  (v) Indian Christians
 (vi) Anglo-Indians

The representation of these communities in the Executive shall be, as far as possible, a reflection of their strength in the Legislature.

I may add that two of my Hindu colleagues in the Executive Council have in the memorandum they have presented to you this morning expressed that the representation given to the Scheduled Castes in His Majesty's Government's proposals is inadequate and unfair. What shocks me (is) that His Majesty's Government with all their profession of being trustees for the Scheduled Castes and contrary to their repeated declarations should have treated their wards in such an ill-liberal, unfair and unjust manner and far worse than enlightened Hindu opinion would have done. I feel it, therefore, my bounden and sacred duty to oppose the proposal by every means at my command. The proposal means a death-knell to the Untouchables and will have the effect of liquidating their efforts over the last 50 years for their emancipation. If His Majesty's Government notwithstanding its many pronouncements wish to hand over the fate of the Untouchables to the tender mercies of Hindu-Muslim combine, His Majesty's Government may well do it. But, I cannot be a party to the suppression of my people. The conclusion to which I have come is to ask His Majesty's Government to redress the wrong and to give to the Untouchables at least 3 seats in the new Executive Council. If His Majesty's Government is not prepare(d) to grant this, then His Majesty's Government should know that I cannot be a member of the newly-constituted Executive Council, even if I was offered a place in it. The Untouchables have been looking forward to a full recognition of their political rights for some time past. I have no doubt that they will be stunned by the decision of His Majesty's Government. And I would not be surprised if the whole of the Scheduled Castes decided as a matter of protest not to have anything to do with the new Government. I am sure their disillusionment will bring about a parting of the ways. This is what I anticipate will be the result of His Majesty's Government's proposals, if they are not revised. So far as I myself am concerned, my decision is made. I may be told that this is not the final shape of things. This is only an interim arrangement. I have been long enough in politics to know concessions and adjustments more (once) made grows into vested rights and how wrong settlements once agreed upon become precedents for future settlement. I cannot, therefore, allow grass to grow under my feet. If I have capacity to judge aright, I visualize that the distribution of seats though it begins as a temporary arrangement will end by becoming permanent. Rather than be left to regret towards the end, I feel I must lodge my protest against it at the very beginning.

It may well be that His Majesty's Government may not mind my eclipse and even the eclipse of the Scheduled Castes from the future Government of India: nor regret the consequent parting of the ways between the British Government in this country and the Scheduled Castes. But I believe it is only fair that His Majesty's Government should know what I have to say about the subject. I have, therefore, to request you to communicate to His Majesty's Government my proposal for increase in the representation of the Scheduled Castes in the Executive Council and the course of action I propose to take if the proposal is rejected by them.

I am,

Yours Sincerely,
B.R. Ambedkar.

23

Memorandum Submitted to the Cabinet Mission*
5 April 1946

PART I. GENERAL

The Working Committee of the All-India Scheduled Castes Federation at its meetings held in Delhi on 2nd April 1946, having given its best consideration to the question of helping the Cabinet Mission to achieve the purpose which it has in view, namely, to make India a self-governing country:

Resolves to place before the Mission its considered views on the problem of how best to achieve the said purpose in a manner which will not merely grant freedom to the Hindu majority but will also free the minority communities and Scheduled Castes in particular from the tyranny of the majority community, which not being political is not liable to be altered and which being communal is a majority fixed for ever.

The Working Committee cannot refrain from repudiating the insinuation made against the Scheduled Castes that they have been putting a veto on the political advancement of India. In the opinion of the Working Committee there can be no doubt that responsibility for holding up political advancement of India lies entirely upon the majority community which has arrogantly and unjustifiably claimed to itself the right to determine what safeguards the minority communities and in particular the Scheduled Castes should have and has never cared, indeed has always avoided to produce its blueprint of the safeguards for the minority communities and for the Scheduled Castes. All that the Scheduled Castes have done is to insist—and will not hesitate to do so in future—firstly, upon the inclusion of proper safeguards in the Constitution itself for the protection of their rights and liberties and

*BAWS 2003, vol. 17, no. 2: 171–81.

secondly, upon the acceptance by the majority of their right to determine the nature and character of the safeguards they want.

The Working Committee thinks it unnecessary to state to the Mission that this stand taken by the Scheduled Castes has been accepted by His Majesty's Government as just and binding upon them as will be seen from the pledges given to the Scheduled Castes by the representatives of His Majesty's Government from time to time in unequivocal terms. The Working Committee trusts that the Mission, in the final conclusions that may be reached as a result of the negotiations it has launched upon, will not depart from the pledges given to the Scheduled Castes and will not, in their hurry to settle, allow any other party to dictate to the Scheduled Castes what safeguards they should have.

Before proceeding to set out its views on the various issues arising out the purpose of the Mission, the Working Committee desires to draw the attention of the Mission to the results of the primary elections which have recently taken place in different Provinces, especially because these elections have conclusively proved that the All-India Scheduled Castes Federation is the only organization, which can claim to speak for the Scheduled Castes of India, and that neither the Congress nor any of the mushroom organizations has any right to speak on their behalf.

Part II. Views on Final Constitution for Free India

In regard to the final Constitution of a free India, the Working Committee of the Federation desires to make it plain to the Mission that the Scheduled Castes will never accept any Constitution which does not contain the following safeguards:

1. True and adequate representation in all the Legislature—Central and Provincial
2. True and adequate representation in all the Executives—Central and Provincial
3. Provision for election through Separate Electorates
4. Adequate representation in the Public Services
5. Adequate representation on the Public Service Commission—Federal and Provincial
6. Provision of adequate sum in the annual budgets of the Provincial and Central Government for the higher education of the Scheduled Castes
7. Provision for new and separate settlements

Without in any way minimizing the importance and necessity of any of the foregoing safeguards, the Working Committee regards (1) the provision for Separate Electorates, (2) provision for adequate representation in the Legislature, in the Executive and in the Services and (3) provision for new and separate settlements, as the most fundamental.

As regards the provision for Separate Electorates, the Working Committee invites the attention of the Mission to the following facts:

1. This demand is not a new demand. It was put forth at the Round Table Conference by the representatives of the Scheduled Castes.
2. Mr. Gandhi had strongly opposed it. But notwithstanding his opposition, His Majesty's Government felt convinced of the necessity of Separate Electorates for the Scheduled Castes, and by their Communal Award of 1932, did grant to the Scheduled Castes Separate Electorates.
3. Before the system of Separate Electorates could come into operation Mr. Gandhi declared that he would fast unto death if the Separate Electorates granted to the Scheduled Castes were not withdrawn and did actually enter upon such a fast. The Scheduled Castes under the pressure of Mr. Gandhi's fast-unto death were coerced into giving up their Separate Electorates.
4. The Poona Pact, which took the place of the Communal Award, (1) has saddled the Scheduled Castes with two elections: (a) Primary and (b) Final, the former through Separate Electorates and the latter through Joint Electorates, and (2) has placed the small number of Scheduled Caste voters in joint constituencies at the mercy of a vast number of caste-Hindu voters.
5. The results of the final elections, as compared with those of the primary elections have conclusively proved that the system of Joint Electorates and reserved seats has made a mockery of the right given to the Scheduled Castes to send their true representatives to the Legislature and is a fraud upon the Scheduled Castes.

If the Scheduled Castes have not been able to send a single candidate to the Provincial Legislatures, who is elected by the votes of the Scheduled Castes and who can therefore be said to be the true representative of the Scheduled Castes, it is because the Joint Electorates in which seats have been reserved for the Scheduled Castes have, by reason of the enormous disparity in the voting strength of the Scheduled Castes and the caste-Hindus, become rotten boroughs from the point of view of the Scheduled Castes and pocket boroughs from the point of view of caste-Hindus, who have been able to put up Scheduled Caste candidates, wishing to be their tools and get them elected in the Joint Electorates exclusively with caste-Hindu votes.

Having regard to the bitter experience of the system of Joint Electorates which the Scheduled Castes have had in the past, the Working Committee desires to convey to the Mission the deep seated conviction of the Scheduled Castes that the need of restoring Separate Electorates has become paramount, as they believe and rightly that Separate Electorates form the only guarantee against the nullification by the caste-Hindus of their constitutional safeguards and that without Separate Electorates no amount of political safeguards will be of any avail to the Scheduled Castes.

On the question of provision for adequate representation in the Legislature, Executive and Services, the Working Committee condemns outright the offer of token representation often made to the Scheduled Castes and expresses its strong opposition to the grant of weightage to other minorities which cannot but deprive the Scheduled Castes of their due share. The Working Committee wishes to emphasize the fact that the Scheduled Castes form the third important element in the national life of India and that they will not be satisfied unless they are given substantial representation in accordance with their need and their numbers.

The Working Committee would be happy if it could convey to the Mission the horror the Scheduled Castes feel at the mere thought of Police and Revenue Services, manned as they are entirely by caste-Hindus, who are oppressing, tyrannizing and discriminating against, the Scheduled Castes even when they are working under the British Government, deriving further support for their acts of tyranny and oppression from a Legislature and an Executive dominated by caste-Hindus. Unless provision is made for a substantial representation of the Scheduled Castes in the Legislature, Executive and Public Services, there can be no safety to the Scheduled Castes, surrounded as they will be by an indifferent Legislature, a pro-Hindu Executive and an anti-Scheduled Caste Policy.

As to the provision for separate settlements, it is the considered opinion of the Working Committee that:
1. The existing village system has the effect of making the Scheduled Castes in the villages slaves of the caste-Hindus. And if notwithstanding that the Penal Code does not recognize slavery,

the Scheduled Castes in every village all over India are in fact the slaves of the Hindus, it is because of the village system. Indeed, a more effective method of enforcing slavery upon the Untouchables could not have been devised.

2. The existing village system under which everyone knows who is a touchable and who is an Untouchable, has the effect of making Untouchability permanent. Indeed, a more effective method of making Untouchability permanent could not have been found.

3. Under the village system—

   (a) The Scheduled Castes are not allowed to live inside the village. They have to live on the outskirts. They are not allowed to take water from the village well. They are not allowed to send their children to the village schools. No barber in the village will shave them. They are a community apart, with no sort of communion with the caste-Hindu residents of the village.

   (b) They have no independent means of livelihood. They own no land. There is no avenue open to them for earning an independent living. The Hindu village is the only market they have. But no Hindu can buy from them. A majority of them live by begging food from their Hindu patrons in the village. They form a mass of landless labour, utterly destitute, a class of hereditary paupers, waiting to eke out such livelihood as they can from such employment and on such wages as the Hindu landowners may give.

   (c) They have to do forced labour day in and day out on pain of being driven away from their quarters by the Hindu landholders, who look upon them as a cheap labour force, on which all of them can draw, and are, therefore, always ready to combine against the Scheduled Castes.

   (d) They have to live a life of degradation, dishonour and ignominy from generation to generation. It is a state of eternal perdition. They cannot wear clean clothes, they cannot wear ornaments, they cannot eat rich food, they cannot sit on a chair in the presence of a Hindu and they must do all the dirty jobs.

   (e) The tyranny of the village Hindus upon the Scheduled Castes is so great and has become so pervasive that as the last election has shown, the Scheduled Castes cannot even exercise their right to vote for a candidate of their choice, if the Hindu villagers do not like him.

(f) The village system makes any progress on the part of Scheduled Castes impossible inasmuch as it enables the Hindus to use that most formidable weapon of social boycott with which they always threaten the Scheduled Castes and which they use to hold them down and compell them to abandon any act or movement however beneficial it may be from the point of view of the Scheduled Castes, if it happens to offend Hindu interests or Hindu sentiments.

So long as this village organization remains unbroken, there can be no doubt that the Scheduled Castes will continue to remain the Untouchables, subject to the tyranny and oppression of the caste-Hindus and will never be able to enjoy free, full and honourable life. The Working Committee has, after long and mature deliberation, come to the conclusion that for the better protection of the Scheduled Castes from the tyranny and oppression of the caste-Hindus, which may assume vast magnitude under *Swaraj,* which is only another name for Hindu *Raj,* and to enable the Scheduled Castes to develop to their fullest manhood, to give them economic and social security, as also to pave the way for the removal of untouchability, radical change must be made in the village system if the Scheduled Castes are to be freed from the ills from which they are suffering for so many centuries at the hands of the Hindus. Realizing the necessity of a change being made in the village system, the Working Committee holds that it is imperative to make provision in the Constitution of India along the following lines:

1. The Constitution should provide for the transfer of the Scheduled Castes from their present habitations and form separate Scheduled Castes villages, away from and independent of Hindu villages.

2. For the settlement of the Scheduled Castes in new villages a provision should be made in the Constitution for the establishment of a Settlement Commission,

3. All Government land, which is cultivable and which is not occupied, shall be handed over to the commission to be held in trust for the purpose of making new settlements of the Scheduled Castes.

4. The Commission should be given the right to purchase new land from private owners in fulfillment of the scheme of settlement for the Scheduled Castes.

5. The Constitution should impose an obligation upon the Central Government to grant to the Settlement Commission a minimum sum of Rupees five crores per annum to enable the Commission to carry out their duty in this behalf.

Part III. Treaty Between India and H.M.G. (His Majesty's Government)

The Working Committee has given its best consideration, to the proposal of a treaty between Free India and His Majesty's Government. The Working Committee understands that the idea behind the Treaty is to give protection to the minorities and to other interests to whom His Majesty's Government has given pledge, even after India has become independent. The Working Committee while appreciating the intention behind the proposal of a Treaty, is unable to follow how it is possible to have such a Treaty overriding the Constitution, having regard to the fact that India is to be a free and independent country, and if the Treaty is not to override the Constitution, of what good can it be to the minorities. The Working Committee has come to the conclusion that the Scheduled Castes would prefer to have their safeguards embodied in the Constitution instead of being set out in a treaty, which has no binding force....

24

Letter to PM Attlee to Restore Separate Electorates*
12 August 1946

My dear Attlee,

Thank you for your letter of the 1st August 1946. I did not expect you to find time to reply to my letter of the 1st July 1946. I am therefore grateful to you for your having found time to let me know your views about the points that I had raised in my letter.

I am afraid I cannot accept your justification for the revision of the policy followed by His Majesty's Government in the Simla Conference of 1945 nor of the Mission's method of treating the Scheduled Castes. I cannot help saying that Mr. Alexander's statement in the House of Commons that the majority of the Scheduled Castes are with the Congress is an atrocious statement and has no foundation in truth. This is not only my view but the view of every Englishman in India. If you only consult Sir Edward Benthall who is now in England, I am sure he will support me.

With regard to the analysis you have given of the result of the achievements of the Federation in the Primary Election, all I can say is that you have misunderstood the situation and I am afraid no outsider who does not know the significance of the facts or the method of the election will be able to understand what they mean without proper explanation. The main ground of my charge against the Mission is that when the other side of the picture were (was) presented by the Congress, it was their bounden duty to have called me and to have asked for an explanation. This, the Mission did not do, which they were in justice bound to do. If I had failed to give them satisfactory explanation then they would have been justified in the conclusion to which they came. That the Mission was grossly misinformed is proved by my election to the Constituent Assembly from Bengal. The Cabinet Mission stated in the House of Commons that my influence was confined to Bombay and C.P. How is it then that I was elected from Bengal? In connection with my election, I would like to impress upon you three facts: One is that I did not merely scrape through but I came at the top of the poll beating even Mr. Sarat Chandra Bose, the topmost Bengalee leader of the Congress Party. Secondly, I am in no way connected by communal ties with the Scheduled Castes community of Bengal. They are of different caste to which I belong. In fact the people of my caste do not exist in Bengal at all and yet the Bengalee Scheduled Castes supported me, so strongly that I was able to come first. Thirdly, though the Scheduled Castes in Bengal had been returned on the Congress ticket yet they broke the rule of their Party not to vote for anybody except for Congressmen and voted for me. Does this prove that I have no following in Bengal? I am sure if the Cabinet Mission are honest in their conclusion, they ought to revise the erroneous opinion which they have expressed in the House of Commons and revise the view and give proper recognition to the Federation.

With regard to the status of the Scheduled Castes in the Minority Advisory Committee, I am glad to have an assurance that the British Cabinet considers the Scheduled Castes to be an important minority. I am afraid that I must again repeat that unless and until the Cabinet Mission were to make a public declaration, this view will not help the Scheduled Castes. I say this because, as you will see, (in) the last letter which Maulana Abul Kalam Azad wrote to the Viceroy on behalf of the Congress before the negotiations broke down he emphatically challenged the view that the Scheduled Castes were a minority. The Scheduled Castes fear that if this view is not corrected by the British Cabinet in time, the Scheduled Castes' case may not be considered in the Advisory Committee which is bound to be packed by Congressmen. The danger of their being relegated to the position of a social group within the Hindus as distinguished from a minority, appears to be most certain in view of the recent pronouncement of Mr. Gandhi who evidently thinks that he can now do anything he likes with the Scheduled Castes in view of the fact that the British Government have refused to lend them their support.

In these circumstances, I would press upon you to reconsider the matter and make a declaration that the Scheduled Castes are an important minority to avert a possible danger to their future position in the new Constitution.

I am sorry to read that you cannot hold out any hope of the Scheduled Castes getting two seats in the Interim Government. I do not see any justification for this denial. Both on the ground of their numbers and also as compared to the assurance given at the time of the last Simla Conference of 1945, they are entitled to better treatment than is proposed to be given to the Sikhs and other smaller minorities. I should think that the claim made by me was more than justified.

With kind regards,

Yours sincerely,
B.R. Ambedkar

25

Cabinet Mission and the Untouchables*
14 October 1946

Karachi, 14 October 1946,
Dr. B.R. Ambedkar, Scheduled Castes Leader and Former Member
of the Viceroy's Executive Council, arrived in Karachi by air from
Bombay on his way to London today.

Dr. Ambedkar said that he was proceeding on a political mission
and would meet Mr. C.R. Attlee, Prime Minister, and Mr. Churchill
and discuss Indian constitutional matters with them. He declined to
be drawn into any further discussion or to clarify the details of his
mission—A.P.I.

Dr. B.R. Ambedkar prepared and carried following Memorandum
for circulation—Editors

The Cabinet Mission in their Statement of 10th May set out their Interim
and Long-term proposals for the solution of the political deadlock in India.
The most galling and astounding feature of their proposals is their refusal to
recognise the Untouchables as a separate and distinct element in the national
life of India. The Mission has so completely ignored the Untouchables that
not even once have they mentioned them in their long statement. To what
extent the Cabinet Mission has gone in ignoring the Untouchables will be
apparent from the following:—

1. The Untouchables have not been given the right to nominate their
   representatives in the Central Executive as have been done in the case of
   the Sikhs and the Muslims. In the present Interim Government they have
   got two representatives of the Scheduled Castes neither of them owe any
   allegiance or obligation to the Scheduled Castes. One is nominated by
   the Congress and the other is nominated by the Muslim League.
2. In the interim Government, the Untouchables have not been given a
   fixed quota of representation as was done in the case of the Muslims. At
   the Simla Conference of 1945 it was agreed that Scheduled Castes should

have at least two members in a Cabinet of 14. The reason for a change of front between 1945 and 1946 is not known.

3. They have not been given the right to separate representation in the Constituent Assembly. The Cabinet Mission's decision constitutes a departure from established policy of H.M.G.

The decision of the Cabinet Mission has not only done a grave wrong to the Untouchables but it has registered a serious departure from the principles which have guided H.M.G. in its policy regarding Indian politics and regarding the position of the Untouchables.

1. Before 1920, the Constitutional changes in the Government of India were made by the British Government on their own authority and in accordance with their own wishes. It was for the first time that in 1920 the British Government decided to frame the Constitution of India in consultation with Indians. Accordingly, a Round Table Conference was called to which Indians were invited. Among the Indians, there were representatives of the Untouchables who were invited separately and independently of the Congress or of any other political party.

2. Mr. Gandhi, the Congress representative, at the Round Table Conference fought against the recognition of the Untouchables as a separate element in the national life of India and contended that they were part of the Hindus and were therefore not entitled to separate representation. The British Government over-ruled Mr. Gandhi and by their Award recognized that the Untouchables were a separate and distinct element in the national life of India and were therefore entitled to the same safeguards as the other minorities of India such as the Muslims, Indian Christians etc.

3. The British Government adhered to this principle in the Simla Conference which was held in June 1945. Among the Indians invited to that Conference, there was a representative of the Untouchables who again was invited separately and independently of the Congress or any other political party.

4. It may be said that in the Constituent Assembly which formed part of the Cripps proposals of 1942, there was no provision for separate representation of the Untouchables and that therefore, the present proposals of the Cabinet Mission cannot be said to mark a departure. The answer is that they do. In the Cripps Proposals of 1942, it

is not that the Untouchables alone were not given separate representation. The fact is that no minority community was given separate representation in the Constituent Assembly. But in the Constitution of the Constituent Assembly of the Cabinet Mission, the Muslims and the Sikhs have been given separate recognition and separate representation which is denied to the Untouchables. It is this discrimination which constitutes the wrong of which the Untouchables are complaining.

The inequity of the proposals of the Cabinet Mission thus lies in the fact that it departs from the policy of recognizing the Untouchables as a separate element in the national life of India and discriminates them by not recognizing them while recognizing the Muslims and Sikhs.

How the Cabinet Mission's Decision Abrogates the Pledges Given by H.M.G to the Untouchables

The non-recognition of the Untouchables as a separate element by the Cabinet Mission is contrary to the pledges given to them by and on behalf of the British Government. The following are some of the pledges worth mentioning.

* * *

Nor must we forget the essential necessity in the interests of Indian unity, of the inclusion of the Indian States in any Constitutional Schemes.

I need refer only two of them—the great Muslim minority and the Scheduled Castes—there are the guarantees that have been given to the minorities in the past; the fact that their position must be safeguarded, and that those guarantees must be honoured.

—Extract from the speech made by Lord Linlithgow,
at the Orient Club, Bombay on 10 January 1940

***

These are two main points which have emerged. On these two points, His Majesty's Government now desire me to make their position clear. The first is as to the position of the minorities in relation to any future Constitutional Scheme. ... It goes without saying that they (H. M. Government) could not contemplate the transfer of their present responsibilities for the peace and welfare of India to any system of Government whose authority is directly denied by large and powerful elements in India's national life. Nor could they be parties to the coercion of such elements into submission to such a Government.

—Extract from the Statements by Lord Linlithgow on 8 August 1940

***

Congress leaders ... have built up a remarkable organization, the most efficient political machine in India ... if only they had succeeded. If the Congress could in fact speak, as it professes to speak, for all the main elements in India's national life, then however advanced their demands, our problem would have been in many respect far easier than it is today. It is true that they are numerically the largest single party in British India, but their claim in virtue of that fact to speak for India is utterly denied by very important elements in India's complex national life. These others assert their right to be regarded not as mere numerical minorities but as separate constituent factors in any future Indian policy. The foremost among these elements stands the great Muslim community. They will have nothing to do with a Constitution framed by a Constituent Assembly elected by a majority vote in geographical constituencies. They claim the right in any constitutional discussions to be regarded as an entity against the operations of a mere numerical majority. The same applies to the great body what are known as the Scheduled Castes who feel, in spite of Mr. Gandhi's earnest endeavours on their behalf, that as a community, they stand outside the main body of the Hindu community which is represented by the Congress.

—Extract from the speech by the Rt. Hon'ble Mr. L.S. Amery, Secretary of State for India, in the House of Commons on 14 August 1940

***

Without recapitulating all these reasons in detail, I should remind you that His Majesty's Government at that time made it clear:—

(a) That, their offer of unqualified freedom after the hostilities was made conditional upon the framing of a Constitution agreed by the main elements of India's national life and the negotiation of the necessary treaty arrangements with this Majesty's Government;

(b) That, it is impossible during the period of hostilities to bring about any change in the Constitution by which means alone a 'National Government' such as you suggest could be made responsible to the Central Assembly.

The object of these conditions was to ensure the fulfillment of their duty to safeguard the interest of the racial and religious minorities, of the Depressed Classes and their treaty obligations to the Indian states.

—Extract from the letter by Lord Wavell to Mr. Gandhi,
dated 15 August 1944

The Cabinet Mission's proposal not to give separate representation to the Untouchables is not the result of their individual judgment arrived at on an honest examination of the relevant facts. On the other hand, what the Mission has done is to pamper to the prejudices of Mr. Gandhi. Mr. Gandhi is vehemently opposed to the recognition of the Untouchables as a separate element in the national life of India. He opposed their recognition at the Round Table Conference. When he found that notwithstanding his opposition they were recognized as a separate element by the Communal Award of Mr. Ramsay Macdonald he threatened to fast unto death if the separate recognition of the Untouchables was not withdrawn. Again in 1945 at the First Simla Conference Mr. Gandhi raised his opposition when he found that H.M.G. had given separate recognition to the Untouchables. The Cabinet Mission were anxious to make a success of their proposals. That was not possible unless they could secure the consent of Mr. Gandhi. Mr. Gandhi demanded his price and mission gave it. That price was the sacrifice of the separate political existence of the Untouchables. Indeed one can go further and say that the proposals of the Cabinet Mission, so far as the minorities are concerned, are nothing but the reproduction of Mr. Gandhi's formula which he resounded at the Second Round Table Conference. Mr. Gandhi said that he would recognize only three communities for political purposes (1) Hindus, (2) Muslims and (3) Sikhs. The Mission's formula is a mere copy of Mr. Gandhi's formula. There is no other explanation.

Grounds Urged by the Cabinet Mission in Justification of its Decision

For justifying their decision not to recognize the Untouchables as a separate element the Cabinet Mission has relied upon the results of the elections to the Provincial Legislative Assemblies which took place in February 1948. In the course of the debate in Parliament on the Cabinet Mission's proposals which took place on 18th July 1946, the members of the Mission have tried to make out the following points:—

1. That, in the election, the Congress captured all seats reserved for the Untouchables; that therefore the Congress represented the Untouchables. That being the case there was no justification for giving separate representation to the Untouchables.
2. That, the following of the All-India Scheduled Castes Federation and my own was confined only to Bombay and Central Provinces.

FUTILITY OF THE GROUNDS

These are monstrous propositions and will not stand an honest scrutiny. The Cabinet Mission, to start with committed a great mistake in adopting the results of the election as a basis for assessing the representative character of the Congress. In doing so, the Mission failed to take into account the following circumstances:—

1. The Hindu electorate was throughout the war intensely anti-British and although it did war work it did not do it willingly. The Congress Party which was anti-British and had non-co-operated with the war effort was a hot favourite of the Hindu electorate. The other parties particularly the Scheduled Castes suffered in the election because they were pro-British and had co-operated in the war effort.

2. Just before the date fixed for election, the Viceroy and the Commander-in-Chief staged the trial of the I.N.A. men. The Congress at once took up the cause of the I.N.A. men and made it an election issue. The trial was the principal factor which enhanced the influence of the Congress which was on the wane.

3. The issue over which the election was fought was Independence and Quit India. The nature of the future Constitution of India was never the issue. If it had been the issue the Congress would never have got the majority it did.

4. The Cabinet Mission did not take into account the open hostility shown by the Returning Officers and the Polling Officers—all of whom were caste-Hindus—against the Scheduled Caste candidates who were opposing the Congress. They went to the length of rejecting their nomination papers and refusing to issue ballot papers. The Cabinet Mission did not take into account the degree of terrorism and intimidation to which the Untouchable voters were subjected by the caste-Hindus on the ground that they were not prepared to vote for the Congress candidates. In the Agra City 40 houses of the Untouchables were burnt down. In Bombay one man from the Untouchable was murdered and in the moffusil Untouchable voters in hundreds of villages were not allowed to go to the polling stations. In Nagpur a Police Officer became so much of a partisan of the Congress that he fired without the permission of the Magistrate on a crowd of Untouchable voters just to frighten them away. There were innumerable such cases all over India.

If the Cabinet Mission had taken into account these circumstances they would have realized that the success of the Congress at the elections was due to purely advantageous circumstances. The results of the elections held under such circumstances should not have been taken as a justification for not giving separate representation to the Untouchables in the Constituent Assembly.

How the Mission Adopted a False Criterion for its Decision

The criterion adopted by the Mission to decide whether the Congress did or did not represent the Untouchables was how many seats reserved for Untouchables were won by the Congress in the final election. This criterion was a false criterion because the results of the final elections are beyond the control of the Untouchables. Under the Poona Pact the final elections are determined by the Hindu votes. The true criterion which the Mission should have adopted was to find out how the Untouchables voted, how many votes were cast in favour of the Congress and how many against the Congress. This can be judged from the results of the primary elections only and not from the results of the final elections. For in the primary election only the Untouchables vote. If the results of the primary elections are taken as a basis, the decision of the Cabinet Mission, would be found to be absurd and contrary to facts. For only 28 per cent of the votes polled in the Primary elections were cast in favour of the Congress and 72 per cent against it.

It is said if the Untouchables felt that they were not in the Congress they should have had a Primary election for every one of the 151 seats reserved for them. As a matter of fact, there were Primary elections for 43 seats only all throughout India. Why did the Untouchables not stage a Primary election for the rest of the 108 seats?

The argument is absurd for the following reasons:

1. Primary election is not obligatory. It becomes obligatory only when there are more than four candidates contesting one seat. It is not realized that anyone who stands for Primary election must also face the necessity of having to stand for Final election. The inability of the Untouchables to bear the expense of double election makes it very difficult to induce members of the Untouchable communities to stand for Primary election. The fact that there have been Primary elections only for 43 seats cannot be made the

basis for the inference that the Untouchables do not claim to be separate from the Congress.

2. It is the Congress who must be asked as to why it did not put up 4 candidates in every constituency in the Primary elections. For if the Congress claims to represent the Untouchables, it should have put up more than 4 candidates on Congress ticket in every constituency and brought about Primary elections in each of the 151 constituencies and ousted every other party from coming into the Final election. The Congress did not do this. On the other hand, even in the 43 Primary elections, the Congress put up only one candidate in each constituency on the off-chance of his coming within the first 4 and then getting him returned in the Final Election with the Hindu votes. This shows that the Congress knew that the Untouchables had no confidence in the Congress.

3. It is only in 1937 that the Untouchables for the first time got their right to vote. It is only after 1937 that the Untouchables started organizing themselves for conducting elections. From the mere fact that Scheduled Castes Federation was outmatched by the Congress in the elections, it is wrong to conclude that the Untouchables are with the Congress. The Cabinet Mission ought to have made allowance from the unequal strength of the Congress and the Scheduled Castes Federation in fighting elections drawing any conclusions adverse to the Federation from the results of the elections.

FUTILITY OF THE GROUNDS URGED BY THE MISSION IN JUSTIFICATION OF THEIR DECISION

The members of the Cabinet Mission argued that Dr. Ambedkar's following was confined to the Scheduled Castes in the Bombay Presidency and the Central Provinces only. There is no foundation for this statement. The Scheduled Castes Federation is functioning in other Provinces as well and it has won there in notable electoral successes, as great as, if not greater than, in Bombay and the Central Provinces. In making this statement the Mission has failed to take into account the single victory Dr. Ambedkar obtained in the election to the Constituent Assembly. He stood as a candidate from the Bengal Provincial Legislative Assembly. He topped the poll as the general seats were concerned, beating even Mr. Sarat Chandra Bose the Leader of the Congress

Party. If Dr. Ambedkar has no influence outside Bombay and Central Provinces how did he get elected from Bengal? It must be further remembered that there are 30 seats for the Scheduled Castes in the Bengal Provincial Assembly. Out of the 80 as many as 28 were elected on the Congress ticket. Of the two who belonged to his party one fell ill on the day of the election. Notwithstanding this Dr. Ambedkar topped the poll. This could not have happened unless the Scheduled Caste members of Bengal elected on the Congress ticket had voted for him. It must also be remembered that Scheduled Castes in Bengal do not belong to the community to which Dr. Ambedkar belongs. This shows that even those Scheduled Caste members who belong to the Congress and who do not belong to his community regard him as the leader of the Scheduled Castes. This completely disproves the statement made by the members of the mission.

The member of the Cabinet Mission argued that for the sake of maintaining uniformity in the composition of the Constituent Assembly they had to adopt in the case of the Untouchables the result of the Final elections as they had done in the case of the other communities. The argument is a form of special pleading which has no force. The mission knew the final election of the Muslims, the Indian Christians and the Sikhs was by Separate Electorates. The Final election of the Scheduled Castes was not by Separate Electorates. Consequently, for the sake of uniformity the Mission should have taken the results of the Primary elections for giving representation to the Untouchables in the Constituent Assembly. The Mission was bound to do so because it was admitted by Sir Strafford Cripps in the debate that the system of election of the Untouchables as determined by the Poona Pact was in inequitous. Why did the Mission then adopt it as a basis for its decision?

WHAT COULD BE DONE TO SAVE THE UNTOUCHABLES FROM IMPENDING PERIL?

The Cabinet Mission has by the Constitution of the Constituent Assembly left the Untouchables entirely at the mercy of the caste-Hindus who have an absolute majority in it. The Untouchables want the restoration of Separate Electorates given to them by the Communal Award by H.M.G. and the abrogation of the Poona Pact which was forced upon them by coercion practised by Mr. Gandhi through his fast unto death. This, the Hindus are bound to oppose. In reply to the criticism that they have been left to the mercy of the Hindu majority the Cabinet Mission has been advertising their proposal for an Advisory Committee on Minorities as a means of safeguarding minority rights. Anyone who examines the powers and Constitution of the Advisory Committee will know that the body is worse than useless.

1. In its composition it is only a pale reflection of the Constituent Assembly. The Hindus will dominate it in the same way as they do the Constituent Assembly;

2. The fact that there will be a certain number of Untouchables in the Constituent Assembly as well as in the Advisory Committee elected by the goodwill of the Congress can be of no help to them for the Untouchable members of the Assembly and of the Committee are but the creatures of the Hindus;

3. The decisions on questions relating to the minority protection by the Advisory Committee are left to the bare majority which means that the decision will be taken by the caste-Hindus and imposed on the minorities.

4. The decision of the Advisory Committee even if they are favourable are no more than recommendations. They are not binding on the Constituent Assembly.

The device of an Advisory Committee is thus a hoax if not a humbug and cannot be relied upon to counteract the mischief the Hindu majority may do to the cause of the minorities. The Hindu majority has singled out the Untouchables for their malicious intention and seems to be determined to deprive them of the right to claim the political safeguards which are due to a minority. This is apparent from the letter addressed by the Congress on 25th June 1946 (Item 21 inCmd.6861). In that letter the Congress has taken the stand that the Untouchables are not a minority. This is an astounding proposition. For according to Mr. Gandhi's owned mission in his weekly called the *Harijan* of 21st October 1939 the Untouchables were the only real minority in India. The Congress has thus taken a complete somersault. The stand now taken by the Congress is contrary to the underlying principles of the Government of India Act, 1935, which recognizes them as a minority. What mischief is contemplated by this somersault it is not possible to know. If the Congress does not regard the Untouchables to be a minority it is possible that the Constituent Assembly might refuse to give them the same safeguards which it might agree to give to the other minorities. The Advisory Committee cannot therefore save the Untouchables from peril.

Parliament must, therefore, intervene to see that the position of the Untouchables is not jeopardized. This Parliament must do, not merely because of the pledges it has given but also because of the fact that the discussions of the Constituent Assembly are not subject to ratification.

What can Parliament do ? The Untouchables would like that the wrong done to them in regard to the Interim Government be redressed. They would like their quota fixed. They would like to be given the right to nominate their representatives to the Executive Council. These rights are not new claims. They are vested rights of the Untouchables which were recognized as late as the Simla Conference of 1945. They realize that this wrong maybe difficult to redress now. But if circumstances change and the Government is reconstituted they expect Parliament to press H.M.G. to right this wrong.

Much can be done now to save the Untouchables from the injury which the Constituent Assembly, dominated by the caste-Hindus who are determined to deprive the Untouchables of their political safeguards may do. To prevent this mischief the following steps could be taken:—

1. Press H.M.G. to make a declaration that they regard the Untouchables as a minority.

    This is essential in view of the stand taken by the Congress in its letter of the 25th June 1946 (Item 21 in Cmd. 6861). This is all the more necessary because the Viceroy in his reply to the Congress dated 27th June 1946 (Item 38 in Cmd. 6861) has avoided giving a specific denial to the contention of the Congress that the Untouchables are not a minority. If the Government is not pressed to make a declaration now the Untouchables will suffer in two ways:—

    (a) The Constituent Assembly dominated by the Hindus will deny them the rights of the minority.

    (b) H.M.G. will be free not to come to their rescue on the ground that they were not committed to regard the Untouchables as a minority.

2. Press for a declaration as to whether H.M.G. will institute machinery, if so of what sort, to examine whether the safeguards for minorities framed by the Constituent Assembly are adequate and real.

(a) In their Supplementary Statement dated 25th May 1946 (Cmd. 6835) the Cabinet Mission says:

When the Constituent Assembly has completed its labours, His Majesty's Government will recommend to Parliament such action as may be necessary for the cessation of sovereignty to the Indian People, subject only of two matters which are mentioned in the statement and which we believe, are not controversial, namely: adequate provision for the protection of the minorities (Paragraph 20 of the statement) and willingness to conclude a treaty with H.M.G. to cover matters arising out of the transfer of power (Paragraph 22 of the statement).

The idea behind this paragraph is not quite clear. It is necessary to press H.M.G. to clarify their intention.

(b) If the words 'subject to' mean that H.M.G. reserve to themselves the right to examine the safeguards for the minorities framed by the Constituent Assembly in order to find out whether they are adequate and real it is necessary to press H.M.G. to state what machinery they propose to institute for such an inquiry. The machinery of a Joint Parliamentary Committee with power to examine witnesses from minorities communities would be most appropriate. There is a precedent for it. A Joint Parliamentary Committee was appointed when the Government of India Act of 1935 was on the anvil. There would be nothing wrong in following the precedent in dealing with the report of the Constituent Assembly.

3. Press H.M.G. to declare if they will insist upon the Constitution framed by the Constituent Assembly containing clause circumscribing the power of the future Indian Legislature to do away with minority safeguard by bare majority.

(a) Neither the first Statement of the Cabinet Mission of 16 May 1946 nor the Supplementary Statement of 25 May 1946 deal with the question of providing against the Legislature of a Free India altering the Constitution and abrogating the clauses dealing with the protection of minorities. There is no use in Parliament introducing safeguards if these safeguards can be done away with by the Indian Legislature. The only safeguards against such action is to see that the Constitution framed by the Constituent Assembly contains clauses putting limitations on the Constituent powers of the Indian Legislature and prescribing conditions precedent to be fulfilled before alterations in minority safeguards are made. Such provisions exist in the Constitution of U.S.A. and Australia.

(b) Though this is a matter of vital importance to the minorities the Cabinet Mission has given no thought to the subject. It is necessary to press H.M.G. as to what they have to say on this question.

Dr. B.R. Ambedkar

Part IV

India's Constitution
Safeguards Against Social Discrimination and Economic Exploitation, 1947–50

Introduction

In this part, Ambedkar's efforts to put inclusive policies for the excluded groups during the Constitution-making for free India by the Constituent Assembly have been discussed. It was the time when the future course of history was to be set in motion. It was in this context that Ambedkar presented a memorandum on the safeguards of SCs to the Constituent Assembly on behalf of the All India Scheduled Castes Federation. He was also appointed the Chairman of the Drafting Committee of the Assembly on 23 December 1947. Thus he intervened in the following ways, while Constituent Assembly was in action:

1. On the Aims and Objectives of the Constitution: 9 December 1946
2. States and Minorities: What Are Their Rights and How to Secure Them in the Constitution of Free India (Memorandum Submitted to the Constituent Assembly on the Safeguards for the Scheduled Castes on Behalf of All India Scheduled Caste Federation): 15 March 1947
3. Constitutional Safeguards for the Scheduled Castes (Debates in the Constituent Assembly): 1947–50.

While articulating the aims and objectives of the proposed Constitution (*BAWS* 1994, vol. 13: 8–9), Ambedkar pointed out the flaws contained in it. These flaws were namely mention of rights to the citizens but lack of remedies and in the absence of socialistic economy, social, economic, and political justice was not possible. The Memorandum presented to the Constituent Assembly (*BAWS* 1979, vol. 1: 381–450) could be termed as a small constitution for the protection of common citizenry and attempted to establish social democracy and state socialism. Apart from mentioning general safeguards, it also had special section on the protection of SCs. These safeguards can be divided into following categories:

1. Social Safeguards Against Discrimination and Social Boycott
   a. Political Safeguards for Representation in the Legislatures and Executive
   b. Educational Safeguards

   c. Public Service Safeguards
   d. Establishment of Separate Settlements for the SCs
   e. Safeguards Against the Amendments of the Safeguards
2. Safeguards Against Economic Exploitation

Now, we observe that Ambedkar's proposals had become more clear, systematic, and forthright with arguments more focused and sharpened. While proposing protection against discrimination, he argued that government officials and private employers were in a habit of discrimination on the basis of race, creed, social status, etc. and it needed to be treated as an offence as it adversely affected SCs primarily.

On the issue of political safeguards after thorough analysis of Poona Pact[1] the proposal of Separate Electorates was reiterated with adult franchise and cumulative voting system so that true representatives are elected and all the adults participate in their election and SCs determine not only their own representatives but have a say in electing the others to the legislative bodies. He proposed political representation not only in the Legislature but also in the Executive as per their population.

For the education of the SCs, the government was to take special responsibility and make adequate provisions in the budgets of the State and the Central governments. Here, the responsibility for secondary and college education was put on the States and to fund foreign education of the SCs on the Union government. However, the responsibility of primary education was bestowed upon the State governments with a fixed amount as per population. It was argued that these demands were not new but contained in the Poona Pact; the only addition was regarding the fixation of amount as per the population of the SCs, was argued by him.

On the representation in Public Services, the demands were (1) proportional representation to their population, (2) compulsory recruitment with minimum qualifications, education, age, continuing the concessions on the basis of Resolutions of 1934 and 1943, and, (3) having one member of SCs in the Public Service Commission or the Committee constituted for filling up of vacancies.

The demand for separate settlements also was not a new demand because it was put in the Memorandum to the Cabinet Mission Plan submitted by Ambedkar.

The section on the safeguards against the amendments in the safeguards can be termed as the guarantee of the guarantees because when Ambedkar proposed equal rights to the SCs as citizens, he also added the guarantees to protect their rights because without guarantees, rights have no meaning in case of their violation. And it was in this light that Ambedkar proposed safeguards to amend the provisions containing protection of SCs. His propositions were—(1) passing of such a resolution by the Popular Chamber, (2) no resolution of amendment to be moved before twenty-five years of Constitutional operation, (3) if such a resolution was passed the Legislature would be dissolved and new election to take place and the same resolution to be passed by the new Legislature by two-third majority of the House including the two-third majority of the SC members of the House. The argument behind was the arrangements existing in South Africa and Canada due to problem of communal majority and communal minority prevalent in these countries.

These safeguards were also to be adopted by the Indian States who wished to be included into the Union of India. And there was nothing odd in this because the joining States had to function as per the new Constitution, was argued by Ambedkar.

While submitting the Memorandum to the Constituent Assembly on the 'States and Minorities' to safeguard the interests of the SCs and other minorities, Ambedkar was not the Chairman of the Drafting Committee. It was in late 1947 that he assumed this office. The wisdom of the Constituent Assembly had by now become favourable to the policy of reservation, where on the political front the seats were reserved for those sections in the Parliament and the State Assemblies.

On the question of reservations in Public Services, the wisdom of the Constituent Assembly was in favour of some safeguards for the SCs. However, there was difference of opinion on the methods to be adopted. Ambedkar summarizing the opinion of the House made two points namely that there shall be equality of opportunity for all the citizens and, there must at the same time be a provision made for the entry of certain communities which have so far been outside the administration. After a rigorous discussion on the issue, during the third reading on the Article 16 the word 'Backward' instead Minorities was inserted and specific safeguards for the claims of the SCs/STs were provided in the Article 335.

So far as the major achievements of this period, it was the phase which significantly introduced inclusive policies to address the discrimination and exclusion of the SCs/STs in particular and other marginalized sections like Backward Classes in general. The significant achievements of this period had been various articles to safeguard the interests of these communities including Article 17 for the abolition of untouchability, Article 16 (4) which provides the State will make provision in the reservation of 1982 appointments or posts in the services under the State in favour of 'Backward Classes citizens', Article 46 asking the State to promote with special care the educational and economic interests of the weaker sections of the people, and in particular, of the SCs and STs, Article 330 and 332 for reservation of seats for SCs and the STs in the Peoples House and Legislative Assemblies of the States respectively, Article 335 for entertaining the claims of the members of the SC and ST in consistent with the maintenance of efficiency and administration in the making of appointments to services and posts in connection with the affairs of the Union or of a State, Article 338 mentioning that there shall be a special officer for the SCs and STs to be appointed by the President and to investigate all matters relating to the safeguards provided for the SCs and STs and report to the President upon the working of those safeguards, Article 340 for appointing a Commission to investigate the conditions of the Backward Classes etc.

During this phase we observe widening of Ambedkar's formulations and the actual policy measures. The most significant contribution of Ambedkar had been the proposal through the Memorandum known as 'States and Minorities' submitted to the Constituent Assembly. In this, various measures were suggested as remedies against social discrimination, the focus of which was on equal participation of SCs in multiple spheres. As a remedy against economic exploitation, he proposed to adopt State Socialism as a policy of the State as a general solution to the problem of poverty and economic exploitation. Through this policy he expected to emancipate the poor in general and SCs in particular and compensate for their historical exclusion.

26

On the Aims and Objectives of the Constitution*
9 December 1946

Dr. Ambedkar: ... The Resolution suffers from certain other lacunae. I find that this part of the Resolution, although it enunciates certain rights, does not speak of remedies. All of us are aware of the fact that rights are nothing unless remedies are provided whereby people can seek to obtain redress when rights are invaded. I find a complete absence of remedies. Even the usual formula that no man's life, liberty and property shall be taken without the due process of law, finds no place in the Resolution. These fundamental rights set out are made subject to law and morality. Obviously what is law, what is morality will be determined by the Executive of the day and when the Executive may take one view another Executive may take another view and we do not know what exactly would be the position with regard to fundamental rights, if this matter is left to the Executive of the day. Sir, there are here certain provisions which speak of justice, economical, social and political. If this Resolution has a reality behind it and a sincerity, of which I have not the least doubt, coming as it does from the Mover of the Resolution, I should have expected some provision whereby it would have been possible for the State to make economic, social and political justice a reality and I should have from that point of view expected the Resolution to state in most explicit terms that in order that there may be social and economic justice in the country, that there would be nationalisation of industry and nationalization of land, I do not understand how it could be possible for any future Government which believes in doing justice socially, economically and politically, unless its economy is a socialistic economy. Therefore, personally, although I have no objection to the enunciation of these propositions, the Resolution is, to my mind, somewhat disappointing. I am however prepared to leave this subject where it is with the observations I have made....

BAWS 1994, vol. 13: 8–9.

27

States and Minorities*—Memorandum Submitted to the Constituent Assembly on the Safeguards for the Scheduled Castes
15 March 1947

Proposed Article II. Detailed Analysis

Article II, Section I—Fundamental Rights of Citizens
Article II, Section II—Remedies Against Invasion of
Fundamental Rights

Clause 1.	Judicial Protection
Clause 2.	Protection Against Unequal Treatment
Clause 3.	Protection Against Discrimination
Clause 4.	Protection Against Economic Exploitation

Article II, Section III—Provisions for the Protection
of Minorities

Clause 1.	Protection Against Communal Executive
Clause 2.	Protection Against Social and Official Tyranny
Clause 3.	Protection Against Social Boycott
Clause 4.	Authority and Obligation of the Union and State Governments to Spend Money for Public Purposes Including Purposes Beneficial to Minorities

Article II, Section IV—Safeguards for the Scheduled Castes
Part I—Guarantees

Clause 1.	Right to Representation in the Legislature and in the Local Bodies
Clause 2.	Right to Representation in the Executive
Clause 3.	Right to Representation in Services

*BAWS 1979, vol. 1: 391–450.

Part II—Special Responsibilities
Clause 1.   For Higher Education
Clause 2.   For Separate Settlements

Part III—Sanction for Safeguards and Amendment of Safeguards
Clause 1.   Safeguards to be Embodied in the Constitution
Clause 2.   Amendment of Safeguards

Part IV—Protection of Scheduled Castes in Indian States
Part V—Interpretation

ARTICLE II—SECTION II

REMEDIES AGAINST INVASION OF FUNDAMENTAL RIGHTS

The United States of India shall provide...

Clause 2. *Protection Against Unequal Treatment*

That the authority of the Legislature and the Executive of the Union as well as of every State throughout India shall be subject to the following limitations:

It shall not be competent for any Legislature or Executive in India to pass a law or issue an order, rule or regulation so as to violate the following rights of the subjects of the State:

1. To make and enforce contracts, to sue, be parties, and give evidence, to inherit, purchase, lease, sell, hold and convey real and personal property.
2. To be eligible for entry into the civil and military employ and to all educational institutions except for such conditions and limitations as may be necessary to provide for the due and adequate representation of all classes of the subjects of the State.
3. To be entitled to the full and equal enjoyment of the accommodations, advantages, facilities, educational institutions, privileges of inns, rivers, streams, wells, tanks, roads, paths, streets, public conveyances on land, air and water, theatres and other places of public resort or amusement except for such conditions and limitations applicable alike to all subjects of every race, class, caste, colour or creed.

4. To be deemed fit for and capable of sharing without distinction the benefits of any religious or charitable trust dedicated to or created, maintained or licensed for the general public or for persons of the same faith and religion.
5. To claim full and equal benefit of all laws and proceedings for the security of persons and property as is enjoyed by other subjects regardless of any usage or custom or usage or custom based on religion and be subject to like punishment, pains and penalties and to none other.

Clause 3. Protection Against Discrimination

1. Discrimination against citizens by Government officers in Public administration or by private employers in factories and commercial concerns on the ground of race or creed or social status shall be treated as an offence. The jurisdiction to try such cases shall be vested in a tribunal to be created for the purpose.
2. The Union Legislature shall have the right as well as the obligation to give effect to this provision by appropriate legislation.

Clause 4. Protection Against Economic Exploitation

The United States of India shall declare as a part of the law of its constitution—

1. That industries which are key industries or which may be declared to be key industries shall be owned and run by the State.
2. That industries which are not key industries but which are basic industries shall be owned by the State and shall be run by the State or by Corporations established by the State.
3. That Insurance shall be a monopoly of the State and that the State shall compel every adult citizen to take out a life insurance policy commensurate with his wages as may be prescribed by the Legislatures.
4. That agriculture shall be State Industry.
5. That State shall acquire the subsisting rights in such industries, insurance and agricultural land held by private individuals, whether as owners, tenants or mortgagees and pay them compensation in the form of debenture equal to the value of his or her right in the land. Provided that in reckoning the value of land, plant or security no account shall be taken of any rise therein due to emergency, of any potential or unearned value or any value for compulsory acquisition.

6. The State shall determine how and when the debenture holder shall be entitled to claim cash payment.

7. The debenture shall be transferable and inheritable property but neither the debenture-holder nor the transferee from the original holder nor his heir shall be entitled to claim the return of the land or interest in any industrial concern acquired by the State or be entitled to deal with it in any way.

8. The debenture-holder shall be entitled to interest on his debenture at such rate as may be defined by law, to be paid by the State in cash or in kind as the State may deem fit.

9. Agricultural industry shall be organized on the following basis:
   (i) The State shall divide the land acquired into farms of standard size and let out the farms for cultivation to residents of the village as tenants (made up of group of families) to cultivate on the following conditions:
      (a) The farm shall be cultivated as collective farm
      (b) The farm shall be cultivated in accordance with rules and directions issued by Government
      (c) The tenants shall share among themselves in the manner prescribed the produce of the farm left after the payment of charges properly leviable on the farm
   (ii) The land shall be let out to villagers without distinction of caste or creed and in such manner that there will be no landlord, no tenant and no landless labourer.
   (iii) It shall be the obligation of the State to finance the cultivation of the collective farms by the supply of water, draft animals, implements, manure, seeds, etc.
   (iv) The State shall be entitled to—
      (a) To levy the following charges on the produce of the farm:
         (i) a portion for land revenue
         (ii) a portion to pay the debenture-holders
         (iii) a portion to pay for the use of capital goods supplied
      (b) To prescribe penalties against tenants who break the conditions of tenancy or willfully neglect to make the best use of the means of cultivation offered by the State or otherwise act prejudicially to the scheme of collective farming.

10. The scheme shall be brought into operation as early as possible but in no case shall the period extend beyond the tenth year from the date of the Constitution coming into operation.

Article II—Section III

Provisions for the Protection of Minorities

The Constitution of United States of India shall provide:

Clause 1. Protection Against Communal Executive

1. That the Executive—Union or State shall be non-parliamentary in the sense that it shall be removable before the term of Legislature.
2. Members of the Executive if they are not members of the Legislature shall have the right to sit in the Legislature, speak, vote and answer questions.
3. The Prime Minister shall be elected by the whole House by single transferable vote.
4. The representatives of different minorities in the Cabinet shall be elected by members of each minority community in the Legislature by single transferable vote.
5. The representatives of the majority community in the Executive shall be elected by the whole House single transferable vote.
6. A member of the Cabinet may resign his post on a censure motion or otherwise but shall not be liable to be removed except on impeachment by the House on the ground of corruption or treason....

Clause 3. Protection Against Social Boycott

That social boycott, promoting or instigating a social boycott or threatening a social boycott as defined below shall be declared to be an offence:

1. *Boycott Defined*—A person shall be deemed to boycott another who—
   (a) refuses to let or use or occupy any house or land, or to deal with, work for hire, or do business with another person, or to render to him or receive from him any service, or refuses to do any of the said things on the terms on which such things should commonly be done in the ordinary course of business, or
   (b) abstains from such social, professional or business relations as he would, having regard to such existing customs in the community which are not inconsistent with any fundamental right or other rights of citizenship declared in the Constitution, ordinarily maintain with such person, or

(c) in any way injures, annoys or interferes with such other person in the exercise of his lawful rights.

2. *Offence of Boycotting*—Whoever, in consequence of any person having done any act which he was legally entitled to do or of his having omitted to do any act which he was legally entitled to omit to do, or with intent to cause any person to do any act which he is not legally bound to do or to omit to do any act which he is legally entitled to do, or with intent to cause harm to such person in body, mind, reputation or property, or in his business or means of living, boycotts such person or any person in whom such person is interested, shall be guilty of offence of boycotting.

Provided that no offence shall be deemed to have been committed under this Section, if the Court is satisfied that the accused person has not acted at the instigation of or in collusion with any other person or in pursuance of any conspiracy or of any agreement or combination to boycott.

3. *Offence of Instigating or Promoting a Boycott*—Whoever—
   (a) publicly makes or publishes or circulates a proposal for, or
   (b) makes, publishes or, circulates any statement, rumour or report with intent to, or which he has reason to believe to be likely to cause, or
   (c) in any other way instigates or promotes the boycotting of any person or class of persons, shall be guilty of the offence of instigating or promoting a boycott.

   Explanation—An offence under this clause shall be deemed to have been committed although the person affected or likely to be affected by any action of the nature referred to herein is not designated by name or class but only by his acting or abstaining from acting in some specified manner.

4. *Offence of Threatening a Boycott*—Whoever, in consequence of any person having done any act which he was legally entitled to do or of his having omitted to do any act which he was legally entitled to omit to do, or with intent to cause any person to do any act which he is not legally bound to do, or to omit to do any act which he is legally entitled to do, threatens to cause such person or any person in whom such person is interested, to be boycotted shall be guilty of the offence threatening a boycott.

Exception—*It is not Boycott—*
(i) To do any act in furtherance of a *bona fide* labour dispute.
(ii) To do any act in the ordinary course of business competition.

All these offences shall be deemed to be cognizable offences. The Union Legislature shall make laws prescribing punishment for these offences.

ARTICLE II—SECTION IV

SAFEGUARDS FOR THE SCHEDULED CASTES

Part I—Guarantees

The Constitution of the United States of India shall guarantee to the Scheduled Castes the following rights:

Clause 1. *Right to Representation in the Legislature*

(i) *Quantum of Representation—*(a) (i) The Scheduled Castes shall have minimum representation in the Legislature—Union and State—and if there be a group Constitution then in the group Legislature equal to the ratio of their population to the total population. Provided that no other minority is allowed to claim more representation than what is due to it on the basis of its population. Provided that no other minority is allowed to claim more representation than what is due to it on the basis of its population.

(ii) The Scheduled Castes of Sind and N.W.F. Provinces shall be given their due share of representation.

(iii) Weightage where it becomes necessary to reduce a huge communal majority to reasonable dimensions shall come out of the share of the majority. In no case shall it be at the cost of another minority community.

(iv) Weightage carved out from the share of majority shall not be assigned to one community only. But the same shall be divided among all minority communities equally or in inverse proportion to their—
(1) economic position,
(2) social status, and
(3) educational advance.

There should be no representation to special interests. But if the same is allowed it must be taken out of the share of representation given to that community to which the special interest belongs.

(2) *Method of Election—*

(A) For Legislative Bodies
 (a) The system of election introduced by the Poona Pact shall be abolished.
 (b) In its place, the system of *Separate Electorates* shall be substituted.
 (c) Franchise shall be adult franchise.
 (d) The system of voting shall be cumulative.

(B) For Local Bodies
The principles for determining the quantum of representation and the Method of election for Municipalities and Local Boards shall be the same as that adopted for the Union and State Legislatures.

Clause 2. Right to Representation in the Executive

1. The Scheduled Castes shall have minimum representation in the Executive—Union and State—and if there be a group Constitution then in the group Executive equal to the ratio of their population to the total population. Provided that no minority community is allowed to claim more than its population ratio.
2. Weightage where it becomes necessary to reduce a huge majority to reasonable dimensions shall come out of the share of the majority community. In no case shall it be at the cost of another minority community.
3. Weightage carved out from the share of the majority shall not be assigned to one community only. But the same shall be divided among all minorities equally or in inverse proportion to:
   (i) their economic position,
   (ii) social status, and
   (iii) educational advance.

Clause 3. Right to Representation in Services

 (a) The quantum of representation of the Scheduled Castes in the Services shall be as follows:

(i) *In the Union Services*—In proportion to the ratio of their population to the total population in India or British India as the case may be.

(ii) *In the State and Group Services*—In proportion to their population in the State or Union.

(iii) *In the Municipal and Local Board Services*—In proportion to their population in the Municipal and Local Boards areas:

Provided that no minority community is allowed to claim more than its population ratio of representation in the Services.

(b) Their right to representation in the Services shall not be curtailed except by conditions relating to minimum qualifications, education, age.

(c) The conditions prescribed for entry in Services shall not abrogate any of the concessions given to the Scheduled Castes by the Government of India in their Resolutions of 1942 and 1945.

(d) The method of filling up the vacancies shall conform to the rules prescribed in the Government of India Resolutions of 1942 and 1946.

(e) On every Public Services Commission or a Committee constituted for filling vacancies, the Scheduled Castes shall have at least one representative.

Part II—Special Responsibilities

That the United States of India shall undertake the following special responsibilities for the betterment of the Scheduled Castes:

Clause 1. Provisions for Higher Education

1. Governments—Union and State—shall be required to assume financial responsibility for the higher education of the Scheduled Castes and shall be required to make adequate provisions in their budgets. Such provisions shall form the first charge on the Education Budget of the Union and State Government.

2. The responsibility for finding money for secondary and college education of the Scheduled Castes in India shall be upon the State Governments and the different States shall make a provision in their annual budgets for the said purpose in proportion to the population of the Scheduled Castes to the total budget of the States.

3. The responsibility for finding money for foreign education of the Scheduled Castes shall be the responsibility of the Union Government and the Union Government shall make a provision of rupees 10 lakhs per year in its annual budget in that behalf.
4. These special grants shall be without prejudice to the right of the Scheduled Castes to share in the expenditure incurred by the State Government for the advancement of primary education for the people of the State.

Clause 2. Provision for New Settlements

1. The following provision shall be made in the Constitution of the Union Government:
   (i) There shall be a Settlement Commission under the new Constitution to hold uncultivated lands belonging to the State in trust for Settlement of the Scheduled Castes in separate villages.
   (ii) The Union Government shall set apart annually a fund of Rs. 5 crores for the purpose of promoting the scheme of settlement.
   (iii) That the Commission shall have the power to purchase any land offered for sale and use it for the said purpose.
2. The Union Government shall from time to time pass such legislation as may be necessary for the Commission to carry out its functions.

Part III—Sanction for Safeguards and Amendment of Safeguards
Clause 1. Sanction for Safeguards

The Constitution of the United States shall provide that—

The United States of India undertakes to give the safeguards contained in Article II Section IV a place in the Constitution and make them a part of the Constitutional Law of India.

Clause 2. Mode of Amendment of Safeguards

The provisions for the Scheduled Castes shall not be altered, amended or abrogated except in the following manner:

Any amendment or abrogation of Section IV of Article II or any part thereof relating to the Scheduled Castes shall only be made by a Resolution passed in the manner prescribed below by the more Popular Chamber of the Union Legislature:

(i) Any proposal for amendment or abrogation shall be initiated in the form of a Resolution in the more Popular Chamber of the Union Legislature,

(ii) No such Resolution shall be moved—

    (a) unless 25 years have elapsed after the Constitution has come into operation and has been worked; and

    (b) unless six months' notice has been given to the House by the mover of his intention to move such a Resolution.

(iii) On the passing of such a Resolution, the Legislature shall be dissolved and a new election held.

(iv) The original Resolution in the form in which it was passed by the previous Legislature shall be moved afresh in the same House of the newly elected Union Legislature.

(v) The Resolution shall not be deemed to have been carried unless it is passed by a majority of two-thirds of the members of the House and also two-thirds of members of the Scheduled Castes who have been returned through Separate Electorates.

Part IV—Protection of Scheduled Castes in the Indian States

The Constitution of the United States shall provide that the admission of the Indian States into the Union shall be subject to the following condition:

All provisions relating to the Scheduled Castes contained in Section IV of Article II of the Constitution of the United States of India shall be extended to the Scheduled Castes in the Indian States. Such a provision in the Constitution of an Indian States shall be a condition precedent for its admission into the Union.

Part V—Interpretation

Scheduled Castes a Minority

I. For the purpose of Article II the Scheduled Castes, as defined in the Government of India Scheduled Caste Order, 1936, issued under the Government of India Act, 1935, shall be deemed to be a minority.

Scheduled Castes and Change of Domicile

II. For the purposes of Article II a Caste which is a Scheduled Caste in one State shall be treated as Scheduled Caste in all States of the Union.

EXPLANATORY NOTES [TO THE CLAUSES]

Protection Against Unequal Treatment (Article II—Section II, Clause 2)

It is difficult to expect that in a country like India where most persons are communally minded those in authority will give equal treatment to those outside their community. Unequal treatment has been the inescapable fate of the Untouchables in India. The extract [mentioned in Chapter 9] from the Proceedings of the Board of Revenue of the Government of Madras No. 723 dated 5th November, 1892, illustrates the sort of unequal treatment which is meted out to the Scheduled Castes by Hindu Officers.

The Punjab Land Alienation Act is another illustration of unequal treatment of the Untouchables by the Legislature.

Many other minority communities may be suffering from similar treatment at the hands of the majority community. It is therefore necessary to have such a provision to ensure that all citizens shall have equal benefit of Laws, Rules and Regulations.

The provisions of Clause 2 are borrowed from Civil Rights Protection Act, 1866, and of March 1st, 1875 passed by the Congress of the United States of America to protect the Negroes against unequal treatment.

Protection Against Discrimination (Article II—Section II, Clause 3)

Discrimination is another menace which must be guarded against if the Fundamental Rights are to be real rights. In a country like India where it is possible for discrimination to be practised on a vast scale and in a relentless manner Fundamental Rights can have no meaning. The remedy follows the lines adopted in the Bill which was recently introduced in the Congress of the U.S.A. the aim of which is to prevent discrimination being practised against the Negroes.

Protection Against Economic Exploitation (Article II—Section II, Clause 4)

The main purpose behind the clause is to put an obligation on the State to plan the economic life of the people on lines which would lead to highest point of productivity without closing every avenue to private enterprise, and also provide for the equitable distribution of wealth.

[Mentioned in Chapter 9.]

The plan set out in the clause proposes State ownership in agriculture with a collectivized method of cultivation and a modified form of State Socialism in the field of industry. It places squarely on the shoulders of the State the obligation to supply capital necessary for agriculture as well as for industry. Without the supply of capital by the State neither land nor industry can be made to yield better results. It also proposes to nationalize insurance with a double objective. Nationalized Insurance gives the individual greater security than a private insurance Firm does inasmuch as it pledges the resources of the State as a security for the ultimate payment of his insurance money. It also gives the State the resources necessary for financing its economic planning in the absence of which it would have to resort to borrowing from the money market at a high rate of interest. State Socialism is essential for the rapid industrialization of India. Private enterprise cannot do it and if it did it would produce those inequalities of wealth which private capitalism has produced in Europe and which should be a warning to Indians. Consolidation of Holdings and Tenancy Legislation are worse than useless. They cannot bring about prosperity in agriculture. Neither Consolidation nor Tenancy Legislation can be of any help to the 60 millions of Untouchables who are just landless labourers. Neither Consolidation nor Tenancy Legislation can solve their problem. Only collective farms on the lines set out in the proposal can help them. There is no expropriation of the interests concerned. Consequently there ought to be no objection to the proposal on that account.

The plan has two special features. One is that it proposes State Socialism in important fields of economic life. The second special feature of the plan is that it does not leave the establishment of State Socialism to the will of the Legislature. It establishes State Socialism by the Law of the Constitution and thus makes it unalterable by any act of the Legislature and the Executive.

Students of Constitutional Law will at once raise a protest. They are sure to ask: Does not the proposal go beyond the scope of the usual type of Fundamental Rights? My answer is that it does not. If it appears to go beyond it is only because the conception of Fundamental Rights on which such criticism is based is a narrow conception. One may go further and say that even from the narrow conception of the scope of the Constitutional Law as comprising no more than Fundamental Rights the proposal can find ample justification. For what is the purpose of prescribing by law the shape and form of the economic structure of society? The purpose is to protect the liberty of the individual from invasion by other individuals which is the object of enacting Fundamental Rights. The connection between individual liberty and the shape and form of the economic structure of society may not be apparent to everyone. Nonetheless the connection between the two is real. It will be apparent if the following considerations are borne in mind.

Political Democracy rests on four premises which may be set out in the following terms:

1. The individual is an end in himself
2. That the individual has certain inalienable rights which must be guaranteed to him by the Constitution
3. That the individual shall not be required to relinquish any of his constitutional rights as a condition precedent to the receipt of a privilege
4. That the State shall not delegate powers to private persons to govern others.

Anyone who studies the working of the system of social economy based on private enterprise and pursuit of personal gain will realize how it undermines, if it does not actually violate, the last two premises on which Democracy rests. How many have to relinquish their constitutional rights in order to gain their living? How many have to subject themselves to be governed by private employers?

Ask those who are unemployed whether what are called Fundamental Rights are of any value to them. If a person who is unemployed is offered a choice between a job of some sort, with some sort of wages, with no fixed hours of labour and with an interdict on joining a union and the exercise of his right to freedom of speech, association, religion, etc., can there be any doubt as to what his choice will be. How can it be otherwise? The fear of starvation, the fear of losing a house, the fear of losing savings if any, the fear of being compelled to take children away from school, the fear of having to be a burden on public charity, the fear of having to be burned or buried at public cost are factors too strong to permit a man to stand out for his Fundamental Rights. The unemployed are thus compelled to relinquish their Fundamental Rights for the sake of securing the privilege to work and to subsist.

What about those who are employed? Constitutional lawyers assume that the enactment of Fundamental Rights is enough to safeguard their liberty and that nothing more is called for. They argue that where the State refrains from intervention in private affairs—economic and social—the residue is liberty. What is necessary is to make the residue as large as possible and State intervention as small as possible. It is true that where the State refrains from intervention what remains is liberty. But this does not dispose of the matter. One more question remains to be answered. To whom and for whom is this liberty? Obviously this liberty is liberty to the landlords to increase rents, for capitalists to increase hours of work and reduce rate of wages. This must be so. It cannot be otherwise. For in an economic system employing armies of workers, producing goods *en masse* at regular intervals some one must make rules so that workers will work and the wheels of industry run on. If the State does not do it the private employer will. Life otherwise will become impossible. In other words what is called liberty from the control of the State is another name for the dictatorship of the private employer.

How to prevent such a thing happening? How to protect the unemployed as well as the employed from being cheated out of their Fundamental Rights to life, liberty and pursuit of happiness? The useful remedy adopted by democratic countries is to *limit* the power of Government to impose arbitrary restraints in political domain and to *invoke* the ordinary power of the Legislature to restrain the more powerful individual from imposing arbitrary restraints on the less powerful in the economic field. The inadequacy and the futility of the plan has been well established. The successful invocation by the less powerful of the authority of the Legislature is a doubtful proposition. Having regard to the fact that even under adult suffrage all Legislatures and Governments are controlled by the more powerful an appeal to the Legislature to intervene is a very precarious safeguard against the invasion of the liberty of the less powerful. The plan follows quite a different method. It seeks to limit not only the power of Government to impose arbitrary restraints but also of the more powerful individuals or to be more precise to eliminate the possibility of the more powerful having the power to impose arbitrary restraints on the less powerful by withdrawing from the control he has over the economic life of people. There cannot be slightest doubt that of the two remedies against the invasion by the more powerful of the rights and liberties of the less powerful the one contained in the proposal is undoubtedly the more effective. Considered in the light of these observations the proposal is essentially a proposal for safeguarding the liberty of the individual. No Constitutional lawyer can therefore object to it on the ground that it goes beyond the usual scope of Constitutional Law.

So far as the plan has been considered purely as a means of safeguarding individual liberty. But there is also another aspect of the plan which is worthy of note. It is an attempt to establish State Socialism without abrogating Parliamentary Democracy and without leaving its establishment to the will of a Parliamentary Democracy. Critics of State Socialism and even its friends are bound to ask why make it a part of the Constitutional Law of the land? Why not leave it to the Legislature to bring it into being by the ordinary process of Law. The reason why it cannot be left to the ordinary Law is not difficult to understand. One essential condition for the success of a planned economy is that it must not be liable to suspension or abandonment. It must be permanent. The question is how this permanence can be secured. Obviously it cannot be secured under the form of Government called Parliamentary Democracy. Under the system of Parliamentary Democracy, the policy of the Legislature and of the Executive is the policy of the majority for the time being. Under the system of Parliamentary Democracy the majority in one election may be in favour of State Socialism in Industry and in Agriculture. At the next election the majority may be against it. The anti-State Socialism majority will use its Law-making power to undoing the work of the pro-State Socialism majority and the pro-State Socialism majority will use its Law-making power to doing over again what has been undone by their opponents. Those who want the economic structure of society to be modeled on State Socialism must realize that they cannot leave the fulfillment of so fundamental a purpose to the exigencies of ordinary Law which simple majorities—whose—political fortunes are never determined by rational causes—have a right to make and unmake. For these reasons Political Democracy seems to be unsuited for the purpose.

What is the alternative? The alternative is Dictatorship. There is no doubt that Dictatorship can give the permanence which State Socialism requires as an essential condition for its fructification. There is however one fact against Dictatorship which must be faced. Those who believe in individual freedom strongly object to Dictatorship and insist upon Parliamentary Democracy as a proper form of Government for a Free Society. For they feel that freedom of the individual is possible only under Parliamentary Democracy and not under Dictatorship. Consequently those who want freedom are not prepared to give up Parliamentary Democracy as a form of Government. However, much they may be anxious to have State Socialism they will not be ready to exchange Parliamentary Democracy for Dictatorship even though the gain by such an exchange is the achievement of State Socialism. The problem therefore is to have State Socialism without Dictatorship, to have State Socialism with Parliamentary Democracy. The way out seems to be to retain Parliamentary Democracy and to prescribe State Socialism by the Law of the Constitution so that it will be beyond the reach of a Parliamentary majority to suspend, amend or abrogate it. It is only by this that one can achieve the triple object, namely, to establish Socialism, retain Parliamentary Democracy and avoid Dictatorship.

The proposal marks a departure from the existing Constitutions whose aim is merely to prescribe the form of the political structure of society leaving the economic structure untouched. The result is that the political structure is completely set at naught by the forces which emerge from the economic structure which is at variance with the political structure.

Those who want Socialism with Parliamentary Democracy and without Dictatorship should welcome the proposal.

The soul of Democracy is the doctrine of one man, one value. Unfortunately, Democracy has attempted to give effect to this doctrine only so far as the political structure is concerned by adopting the rule of one man, one role which is supposed to translate into fact the doctrine of one man, one value. It has left the economic structure to take the shape given to it by those who are in a position to mould it. This has happened because Constitutional lawyers have been dominated by the antiquated conception that all that is necessary for a perfect Constitution for Democracy was to frame a Constitutional Law which would make Government responsible to the people and to prevent tyranny of the people by the Government. Consequently, almost all Laws of Constitution which relate to countries which are called democratic stop with Adult Suffrage and Fundamental Right. They have never advanced to the conception that the Constitutional Law of Democracy must go beyond Adult Suffrage and Fundamental Rights. In other words, old time Constitutional lawyers believed that the scope and function of Constitutional Law was to prescribe the shape and form of the political structure of society. They never realized that it was equally essential to prescribe the shape and form of the economic structure of society, if Democracy is to live up to its principle of one man, one value. Time has come to take a bold step and define both the economic structure as well as the political structure of society by the Law of the Constitution. All countries like India which are latecomers in the field of Constitution-making should not copy the faults of other countries. They should profit by the experience of their predecessors.

Protection Against Communal Executive (Article II—Section III, Clause I)

In the Government of India Acts of 1919 and 1935 the model that was adopted for framing the structure of the Executive in the Provinces and in the Centre was of the British type or what is called by Constitutional Lawyers Parliamentary Executive as opposed to the American type of Executive which in contradistinction of the British type is called Non-Parliamentary Executive. The question is whether the pattern for the Executive adopted in the two Acts should be retained or whether it should be abandoned and if so what model should be adopted in its place. Before giving final opinion on this issue it would be desirable to set out the special features of the British type of the Executive and the consequences that are likely to follow if it was applied to India.

The following may be taken to be the special features of British or the Parliamentary Executive:

1. It gives a party which has secured a majority *in* the Legislature the right to form a Government.
2. It gives the majority party the right to exclude from Government persons who do not belong to the Party.
3. The Government so formed continues in office only so long as it can command a majority in the Legislature. If it ceases to command a majority it is bound to resign either in favour of another Government formed out of the existing Legislature or in favour of a new Government formed out of a newly elected Legislature.

As to the consequences that would follow if the British System was applied to India the situation can be summed up in the following proposition:

1. The British system of Government by a Cabinet of the majority party rests on the premise that the majority is a political majority. In India the majority is a communal majority. No matter what social and political programme it may have the majority will retain its character of being a communal majority. Nothing can alter this

fact. Given this fact it is clear that if the British System was copied it would result in permanently vesting Executive power in a Communal majority.

2. The British System of Government imposes no obligation upon the Majority Party to include in its cabinet the representatives of Minority Party. If applied to India the consequence will be obvious. It would make the majority community a governing class and the minority community a subject race. It would mean that a communal majority will be free to run the administration according to its own ideas of what is good for the minorities. Such a state of affairs could not be called democracy. It will have to be called imperialism.

In the light of these consequences it is obvious that the introduction of British type of the Executive will be full of menace to the life, liberty and pursuit of happiness of the minorities in general and of the Untouchables in particular.

The problem of the Untouchables is a formidable one for the Untouchables to face. The Untouchables are surrounded by a vast mass of Hindu population which is hostile to them and which is not ashamed of committing any inequity or atrocity against them. For a redress of these wrongs which are matters of daily occurrence, the Untouchables have to call in the aid of the administration. What is the character and composition of this administration? To be brief, the administration in India is completely in the hands of the Hindus. It is their monopoly. From top to bottom they control it. There is no Department which is not dominated by them. They dominate the Police, the Magistracy and the Revenue Services, indeed any and every branch of the Administration. The next point to remember is that the Hindus in the administration have the same positive anti-social and inimical attitude to the Untouchables which the Hindus outside the administration have. Their one aim is to discriminate against the Untouchables and to deny and as deprive them not only of the benefits of Law, but also of the protection of the Law against tyranny and oppression. The result is that the Untouchables are placed between the Hindu population and the Hindu-ridden administration, the one committing wrong against them and the other protecting the wrong-doer, instead of helping the victims....

These are special considerations against the introduction of the British System of Executive, which have their origin in the interests of the minorities and the Scheduled Castes. But there is one general consideration which can be urged against the introduction of the British Cabinet System in India. The British Cabinet System has undoubtedly given the British people a very stable system of Government. Question is will it produce a stable Government in India? The chances are very slender. In view of the clashes of castes and creeds there is bound to be a plethora of parties and groups in the Legislature in India. If this happens it is possible, nay certain, that under the system of Parliamentary Executive like the one that prevails in England under which the Executive is bound to resign upon an adverse vote in the Legislature, India may suffer from instability of the Executive. For it is the easiest thing for groups to align and realign themselves at frequent intervals and for petty purposes and bring about the downfall of Government. The present solidarity of what are called the Major Parties cannot be expected to continue. Indeed as soon as the problem of the British in India is solved the cement that holds these parties together will fall away. Constant overthrow of Government is nothing short of anarchy. The present Constitution has in it Section 93 which provides a remedy against it. But Section 93 would be out of place in the Constitution of a free India. Some substitute must therefore be found for Section 93.

Taking all these considerations together there is no doubt that the British type of the Executive is entirely unsuited to India.

The form of the Executive proposed in the clause is intended to serve the following purposes:

1. To prevent the majority from forming a Government without giving any opportunity to the minorities to have a say in the matter,
2. To prevent the majority from having exclusive control over administration and thereby make the tyranny of the minority by the majority possible.
3. To prevent the inclusion by the Majority Party in the Executive representatives of the minorities who have no confidence of the minorities,
4. To provide a stable Executive necessary for good and efficient administration.

The clause takes the American form of Executive as a model and adapts it to Indian conditions especially to the requirements of minorities. The form of the Executive suggested in the proposal cannot be objected to on the ground that it is against the principle of responsible Government. Indians who are used to the English form of Executive forget that this is not the only form of democratic and responsible

Government. The American form of Executive is an equally good type of democratic and responsible form of Government. There is also nothing objectionable in the proposal that a person should not be qualified to become a Minister merely because he is elected to the Legislature. The principle that a member of the Legislature before he is made a Minister should be chosen by his constituents was fully recognized by the British Constitution for over hundred years. A member of Parliament who was appointed a Minister had to submit himself for election before taking up his appointment. It was only lately given up. There ought therefore to be no objection to it on the ground that the proposals are not compatible with responsible Governments. The actual proposal is an improved edition of the American form of Government, for the reason that under it members of the Executive can sit in the Legislature and have a right to speak and answer questions.

Protection Against Social Boycott (Article II—Section III, Clause 3)

Social boycott is always held over the heads of the Untouchables by the caste-Hindus as a sword of Damocles. Only the Untouchables know what a terrible weapon it is in the hands of the Hindus. Its effects and forms are well described in the Report made by a Committee appointed by the Government of Bombay in 1928 to investigate the grievances of the Depressed Classes and from which the following extracts are made. It illuminates the situation in a manner so simple that everybody can understand what tyranny the Hindus are able to practice upon the Untouchables. The Committee said:

Although we have recommended various remedies to secure to the Depressed Classes their rights to all public utilities we fear that there will be difficulties in the way of their exercising them for a long time to come. The first difficulty is the fear of open violence against them by the orthodox classes. It must be noted that the Depressed Classes form a small minority in every village, opposed to which is a great majority of the orthodox who are bent on protecting their interests and dignity from any supposed invasion by the Depressed Classes at any cost. The danger of prosecution by the Police has put a limitation upon the use of violence by the orthodox classes and consequently such cases are rare.

The second difficulty arises from the economic position in which the Depressed Classes are found today. The Depressed Classes have no economic independence in most parts of the Presidency. Some cultivate the lands of the orthodox classes as their tenants at will. Others live on their earnings as farm labourers employed by the orthodox classes and the rest subsist on the food or grain given to them by the orthodox classes in lieu of service rendered to them as village servants. We have heard of numerous instances where the orthodox classes have used their economic power as a weapon against those Depressed Classes in their villages, when the latter have dared to exercise their rights, and have evicted them from their land, and stopped their employment and discontinued their remuneration as village servants. This boycott is often planned on such an extensive scale as to include the prevention of the Depressed Classes from using the commonly used paths and the stoppage of sale of the necessities of life by the village Bania. According to the evidence, sometimes small causes suffice for the proclamation of a social boycott against the Depressed Classes. Frequently it follows on the exercise by the Depressed Classes of their right to use the common well, but cases have been by no means rare, where a stringent boycott has been proclaimed simply because a Depressed Class man has put on the sacred thread, has bought a piece of land, has put on good clothes or ornaments, or has carried a marriage procession with a bridegroom on the horse through the public street.

This was said in 1928. Lest it should be regarded as a phase which has now ended, I reproduce below a copy of a petition by the Untouchables of the village Kheri Jessore in the Punjab addressed to the Deputy Commissioner of the Rohtak District in February 1947 and a copy of which was sent to me. It reads as follows:

From
The Scheduled Caste People (Chamars),
Village Kheri Jessore, Tehsil and District Rohtak.

To
The Deputy Commissioner,
Rohtak District, Rohtak.

Sir,

We, the following Scheduled Caste (Chamars) of the Village Kheri Jessore, beg to invite your kind attention to the hard plight, we are put to, due to the undue pressure and merciless treatment by the caste-Hindu Jats of this village.

It was about four months back that the Jats of the village assembled in the Chopal and told us to work in the fields on a wage in kind of one bundle of crops, containing only about one seer of grains per day per man instead of food at both times and a load of crops, and annas 8 in addition which we used to get before above announcement was made. As it was too little and insufficient to meet both ends, we refused to go to work. At this they were enraged and declared a Social Boycott on us. They made a rule that our cattle would not be allowed to graze in the jungle unless we would agree to pay a tax not leviable under Government for the animals, which they call as 'Poochhi'. They even do not allow our cattle to drink water in the village pool and have prevented the sweepers from cleaning the streets where we live so that heaps of dust and dirt are lying there which may cause some disease if left unattended to. We are forced to lead a shameful life and they are always ready to beat us and to tear down our honour by behaving indecently towards our wives, sisters and daughters. We are experiencing a lot of trouble of the worst type. While going to the school, the children were even beaten severely and in a merciless manner.

We submitted an application detailing the above facts to yourself but we are sorry that no action has been taken as yet.

It is also for your kind consideration that the Inspector of Police and Tehsildar of Rohtak, whom we approached in this connection, made a careless investigation and in our opinion, no attention was paid to redress the difficulties of the poor and innocent persons.

We, therefore, request your good self to consider over the matter and make some arrangement to stop the merciless treatment and threats which the Jats give us in different ways. We have no other approach except to knock at your kind door and hope your honour will take immediate steps to enable us to lead an honourable and peaceful life which is humanity's birthright.

We beg to remain,

Sir,
Your most obedient servants,
Scheduled Caste People (Chamars), of Village Kheri Jessore,
Tehsil and District Rohtak.
Thumb Impressions.

Copy forwarded to the Hon'ble Dr. B.R. Ambedkar
Western Court, New Delhi.
Received on 1st February 1947.

This shows that what was true in 1928 is true even today. What is true of Bombay is true of the whole of India. For evidence of the general use of boycott by the Hindus against the Untouchables one has only to refer to the events that occurred all over India in the last elections to the Provincial Legislatures. Only when boycott is made criminal will the Untouchables be free from being the slaves of the Hindus.

The weapon of boycott is nowadays used against other communities besides the Scheduled Castes. It is therefore in the interests of all minor communities to have this protection.

The provisions relating to boycott are taken bodily from the Burma Anti-Boycott Act, 1922.

Right to Representation in the Legislature and in the Local Bodies (Article II—Section IV, Part I Clause 1)

There is nothing new in this clause. The right to representation in the Legislature is conceded by the Poona Pact. The only points that require to be reconsidered relate to (1) Quantum of Representation, (2) Weightage and (3) The System of Electorates.

Quantum

The quantum of representation allowed to the Scheduled Castes by the Poona Pact is set out in Clause 1 of the Pact. The proportion set out in the Pact was fixed out of the balance of seats which remained after (i) the share of the other communities had been taken out; (ii) after weightage to other communities had been allotted, and (iii) after seats had been allocated to special interests. This allotment of seats to the Scheduled Castes has resulted in great injustice. The loss due to seats taken out as weightage and seats given to special interests ought not to have been thrown upon the Scheduled Castes. The allotment of those seats had already been made by the Communal Award long before the Poona Pact. It was therefore not possible then to rectify this injustice.

Weightage

There is another injustice from which the Scheduled Castes have been suffering. It relates to their right to a share in weightage.

As one can see the right to weightage has become a matter of double controversy. One controversy is between the majority and the minorities, the other is a matter of controversy between the different minorities.

The first controversy relates to the principle of weightage. The majority insists that the minority has no right to representation in excess of the ratio of its population to the total population. Why this rule is insisted upon by the majority it is difficult to understand. Is it because the majority wants to establish its own claim to population ratio so that it may always remain as a majority and act as a majority? Or is it because of the fact that a minority no matter how much weightage was given to it must remain a minority and cannot alter the fact that the majority will always be able to impose its will upon it. The first ground leads to a complete negation of the basic conception of majority rule which if rightly understood means nothing more than a decision of the majority to which the minority has reconciled itself. This cannot be the intention of the majority. One must put a more charitable construction and assume that the argument on which the contention of the majority rests is the second and not the first. That a minority even with weightage will remain a minority has to be accepted in view of the insistence of a communal majority to remain a majority and to claim the privileges of a political majority which it is not. But surely there is a difference between a defeat which is a complete rout and a defeat which is almost victory though not a victory. Cricketers know what difference there is between the defeat of a team by a few runs, a defeat by a few wickets and a defeat by one whole innings. The defeat by one whole innings is a complete frustration which a defeat by a few runs is not. Such a frustration, when it comes about in the political life of a minority depresses and demoralizes and crushes the spirit of the minority. This must be avoided at any price. Looked at from this point of view there is no doubt that the rule of population—ratio—representation insisted upon by the majority is wrong. What a minority needs is not more representation but effective representation.

And what is effective representation? Obviously the effectiveness of representation depends upon its being large enough to give the minority the sense of not being entirely overwhelmed by the majority. Representation according to population of a minority or of the minorities combined may be effective by reason of the fact that the population of a minority where there is only one or of the combined minorities where there are many is large enough to secure effective minority representation. But there may be cases where the population of a minority or of the minorities combined is too small to secure such effective representation if the population ratio of a minority is taken as an inflexible standard to determine its quantum of representation. To insist upon such a standard is to make mockery of the protection to the minority which is the purpose behind the right to representation which is accepted as the legitimate claim of a minority. In such cases weightage which is another name for deduction from the quantum of representation which is due to the majority on the basis of its population becomes essential and the majority if it wishes to be fair and honest must concede it. There can therefore be no quarrel over the principle of weightage. On this footing the controversy becomes restricted to the question, how is the magnitude of weightage to be determined? This obviously is a question of adjustment and not of principle.

There can therefore be no manner of objection to the principle of weightage. The demand for weightage is however a general demand of all the minorities and the Scheduled Castes must join in it where the majority is too big. What is however wrong with the existing weightage is unequal distribution among the various minorities. At present, some minorities have secured a lion's share and some like the Untouchables have none. This wrong must be rectified by a distribution of the weightage on some intelligible principles.

Electorates

The method of election to the seats allotted to the Scheduled Castes is set out in clauses (2) to (4) of the Poona Pact. It provides for two elections: (1) Primary election and (2) Final election. The Primary election is by a Separate Electorate of the Scheduled Castes. It is only a qualifying election and determines who is entitled to stand in the Final election on behalf of the Scheduled Castes for the seats reserved to them. The Final election is by a Joint Electorate in which both caste-Hindus and the Scheduled Castes can vote and the final result is determined by their joint vote.

Clause 5 of the Poona Pact has limited the system of Primary election to ten years which means that any election taking place after 1947 will be by a system of Joint Electorates and reserved seats pure and simple.

Even if the Hindus agreed to extend the system of double election for a further period it will not satisfy the Scheduled Castes. There are two objections to the retention of the Primary election. Firstly, it does not help the Scheduled Castes to elect a man who is their best choice ... the Scheduled Caste candidate who tops the poll in the Primary election fails to succeed in the Final election and the Scheduled Caste candidate who fails in the Primary election tops the poll in the Final election. Secondly, the Primary election is for the most part a fiction and not a fact. In the last election, out of 151 seats reserved for the Scheduled Castes there were Primary elections only in 43. This is because it is impossible for the Scheduled Castes to bear the expenses of two elections—Primary and Final. To retain such a system is worse than useless.

Things will be much worse under the system of Joint Electorates and reserved seats which will hereafter become operative under the terms of the Poona Pact. This is no mere speculation. The last election has conclusively proved that the Scheduled Castes can be completely disfranchised in a Joint Electorate.... As the Simon Commission has observed, the device of the reserved seats ceases to be workable where the protected community constitutes an exceedingly small fraction of any manageable constituency. This is exactly the case of the Scheduled Castes. This disparity cannot be ignored. It will remain even under adult suffrage. That being the case, a fool-proof and a knave-proof method must be found to ensure real representation to the Scheduled Castes. Such a method must involve the abolition of—

1. the Primary election as a needless and heavy encumbrance; and
2. the substitution of Separate Electorates.

One of the issues which has embittered the relations between the Hindus and the Scheduled Castes in the political field is the issue of electorate. The Scheduled Castes are insisting upon Separate Electorates. The Hindus are equally insistent on opposing the demand. To arrive at a settlement on this issue—without which there can be no peace and amity between the Hindus and the Scheduled Castes—it is necessary to determine who is right and who is wrong and whether the opposition is based on rational grounds or is based on mere prejudice.

The grounds which are generally urged against the demand of the Scheduled Castes for Separate Electorates are:

1. that the Scheduled Castes are not a minority;
2. that the Scheduled Castes are Hindus and therefore they cannot have Separate Electorates;
3. that Separate Electorates will perpetuate untouchability;
4. that Separate Electorates are anti-national; and
5. that Separate Electorates enable British Imperialism to influence the communities having Separate Electorates to act against the interests of the country.

Are these arguments valid?

1. To say that the Scheduled Castes are not a minority is to misunderstand the meaning of the word 'minority'. Separation in religion is not the only test of a minority. Nor is it a good and efficient test. Social discrimination constitutes the real test for determining whether a social group is or is not a minority. Even Mr. Gandhi thought it logical and practical to adopt this test in preference to that of religious separation. Following this test, Mr. Gandhi in an editorial under the heading. 'The Fiction of Majority' in the *Harijan*

dated 21st October 1939 has given his opinion that the Scheduled Castes are the only real minority in India.

2. To argue that the Scheduled Castes are Hindus and therefore cannot demand Separate Electorates is to put the same argument in a different form. To make religious affiliation the determining factor for constitutional safeguards is to overlook the fact that the religious affiliation may be accompanied by an intense degree of social separation and discrimination. The belief that Separate Electorates go with separation in religion arises from the fact that those minorities who have been given Separate Electorates happen to be religious minorities. This, however, is not correct. Muslims are given Separate Electorates not because they are different from Hindus in point of religion. They are given Separate Electorates because—and this is the fundamental fact—the social relations between the Hindus and the Musalmans are marked by social discrimination. To put the point in a somewhat different manner, the nature of the electorates is determined not by reference to religion but by reference to social considerations. That it is social considerations and not religious affiliation or disaffiliation which is accepted as the basis of determining the nature of the electorates is best illustrated by the arrangements made under the Government of India Act (1935) for the Christian community in India. The Christian community is divided into three sections—Europeans, Anglo-Indians and Indian Christians. In spite of the fact that they all belong to the same religion, each section has a Separate Electorate. This shows that what is decisive is not religious affiliation but social separation.

3. To urge that Separate Electorates prevent solidarity between the Untouchables and the caste-Hindus is the result of confused thinking. Elections take place once in five years. Assuming there were Joint Electorates, it is difficult to understand how social solidarity between the Hindus and the Untouchables can be promoted by their devoting one day for voting together when out of the rest of the five years they are leading severally separate lives? Similarly, assuming that there were Separate Electorates it is difficult to understand how one day devoted to separate voting in the course of five years can make for greater separation than what already exists? Or contrary-wise, how can one day in five years devoted to separate voting prevent those who wish to work for their union

from carrying out their purposes. To make it concrete, how can Separate Electorate for the Untouchables prevent inter-marriage or inter-dining being introduced between them and the Hindus? It is therefore futile to say that Separate Electorates for the Untouchables will perpetuate separation between them and the Hindus.

4. To insist that Separate Electorates create anti-national spirit is contrary to experience. The Sikh have Separate Electorates. But no one can say that the Sikhs are anti-national. The Muslims have had Separate Electorates right from 1909. Mr. Jinnah had been elected by Separate Electorates. Yet, Mr. Jinnah was the apostle of Indian Nationalism up to 1935. The Indian Christians have Separate Electorates. Nonetheless a good lot of them have shown their partiality to the Congress if they have not been actually returned on the Congress ticket. Obviously, nationalism and anti-nationalism have nothing to do with the electoral system. They are the result of extra electoral forces.

5. This argument has no force. It is nothing but escapism. Be that as it may, with free India any objection to Separate Electorates on such a ground must vanish.

The reason why the arguments advanced by the opponents of Separate Electorates do not stand the scrutiny of logic and experience is due entirely to the fact that their approach to the subject is fundamentally wrong. It is wrong in two respects:

1. They fail to realize that the system of electorates has nothing to do with the religious nexus or communal nexus. It is nothing but a mechanism to enable a minority to return its true representative to the Legislature. Being a mechanism for the protection of a minority it follows that whether the electorate should be joint or separate must be left to be determined by the minority.

2. They fail to make any distinction between the demand for Separate Electorates by a majority community and a similar demand made by a minority community. A majority community has no right to demand Separate Electorates. The reason is simple. A right by a majority community to demand Separate Electorates is tantamount to a right to establish the Government of the majority community over the minority community without the consent of the minority. This is contrary to the well-established doctrine of democracy that government must be with the consent of the governed. No such evil consequence follows from the opposite principle namely that

a minority community is entitled to determine the nature of the electorates suited to its interests, because there is no possibility of the minority being placed in a position to govern the majority.

A correct attitude towards the whole question rests on the following axioms:

1. The system of electorates being a devise for the protection of the minority, the issue whether the electoral system should be the Joint Electorate or Separate Electorate must be left to the wishes of the minority. If it is large enough to influence the majority it will choose Joint Electorates. If it is too small for the purpose, it will prefer Separate Electorates for fear of being submerged.

2. The majority, being in a position to rule can have no voice in the determination of the system of electorates. If the minority wants Joint Electorates, the majority must submit itself to Joint Electorates. If the minority decides to have Separate Electorates for itself the majority cannot refuse to grant them. In other words, the majority must look to the decision of the minority and abide by it.

Right to Representation in the Executive (Article II—Section IV, Part I Clause 2)

This demand may appear to be outside the Poona Pact in as much as the Poona Pact made no provision for it. This would not be correct. As a matter of fact, if no provision was made, it was because there was no need to make such a provision. This was due to two reasons: *Firstly,* it was due to the fact that at the time when the Poona Pact was made no community was guaranteed by Law a specific quantum of representation in Executive, *Secondly,* the representation of the communities in the Executive was left to a convention which the Governor by his instrument of instructions was required to see observed. Experience has shown that the quantum of representation of the Scheduled Castes in the Executive should now be fixed.

Right to Representation in Services (Article II—Section IV, Part I Clause 3)

This is not a new demand. Clause 8 of the Poona Pact guarantees to the Scheduled Castes fair representation in Public Services. It does not, however, define the quantum of representation. The demand has been admitted by the Government of India as legitimate and even the quantum of representation has been defined. All that remains is to give it a statutory basis.

Special Responsibilities for Higher Education (Article II— Section IV, Part II Clause 1)

This is not a new demand. Clause 9 of the Poona Pact guarantees that an adequate sum shall be earmarked for the education of the Scheduled Castes. It does not define the quantum. All that the demand does is to define the quantum of liability the State should take. In this connection reference may be made to Section 83 of the Government of India Act, 1935, which relates to the education of the Anglo-Indians and Europeans and to the grants made to the Aligarh and Benaras Hindu Universities by the Central Government.

Special Responsibilities for Separate Settlements (Article II— Section IV, Part II Clause 2)

This is a new demand but is justified by circumstances. At present, the Hindus live in the village and the Untouchables live in the ghettoes. The object is to free the Untouchables from the thraldom of the Hindus. So long as the present arrangement continues it is impossible for the Untouchables either to free themselves from the yoke of the Hindus or to get rid of their untouchability. It is the close knit association of the Untouchables with the Hindus living in the same villages which marks them out as Untouchables and which enables the Hindus to identify them as being Untouchables. India is admittedly a land of villages and so long as the village system provides an easy method of marking out and identifying the Untouchables, the Untouchable has no escape from untouchability. It is the system of the village plus the Ghetto which perpetuates untouchability and the Untouchables therefore demand that the nexus should be broken and the Untouchables who are as a matter of fact socially separate should be made separate geographically and territorially also, and be settled into separate villages exclusively for Untouchables in which the distinction of the high and the low and of Touchable and Untouchable will find no place.

The second reason for demanding separate settlements arises out of the economic position of the Untouchables in the villages. That their condition is most pitiable no one will deny. They are a body of landless labourers who are entirely dependent upon such employment as the

Hindus may choose to give them and on such wages is the Hindus may find it profitable to pay. In the villages in which they live they cannot engage in any trade or occupation, for owing to untouchability no Hindu will deal with them. It is therefore obvious that there is no way of earning a living which is open to the Untouchables so long as they live in a ghetto as a dependent part of the Hindu village.

This economic dependence has also other consequences besides the condition of poverty and degradation which proceeds from it. The Hindu has a code of life, which is part of his religion. This code of life gives him many privileges and heaps upon the Untouchable many indignities which are incompatible with the dignity and sanctity of human life. The Untouchables all over India are fighting against the indignities and injustices which the Hindus in the name of their religion have heaped upon them. A perpetual war is going on every day in every village between the Hindus and the Untouchables. It does not see the light of the day. The Hindu Press is not prepared to give it publicity lest it should injure the cause of their freedom in the eyes of the world. The existence of a grim struggle between the Touchables and the Untouchables is however a fact. Under the village system the Untouchables has found himself greatly handicapped in his struggle for free and honorable life. It is a contest between the Hindus who are economically and socially strong and the Untouchables who are economically poor and numerically small. That the Hindus most often succeed in suppressing the Untouchables is due to many causes. The Hindus have the Police and the Magistracy on their side. In a quarrel between the Untouchables and the Hindus the Untouchables will never get protection from the Police and justice from the Magistrate. The Police and the Magistracy naturally love their class more than their duty. But the chief weapon in the armoury of the Hindus is economic power which they possess over the poor Untouchables living in the village. The proposal may be dubbed escapism. But the only alternative is perpetual slavery.

Sanctions for Safeguards and Amendment of Safeguards to be embodied in the Constitution (Article II—Section IV, Part III Clause 1)

No country which has the problem of communal majority and communal minority is without some kind of an arrangement whereby they agree to share political power. South Africa has such an understanding. So has Canada. The arrangement for sharing political power between the English and the French in Canada is carried to the minutes office. In referring to this fact Mr. Porritt in his book *Evolution of the Dominion of Canada* says:

Conditions at Ottawa, partly due to race and language, and partly due to long prevailing ideas as to the distribution of all government patronage, have militated against the Westminster precedent of continuing a member in the chair for two or three parliaments, regardless of the fortunes of political parties at general elections. There is a new speaker at Ottawa for each new House of Commons; and it has long been a custom that when one political party continues in power for two or three parliaments, if the speaker in one parliament is of British extraction the next one shall be a French-Canadian.

It is a rule also that the offices of speaker and of deputy speaker can at no time be held by men of the same race. If the speaker is a French-Canadian, the deputy speaker, who is also Chairman of committees, must be an English-speaking Canadian; for the rule of the House is that the member elected to serve as deputy speaker shall be required to possess the full and practical knowledge of the language which is not that of the speaker for the time being.

The clerkship and the assistant clerkship of the House, and the offices of sergeant-at-arms and deputy sergeant-at-arms—all appointive as distinct from elective offices—are, by usage, also similarly divided between the two races.

Nearly all the offices, important and unimportant, connected with parliament, with the Senate as well as with the House, are distributed in accordance with these rules or usages. A roll call of the staffs of the two Houses, including even the boys in knickerbockers who act as pages, would contain the names of almost as many French-Canadians as Canadians of British ancestry.

The rules and usages by virtue of which this distribution of offices is made are older than Confederation. They date back to the early years of the United Provinces, when Quebec and Ontario elected exactly the same number of members to the Legislature, and when these were the only provinces in the union.

Quebec today elects only 65 of the 234 members of the House of Commons. Its population is not one-fourth of the population of the Dominion. Its contribution to Dominion revenues does not exceed one-sixth. But an equal division of the offices of the House of Commons is regarded by Quebec as necessary to the preservation of its rights and privileges; and so long as each political party, when it is in power, is dependent on support from French-Canada, it will be nearly as difficult to ignore the claim of Quebec to these parliamentary honours and offices as it would be to repeal the clause in the British North America Act that safeguards the separate schools system.

Unfortunately for the minorities in India, Indian Nationalism has developed a new doctrine which may be called the Divine Right of the Majority to rule the minorities according to the wishes of the majority. Any claim for the sharing of power by the minority is called communalism while the monopolizing of the whole power by the majority is called Nationalism. Guided by such a political philosophy the majority is not prepared to allow the minorities to share political power nor is it willing to respect any convention made in that behalf as is evident from their repudiation of the obligation (to include representatives of the minorities in the Cabinet) contained in the Instrument of Instructions issued to the Governors in the Government of India Act of 1935. Under these circumstances there is no way left but to have the rights of the Scheduled Castes embodied in the Constitution.

Sanctions for Safeguards and Amendment of Safeguards to be Embodied in the Constitution (Article II—Section IV, Part III Clause 2)

This is not a new demand. It replaces Clause 6 of the Poona Pact which provides that the system of representation for the Scheduled Castes by reserved seats shall continue until determined by mutual consent between the communities concerned in the settlement. Since there is no safe method of ascertaining the will of the Scheduled Castes as to how to amend and alter the safeguards provided for them it is necessary to formulate a plan which will take the place of Clause 6 of the Pact. Provisions having similar objectives to those contained in the proposal exist in the Constitution of Australia, America and South Africa.

In dealing with a matter of this sort two considerations have to be borne in mind. One is that it is not desirable to rule out the possibility of a change in the safeguards being made in the future by the parties concerned. On the other hand it is by no means desirable to incessant struggle over their revision. If the new Union and State Legislatures are to address themselves successfully to their responsibilities set out in the Preamble it is desirable that they should not be distracted by the acute contentions between religions and classes which questions of change in the safeguards are bound to arise. Hence a period of twenty-five years has been laid down before any change could be considered.

Sanctions for Safeguards and Amendment of Safeguards to be embodied in the Constitution (Article II—Section IV, Part IV)
The object of this provision is to see that whatever safeguards are provided for the Scheduled Castes in British India are also provided for the Scheduled Castes in the Indian States. The provision lays down that an Indian State seeking admission to the Union shall have to satisfy that its Constitution contains these safeguards.

Part V—Interpretation
Whether the Scheduled Castes are a minority or not has become a matter of controversy. The purpose of First Provision is to set this controversy at rest. The Scheduled Castes are in a worse position as compared to any other minority in India. As such they require and deserve much more protection than any other minority does. The least one can do is to treat them as a minority.

The purpose of Second Provision is to remove the provincial bar. There is no reason why a person who belongs to Scheduled Castes in one Province should lose the benefit of political privileges given by the Constitution merely because he happens to change his domicile.

28

Constitutional Safeguards for the Scheduled Castes
1947–50

ARTICLE 10 (DRAFT CONSTITUTION) (*BAWS* 1994, VOL. 13: 391–4)

...To come to the other question which has been agitating the members of this House, viz., the use of the word 'backward' in clause (3) of Article 10. I should like to begin by making some general observations so that members might be in a position to understand the exact import, the significance and the necessity for using the word 'backward' in this particular clause. If members were to try and exchange their views on this subject, they will find that there are three points of view which it is necessary for us to reconcile if we are to produce a workable proposition which will be accepted by all. Of the three points of view, the first is that there shall be equality of opportunity for all citizens. It is the desire of many Members of this House that every individual who is qualified for a particular post should be free to apply for that post, to sit for examinations and to have his qualifications tested so as to determine whether he is fit for the post or not and that there ought to be no limitations, there ought to be no hindrance in the operation of this principle of equality of opportunity. Another view mostly shared by a section of the House is that, if this principle is to be operative and it ought to be operative in their judgment to its fullest extent there ought to be no reservations of any sort for any class or community and all citizens, if they are qualified, should be placed on the same footing of equality so far as the Public Services are concerned. That is the second point of view we have. Then we have quite a massive opinion which insists that, although theoretically it is good to have the principle that there shall be equality of opportunity, there must at the same time be a provision made for the entry of certain communities which have so far been outside the administration. As I said, the Drafting Committee had to produce a formula which would reconcile these three points of view, firstly, that there shall be equality of opportunity, secondly that there shall be reservations in favour of certain communities which have not so far had a 'proper look-in' so to say into the administration. If honourable Members will bear these facts in mind—the three principles, we had to reconcile, they will see that no better formula could be produced than the one that is embodied in sub-clause (3) of Article 10 of the Constitution; they will find that the view of those who believe and hold that there shall be equality of opportunity, has been embodied in sub-clause (1) of Article 10. It is a generic principle. At the same time as I said, we had to reconcile this formula with the demand made by certain communities that the administration which has now for historical reasons been controlled by one community or a few communities, that situation should disappear and that the others also must have an opportunity of getting into the Public Services. Supposing, for instance, we were to concede in full the demand of those communities who have not been so far employed in the Public Services to the fullest extent, what would really happen is, we shall be completely destroying the first proposition upon which we are all agreed, namely, that there shall be an equality of opportunity. Let me give an illustration. Supposing, for instance, reservations were made for a community or a collection of communities, the total of which came to something like 70 per cent of the total posts under the State and only 30 per cent were retained as the unreserved. Could anybody say that the reservation of 30 per cent we open to general competition would be satisfactory from the point of view of giving effect to the first principle, namely, that there shall be equality of opportunity? It cannot be in my judgment. Therefore, the seats to be reserved if the reservation is to be consistent with sub-clause (1) of Article 10 must be confined to a minority of seats. It is then only that the first principle could find its place in the Constitution and effective in operation. If honourable Members understand this position that we have to safeguard two things namely, the principle of equality of opportunity and at the same time satisfy the demand of communities which have not so far representation in the State, then, I am sure they will agree that unless you use some such qualifying phrase as 'backward' the exception made in favour of reservation will ultimately eat up the rule altogether. Nothing of the rule will remain. That I think if I may say so, is the justification why the Drafting Committee undertook on its own shoulders the responsibility of introducing the word 'backward', which I admit, did not originally find a place in the fundamental right in the way in which it was passed by this Assembly. But I think honourable Members will realize that the Drafting Committee which has been ridiculed on more than one ground for producing sometimes a loose draft, sometimes something which is not appropriate and so on, might have opened itself to further attack that they produced a Draft Constitution in which the exception was so large, that it left no room for the rule to operate. I think that is sufficient to justify why the word 'backward' has been used.

... With regard to the minorities, there is a special reference to that in Article 296, where it has been laid down that some provision will be made with regard to the minorities. Of course we did not lay down any proportion. That is quite clear from the section itself, but we have not altogether omitted the minorities from consideration. Somebody asked me: 'What is a backward community'? Well, I think any one who reads the language of the draft itself will find that we have left to be determined by each local Government. A backward community is a community which is backward in the opinion of the Government. My honourable Friend Mr. T.T. Krishnamachari asked me whether this rule will be justifiable. It is rather difficult to give a dogmatic answer. Personally I think it would be a justifiable matter. If the local Government included in this category of reservations such a large number of seats; I think one could very well go to the Federal Court and the Supreme Court and say that the reservation is of such a magnitude that the rule regarding equality of opportunity has been destroyed and the court will then come to the conclusion whether the local Government or the State Government has acted in a reasonable and prudent manner. Mr. Krishnamachari asked who is a reasonable man and who is a prudent man? These are matters of litigation. Of course, they are matters of litigation, but my honourable Friend, Mr. Krishnamachari will understand that the words 'reasonable persons and prudent persons have been used in very many laws and if he will refer only to the Transfer of Property Act, he will find that in very many cases the words "a reasonable person and a prudent person" have very well been defined and the court will not find any difficulty in defining it. I hope therefore that the amendments which I have accepted, will be accepted by the House.

ARTICLE 320: RESERVATION IN PUBLIC SERVICES (*BAWS* 1994, VOL. 13: 843–6)

... The only point that remains for me to say anything about is the question that is raised about the Scheduled Castes and the Backward Classes. I think I might say that enough provision has been made, both in Article 296 which we have to consider at a later stage and in Article 10, for safeguarding the interests of what are called the Scheduled Castes, the Scheduled Tribes and the Backward Classes. I do not think that any purpose will be served by making a provision whereby it would be obligatory upon the President to appoint a member of what might be called either a Scheduled Caste, or Scheduled Tribe or a member belonging to the Backward Classes....

The function of a member of the Public Service Commission is a general one. He cannot be there to protect the interests of any particular class. He shall have to apply his mind to the general question of finding out who is the best and the most efficient candidate for an appointment. The real protection, the real method of protection is one that has been adopted, namely, to permit the Legislature to fix a certain quota to be filled by these classes. I am also asked to define what are Backward Classes. Well, I think the words 'Backward Classes' so far as this country is concerned is almost elementary. I do not think that I can use a simpler word than the word 'Backward Classes'. Everybody in the province knows who are the Backward Classes, and I think it is, therefore, better to leave the matter as has been done in this Constitution, to the Commission which is to be appointed which will investigate into the conditions of the state of society, and to ascertain which are to be regarded as Backward Classes in this country....

But in the meantime, there is no prohibition on any provincial government to make provisions for what are called the Backward Classes. They are left quite free, by Article 10. Therefore, my submission is that there is no fear that the interests of the Backward Classes or the Scheduled Castes will be overlooked in the recruitment to the services. As my Friend Pandit Kunzru has said, the articles I have presented to the House are certainly a very great improvement upon what the articles were before in the Draft Constitution. We have, if I may say so for myself, studied a great deal the provisions in the Canadian law and the provisions in the Australian law, and we have succeeded, if I may say so, in finding out a via *media* which I hope the House will not find any difficulty in accepting.

ARTICLE 330: POLITICAL RESERVATIONS (*BAWS* 1994, VOL. 13: 848–9)

...There are just three points which, I think, call for a reply. One point is the one which is raised by Mr. Laskar by his amendment. His amendment is to introduce the words 'save in the case of the Scheduled Castes in Assam'. I have completely failed to understand what he intends to do by the introduction of these words. If these words were introduced it would mean that the Scheduled Castes in Assam will not be entitled to get the representation which the article proposes to give them in the Lower House of the Central Parliament, because if the words stand as they are, 'save in the case of the Scheduled Castes in Assam' unaccompanied by any other provision, I cannot see what other effect it would have except to deprive the Scheduled Castes of Assam of the right to representation which has been given to them. If I understand him correctly, I think the matter, which he has raised, legitimately refers to Article 67B of the Constitution which has already been passed. In that article it has been provided that the ratio of representation in the Legislature should have a definite relation to certain population figures. It has been laid down that the representation in the Lower House at the Centre shall be not less than one representative for every 7, 50, 000 people, or not more than one representative for a population of 5, 00, 000. According to what he was saying—and I must confess that it was utterly impossible for me to hear anything that he was saying—but if I gathered the purport of it, he seems to be under the impression that on account of the division of Sylhet district the population of the Scheduled Castes in Assam has been considerably reduced and that there may not be any such figure as we have laid down, namely 7, 50, 000 or 5, 00, 000, with the result that he feels that the Scheduled Castes of Assam will not get any representation. But I should like to tell him that it applies to the constituency. What it means is that if a constituency consists of 7, 50, 000 people, that constituency will have one seat. It may be that within that constituency the population of the Scheduled Castes is much smaller, but that would not prevent either the Delimitation Committee or Parliament from allotting a seat for the Scheduled Castes in that particular area. His fear, therefore, in my judgment, is utterly groundless.

Then I come to the amendment moved by Sardar Hukam Singh in which he suggests that provision ought to be made whereby the Scheduled Castes and the Scheduled Tribes would be entitled to contest seats which are generally not reserved for the Scheduled Castes or the Scheduled Tribes. He said that the Drafting Committee has made a deliberate omission. I do not think that is correct. It is accepted that the Scheduled Castes and the Scheduled Tribes shall be entitled to contest seats which are not reserved seats, which are unreserved seats. That is contained in the report of the Advisory Committee which has already been accepted by the House. The reason why that particular provision has not been introduced in Article 292 is because it is not germane at this place. This proposition will find its place in the law relating to election with which this Assembly or the Assembly in its legislative capacity will have to deal with. He therefore need have no fear on that ground.

With regard to the point raised by my Friend Mr. Pillai that the population according to which seats are to be reserved should be estimated by a fresh census, that matter has been agitated in this House on very many occasions. I then said that it was quite impossible for the Government to commit itself to taking a fresh census but the Government has kept its mind open. If it is feasible the government may take a fresh census in order to estimate the population of the Scheduled Castes or the Scheduled Tribes in order to calculate the total representation that they would be entitled to in accordance with the provisions of Article 292. The Government is also suggesting that if in any case it is not possible to have a fresh census, they will estimate the population of these communities on the basis of the voters' strength which may be calculated from them, in which case we might be able to arrive at what might be called a rough and ready estimate of the population I do not think it is possible for me to go beyond that.

ARTICLE 334: TIME-LIMIT FOR POLITICAL RESERVATIONS (*BAWS* 1994, VOL. 13: 850–3)

... with regard to the question raised by Mr. Naziruddin Ahmad, one part of it has been, I think, met by the amendment moved by my Friend Mr. Krishnamachari which I also accept. I am not at all clear in my own mind at the present stage whether the words in the clause mean that the time-limit should begin to operate from the commencement of the Constitution or whether from the date of the first election to the new Parliament. But all I can say at this stage is that that is a matter which the Drafting Committee will consider and if it is necessary, they will bring about some amendment to carry out the intention that the period should be from the date of the first meeting of the Parliament.

With regard to the other arguments which have been used by my friends Mr. Muniswami Pillai and Mr. Monomohan Das, I am sorry it is not possible to accept that amendment. Their proposal is that while they are prepared to leave the clause as it is, they propose to vest Parliament with the power to alter this clause by further extension of the period of ten years. Now first of all we have, as I said, introduced this matter in the Constitution itself, and I do not think that we should permit any change to be made in this, except by the amendment of the Constitution itself.

I would like to say one or two words on the remarks of Scheduled Castes who have spoken in somewhat passionate and vehement terms on the limitation imposed by this article. I have to say that they have really no cause for complaint, because the decision to limit the thing to ten years was really a decision which has been arrived at with their consent. I personally was prepared to press for a larger time, because I do feel that so far as the Scheduled Castes are concerned, they are not treated on the same footing as the other minorities. For instance, so far as I know the special reservations for the Musalmans started in the year 1892; so to say, the beginning was made then. Therefore, the Muslims had practically enjoyed these privileges for more or less sixty years. The Christians got this privilege under the Constitution of 1920 and they have enjoyed it for 28 years. The Scheduled Castes got this only in the Constitution of 1935. The commencement of this benefit of special reservation practically began in the year 1937 when that Act came into operation. Unfortunately for them, they had the benefit of this only for two years, for from 1939 practically up to the present moment, or up to 1946, the Constitution was suspended and the Scheduled Castes were not in a position to enjoy the benefits of the privileges which were given to them in the 1935 Act, and it would have been quite proper I think, and generous on the part of this House to have given the Scheduled Castes a longer term with regard to these reservations. But, as I said, it was all accepted by the House. It was accepted by Mr. Nagappa and Mr. Muniswami Pillai, all these Members, if I may say so—I am not making any complaint—were acting on the other side, and I think it is not right now to go back on these provisions. If at the end of the ten years, the Scheduled Castes find that their position has not improved or that they want further extension of this period, it will not be beyond their capacity or their intelligence to invent new ways of getting the same protection which they are promised here.

... For the Scheduled Tribes I am prepared to give far longer time. But all those who have spoken about the reservation to the Scheduled Castes or to the Scheduled Tribes have been so meticulous that the thing should end by ten years. All I want to say to them, in the words of Edmund Burke, is 'Large Empires and small minds go ill together'.

ARTICLE 30 (DRAFT CONSTITUTION): (ECONOMIC DEMOCRACY) *(BAWS* 1994, VOL. 13: 350–3)

... I see that there is a great deal of misunderstanding as to the real provisions in the Constitution in the minds of those members of the House who are interested in this kind of directive principles. It is quite possible that the misunderstanding or rather inadequate understanding is due to the fact that I myself in my opening speech in support of the motion that I made, did not refer to this aspect of the question. That was because, not that I did not wish to place this matter before the House in a clear-cut fashion, but my speech had already become so large that I did not venture to make it more tiresome than I had already done; but I think it is desirable that I should take a few minutes of the House in order to explain what I regard as the fundamental position taken in the Constitution. As I stated, our Constitution as a piece of mechanism lays down what is called parliamentary democracy. By parliamentary democracy we mean 'one man, one vote'. We also mean that every Government shall be on the anvil, both in its daily affairs and also at the end of a certain period when the voters and the electorate will be given an opportunity to assess the work done by the Government. The reason why we have established in this Constitution a political democracy is because we do not want to install by any means whatsoever a perpetual dictatorship of any particular body of people. While we have established political democracy, it is also the desire that we should lay down as our ideal economic democracy. We do not want merely to lay down a mechanism to enable people to come and capture power. The Constitution also wishes to lay down an ideal before those who would be forming the Government. That ideal is economic democracy, whereby, so far as I am concerned, I understand to mean; 'one man, one vote'. The question is: Have we got any fixed idea as to how we should bring about economic democracy? There are various ways in which people believe that economic democracy can be brought about; there are those who believe in having a socialistic state as the best form of economic democracy; there are those who believe in the communistic idea as the most perfect form of economic democracy.

Now, having regard to the fact that these various ways by which economic democracy may be brought about, we have deliberately introduced in language that we have used, in the directive principles, something which is not fixed or rigid. We have left enough room for people of different ways of thinking, with regard to the reaching of the ideal of economic democracy, to strive in their own way, to persuade the electorate that it is the best way of reaching economic democracy, the fullest opportunity to act in the way in which they want to act Sir, that is the reason why the language of the articles in Part IV is left in the manner in which this Drafting Committee thought it best to leave it. It is no use giving a fixed, rigid form to something which is not rigid, which is fundamentally changing and must, having regard to the circumstances and the times, keep on changing. It is, therefore, no use saying that the directive principles have no value. In my judgment, the directive principles have a great value, for they lay down that our ideal is economic democracy. Because we did not want merely a parliamentary form of Government to be instituted through, the various mechanisms provided in the Constitution, without any direction as to what our economic ideal, as to what our social order ought to be, we deliberately included the Directive Principles in our Constitution. I think, if the friends who are agitated over this question bear in mind what I have said just now that our object in framing this Constitution is really two-fold: (i) to lay down the form of political democracy, and (ii) to lay down that our ideal is economic democracy and also to prescribe that every Government whatever, it is in power, shall strive to bring about economic democracy, much of the misunderstanding under which most members are labouring will disappear.

My friend Mr. Tyagi made an appeal to me to remove the word 'strive', and phrases like that. I think he has misunderstood why we have used the word 'strive'. The word 'strive' which occurs in the Draft Constitution, in my judgment, is very important. We have used it because our intention is that even when there are circumstances which prevent the Government, or which stand in the way of the Government giving effect to these Directive Principles, they shall, even under hard and unpropitious circumstances, always strive in the fulfilment of these Directives. That is why we have used the word 'strive'. Otherwise, it would be open for any Government to say that the circumstances are so bad, that the finances are so inadequate that we cannot even make an effort in the direction in which the Constitution asks us to go. I think my friend Mr. Tyagi will see that the word 'strive' in the context is of great importance and it would be very wrong to delete it. As to the rest of the amendments, I am afraid I have to oppose them....

NOTES

1. Ambedkar explained the disadvantages of the Poona Pact which are part of Appendix of 'States and Minorities' as follows and concluded:
    (i) That every of the Scheduled Caste candidate who became successful in the Final election (there were to be two elections—Primary and Final) owed his success to the votes of the caste-Hindus and not of the Scheduled Castes. A great many of them came to the top of the poll and secured votes equal to and in some cases larger than those obtained by caste-Hindu candidates. Secondly, in very few constituencies was the successful Scheduled Caste candidate required to rely on reservation. This is a most unexpected phenomenon. Anyone who compares the voting strength of the Scheduled Castes with the voting strength of the caste-Hindus in the different constituencies would realize that the voting strength of the Scheduled Castes is so small that such a phenomenon could never have occurred if only the Scheduled Castes voters had voted for the Scheduled Caste candidates. That they have occurred is proof positive that the success of the Scheduled Caste candidate in the Final election is conditioned by the caste-Hindu votes.
    (ii) That comparing the results of the Primary election with those of the Final election the Scheduled Caste candidate who was elected in the Final election was one who had failed in the Primary election (if the Primary election be treated as a Final election and the constituency be treated as a single-member constituency).
    (iii) Owing to the extreme disparity between the voting strength of the Hindus and the Scheduled Castes—disparity which will not disappear even under adult suffrage—a system of Joint Electorates will not succeed in giving the Scheduled Castes the chance of returning their true representatives.

(iv) The Poona Pact has completely disfranchised the Scheduled Castes inasmuch as candidates whom they rejected in the Primary elections—which is a true index of their will—have been returned in the Final election by the votes of the caste-Hindus.

The Poona Pact is thus fraught with mischief. It was accepted because of the coercive fast of Mr. Gandhi and because of the assurance given at the time that the Hindus will not interfere in the election of the Scheduled Caste (for detailed version See *BAWS* 1979, vol. 1: 431–46).

Text of Poona Pact

The following is the text of the agreement:—

1. There shall be seats reserved for the Depressed Classes out of the general electorate seats in the Provincial Legislatures as follows:

   Madras 30; Bombay with Sind 15; Punjab 8; Bihar and Orissa 18; Central Provinces 20; Assam 7; Bengal 30; United Provinces 20; Total 148.

   These figures are based on the total strength of the Provincial Councils, announced in the Prime Minister's decision.

2. Election to these seats shall be by Joint Electorates subject, however, to the following procedure:

   All the members of the Depressed Classes, registered in the general electoral roll in a constituency, will form an electoral college, which will elect a panel of four candidates belonging to the Depressed Classes for each of such reserved seats, by the method of the single vote; the four persons getting the highest number of votes in such primary election, shall be candidates for election by the general electorate.

3. Representation of the Depressed Classes in the Central Legislature shall likewise be on the principle of Joint Electorates and reserved seats by the method of primary election in the manner provided for in Clause 2 above, for their representation in the Provincial Legislatures.

4. In the Central Legislature, eighteen per cent of the seats allotted to the general electorate for British India in the said Legislature shall be reserved for the Depressed Classes.

5. The system of primary election to a panel of candidates for election to the Central and Provincial Legislatures, as herein before mentioned, shall come to an end after the first ten years, unless terminated sooner by mutual agreement under the provision of Clause 6 below.

6. The system of representation of the Depressed Classes by reserved seats in the Provincial and Central Legislatures as provided for in Clauses 1 and 4 shall continue until determined by mutual agreement between the communities concerned in the settlement.

7. Franchise for the Central and Provincial Legislatures for the Depressed Classes shall be as indicated in the Lothian Committee Report.

8. There shall be no disabilities attaching to any one on the ground of his being a member of the Depressed Classes in regard to any elections to local bodies or appointment to the Public Services. Every endeavour shall be made to secure fair representation of the Depressed Classes in these respects, subject to such educational qualifications as may be laid down for appointment to the Public Services.

9. In every province out of the educational grant, an adequate sum shall be earmarked for providing educational faculties to the Members of the Depressed Classes.

Part V

Post-Constitution Reflections: 1951–6

Introduction

This section deals with the contributions of Ambedkar after formulation of a concrete reservation policy and other safeguards adopted by the Constitution of India. This was the phase where the flaws in the execution and the need to conceptualize the areas left out in the Constitution were coming to the fore. Following have been the interventions in the last phase of his life:

1. Constitution (First Amendment) Bill: 16 May 1951.
2. Scheduled Castes Emancipation—(Draft Manifesto of Scheduled Caste Federation): 6 October 1951.
3. On Report of the Commissioner for the Scheduled Castes and Tribes (Debate in Parliament): 6 September 1954.
4. On Majorities and Minorities (Thoughts on Linguistic States): 23 December 1955.

The first intervention by Ambedkar in the post-Constitution period comes on judicial interpretation of Article 16(4) of the Constitution vis-à-vis the communal Government Order of Madras government involving reservation for the Backward Classes in the educational institutions. It was in the light of the judgment by the Supreme Court that the Constitution (First Amendment) Bill (*BAWS* 1997, vol. 15: 329–34) was introduced by Ambedkar as Law Minister which also introduced Article 15(4) to legislate any special provision for the advancement of any socially and educationally Backward Classes of citizens or for the SCs and the STs.

The second intervention was in the form of the election manifesto of the Scheduled Castes Federation (*BAWS* 2003, vol. 17: 385–403) in the context of the first general election of India. This can be divided into three parts where first deals with the Principles of the Party, second with the Policy of the Party and the third with the Programme of the Party. It clearly mentioned that the equality of opportunity will be upheld for every Indian but it will be subject to the provision that those who had none in the past shall have priority over those who had. It was to supplement the redemption from oppression and exploitation of man

by another man, of one class by another class and of nation by another
nation. On the policy front of the party, he categorically mentioned
that it will not be tied to any 'ism' but to adopt any plan of social and
economic betterment of the people provided it is consistent with its
principles. While outlining the programme, the British legacy was
told to be having both its credit and debit side. The credit was in the
uniform system of law, justice, and administration. Whereas the debit
was in the maintenance of the archaic social system, maintenance of
the privileged class in education and in the Services—both Civil and
Military, complete neglect of the Untouchables, of the Backward Classes
and of the Tribal People and impoverization of the country.

In the programme of the party, the first priority was given to
education next to the Services in Civil and Military administration.
The focus of education was said to be neither primary nor secondary
but advanced education of such high order both in and outside the
country, which will enable these classes to fit themselves for taking hold
of administration. In the matter of services, reservation will be insisted
upon subject to minimum qualifications to eliminate communalism
rampant in these services due to dominance of privileged sections.
On the poverty front, it was mentioned that in spite of considerable
development of industries, there had been little change in the occupational
structure of the social groups. It was suggested that the landless labour
could be handed over the cultivable wasteland of 93 million acres and
the necessary infrastructure be provided by the State.

As mentioned earlier, the Commissioner for SCs/STs had been
appointed to monitor the safeguards provided in the Constitution of
India. He was to present the reports to the Parliament. Participating
on the report for 1953 (*BAWS* 1997, vol. 15: 895–918), Ambedkar for
the first time commented on the functioning of the existing measures.
The progress on the education front was termed to be satisfying but it
was argued that in 1942, it was agreed that the responsibility of education
of the SCs up to the university standard in India was to be borne by the
provincial governments and the contribution of Government of India
will be towards their education in foreign countries but it was withheld
when Rajagopalachary became the Education Minister and it should
be resumed. On the other hand the scholarships on the basis of minimum
of 50 per cent marks (done through a Circular of the Ministry) should
have no relationship for the SC students because the studying conditions
were not conducive for them was argued by him.

Terming the phrase 'unsuitable' as a very ambiguous phrase, Ambedkar argued that this phrase had been used by all the Public Service Commissions and appointing authorities to end the matter then and there to keep out the SC candidates but what about its use in the Army services at lower ranks where much intellectual caliber was not expected, needed special attention of the government. He also observed that not even a single SC candidate was chosen by the Public Service Commission for the Indian Administrative and Police Services till 1951 and only after his own intervention one such candidate was selected.

On the economic emancipation of the SCs, he maintained that as the government has not taken land into its own hands and created land proprietors so now it could not take away the land and distribute equally among the masses. So the only way out was to amend the Constitution and put the cultivation of wasteland within the purview of Central government so that it was utilized for the benefit of the landless. The second suggestion was to levy the salt tax and develop the wasteland and settling the SCs on that land. He even suggested that the money from salt tax could be kept out of budget and be spent on a scheme in the name of Mahatma Gandhi like 'Gandhi Welfare Scheme' that will give relief to the people whom he wanted to elevate.

There had been yet another occasion when Ambedkar participated in the debates of Rajya Sabha on the social exclusion of SCs and it was while a discussion on Untouchability Offences Bill introduced in 1954. Here, he argued for strict strictures to check the commission of atrocities and take specific measure against the social ostracism that was emphasized at the RTCs as well.

While writing on the linguistic states in 1955 (*BAWS* 1979, vol. 1: 167–70) Ambedkar probably in his last observations on the equal access to the SCs expressed himself. Here, he argued that caste has converted people into majority and minority. Moreover the majority in India is not a political majority rather a communal majority that cannot be transformed or changed as it is fixed.

Though, he had analysed the results of 1937 elections after the Poona Pact (*BAWS* 1990, vol. 9: 146–65) and suggested and struggled for restoration of Separate Electorates throughout 1940s but in vain. The Constitution-making process itself started with an agreement that the minorities including the SCs will not demand Separate Electorates and the majority would agree for reserved constituencies. Dissatisfied with the political representation that had been imposed upon the SCs,

Ambedkar had been emphasizing on alternative modes sometimes in the form of Separate Electorates and plural member constituencies or multi-member constituencies. Once again, he spoke in favour of multi-member constituencies with cumulative voting system in place of Joint Electorates but without much elaboration.

During this phase, Ambedkar seems dissatisfied on majority of the issues except the progress and policies on the education front. Whether it is political representation in the Legislatures due to Joint Electorates or the representation in the Public Services or the prevalent social exclusion of the SCs in multiple spheres, he seems to be discontented. He re-emphasized that State has to play an important role as Interventionist State in the spheres of Land, Industry and Insurance so that the poor and the socially discriminated groups are protected from the monopoly resources for equitable distribution and inclusive development.

29

Constitution (First Amendment) Bill*
16 May 1951

The Minister of Law (Dr. Ambedkar): ... I thought it incumbent on my part to intervene in this debate and to clarify the position so as to dispel the two arguments which had been used in the course of the debate, that there was no necessity for the amendment of the Constitution, and secondly, that Government could wait and give the country and the public larger and longer time and should not rush through this measure. In the observations that I propose to make, I will take the Bill clause by clause and try to explain the necessity for making the changes which the Bill proposes to make.

I will begin with clause 2 of the Bill. Clause 2 of the Bill proposes to amend Article 15. The necessity for the amendment of Article 15 has arisen on account of the judgments recently delivered by the Supreme Court in two cases which came up before them from the Madras State. One case was Madras *vs.* Shrimati Champakam Dorairajan and the other was Venkatraman *vs.* the State of Madras. In the case of Venkataraman the article involved was articled clause (4) and in the case of Shrimati Champakam the article involved was article 29, clause (2). In the one case the question involved was the reservation for Backward Classes in Public Services and in the other case, the question involved was the reservation for Backward Classes in educational institutions. The question turned upon what is known in the Madras Presidency and elsewhere as the Communal G.O. The argument on which the Communal G.O. of the Madras Government was declared to be void and invalid was this. It was said by the Supreme Court that Article 29, clause (2), did not have a saving clause like clause (4) attached to Article 16. As the House will remember under clause (4) of Article 16, a special provision is made that Article 16 shall not stand in the way of the Government making a suitable provision for the representation

of Backward Classes in the services. Such a provision of course is not
to be found in Article 29. With regard to Article 16, clause (4), the
Supreme Court came to the conclusion that it involved discrimination
on the ground of caste and therefore it was invalid. I have carefully
studied both these judgments of the Supreme Court and with all
respect to the judges of the Supreme Court I cannot help saying that
I find this judgment to be utterly unsatisfactory.

... My view is that in Article 29, clause (2), the most important word
is only No distinction shall be made on the ground only of race, religion
or sex. The word 'only' is very important. It does not exclude any
distinction being made on grounds other than those mentioned in
this article and I respectfully submit that the word only did not receive
the same consideration which it ought to have received.

Then with regard to Article 16, clause (4), my submission is this
that it is really impossible to make any reservation which would not
result in excluding somebody who has a caste. I think it has to be borne
in mind and it is one of the fundamental principles which I believe is
stated in Mulla's last edition on the very first page that there is no Hindu
who has not a caste. Every Hindu has a caste—he is either a Brahmin
or a Mahratta or a Kunby or a Kumbhar or a carpenter. There is no
Hindu—that is the fundamental proposition—who has not a caste.
Consequently, if you make a reservation in favour of what are called
Backward Classes which are nothing else but a collection of certain
castes, those who are excluded are persons who belong to certain castes.
Therefore, in the circumstances of this country, it is impossible to
avoid reservation without excluding some people who have got a caste.
On these points I do not think personally that the judgment is a
very satisfactory judgment. In this connection I would like to state,
notwithstanding what the House and some Members are saying, that
I have often in the course of my practice told the presiding judge in
very emphatic terms that I am bound to obey his judgment but I am
not bound to respect it. That is the liberty which every lawyer enjoys
in telling the judge that his judgment is wrong and I am not prepared
to give up that liberty. I have always told the judges before whom I
practised that that is my view of the matter. Now the point has to be
borne in mind that in Article 46 of the Directive Principles an obligation
has been laid upon the Government to do everything possible in order
to promote the welfare and the interest of what are called the weaker
sections of the public by which I understand to mean the Backward

Classes or such other classes who are for the moment not able to stand on their legs—the scheduled castes and the scheduled tribes. It is therefore incumbent not merely on the Government but upon this Parliament to do everything in its hands to see that article 46 is fulfilled and if that fulfilment is to come, I can not see how one can escape an amendment so as to prevent Article 29, clause (2), and Article 16, clause (4) being interpreted in the way in which it has been interpreted and being made to block the advancement of the people who are spoken of as the weaker class. That is the necessity for amending Article 15....

30

Scheduled Castes Emancipation
Draft Manifesto*
6 October 1951

Scheduled Caste Federation is an All India political party of Scheduled Castes, established by the Scheduled Caste. In the following pages an attempt is made to set out (1) its Principles, (2) its Policy, (3) its Programmes and (4) its terms of Co-operation with other political parties.

PRINCIPLES OF THE PARTY

The attitude of the Party in public affairs will be governed by the following principles:

1. It will treat all Indians not only as being equal before the law but as being entitled to equality and will accordingly foster equality where it does not exist and uphold it where it is denied.

2. It will regard every Indian as an end in himself with a right to his own development in his own way and the State as only a means to that end.

3. It will sustain the right of every Indian to freedom—religious, economic and political—subject to such limitations as may arise out of the need for the protection of the interests of other Indians or the State.

4. It will uphold the right of every Indian to equality of opportunity subject to the provision that those who have had none in the past shall have priority over those who had.

5. It will keep the State ever aware of its obligation to make every Indian free from want and free from fear.

6. It will insist on the maintenance of liberty, equality and fraternity and will strive for redemption from oppression and exploitation of man by man, of class by class and of nation by nation.

*BAWS 2003, vol. 17: 385–403.

7. It will stand for the Parliamentary System of Government as being the best form of Government both in the interest of public and in the interest of the individual.

There are two considerations which should be borne in mind in assessing the implication and sincerity behind these principles. The first consideration is that these principles though adopted by the Federation are for the benefit of all the downtrodden humanity in India. The Federation in that sense cannot be accused of being a communal organization. It may be that it is not open to all, nonetheless it is out to serve all and co-operate with all who prove worthy of co-operation.

There may not be anything new in the Principles of the Scheduled Castes Federation. They will be found in the manifestoes of most political parties. But there are two considerations which distinguish the Federation from other political parties. The first consideration is that the principles of the Federation are not adopted by the Federation merely to look politically respectable or merely to delude the voters. They are natural to the Federation. They are borne out of the social condition of the Scheduled Castes. The Scheduled Castes Federation cannot exist without adopting these principles and without holding up to those principles and living up to them. The principles of the Scheduled Castes Federation are the life book of the Scheduled Castes Federation. They are not the external marks of a political faith. They are the outward register of the inward feeling. They are not cloak worn for the purpose of winning the election. Many parties may adopt these principles. But no party can be so true to the principles as the Scheduled Castes Federation. This is the second consideration in valuing the principles of the Federation.

THE POLICY OF THE PARTY

The policy of the Party will be to try to give effect to the principles set out above. The policy of the Party is not tied to any particular dogma or ideology such as Communism, Socialism, Gandhism, or any other ism. The Party will be ready to adopt any plan for the social and economic betterment of the people irrespective of its origin and provided it is consistent with its principles. Its outlook on life will be purely rational and modern, emperistic and not academic.

The Programme of the Party

Old Problems

The programme of any political party in India must be integrally connected with the legacy left by the British. The legacy of the British has its credit side, and also its debit side. On the credit side must be reckoned (1) a uniform system of law, (2) a uniform system of justice, and (3) a uniform system and administration. On the debit side must be reckoned (1) maintenance of the archaic social system prevalent among the people of the country, (2) maintenance of the privileged class in education and in the Services, both Civil and Military, (3) complete neglect of the Untouchables, of the Backward Classes and of the Tribal People, (4) impoverization of the country.

Problem of Raising the Backward Classes

The Scheduled Castes Federation will fight for the raising of the Backward Classes, the Untouchables and the Tribal people both in the matter of Education and Services. This will receive topmost priority in the plan of action by the Federation and will be treated as fundamental. Neither delay nor want of means will be allowed to stand in the way of carrying this part of the Programme into effect. The sort of Education which the Scheduled Castes Federation has in mind with regard to these classes is not primary education, not even secondary education. What it has in mind is advanced education of such high order, both in this country and outside, which will enable these classes to fit themselves for taking hold of administration. Similarly, in the matter of services, the Scheduled Castes Federation will insist on reservation, subject to minimum qualifications, so long as these classes are not able to find their place in the Civil and Military services of the country. Today there is rampant a worst sort of communalism in the Civil and Military services of the country by the higher classes. The services have become the monopoly of a few communities. When the lower classes are trying to break this monopoly by demanding that they who are at present excluded from services, are decried as communalists. The Scheduled Castes Federation will not allow this perverted logic to stand in the way of the non-privileged classes in the way of the fulfillment of their demand for occupying their rightful place in the affairs of this country.

The Scheduled Castes Federation believes that the gulf between the higher classes and the lower classes in this country is already very great. This gulf has already created a good deal of enmity between them. The murders, arsons and loot that were committed by members of the lower classes against members of the higher classes in 1948 in certain parts of India after the murder of Mr. Gandhi shows how deep rooted this enmity is.

The Scheduled Castes Federation is firmly of opinion that to remove the cause of this enmity is to give the lower classes the higher education and to open to them the door of services is the only solution of this problem. The artificial distinction between higher classes and lower classes based on birth must come to an end soon. But it cannot come to an end except by raising the lower classes to the level of the higher classes in the matter of education.

The Problem of Poverty

The economic condition of India has been described by the Planning Commission in very realistic terms. It says:

1. The population of the Indian Union (excluding Jammu and Kashmir) has increased from 235.5 million in 1901 to 356.9 million in 1951—an increase of about 52 per cent over the half-century. The rate of increase for the first two decades was relatively low, but it has risen since then. Between 1921 and 1931, the increase was 11 per cent; for 1931–41, it was 14.3 per cent; and, for 1941–51, it was 13.4 per cent.

2. There has been very little change in the occupational structure, despite considerable development of industries. In 1911, about 71 per cent of the working population was engaged in agriculture. For 1948, the National Income Committee puts this figure at about 68.2 per cent. Agriculture affords employment for only a part of the year, so that a large proportion of the workers engaged in this occupation are more or less idle for the rest of the year. There is thus a great deal of chronic under-employment in the country.

3. Sown area per person has shown a steady tendency to decline. For British India, sown area per person went down from 0.88 acre in 1911–12 to 0.72 acre in 1941–42. For 1948, i.e., after partition, the estimated sown area per person in the Indian Union works out at 0.71 acre. Evidence as to the trend of yields per acre is not conclusive. From some of the published figures available, it would appear that in respect of certain food crops, at any rate, the trend has been downward. It is difficult to assess the over-all trend of productivity in agriculture, but the broad picture that emerges suggests conditions of stagnation in this respect.

The problem of poverty is thus a double edged problem. From one point of view it is a problem of more production both in Agriculture and in Industry. From another point of view, it is a problem of controlling the excessive growth of population. Both sides are equally important. The Scheduled Castes Federation proposes to fight the battle against poverty on both the fronts.

For the purpose of reducing population, it would advocate an intensive propaganda in favour of birth-control among the people. It will advocate the opening of birth control clinics in different parts of the country. It regards the growing rate in the increase of population in the country so grave an evil that it would not hesitate to advocate more drastic methods of controlling it.

For the purpose of increasing production, the Scheduled Castes Federation will not be bound by any dogma or any pattern. The pattern of industrial enterprise will be a matter regulated by the needs of the time and circumstances. Where national undertaking of an industry is possible and essential, the Scheduled Castes Federation will support national undertaking. Where private enterprise is possible and national undertaking not essential, private enterprise will be allowed. Looking at the intense poverty of the people of this country no other consideration except that of greater production and still greater production can be the primary and paramount condition. A pre-conceived pattern of industry cannot be the primary or paramount consideration. The remedy against poverty is more production and not the pattern of production. Once reservation, the Scheduled Castes Federation must however make. Any scheme of production must in the view of the Scheduled Castes Federation remain subject to one overriding consideration namely that there should be no exploitation of the working classes.

While the rapid industrialization of the country is very essential in the opinion of the Federation agriculture is bound to remain the foundation of India's economy. Any scheme of increased production which does not take into account the re-construction of Indian agriculture is doomed to disappointment.

The Federation holds that for increased production in agriculture the following plan must be adopted:—

1. Agriculture must be mechanized. Agriculture in India can never become prosperous so long as the method of cultivation remains primitive.

2. To make mechanized farming possible, cultivation on small holdings must be replaced by large farms.
3. To increase the yield, there must be provision for adequate manuring and for the supply of healthy seeds.

It is not possible for the average agriculturist to adopt this plan and work upon it. He has no means to bear the cost involved in the plan. The Scheduled Castes Federation believes that the plan should be put into effect by the State. The first item in this plan should be the responsibility of the State. The State should supply all the mechanized equipment to the farmer on hire and at a rental to be recovered along with the land revenue.

With numerous small holdings, the problem of creating large scale farms becomes very difficult. But the problem must be solved either by introducing Co-operative farms or collective farms.

Although India is an agricultural country, there are a vast number of people who are just landless labourers, who are ekeing out a miserable living and who are exploited by cultivators and majority of whom are Untouchables and other Backward Classes. There is no need why this body of landless labourers should be left to their fate resulting in their misery and in the poverty of the country. This is all the more regrettable because the situation is not beyond remedy....

The prosperity of the agriculturist must depend upon the maintenance of forest belts spread over the country. Without forest belts proper degree of rainfall will not be assured and agriculture in India will continue to be the gamble in rain as it has always been in the past. The Federation would urge for more and more afforestation of the uncultivable wasteland.

Agriculture in the narrow sense of the term can never be a profitable pursuits. It must be supplemented by subsidiary industries which are called cottage industries. But no cottage industry worth the name will be possible without an adequate supply of electricity. Generation of electricity is in the opinion of the Scheduled Castes Federation the foundation of economic prosperity of India and the Scheduled Castes Federation will strive for the realization of the river valley projects, the purpose of which is to provide irrigation, to produce electricity and to stop floods.

Just as land has been neglected so also landless labourers have been neglected. The Federation will reserve land out of uncultivated land or reclaimed land for the benefit of landless labourers and will also introduce for them the principle of minimum wages....

QUESTION OF RESOURCES

Programme is not a mere matter of words or ideas. If it is to be put into action, it is necessary to find the necessary finance. Nobody will take a Party's programme seriously unless and until the Party is able to show how it is going to foot the bill.

Although the amount required for the programme set out by the Federation is by no means small, the financial problem is not unmanagable. The Scheduled Castes Federation suggests the following ways of raising finances for the development of the country:—

1. Reduction of Expenditure over the Army
2. Re-levy of the Salt tax
3. Abolition of prohibition and the saving of Excise Revenue
4. Nationalisation of Insurance

The total revenues of the Government of India are about Rs. 350 crores out of this the Army is eating up more than 50 per cent of the Revenues or nearly Rs. 180 crores per annum. This is a colossal expenditure on defence in a country where people are dying of starvation. On the basis of the settlement of the Kashmir issue in the way suggested in the Manifesto and the change in the foreign policy and creation of friendly relations with other foreign nations, there should be no risk in reducing the defence expenditure by Rs. 50 crores per year.

There is no reason why the levy of the Salt tax should not be resumed. The giving up of the levy of the Salt tax was a concession to mere sentiment. It has not made Salt cheap. Instead salt has become very dear. The only thing that has happened is that the State has lost a valuable source of revenue which used to produce Rs. 11 crores of revenue per year and which has seriously handicapped the State in advancing the development of the country. The incident of the tax on the people will be nothing even if it is levied at a rate which will produce Rs. 30 crores per year.

Prohibition is sheer madness. Its progress must not only be arrested but it must be immediately abolished. It has produced more evils than those it was intended to stop. Manufacture of liquor has become a cottage industry. Formerly only men drank liquor. Now women and children also drink because liquor is manufactured in every home in the presence of women and children. It has produced more crime and worst sort of demoralization of the lower classes....

From the point of equity, there is no justification for prohibition. The cost of prohibition is borne by the general public. Why should the general public be made to pay the cost of reforming a lakh or two of habitual drunkards who could never be reformed? Why should the general public be made to pay the cost of prohibition when the other wants of the public such as education, housing and health are crying for remedy? Why not use the money for development plans? Who has greater priority, the Drunkard or the Hungry? There are pertinent questions to which there is no answer except arrogance and obstinacy. Whatever happens, the policy of prohibition must be reversed and this colossal waste of public money should be put a stop to and the resources utilized for advancing general welfare....

The Scheduled Castes Federation will not only press for nationalization of Insurance; it will make Insurance compulsory for all State and Private Employees. Compulsory Insurance will give security to the individual and funds for the Government for further development....

31

On Report of the Commissioner for the Scheduled Castes and Tribes*
6 September 1954

Dr. B.R. Ambedkar (Bombay):

... I ask the Hon. Home Minister whether he thinks that there is any duty upon him or not. I ask him whether the breaches of the law which are being reported and witnessed by Scheduled Castes or other people are not breaches of the fundamental law and the fundamental rights ? Are not fundamental rights part of the Constitution ? If you are allowing a large mass of bullies and hooligans to trample upon the fundamental rights, are you not bringing the Constitution to contempt? Is it not your duty to create a special department either within the Home Ministry itself or separately for this purpose? The United States has got a Judicial Department, the duty and the function of which is to see that the Constitution and the Federal laws are respected. I think it is high time that the Home Minister realizes that if the Constitution is to function, if it is to be the law of the land, if all people are to recognize it, his duty is to see that it is enforced, and the only way in which he can enforce it is to take upon himself the duty of enforcing it and not leave it even to the State Governments who can never do it, not even to the Police who has no desire to do it, and not even to the Scheduled Castes who have no means to do it. Therefore I hope that he will take the matter more seriously and attend to it in the manner in which a statesman ought to.

Now, I come to the subject matter of education. It is quite satisfactory I must admit, that the Government has been spending annually more and more on the education of the Scheduled Castes. If my friend will forgive my mentioning myself, he will realize that it was for the first time in the year 1942 that the Government of India, at my instance when I was a Member of the Executive Council, accepted that they too had the responsibility for the education of the Scheduled Castes.

BAWS 1997, vol. 15: 895–18.

Theretofore, education was purely a provincial subject. It was only—
so far as the Muslims and Hindus were concerned, that the Government
of India had taken upon themselves the responsibility of supporting
the Aligarh University and the Benares Hindu University by an annual
grant of Rs. 3 lakhs. I raised the question whether the Government;
which had recognized its duty for the Muslim and the Hindus, had
not also a duty for the Scheduled Castes, and the Government of India
agreed that it was a legitimate question and that the answer to that
question could not be except in the affirmative....

...With regard to Army, I find that in certain categories the position
has deteriorated. In 1952 there were two Second Lieutenants belonging
to the scheduled castes. In 1953, the position is 'nil'. Of Junior
Commissioned Officers, in 1952 there were 601. In 1953 the number
is 435. Non-Commissioned Officers, in 1952 there were 3, 273. In
1953, the figure has gone down to 2, 533. Other ranks in 1952, the
number was 22, 288. In 1953 it has gone down to 18, 666. I am quite
unable to understand this deterioration in the position of the scheduled
castes in the Army. The Army, I thought, is the one place where not
much intellectual caliber is necessary, I mean in the other ranks may
be that in the higher staff it is required—much intellectual eminence.
But we are not talking about them. But taking the other ranks, we find
that the figure has gone down from 22, 000 to some 18, 000. Why? The
Army, I understand has been expanding, and with the expansion of the
Army one would naturally expect an increase in the number of scheduled
caste men in the Army. In all other places, you say they are unsuitable.
And that is a very ambiguous phrase. All Public Service commissions
and appointing authorities have learnt that phrase by heart. You simply
say the man is unsuitable and there is an end of the matter. But in the
Army what is there to be unsuitable? What is the unsuitability about?
There you have certain measurement of the chest. There are very few
people among the scheduled castes who would not fulfill that test. Then
you have certain tests of height—some 5 ft. 4 inches or so. Well, I think
all scheduled caste candidates would fill up that height (Interruption).
Very few, there may be, I admit, who may fail. But given these physical
standards of health, chest measurements and height, I should have
thought that almost every scheduled caste man was fit to be in the
military service. And when you are denying them service in other
departments of the Government of India, surely you ought to make
some concession to them in departments like the Army and the Police

where education is not a matter of any considerable moment. But there again you have been behaving in a step-motherly fashion. I do not know whether the Home Department ever takes interest in these figures, or knows them and pursues the matter. Surely, the Commander-in-Chief ought to be asked by them as to why this deterioration has taken place.

... Now, Sir, I come to the question of the economic emancipation of the Scheduled Castes. This, I think along with education and services is the most important thing for the raising of the status of the Scheduled Castes. Now what are the means of raising the economic status of the Scheduled Castes? Obviously the economic emancipation of the Scheduled castes will depend upon the opportunity that they get for what might be called entry into gainful occupation. Unless and until doors are open to them where they can find gainful occupation, their economic emancipation is not going to take place. They are going to remain slaves, if not slaves, serfs of the land-owning classes in the villages. There can be no doubt on that point at all. Now, Sir, out of these gainful occupations I personally feel no doubt that the most important thing on which Government ought to concentrate is the giving of land to the Scheduled Castes. They must be settled on land so that they might obtain independent means of livelihood, cease to be afraid of anybody, walk with their heads erect and live fearlessly and courageously. I think this is a thing which all the Ministers are agreed upon. I take it that the one thing that Government ought to do is to provide land for the Scheduled Castes. Let us take that question. Firstly, is there land available to be given to the Scheduled Castes? Has Government any power to sequester land from those who are owning land now, take it away and give it to the Scheduled Castes? Is it possible for the Scheduled Castes to be finance by the Government in the matter of purchasing lands if land was to be sought? These are the three ways by which land could be given to the Scheduled Castes. Government should by law limit the holding of those who hold land and take away the excess and hand it over to the Scheduled Castes. Secondly the Government may finance the purchase of land if any is to be sold.

Sir, it is clear to everybody that land-holding in India is not merely a matter of economic livelihood. It is a matter of social status. A person holding land has a higher status than a person not holding land. Now it is quite clear that in the villages this matter of economic status is of the utmost importance to everybody. And no Hindu wishes that an Untouchable should possess a piece of land so that he may reach a higher status than his community is entitled to under the social system. Sir, the question of a Scheduled Caste man getting a bit of land in the village seems to me to be utterly impossible. I do not know to what extent the Government will be able to make a law limiting the holdings. There might easily be a revolution. If the Government had, in passing land legislation, instead of giving the title of the property to the peasant, kept the title to themselves as paramount owners of land, they might have been able to pass a law that as the land belonged to the Government nobody would be allowed to hold more than a certain number of acres. But the Government has committed one of the greatest acts of folly in creating these peasant proprietors.

Now, Sir, I am going to make one suggestion to my honourable friend and it is this. I find from the Planning Commission's Report that is very large amount of what might be called cultivable waste is to be found in this country. According to the Planning Commission it is 98 million acres. Now, my suggestion to my friends is this. The Government is going, I understand, to amend the Constitution. They are fond of amending the Constitution. Why have a Constitution at all, I do not understand, if you are amending it every Saturday? However, as you are amending it, I suggest that you amend it and put the cultivation of wasteland in list No. 1 so that it will come within the purview of the Central Government. The State Governments have not got the means of developing that land. They are living like dog in the manger, neither developing it themselves nor allowing anybody else to do it. Therefore there can be nothing wrong in taking over the waste land by amending the Constitution in List No. 1.

The second thing which I am going to suggest is one which many people may not find pleasant but I think there is no harm in suggesting. It is this, you again levy the salt tax. The salt tax was the lightest tax that we had in our country. At the time it was abolished, the revenue was about Rs. 10 crores and it might easily go up to Rs. 20 crores now. No doubt, the abolition of salt tax was done in the memory of Mr. Gandhi. I respect him and I suggest to you that you levy the tax and create a Trust Fund in the name of Mr. Gandhi—Gandhi Trust Fund for the development or settlement of the Untouchables. After all, the Untouchables, according to all of us, were the nearest and dearest to him and there is no reason why Mr. Gandhi may not bless this project from Heaven, namely, levying the tax and using it for the development of wasteland and settling the Scheduled Castes on this waste land.

There is promise but a scope for performance. You know in the game of poker there is a difference between promise and performance. I give you a scheme where there is not only promise but there is also performance. I do not understand why the people of this country should not contribute through the means of the salt tax for the elevation of the Scheduled Castes. You may keep it quite outside the Budget just as a sort of a Gandhi Welfare Scheme which will perpetuate the name of Mr. Gandhi and which will give relief to the people whom he wanted to protect and whom he wanted to elevate. This is my suggestion to the Hon. Home Minister and I hope he will give this matter his most serious consideration....

Sir, there is one other word I should like to say. People might say that I have taken most of the time with the Scheduled Castes. I have not said anything with regard to the tribes and I am not going to say anything, because there are many friends who are more qualified to speak about them than I am, I shall, therefore, not venture to enter that field, but there is one thing which, I think, one can say and should say, because I find there is a good deal of confusion in the minds of the people as regards the relative position of the Scheduled Castes, the tribal castes and the criminal tribes. Now, Sir, with regards to the Scheduled Castes, the position is this: they are prepared—in fact, not prepared—but they are already within the pale of civilization. They are not outside. Their struggle is to achieve equality of opportunity and equality of status. That is their problem. With regard to the tribal people, their problem is totally different. They are outside the Hindu civilization. And the question that has to be considered with regard to these tribal people is this: do they want to come within the Hindu civilization and be assimilated and then acquire equality of status and equality of opportunity? I was talking to many leaders of the tribal communities—many men and women of the tribal community—they seem to be most reluctant to come within the pale of Hindu civilization.

With regard to the criminal tribes, theirs is a purely economic problem: how well can you give them the opportunity to earn a decent living? If they can get the opportunity to earn a decent living, they will cease to be criminals.

Now, Sir, one question asked is this. It seems to me a matter of great regret that the Hindu civilization which is so many years old, some say six thousand years old—many people will not be satisfied with that period probably they want to take it back—never mind about it, let it be six thousand years old—has produced five crores of Untouchables, some two crores of tribal people; and some fifty thousand criminal tribes people. What can one say of this civilization? With a civilization which has produced these results, there must be something very fundamentally wrong, and I think it is time the Hindus looked at it from this point of view—whether they can be proud of the civilization which has produced these communities like the Untouchables, the criminal tribes and the tribal people. I think they ought to think twice— not twice a hundred times—they are conventionally called civilized— whether they could be called civilized with this land of results produced by their civilization.

Sir, I thank you very much for this opportunity.

32

On Majorities and Minorities*
23 December 1955

Politics is nothing if not realistic. There is very little in it that is academic. It is therefore follows that before passing any judgement on any scheme of politics it is essential that one must consider the ground plan.

Someone may ask what do I mean by 'Ground Plan'. To me the ground plan means the social structure of a community to which the political plan is sought to be applied.

It needs no argument to show that the political structure rests on the social structure. Indeed the social structure has a profound effect on the political structure. It may modify it in its working. It may nullify it or it may even make a mockery of it.

In the case of India the social structure is built up on the caste system, the special product of Hindu civilization and culture.

The caste system is so well known that one need not wait to explain its nature. One can straight proceed to show what effect it is likely to have on Linguistic States.

There are some peculiar features of the caste system which must however be noted—

1. Castes are so distributed that in any given area there is one caste which is major and there are others which are small and are subservient to the major caste owing to their comparative smallness and their economic dependence upon the major caste which owns most of the land in the village.
2. The caste system is marked not merely by inequality but is affected by the system of graded inequality. All castes are not on a par. They are one above the other. There is a kind of ascending scale of hatred and a descending scale of contempt.
3. A caste has all the exclusiveness and pride which a nation has. It is therefore not improper to speak of collection of castes as a collection of major and minor nations.

*BAWS 1979, vol. 1: 167–70.

I am sorry, I cannot illustrate these points by reference to facts and figures. The census which is the only source of information on these points fails to help me. The last census omits altogether the caste tables which had been the feature of the Indian census ever since its birth. The Home Minister of the Government of India who is responsible for this omission was of the opinion that if a word does not exist in a dictionary it can be proved that the fact for which the word stands does not exist. One can only pity the petty intelligence of the author.

The consequences of the caste system on politics are quite obvious. The interesting part is to see what effect it has upon election which is the foundation of Representative Government which is reared up on a system of single member constituencies.

The effects may be summarized as follows:

1. Voting is always communal. The voter votes for the candidate of his community and not for the best candidate.
2. The majority community carries the seat by sheer communal majority.
3. The minority community is forced to vote for the candidate of the majority community.
4. The votes of the minority community are not enough to enable the candidate to win the seat against the candidate put up by the majority community.
5. As consequence of social system of graded inequality the voter of the higher (major) communities can never condescend to give his vote to a candidate of a minority community. On the other hand the voter of the minority community who is socially on a lower level takes pride in giving his vote to the candidate of the majority community. That is another reason why a candidate of a minority community loses in election.

... The caste is a nation but the rule of one caste over another may not be admitted to be the same as the rule of one nation over another. But supposing the case is not carried so far but is limited to majority and minority even then the question remains: What right has the majority to rule the minority?

The answer is that whatever the majority does it is right. What complain the minorities can have?

People who rely upon majority rule forget the fact that majorities are of two sorts: (1) Communal majority and (2) Political majority.

A political majority is changeable in its class composition. A political majority grows. A communal majority is born. The admission to a political majority is open. The door to a communal majority is closed. The politics of a political majority are free to all to make and unmake. The politics of a communal majority are made by its own members born in it.

How can a communal majority run away with the title deeds given to a political majority to rule? To give such title deeds to a communal majority is to establish a hereditary Government and make the way open to the tyranny of that majority. This tyranny of the communal majority is not an idle dream. It is an experience of many minorities. This experience to Maharashtrian Brahmins being very recent it is unnecessary to dilate upon it.

What is the remedy? No doubt some safeguards against this communal tyranny are essential. The question is: What can they be? The first safeguard is not to have too large a State. The consequences of too large a State on the minority living within it are not understood by many. The larger the State the smaller the proportion of the minority to the majority. To give one illustration—If Mahavidarbba remained separate, the proportion of Hindus to Muslims would be four to one. In the United Maharashtra the proportion will be fourteen to one. The same would be the case of the Untouchables. A small stone of a consolidated majority placed on the chest of the minority may be borne. But the weight of a huge mountain it cannot bear. It will crush the minorities. Therefore creation of smaller States is a safeguard to the minorities.

The second safeguard is some provision for representation in the Legislature. The old types of remedy provided in the Constitution were (1) certain number of reserved seats and (2) Separate Electorates. Both these safeguards have been given up in the new Constitution. The lambs are shorn of the wool. They are feeling the intensity of the cold. Some tempering of the wool is necessary.

Separate Electorates or reservation of seats must not be resorted to. It would be enough to have plural member constituencies (of two or three) with cumulative voting in place of the system of single-member constituency embodied in the present Constitution. This will allay the fears which the minorities have about Linguistic States.

Bibliography

PRIMARY SOURCES (WRITINGS OF AMBEDKAR)

Ambedkar, B.R. [1916]. 'Castes in India' in Vasant Moon (ed.). 1979. *Dr. Babasaheb Ambedkar: Writings and Speeches.* Vol. 1. Education Department, Government of Maharashtra, pp. 3–22.

———. [1919]. 'Evidence before the Southborough Committee on Franchise' in Vasant Moon (ed.). 1979. *Dr. Babasaheb Ambedkar: Writings and Speeches.* Vol. 1, Education Department, Government of Maharashtra, pp. 245–77.

———. [1928]. 'Statement Concerning the Status of Education of Depressed Classes in the Bombay Presidency', 'Statement Concerning the Safeguards for the Protection of the Depressed Classes as a Minority in the Bombay Presidency and the Changes in the Composition of and the Guarantees from the Bombay Legislative Council Necessary to Ensure the Same under Provincial Autonomy' and 'Evidence of Dr. Ambedkar before the Indian Statutory Commission' in Vasant Moon (ed.). 1982. *Dr. Babasaheb Ambedkar: Writings and Speeches.* Vol. 2. Education Department, Government of Maharashtra, pp. 425–46, 459–90.

———. [1929]. 'Report on the Constitution of the Government of Bombay Presidency' in Vasant Moon (ed.). 1982. *Dr. Babasaheb Ambedkar: Writings and Speeches.* Vol. 2. Education Department, Government of Maharashtra, pp. 337–66, 393–99.

——— and Rao Bahadur R. Srinivasan. [1930]. 'A Scheme of Political Safeguards for the Protection of the Depressed Classes in the Future Constitution of Self-Governing India' Appendix to Report to of Sub-Committee No. III (Minorities), in Vasant Moon (ed.). 1982. *Dr. Babasaheb Ambedkar: Writings and Speeches.* Vol. 2. Education Department, Government of Maharashtra, pp. 546–56.

———. [1930]. Proceeding of Round Table Conference: (1) In the Plenary Session-Fifth Sitting-20th November 1930, Need for Political Power for Depressed Classes. (2) In Sub-Committee No. III (Minorities) Second Sitting, Government of India, in Vasant Moon (ed.). 1982. *Dr. Babasaheb Ambedkar: Writings and Speeches.* Vol. 2. Education Department, Government of Maharashtra, pp. 502–9, 528–45.

_____ and Rao Bahadur R. Srinivasan. [1931]. 'Supplementary Memorandum on the Claims of the Depressed Classes for Special Representation' Appendix to the Report in the Minorities Committee in Vasant Moon (ed.). 1982. *Dr. Babasaheb Ambedkar: Writings and Speeches.* Vol. 2. Education Department, Government of Maharashtra, pp. 669–72.

_____. [1931]. 'Proceeding of the Round Table Conference:' (1) 'Plenary Session-Ninth Sitting—October 1931', 'Provisions for a Settlement of the Communal Problem Put Forward Jointly by Muslims, Depressed Classes etc'—Appendix to the Report in the Minorities Committee—in Vasant Moon (ed.). 1982. *Dr. Babasaheb Ambedkar: Writings and Speeches.* Vol. 2. Education Department, Government of Maharashtra, pp. 659–63, 664–9.

_____. [1932]. 'Note submitted to the Indian Franchise Committee Need for Political Power for Depressed Classes' in Vasant Moon (ed.). 1982. *Dr. Babasaheb Ambedkar: Writings and Speeches.* Vol. 2. Education Department, Government of Maharashtra, pp. 491–502.

_____. [1932]. 'Poona Pact Correspondence with Gandhi and Others', in Vasant Moon (ed.). 1990. *Dr. Babasaheb Ambedkar: Writings and Speeches.* Vol. 9. Education Department, Government of Maharashtra, pp. 74–91.

_____. [1932]. 'Statement on Gandhi's Fast' in Vasant Moon (ed.). 1990. *Dr. Babasaheb Ambedkar: Writings and Speeches.* Vol. 9. Education Department, Government of Maharashtra, pp. 311–17.

_____. [1934]. 'Joint Vs Separate Electorates: Dr. Ambedkar's Via Media' (Statement to *The Times of India*) in Vasant Moon (ed.). 2003. *Dr. Babasaheb Ambedkar: Writings and Speeches.* Vol. 17, no. 2. Education Department, Government of Maharashtra, pp. 290–93.

_____. [1935]. 'Annihilation of Caste' in Vasant Moon (ed.) 1979. *Dr. Babasaheb Ambedkar: Writings and Speeches.* Vol. 1. Education Department, Government of Maharashtra, pp. 25–96.

_____. [1940]. 'Safeguards under Government of India Act and Poona Pact are inadequate', in Vasant Moon (ed.) 2003. *Dr. Baba Saheb Ambedkar: Writings and Speeches.* Vol. 17, no. 3. Educational Department, Government of Maharashtra, p. 61.

_____. [1942]. 'Grievances of the Scheduled Castes' (Memorandum submitted to His Excellency Governor-General of India as Member of the Executive Council) in Vasant Moon (ed.). 1991. *Dr. Babasaheb Ambedkar: Writings and Speeches.* Vol. 10. Education Department, Government of Maharashtra, pp. 405–42.

_____. [1943]. 'The Political Demands of Untouchables' (For the Institute of Pacific Studies) in Vasant Moon (ed.). 1990. *Dr. Babasaheb Ambedkar: Writings and Speeches.* Vol. 9. Education Department, Government of Maharashtra, pp. 403–25.

————. [1945]. 'Communal Deadlock and How to Solve it' in Vasant Moon (ed.). 1979. *Dr. Babasaheb Ambedkar: Writings and Speeches*. Vol. 1. Education Department, Government of Maharashtra, pp. 355–79.

————. [1945]. 'Proposal for the Representation of Scheduled Castes in the Executive Council' (To Lord Wavell on the Transfer of Power to Indians) in Vasant Moon (ed.). 2003. *Dr. Babasaheb Ambedkar: Writings and Speeches*. Vol. 17, no. 2. Education Department, Government of Maharashtra, pp. 166–70.

————. [1946]. 'Memorandum Submitted to the Cabinet Mission by the All India Scheduled Castes Federation' (On the future Constitution of India) in Vasant Moon (ed.). 2003. *Dr. Babasaheb Ambedkar: Writings and Speeches*. Vol. 17, no. 2. Education Department, Government of Maharashtra, pp. 171–81.

————. [1946]. 'Letter to PM Attllee to Restore Separate Electorates' (On the future Constitution of India) in Vasant Moon (ed.). 1991. *Dr. Babasaheb Ambedkar: Writings and Speeches*. Vol. 10. Education Department, Government of Maharashtra, pp. 512–14.

————. [1946]. 'Statement 'How the Cabinet Mission Have Ignored Untouchables?' (*The Times of India*) in Vasant Moon (ed.). 2003. *Dr. Babasaheb Ambedkar: Writings and Speeches*. Vol. 17, no. 2. Education Department, Government of Maharashtra, pp. 263–73.

————. [1946]. 'On the Aims and Objectives of the Constitution' in Vasant Moon (ed.). 1994. *Dr. Babasaheb Ambedkar: Writings and Speeches*. Vol. 13. Education Department, Government of Maharashtra, pp. 8–9.

————. [1946]. 'Who Were Shudras?' in Vasant Moon (ed.). 1994. *Dr. Babasaheb Ambedkar: Writings and Speeches*. Vol. 7. Education Department, Government of Maharashtra, pp. 1–226.

————. [1946]. 'Untouchables or the Children of India's Ghetto and Other Essays on Untouchables and Untouchability: Social-Political-Religious', in Vasant Moon (ed.). 1989. *Dr. Babasaheb Ambedkar: Writings and Speeches*, Vol. 5. Education Department, Government of Maharashtra, pp. 1–445.

————. [1947]. 'States and Minorities: What are their rights and how to secure them in the Constitution of free India, Memorandum submitted on behalf of All India Scheduled Castes Federation' in Vasant Moon (ed.). 1990. *Dr. Babasaheb Ambedkar: Writings and Speeches*. Vol. 9. Education Department, Government of Maharashtra, pp. 391–450.

————. [1948]. 'The Untouchables: Who Were They and Why They Become Untouchables?' in Vasant Moon (ed.). 1994. *Dr. Babasaheb Ambedkar: Writings and Speeches*. Vol. 7. Education Department, Government of Maharashtra, pp. 239–381.

————. [1947–1950]. 'Dr. Ambedkar: The Principal Architect of the Constitution of India', in Vasant Moon (ed.). 1994. *Dr. Babasaheb Ambedkar: Writings and Speeches*. Vol. 13. Education Department, Government of Maharashtra, pp. 350–53, 391–94, 843–53.

———. [1950]. 'Constitution (First Amendment) Bill' in Vasant Moon (ed.) 1997. *Dr. Babasaheb Ambedkar: Writings and Speeches*. Vol. 15. Educational Department, Government of Maharashtra, pp. 329–422.

———. [1951]. 'Scheduled Castes Emancipation-Draft Manifesto' in Vasant Moon (ed.). 2003. *Dr. Babasaheb Ambedkar: Writings and Speeches*. Vol. 17, no. 2. Education Department, Government of Maharashtra, pp. 385–503.

———. [1953]. 'Report of the Commissioner for the Scheduled Castes and Tribes for 1953' (Rajya Sabha Debates) in Vasant Moon (ed.). 1997. *Dr. Babasaheb Ambedkar: Writings and Speeches*. Vol. 15. Education Department, Government of Maharashtra, pp. 895–918.

———. [1955]. 'Majorities and Minorities:Thoughts on Linguistic States' in Vasant Moon (ed.). 1979. *Dr. Babasaheb Ambedkar: Writings and Speeches*, Vol. 1. Education Department, Government of Maharashtra, pp. 167–70.

———. [first published 1987]. 'The Hindu Social Order: Its Essential Features' in Vasant Moon (ed.). *Dr. Babasaheb Ambedkar Writing and Speeches*. Vol. 3. Department of Education, Government of Maharashtra, Bombay, pp. 95–115.

———. [first published 1987]. 'The Hindu Social Order: Its Unique Features' in Vasant Moon (ed.) *Dr. Babasaheb Ambedkar Writings and Speeches*. Vol. 3. Department of Education, Government of Maharashtra, pp.116–29.

SECONDARY SOURCES

Agarwal, R.C. 1998. *Constitutional Development and National Movement in India*. New Delhi: S. Chand and Co.

Allana G. 1988. *The Pakistan Movement: Historic Documents*. Lahore: Islamic Book Service.

Bhalla, A.S. and F. Layepre. 1994. 'A Note on Exclusion'. Geneva: International Institute for Labour Studies (IILS), Mimeo.

Chatterjee, S.K. 1996. *The Scheduled Castes in India*. Vols 1–2. New Delhi: Gyan.

Deshpande, R.S. 2001. 'Caste System and Economic Inequality: Economic Theory and Evidence' in Ghanshyam Shah (ed.). *Dalit Identity and Politics*. New Delhi: Sage, pp. 44–73.

Deshpande, Satish and Yogendra Yadav. 2006. 'Redesigning Affirmative Action-Caste and Benefits in Higher Education'. *Economic and Political Weekly*. Vol. 17, pp. 2419–24.

First Backward Class Commission Report 1955, Government of India.

Fuller, C.J. (ed.). 1996. *Caste Today*. New Delhi: Oxford University Press.

Galanter, Marc. 1984. *Competing Equalities*. New Delhi: Oxford University Press.

Ghosh, Jayati. 2006. 'Case for Caste-based Quotas in Higher Education'. *Economic and Political Weekly*. Vol. 17, pp. 2428–32.

Ghurye, G.S. 1990. *Caste and Race in India*. Bombay: Popular Prakashan.

Haan, De Arjan. 1997. 'Poverty and Social Exclusion: A Comparison of Debates on Deprivation'. Working Paper No. 2, *Poverty Research Unit* at Sussex. Brighton: University of Sussex.

Jaffrelott Christophe. 2003. *India's Silent Revolution: The Rise of Low Castes in Indian Politics*. Delhi: Permanent Black.

——. 2005. *Dr. Ambedkar and Untouchability: Analyzing and Fighting Caste*. New Delhi: Permanent Black.

Jain, Kalpna. 1990. 'A Myth the Muslim Created'. *Indian Express*. 5 October.

Johari, J.C. 1988. *Indian Government and Politics*. Delhi: Vishal.

Keer, Dhahahjoy. 1990. *Dr. Ambedkar: Life and Mission*. Bombay: Popular Prakashan.

Kshirsagar, R.K. 1994. *Political Thought of Babasaheb Ambedkar*. New Delhi: Intellectual Publishing House.

Lal, Deepak. 1988. 'Hindu Equilibrium'. *Cultural Stability and Economic Stagnation*. Vol. I, Oxford: Clarendon.

Lathe, A.B. 1924. *Memoirs of His Highness Shri Sahu Chattrapati Maharaja of Kolhapur*. Bombay.

Lieten, George K. 1979. 'Caste in Class Politics'. *Economic and Political Weekly*. Annual Issue (February).

Maharashitriya Dnyana Kosh, Part VII:644.

Mehta, Bhanu Pratap. 2006. 'Democracy, Disagreement and Merit'. *Economic and Political Weekly* June, 17, pp. 2425–27.

Mendelsohn and Vicziany. 1998. *The Untouchables: Subordination, Poverty and the State in Modern India*. Cambridge: Cambridge University Press.

Mudaliar, Chandra. n.d. *The Kohlapur Movement*. Kohlapur: Shivaji Vidyapith.

Mysore Government Circular No. 218–98 dated 19 /21 January 1895.

Narender Kumar. 2004. *Dalit Policies, Politics and Parliament*. New Delhi: Shipra.

Rodrigues, Valerian. 2002. *The Essential Writings of B.R. Ambedkar*. New Delhi: Oxford University Press.

Saxena, H.S. 1981. *Safeguards for Scheduled Castes and Scheduled Tribes: Founding Fathers' Views*, New Delhi: Uppal Publishing House.

Shah, Ghanshyam et al. 2006. *Untouchability in Rural India*. New Delhi: Sage.

Silver, H. 1994. *Social Solidarity and Social Exclusion: Three Paradigms*. Discussion paper Series No. 69. Geneva: IILS.

Sinha, R.K. 1986. *Alienation Among Scheduled Castes*. Delhi: Manas Publications.

Somanathan, Rohini. 2006. 'Assumptions and Arithmatic of Caste-Based Reservations'. *Economic and Political Weekly*. June, 17, pp. 2436–38.

Special Report. 2000. Karnataka State Commission for Backward Classes (Chairman Ravi Varma), Government of Karnataka.

Srinivas, M.N. (ed.). 1996. *Caste: Its Modern Avatar*. New Delhi: Viking Penguin.

Thorat, Sukhadeo. 1996. 'Ambedkar and the Economics of the Hindu Social order; Under standing its orthodoxy and legacy', in Walter Fernandis (ed.). *The Emerging Dalit Identity*. Delhi: Indian Social Institute, pp. 9–35.

———. 2002. '"Oppression and Denial": Dalit Discrimination in the 1990s'. *Economic and Political Weekly*. 9 February, pp. 574–6.

———. Aryama, Negi, Prashant (ed.). 2005. *Reservation and Private Sector: Quest for Equal Opportunity and Growth*. Jaipur: Rawat.

Vundru, Rajasekhar. 2003. 'The Quest for Equal Opportunity: Walking Through an Era of Reservation', in *Hundred Years of Reservations: Appraisal and Assessment*. Hyderabad: Republican Party of Andhra Pradesh, pp. 69–93.

Index